New Directions in
Interpersonal
Communication
Research

To my colleagues at Michigan State University who make coming to work every day such a pleasure. —SWS

To my children, Brendan, Sheridan, Ashlee, Lisette, Annie, and Robyn, who have seen my strengths and limits as a communicator and taught me to really appreciate the complexities and possibilities of interpersonal communication. —SRW

New Directions in
Interpersonal
Communication
Research

Edited by

Sandi W. Smith
Michigan State University

Steven R. Wilson
Purdue University

Los Angeles • London • New Delhi • Singapore • Washington DC

For information:

SAGE Publications, Inc.
2455 Teller Road
Thousand Oaks, California 91320
E-mail: order@sagepub.com

SAGE Publications India Pvt. Ltd.
B 1/I 1 Mohan Cooperative
   Industrial Area
Mathura Road, New Delhi 110 044
India

SAGE Publications Ltd.
1 Oliver's Yard
55 City Road
London EC1Y 1SP
United Kingdom

SAGE Publications Asia-Pacific
   Pte. Ltd.
33 Pekin Street #02-01
Far East Square
Singapore 048763

Printed in the United States of America

Library of Congress Cataloging-in-Publication Data

New directions in interpersonal communication research/[edited by] Sandi W. Smith, Steven R. Wilson.
   p. cm.
Includes bibliographical references and index.
ISBN 978-1-4129-5940-7 (cloth)
ISBN 978-1-4129-5941-4 (pbk.)
   1. Interpersonal communication. 2. Interpersonal communication—Research. I. Smith, Sandi W. II. Wilson, Steven R.

BF637.C45N45 2009
153.6—dc22   2008039412

Printed on acid-free paper

09   10   11   12   13   10   9   8   7   6   5   4   3   2   1

Acquiring Editor:	Todd R. Armstrong
Editorial Assistants:	Aja Baker
Production Editor:	Sarah K. Quesenberry
Copy Editor:	QuADS Prepress (P) Ltd.
Proofreader:	Jenifer Kooiman
Indexer:	Molly Hall
Typesetter:	C&M Digitals (P) Ltd.
Cover Designer:	Candice Harman
Marketing Manager:	Carmel Schrire

Contents

Acknowledgments

We began talking about this book several years ago at a National Communication Association annual meeting as we sat with Todd Armstrong, Denise Solomon, John Caughlin, and Walid Afifi. We all agreed that exciting research was taking place within the domain of interpersonal communication, but that the diffuse nature of its dissemination might be precluding people from recognizing how much vital work was being done. We are grateful to many who helped us make this book a reality—the journey was filled with unexpected turns and we could not have reached the finish line without many people's support. First and foremost, we thank Todd Armstrong for his editorial skills and good friendship to both of us. Second, we want to thank the authors who came on the journey with us. Several of you commented that this is the first time that you have been asked to step back and look at where you have been and where you intend to head with your life's work. We would also like to thank the following reviewers Dale E. Brashers, University of Illinois at Urbana-Champaign; Daena J. Goldsmith, Lewis & Clark College; Sandra Metts, Illinois State University; Paul Mongeau, Arizona State University; and Jennifer A. Samp, University of Georgia. Of course, we have to thank our families for their support as well. Chuck is a fine husband, chair, colleague, and friend to Sandi. She has dedicated this book to her colleagues at Michigan State University, and that includes faculty members, students, and staff who make her work life such a pleasure there. Patrice is an irreplaceable spouse, colleague, and friend to Steve. He has dedicated this book to his children, who are a crucial source of inspiration, exasperation, and meaning in his life. We both look forward to receiving feedback on the book from our colleagues (faculty and students) at Michigan State and Purdue Universities as well as from many others who we hope will find it to be a useful resource for their teaching and research.

Foreword

Commentary on *New Directions in Interpersonal Communication Research*

Michael E. Roloff

When approached by Sandi and Steve about commenting on the chapters in this volume, I was deeply honored and excited. Their project is an extension of two volumes to which I contributed chapters and one of which I coedited with Gerald R. (GR) Miller (Miller, 1976a; Roloff & Miller, 1987). However, while preparing my comments, I was overcome by a sense of melancholy. Certainly, the chapters are excellent but in thinking about them, I had a strong sense of loss. GR passed away in 1993, and those who worked with him sorely miss his keen intellect, biting and often irreverent humor, pertinent insights, and friendship. Moreover, he was a driving force behind the creation of the earlier volumes, and his opinions would have made a significant contribution to this commentary.

Hence, when preparing my comments, I kept wondering, "What would GR say?" After much deliberation, I heard his voice. Toward the end of his life, GR self-referenced as being an "old buffalo." Although I was always quick to point out his continued vitality, he noted that the term did not imply a lack of energy or useful contribution. Instead, he noted that the old buffalos are those members of the herd that offered wisdom garnered from the past, and their insights are useful for setting future directions. After all, the old buffalos have survived the attacks of countless wolf packs, droughts, fires, hunters, and other such calamities. Although they bear the scars from past mistakes, they know the trails that proved productive as well as those that were dead ends. Their theories may no longer map onto current reality but their data points are voluminous and are useful for understanding trends. Although some in my generation resist being labeled "old," I for one gladly accept the moniker of "old buffalo" and hope that these comments live up to the high standards that GR associated with the term.

My comments are divided into three sections. In the first, I provide history with regard to the two earlier volumes and why the current one comes at an opportune time. Second, I note the themes and contributions arising from the chapters in this volume. Third, I end with some comments about the future.

History

In the summer of 1975, with my freshly minted PhD from Michigan State in hand, I was preparing to leave for my first position at the University of Kentucky. GR stopped by my office to bid farewell and to make an offer. He was going to edit a volume on interpersonal communication that would appear as part of a new series titled *Sage Annual Reviews of Communication Research,* and he asked if I would submit a chapter. The purpose of the volume was to bring together scholars who were researching various aspects of interpersonal communication and, by doing so, provide a stimulus package of ideas and a sense of identity for those working in the area. I was thrilled and especially so when he told me the lineup of contributors, which was composed of a mixture of established and young scholars who were all bright and productive.

In the foreword to the volume, GR acknowledged the diversity evident in the chapters but argued that they provided useful information about how interpersonal communication should be conceptualized, how it should be researched, and the topics worthy of investigation (Miller, 1976b). Although the chapters advanced a number of conceptualizations of interpersonal communication, one that seemed to be predominant was relational communication. Several chapters looked at how relational development is associated with changes in uncertainty (Berger, Gardner, Parks, Schulman, & Miller, 1976), information processing (Duck, 1976), interpersonal influence (Roloff, 1976), and self-disclosure (Gilbert, 1976; Morton, Alexander, & Altman, 1976). Although most chapters focused on communication in close relationships, one looked at the communication that occurred within professional therapeutic relationships (Vaughn & Burgoon, 1976). Because interaction is a defining feature of interpersonal communication, most chapters adopted theoretical frameworks for understanding patterns of interaction, including symbolic interaction (Cushman & Craig, 1976), coordinated management of meaning (Pearce, 1976), systems theory (Cappella, 1976; Millar & Rogers, 1976), uncertainty reduction theory (Berger et al., 1976), and social penetration theory (Morton et al., 1976). Because of the inherent relationship between theory and methods, one chapter focused on statistical methods for studying interaction (Hawes & Foley, 1976). Finally, the chapters identify a number of communication forms to be studied, including self-disclosure (Gilbert, 1976), interpersonal influence (Roloff, 1976), uncertainty reduction strategies (Berger et al., 1976), and nonverbal communication (Harrison, 1976).

Although I do not want to overstate the impact of the volume, the content of the chapters stimulated or at least contributed to a number of subsequent research areas. First, research on relational communication grew as researchers investigated issues such as relationship change (e.g., Baxter & Wilmot, 1983) and how communication varied across types of relationships (e.g., Fitzpatrick, 1983). Second, the study of interpersonal influence became a dominant focus as researchers studied compliance gaining and resistance (see Wheeless, Barraclough, & Stewart, 1983). Uncertainty reduction theory proved to be a useful framework for studying interaction and was part of a move toward studying social cognition and communication (Roloff & Berger, 1982).

By 1985, the study of interpersonal communication was a booming enterprise, and I suggested to GR that it was time he updated the first *Sage Annual.* He agreed but suggested that I take the role of lead editor. We both approached Sara Miller McCune at SAGE Publications, who was excited by the idea, and she encouraged us to submit a proposal to the series editors, James Carey and Peter Miller. In creating the second volume, we wished to revisit some of the ideas raised in the first and introduce some notions that were not foreseen in the first.

Because of page limitations, we were only able to update a few. First, in the initial volume, Cushman and Craig (1976) had argued that interpersonal communication is distinguished from other forms of communication in part because it is a means by which individuals form and validate their self-concepts. Hence, we invited McCall (1987) to overview his role identity model that highlighted the interplay between the self and interaction. Second, as noted earlier, the first volume contained several articles that focused on relational communication. Therefore, we asked Taylor and Altman (1987) to discuss recent research on their social penetration theory, Millar and Rogers (1987) to revisit their research on the dynamics of relational interaction, and Duck (1987) to focus on recent developments on communication and relational decline. In my own chapter, I looked at the implications of social exchange theory for understanding relational communication (Roloff, 1987). Third, we noted the influence of uncertainty reduction theory and asked Berger (1987) to evaluate the theory based on the body of research. Fourth, we wanted chapters that focused on both traditional and new areas of research on communication forms. We asked Derlega, Winstead, Wong, and Greenspan (1987) to extend the self-disclosure chapter in the first book by looking at the relationship between self-disclosure and aspects of social cognition. Since the first volume, the study of interpersonal influence had subdivided into specialties. Hence, we asked Miller, Boster, Roloff, and Seibold (1987) to examine trends and controversies in compliance gaining research and Sillars and Weisberg (1987) to look at conflict management in close relationships. In the first volume, several chapters looked at interaction dynamics, and we asked Kellermann (1987) to look specifically at information exchange and Berscheid (1987) to focus on emotion and communication. Finally, we asked Poole, Folger, and Hewes (1987) to discuss developments in methodologies used for studying interaction.

Did these volumes have lasting impact? I conducted a citation analysis for the volumes and found that both contain chapters that have been cited as recently as 2005. And, they still return royalties albeit small ones, and my family and I remain grateful to those who purchase them!

And a little over 30 years later, Sandi and Steve have edited the most recent installment on perspectives in interpersonal communication. Because of the time frame, two questions emerge. First, why so long? And second, why now? I will posit some answers to both. Although I cannot speak for others, my own lack of initiative stems from several sources. First, the venue in which the first two volumes appeared ceased publication. The last *Sage Annual Review of Communication Research* was published in 1994. The absence of this series was a significant loss in several respects, including the ability of those working in an area to highlight research trends and advance new perspectives. Second, new venues appeared that replaced some aspects of the earlier volumes. Three editions of the *Handbook of Interpersonal Communication* were published that provide useful literature reviews (Knapp & Daly, 2002; Knapp & Miller, 1985, 1994). The *Communication Yearbook* also published literature reviews and meta-analyses on topics related to interpersonal communication. Furthermore, scholars have published theories related to interpersonal communication in *Communication Theory*. Hence, although scattered, one can find some information that previously would have appeared in a volume. Finally, and most important, GR's passing away in 1993 meant the initiator of the volumes was no longer present to oversee new ones.

Why now? The initial volume was created, in part, to provide a sense of identity and community to scholars interested in interpersonal communication.

In 1976, the area was developing a sufficient critical mass to warrant such a move. In 2008, there is a feeling among some that the interpersonal communication area needs another identity-building exercise. Although not appearing in print, some critics have suggested the study of interpersonal communication has lost its edge. They opine that the Internet and rapidly mutating new information technologies have rendered the study of face-to-face interaction quaint and passé. Because of globalization, understanding communication processes between individuals located in geographical proximity is too restrictive and has little of value to say about the new world of virtual relationships and cultural diversity. Our traditional focus on communication in close relationships has made interpersonal scholars indistinguishable with regard to theories and methods from researchers residing in allied fields and disciplines who also study close relationships. And there are some who argue that the ability of interpersonal communication scholars to develop new and exciting ideas has run out. Allegedly, the best and the brightest researchers have migrated elsewhere.

The chapters in this volume clearly indicate that the aforementioned indictments are wrongheaded. In the next section, I will highlight the valuable insights that they provide.

Themes and Contributions

As was the case with the chapters in the preceding volumes, these chapters are quite diverse. They review literature and advance perspectives focused on a variety of communication processes and contexts. To help identify the contributions made by the chapters, I looked at the questions they address. In 1987, Cappella provided a useful framework for understanding the types of questions investigated in interpersonal communication. He privileged interaction as the defining construct of interpersonal communication and noted four levels of questions addressed by scholars. I will use his levels for categorizing the chapters.

Zero-level questions are focused on mapping to the terrain of interpersonal communication. Essentially, the primary tasks are to identify, define, and operationalize the key verbal and nonverbal behaviors enacted during an interaction as well as the time and sequence in which they appear. Unlike the first volumes, these chapters contain little discussion of the key behaviors and time units to be analyzed. In part, this may reflect the maturity of many of the topics. In my mind, zero-level questions are most pertinent in the early stages of investigation when researchers are collecting descriptive data that might be used to identify the constructs about which their theories should be focused. The notable exception in this volume is Chapter 13 by Walther and Ramirez. Because of the rapid pace at which new technologies have emerged and existing ones mutated, there is a necessity to constantly monitor the changing landscape so as to address the utility of theory and validity of prior results.

First-level questions examine the psychological factors that influence the encoding and decoding of interaction features. By and large, these questions are focused on intraindividual predictors of interaction. Cappella (1987) noted that these questions have dominated the study of interpersonal communication and these chapters demonstrate that his observations remain true today. Virtually every chapter has a strong focus on some aspect of the psychological processes that influence an individual's encoding and decoding. In Chapter 8, Burleson has proposed a dual processing account of how comforting messages are constructed. In Chapter 11, Vangelisti and Hampel highlight the processes that cause individuals to feel hurt by messages. Two chapters evidence the continued influence of uncertainty reduction theory but focus on one particular aspect of it such as relational uncertainty (Knobloch, Chapter 4) or broaden its focus to general information seeking (Afifi, Chapter 5). In Chapter 9, Caughlin and Scott advance a goal-driven explanation for the demand-withdrawal interaction pattern. Solomon, Weber, and Steuber (Chapter 6) build on the focus on relational development evident in the earlier volumes and review a program of research that investigates how relational change can create patterns of support and interference.

Second-level questions are focused on patterns of communication evident within interactions. In effect, these questions look at mutual influence as the behavior of one individual is influenced by another. The importance of this mutuality was evident in several chapters in the earlier volumes. In Chapter 10 of the current volume, Burgoon and Levine discuss how deception detection may change during the course of an interaction arising, in part, from the tendencies of individuals to adapt their messages to each other's responses, whereas Caughlin and Scott (Chapter 9) explore how different forms of demanding may elicit different forms of withdrawing (and vice versa), producing more varied patterns than have been recognized in prior work.

Third-level questions examine how social and relational factors influence interactions. Individuals are embedded within larger social units such as cultures, subcultures, communities, and institutionalized relationships that carry within them norms that may influence interaction. In some respects, this has been one of the most neglected aspects of interpersonal communication. This volume contains several chapters that draw links between culture and interpersonal communication. Burgoon and Levine (Chapter 10) posit that culture is a potential moderator in research on deception detection. Meyers discusses the interpersonal communication processes by which individuals are assimilated into organizational culture. In the first volume, Cushman and Craig (1976) distinguished interpersonal communication from cultural communication, in part based on the latter's portrayal of institutions via the mass media. Smith and Granados examine the manner in which close relationships are portrayed on television, which may provide cultural representations of what our relationships are like or should be (Chapter 14). Finally, the chapters by Fitch (Chapter 12) and by Baxter and Braithwaite (Chapter 3) strongly note the manner in which culture influences interpersonal discourse.

Regardless of the questions being addressed, my reading of the chapters leads to several conclusions. First, interpersonal communication scholars continue to make valuable and unique contribution to the understanding of close relationships. We study relational development, relational uncertainty, supportive communication, and relational problems. Although the multidisciplinary nature of inquiry on personal relationships is reflected in each chapter, there is a strong focus on interaction processes, and the programs of research evident in each chapter are conducted by those in communication.

Second, the study of interpersonal communication has extended beyond the context of close relationships. In the first volume, there was a chapter focused on small-group interaction, but the second volume was primarily focused on relational interaction. This set of chapters notes that interactions occur in a variety of contexts and not just in face-to-face settings. Importantly, rather than being rendered obsolete by technology and globalization, interpersonal communication researchers are making valuable contributions.

Third, our research is rigorously conducted and programmatic. Each chapter articulates a theoretical framework, provides appropriate methods, and cites the findings of a coherent body of research. Most impressively, the authors lay out the logic that guided the sequence of projects that were pursued as the program unfolded.

Future

Although I am heartened by the chapters, they also raise a challenge for the future. Our theorizing will need to become more complex. This is not to say that prior theorizing was simplistic but that it tended to focus on a limited set of psychological variables often residing at Cappella's (1987) Level 1.

With the move to incorporate social factors such as culture and relation-ships, we will need to create theories that are grounded in both intraindi-vidual and social processes. Hence, I am a white male approaching 60 years, who resides in a suburb within a large metropolitan area that is part of the Midwest of the United States. I have graduate degrees, and am married with three children and two grandchildren. My wife and I have lived in the same house for 30 years. I am a moderate to high self-monitor who scores high in conscientiousness. The aforementioned cluster of characteristics suggests a number of factors that may account for why my communication may differ from that of others. In effect, I am an individual embedded within several types of relationships, cohorts, communities, and subcultures. From a vari-able analytic perspective, a key question concerns how much of the variance in behavior can be accounted for by the variables at each level and how might they interact with or mediate the impact of each other. Advances in statistics allow such multilevel comparisons, but our theorizing has not kept pace. Researchers who use qualitative and interpretative methods seem to have perspectives that are somewhat better suited for this task but their thinking seems to focus more on the cultural level than at the individual or relational levels.

To move to multilevel theorizing will be difficult. It will require researchers to become expert or at least familiar with the processes evident within each level. To simply argue that we must look at factors associated with individu-als, relationships, or cultures does not say what features of these units are relevant to the question under investigation. To understand the nuances of individuals, relationships, and culture is a challenge. When editing the *Handbook of Communication Science,* Charles Berger and Stephen Chaffee (1987) asked contributors to approach their topic from various levels such as individual, interpersonal, organizational, media, and cultural. I found the task to be formidable even though my topic was relatively narrow (conflict). It required finding and reviewing research conducted in a variety of fields and disciplines, each of which often had unique jargons, methods, and theories. However, those authors who were able to complete the assignment produced chapters that demonstrated the complexity of the construct and the diverse ways in which it is studied. Unfortunately, no multilevel theories resulted from the exercise. It is hoped that this will not be the case now.

Conclusion

At the outset of my comments, I noted that I wondered what GR would say about the chapters in this volume. He certainly would recognize links to chapters contained in the earlier volumes and would be pleased by their continued influence. GR understood the evolving nature of research and would applaud the refinement and progress made in the research areas highlighted in the earlier volumes. He would also find some approaches that were not at all anticipated and would be impressed with the research programs that have developed. Although I am sure that he would vigorously disagree with aspects of some chapters, I am convinced he would say, "A job well done."

Although I am not sure that I would be around to learn from the next volume (especially if it takes 20 years before it appears!!), I am convinced that the chapters in the current volume will stimulate significant strides in interpersonal communication research.

References

Baxter, L., & Wilmot, W. (1983). Communication characteristics of relationships with differential growth rates. *Communication Monographs, 50,* 264–272.

Berger, C. R. (1987). Communicating under uncertainty. In M. E. Roloff & G. R. Miller (Eds.), *Interpersonal processes: New directions in communication research* (pp. 39–62). Newbury Park, CA: Sage.

Berger, C. R., & Chaffee, S. H. (Eds.). (1987). *Handbook of communication science.* Newbury Park, CA: Sage.

Berger, C. R., Gardner, R. R., Parks, M. R., Schulman, L., & Miller, G. R. (1976). Interpersonal epistemology and interpersonal communication. In G. R. Miller (Ed.), *Explorations in interpersonal communication* (pp. 149–172). Beverly Hills, CA: Sage.

Berscheid, E. (1987). Emotion and interpersonal communication. In M. E. Roloff & G. R. Miller (Eds.), *Interpersonal processes: New directions in communication research* (pp. 77–88). Newbury Park, CA: Sage.

Cappella, J. N. (1976). Modeling interpersonal communication systems as a pair of machines coupled through feedback. In G. R. Miller (Ed.), *Explorations in interpersonal communication* (pp. 59–86). Beverly Hills, CA: Sage.

Cappella, J. N. (1987). Interpersonal communication: Definitions and fundamental question. In C. R. Berger & S. H. Chaffee (Eds.), *Handbook of communication science* (pp. 184–238). Newbury Park, CA: Sage.

Cushman, D. P., & Craig, R. T. (1976). Communication systems: Interpersonal implications. In G. R. Miller (Ed.), *Explorations in interpersonal communication* (pp. 37–58). Beverly Hills, CA: Sage.

Derlega, V. J., Winstead, B. A., Wong, P. T. P., & Greenspan, M. (1987). Self-disclosure and relationship development: An attributional analysis. In M. E. Roloff & G. R. Miller (Eds.), *Interpersonal processes: New directions in communication research* (pp. 172–187). Newbury Park, CA: Sage.

Duck, S. (1976). Interpersonal communication in developing acquaintance. In G. R. Miller (Ed.), *Explorations in interpersonal communication* (pp. 127–148). Beverly Hills, CA: Sage.

Duck, S. (1987). How to lose friends without influencing people. In M. E. Roloff & G. R. Miller (Eds.), *Interpersonal processes: New directions in communication research* (pp. 278–298). Newbury Park, CA: Sage.

Fitzpatrick, M. A. (1983). Predicting couples' communication from couples' self-reports. In R. Bostrom (Ed.), *Communication yearbook 7* (pp. 49–82). Beverly Hills, CA: Sage.

Gilbert, S. J. (1976). Empirical and theoretical extension of self-disclosure. In G. R. Miller (Ed.), *Explorations in interpersonal communication* (pp. 197–216). Beverly Hills, CA: Sage.

Harrison, R. P. (1976). The face in face-to-face interaction. In G. R. Miller (Ed.), *Explorations in interpersonal communication* (pp. 217–236). Beverly Hills, CA: Sage.

Hawes, L. C., & Foley, J. M. (1976). Group decisioning: Testing a finite stochastic model. In G. R. Miller (Ed.), *Explorations in interpersonal communication* (pp. 237–255). Beverly Hills, CA: Sage.

Kellermann, K. (1987). Information exchange in social interaction. In M. E. Roloff & G. R. Miller (Eds.), *Interpersonal processes: New directions in communication research* (pp. 188–219). Newbury Park, CA: Sage.

Knapp, M. L., & Daly, J. A. (Eds.). (2002). *Handbook of interpersonal communication* (3rd ed.). Thousand Oaks, CA: Sage.

Knapp, M. L., & Miller, G. R. (Eds.). (1985). *Handbook of interpersonal communication*. Beverly Hills, CA: Sage.

Knapp, M. L., & Miller, G. R. (Eds.). (1994). *Handbook of interpersonal communication* (2nd ed.). Thousand Oaks, CA: Sage.

McCall, G. (1987). The self-concept and interpersonal communication. In M. E. Roloff & G. R. Miller (Eds.), *Interpersonal processes: New directions in communication research* (pp. 63–76). Newbury Park, CA: Sage.

Millar, F. E., & Rogers, L. E. (1976). A relational approach to interpersonal communication. In G. R. Miller (Ed.), *Explorations in interpersonal communication* (pp. 87–104). Beverly Hills, CA: Sage.

Millar, F. E., & Rogers, L. E. (1987). Relational dimensions of interpersonal dynamics. In M. E. Roloff & G. R. Miller (Eds.), *Interpersonal processes: New directions in communication research* (pp. 117–139). Newbury Park, CA: Sage.

Miller, G. R. (Ed.). (1976a). *Explorations in interpersonal communication*. Beverly Hills, CA: Sage.

Miller, G. R. (1976b). Foreword. In G. R. Miller (Ed.), *Explorations in interpersonal communication* (pp. 9–16). Beverly Hills, CA: Sage.

Miller, G. R., Boster, F. J., Roloff, M. E., & Seibold, D. R. (1987). In M. E. Roloff & G. R. Miller (Eds.), *Interpersonal processes: New directions in communication research* (pp. 89–116). Newbury Park, CA: Sage.

Morton, T. L., Alexander, J. F., & Altman, I. (1976). Communication and relationship definition. In G. R. Miller (Ed.), *Explorations in interpersonal communication* (pp. 105–126). Beverly Hills, CA: Sage.

Pearce, W. B. (1976). The coordinated management of meaning: A rules-based theory of interpersonal communication. In G. R. Miller (Ed.), *Explorations in interpersonal communication* (pp. 17–36). Beverly Hills, CA: Sage.

Poole, M. S., Folger, J. P., & Hewes, D. E. (1987). Analyzing interpersonal interaction. In M. E. Roloff & G. R. Miller (Eds.), *Interpersonal processes: New directions in communication research* (pp. 220–256). Newbury Park, CA: Sage.

Roloff, M. E. (1976). Communication strategies, relationships, and relational changes. In G. R. Miller (Ed.), *Explorations in interpersonal communication* (pp. 173–196). Beverly Hills, CA: Sage.

Roloff, M. E. (1987). Communication and reciprocity within intimate relationships. In M. E. Roloff & G. R. Miller (Eds.), *Interpersonal processes: New directions in communication research* (pp. 11–38). Newbury Park, CA: Sage.

Roloff, M. E., & Berger, C. R. (Eds.). (1982). *Social cognition and communication.* Beverly Hills, CA: Sage.

Roloff, M. E., & Miller, G. R. (Eds.). (1987). *Interpersonal processes: New directions in communication research.* Newbury Park, CA: Sage.

Sillars, A. L., & Weisberg, J. (1987). Conflict as a social skill. In M. E. Roloff & G. R. Miller (Eds.), *Interpersonal processes: New directions in communication research* (pp. 140–171). Newbury Park, CA: Sage.

Taylor, D. A., & Altman, I. (1987). Communication in interpersonal relationships: Social penetration processes. In M. E. Roloff & G. R. Miller (Eds.), *Interpersonal processes: New directions in communication research* (pp. 257–277). Newbury Park, CA: Sage.

Vaughn, D. R., & Burgoon, M. (1976). Interpersonal communication in therapeutic settings: Mariah or messiah? In G. R. Miller (Ed.), *Explorations in interpersonal communication* (pp. 255–272). Beverly Hills, CA: Sage.

Wheeless, L. R., Barraclough R., & Stewart, R. (1983). Compliance gaining and power in persuasion. In R. E. Bostrom (Ed.), *Communication yearbook 7* (pp. 105–145). Beverly Hills, CA: Sage.

1

Evolving Trends in Interpersonal Communication Research

Sandi W. Smith

Steven R. Wilson

Two books edited by G. R. Miller, and published by SAGE, revolutionized interpersonal communication research (Miller 1976a; Roloff & Miller, 1987). These volumes set the tone for interpersonal communication research as we know it today. Every researcher who we know bought the books and assigned them in graduate courses. Our copies are literally falling apart from use. There were 11 years between the two Miller volumes, and now 21 years have passed. This is a time that vital, collaborative, and interdisciplinary research with its roots in interpersonal communication is being conducted, and we want to showcase that research in this new volume.

The prior volumes were loosely structured around the themes of explorations in interpersonal communication and interpersonal processes, and here we highlight new directions in interpersonal communication. Miller invited scholars who he thought were doing interesting and important work to explain their research programs—their basic commitments, central concepts, key findings—in a way that engaged readers. We have tried to do the same with this volume by asking the authors to tell the personal stories of their research programs that have roots in interpersonal communication and to provide future directions that this research should take.

1

Our goals for this book crystallized as we talked over the years about the breadth and reach of the study of interpersonal communication. Some of these conversations centered on our mutual roles as chair of the International Communication Association's (ICA) Interpersonal Communication Division and the apparent meshing of interpersonal communication research into many other divisions. Others became clear as we met with colleagues like Denise Solomon, John Caughlin, and Walid Afifi before we began the book. In the sections that follow, we explain our vision for the book, discuss evolving trends in interpersonal communication research, and provide an overview of the sections and chapters of the book that follow.

Vision for the Book

This book is motivated by three interrelated goals. First, we want to showcase interpersonal communication as an area of study where exciting, vital work continues to be done. As Michael Roloff notes in his commentary on this book (Foreword), the 1976 volume played a key role in establishing interpersonal communication as an area of study. Miller's (1976b) foreword to that first volume noted that it was published at a time when scholars were struggling with questions such as "How is the interpersonal communication process to be conceptualized and researched?" and "What aspects of the interpersonal communication process merit research scrutiny?" Thirty years later, these remain important questions; however, well-developed positions now exist regarding how interpersonal communication can be conceptualized as a developmental process involving qualitative shifts in inference making, as a symbolic process involving the presentation of selves, or as an interactional process involving mutual influence, and each position has motivated large bodies of research (see Berger, 2005; Cappella, 1987; Roloff & Anastasiou, 2000). Put simply, in 1976, interpersonal communication was a new and exciting area of study, whereas today, some may not view it as cutting edge. Due to various trends (some identified by Roloff in his commentary to this volume, others which we discuss below), some may even question whether interpersonal communication is still central to our discipline or worthy of research scrutiny.

To dispel such notions, we have invited authors doing exciting work in interpersonal communication to tell the stories of their programs of research, some of which are their life's work, and in which they have a strong personal investment. Like the Miller volumes, we invited not only senior scholars but also individuals earlier in their scholarly career. What all the contributors have in common are research programs that showcase how interpersonal scholarship can simultaneously address fundamentally important questions about communication itself (Burleson, 1992) and pragmatic concerns about families, health, work, technology, culture, and other issues salient in our contemporary society.

Second, we have strived to create a volume that will be useful for a broad audience. Based on this goal, we have asked authors to avoid the somewhat encyclopedic style typically found in three editions of the *Handbook of Interpersonal Communication Research* (Knapp & Daly, 2002; Knapp & Miller, 1985, 1994)—these handbooks are extremely important resources for anyone interested in interpersonal communication, but they often seem dense when first encountered by students and sometimes sacrifice the depth valued by seasoned scholars to adequately cover broad areas of study. To achieve accessibility and depth, we have encouraged authors to tell the stories of their own research programs. Specifically, we asked each contributor to address the following questions:

- What projects with roots in interpersonal communication are you working on right now? What is the purpose of these projects, and what key concepts are being explored? What was it that led you to these projects? How do they build on and/or fill gaps in prior research on interpersonal communication?

- What methods have you employed in these projects? What have you found so far?

- Why are these projects relevant? What central questions/issues about interpersonal communication do they highlight/explore? How do they extend/challenge current theories of interpersonal communication? How do these projects address issues that actually matter to and impact individuals, communities, and the larger society?

- What are you doing right now to move these projects forward? What conceptual, methodological, pragmatic (e.g., resource), and/or ethical challenges are you facing in making progress? How are you addressing these challenges?

- What future directions should be taken in this line of research?

Our third goal is to highlight the permeability of boundaries between interpersonal communication and other areas of communication. The Miller volumes crossed boundaries by inviting contributors from several disciplines, including interpersonal communication, social and clinical psychology, and sociology. Several things have changed since the publication of the two earlier volumes. Large bodies of theory and research have accumulated on topics such as uncertainty management, message production, and interpersonal adaptation (see Berger, 2005; Braithwaite & Baxter, 2008). At the same time, there has been a proliferation of divisions and identifications within the communication discipline (see below). Given these trends, we felt that it is important to cross boundaries within our own discipline. Hence, all the contributors to this volume reside within communication departments, but several might be characterized as divisional "boundary spanners." Some of our contributors are clearly identifiable as interpersonal communication scholars but apply theory and research to topics of interest in other areas; others are scholars whose primary identification may lie in another area but whose theory and research is informed by and/or informs work viewed as central by interpersonal communication scholars.

Given these goals, we envision the primary audience for this book to be faculty and graduate students who consider interpersonal communication one of their areas of interest. We hope the book will be one that any faculty member who teaches graduate and/or upper-level undergraduate courses in interpersonal communication feels compelled to own, as was the case with the Miller and Roloff books. We hope that it is adopted widely as a text in graduate-level courses on interpersonal communication and perhaps also in senior-level undergraduate courses. Graduate students working on their theses or dissertations in interpersonal communication also should be attracted to this compilation of cutting-edge research. Secondary audiences for the book are faculty and graduate students in related areas such as family, health, intercultural, mass, and organizational communication who find interest in the "boundary spanner" chapters that apply theory and research with roots in interpersonal communication to these related contexts. We also hope that this work reaches scholars in related disciplines, such as those in social psychology, child and family studies, and sociology who belong to interdisciplinary groups such as the International Association of Relationship Researchers as well as the International Association of Language and Social Psychology.

Evolving Trends

Our goals for this volume have been influenced by evolving trends that we see as present in interpersonal communication research today. We show how a proliferation of identifications, globalization, the focus on the dark side of interpersonal communication, dominant and alternative metatheoretical voices, the increase in funded and applied scholarship, and technology affect interpersonal communication research today and differ from what was occurring in the 1970s and 1980s.

Proliferation of Identifications

The chapters that follow show that interpersonal communication is a phenomenon that can be examined through an evolutionary perspective lens, through dialectic theory, as it is situated on a cultural level, as it occurs in organizations, on television, and online. The definition of interpersonal communication changed fundamentally in 1975 when Miller and Steinberg wrote *Between People* and claimed that there were varied positions on what constitutes interpersonal communication. No matter the level, Miller (1976b) claimed that the focus on interpersonal communication research is dyadic, and there is a symbiotic relationship between interpersonal communication and relational development. These emphases continue today; for example, chapters by Caughlin and Scott (Chapter 9) as well as Fitch (Chapter 12) analyze examples of dyadic interaction, while those by Baxter and Braithwaite (Chapter 3) as well as by Solomon, Steuber, and Weber (Chapter 6) explore how relationships are defined and transformed via communication. Due to the fact that interpersonal communication is a basic process, it is applicable in widespread contexts.

Perhaps this widespread applicability, more than any other reason, has contributed to one of the most fundamental changes in interpersonal communication scholarship over the past 20 years. For example, ICA initially was founded with just 8 divisions, whereas today it includes 19 divisions as well as several interest groups. Not only are there myriad new divisions, but also scholars who would have made Interpersonal Communication their primary, if not only, home when the Miller volumes were published have partially, if not fully, migrated to other divisions. A 2004 network analysis of ICA division membership shows very strong links between membership in the Interpersonal Communication Division and the Health Communication, Language and Social Interaction, Organizational Communication, and Intercultural Communication divisions, with moderate links to Information Systems, Mass Communication, Developmental Communication, and Communication and Instructional Technology. This indicates that most interpersonal communication scholars now have multiple identifications because their work cuts across multiple divisions (for one discussion of the implications for this proliferation of divisions, see Bochner, 2008).

As previously noted, the 1976 and 1987 Miller books featured authors from several disciplines. Those from Communication made their home in the Information Systems and Interpersonal Communication Divisions of ICA primarily. Pearce, Cushman, Craig, Cappella, Millar, Rogers, Duck, Berger, Parks, Miller, Roloff, Harrison, and Burgoon were authors in the 1976 book, and Boster, Seibold, Sillars, Kellermann, Poole, Folger, and Hewes joined many of them again in the 1987 book. Of those authors who are still active today, many of them have become associated with other divisions such as Organizational, Group, Health, and Technology, while others have retained their primary association with Interpersonal Communication. In response to this first trend, we emphasize the boundary-spanning metaphor to highlight how theory and research with its roots in interpersonal communication is informing current work in many areas of study.

Globalization

The world is smaller and more interconnected than it was in 1976 or even 1987, and the resulting trends are reflected in interpersonal communication programs and research. When Steve began his PhD studies at Purdue University in 1984, there were no international students in the graduate program. International students were represented in fields such as Engineering or Agriculture at Purdue at that time, but not in Communication. Today, nearly one third of the Communication graduate students at Purdue are international students, and at last count, they originated from at least 11 different countries (Bangladesh, Canada, Chile, Germany, India, Lebanon, Romania, People's Republic of China, Singapore, South Korea, and Turkey). Communication graduate students at Purdue now have the opportunity to study abroad in northern Italy and to participate in exchanges of faculties and graduate students with universities in Belgium, China, and Dubai, among other places. This type of international diversity and connection is occurring in many graduate programs in the field. Although international students have been part of the Michigan State University (MSU) graduate program for a longer period of time (e.g., Everett Roger's research, funded by USAID, on how international students could become change agents in their own cultures), the diversity of students with interests in interpersonal communication also has increased at MSU over time.

Globalization has not just broadened the nationality of scholars studying interpersonal communication; rather, it has made scholars more reflexive about cultural assumptions underlying theory and research. In the initial volume, Miller (1976b) argued that interactions shift from being non-interpersonal to interpersonal as participants move from relying primarily on shared knowledge about culture and social roles to knowledge of each other as individuals (i.e., persons possessing unique psychological attributes and desires). Despite or perhaps because of this definition, contributors to the first volume paid virtually no attention to culture; indeed, a chapter by Harrison (1976), which reviewed Ekman and Friesen's classic work on cross-cultural similarities in facial displays of affect, is one of the few places where culture is mentioned at all. That Miller's developmental perspective, which equates interpersonal communication with interactions where we really know the other party as an individual, itself reflects a particular cultural view of the self (Kim, 2002; Markus & Kitayama, 1991) became apparent to us (and perhaps to many others) only over time. Culture is also rarely mentioned in the 1987 volume, with the exception of a chapter by Sillars and Weisburg that devoted considerable space to assessing how alternative cultural values regarding expressivity, privacy, and individuality might lead to differing perceptions of the competence of conflict-management strategies across ethnic groups and social classes.

In the past two decades, interpersonal communication scholars, including several contributors to this volume, have conducted research comparing participants from different countries (e.g., Burleson & Mortenson, 2003; Fitch, 1998; Lapinski & Levine, 2000) as well as participants from the United States who are diverse in terms of age, ethnicity, disability status, and social class (e.g., Afifi et al., 2006; Braithwaite & Eckstein, 2003; Wilson, Morgan, Hayes, Bylund, & Herman, 2004). More important, scholars have become increasingly aware that their theories may reflect particular cultural views or values. Two books illustrate this trend. In *Non-Western Perspectives on Human Communication,* Kim (2002) contrasts independent versus interdependent views of the self to highlight the implicit U.S.-centrism that underlies research on a wide range of topics explored by interpersonal scholars, including communication apprehension, conflict management styles, attitude-behavior consistency, deception, self-disclosure, and silence. In her book *Speaking Relationally: Culture, Communication, and Interpersonal Connection,* Fitch (1998) presents a detailed ethnographic analysis of communication and personal relationships in an urban Columbian speech community, and then shows how the interpersonal ideology of connection in this speech community leads to different interpretations and assumptions than those commonly made by interpersonal scholars. Reflecting this trend, many authors in our volume discuss culture as part of their ongoing research programs or plans for future research.

The Dark Side

Prompted by the publication of three edited collections (Spitzberg & Cupach, 1994, 1998, 2007) published in between the Miller volumes and this book, the "dark side" has become an influential metaphor guiding interpersonal communication research. These volumes have drawn attention away from seemingly positive topics such as authenticity, intimacy, and openness that pervaded the early interpersonal communication landscape (Parks, 1982) to also examine dysfunctional and ethically questionable practices such as bullying, deception, hurtful messages, infidelity, stalking, and physical/sexual/verbal aggression—topics that have garnered a great deal of research attention in the past two decades, including by several contributors to this volume. These dark topics also reflect how personal relationships often are represented in contemporary television programming (see Smith & Granados, Chapter 14, this volume).

Yet as Spitzberg and Cupach (2007) note, the dark side metaphor is more than a call to investigate the dysfunctional and ethically objectionable. Instead, it offers a lens for asking more complicated questions that draw attention to

> the ambivalent, multivalent, and multifunctional nature of our needs, goals . . . and courses of action. The dark side seeks acceptance that all social processes unfold in ways that produce both gains and losses, and gains that appear to be losses and losses that appear to be gains. (p. 8)

Thus, seemingly "bright" practices (e.g., assertiveness, self-disclosure, social support) can have negative consequences, whereas seemingly "dark" practices (e.g., avoidance, deception, messages eliciting guilt or shame) can have functional consequences for individuals, relationships, and/or social groups (Kim, 2002; Parks, 1982; Spitzberg & Cupach, 2007). This type of thinking can be found in some chapters from the Miller volumes, such as Morton, Alexander, and Altman's (1976) argument that openness and privacy form a dialectic process that participants regulate as part of the process of achieving a shared relational definition. Dialectical perspectives have had a major impact on interpersonal communication research over the past two decades (see Baxter & Braithwaite, Chapter 3, this volume). Several other contributors also appear to have been influenced by dark-side thinking, such as Burleson's exploration of the conditions under which highly person-centered comforting messages may not be evaluated as much more sensitive or sophisticated than less person-centered messages or Caughlin and Scott's exploration of different forms of demand-withdraw patterns, some of which may not be detrimental to marital or parent/adolescent relationships.

Dominant and Alternative Metatheoretical Voices

Interpersonal communication as an area of study has, from its early days, been influenced by those who advocated taking a social science perspective. Miller himself was a strong proponent of scientific approaches to the study of communication, arguing that such approaches offered feasible, efficacious, and democratic means of acquiring knowledge about communication (Miller, 1981; Miller & Berger, 1978).

Social science perspectives on interpersonal communication scholarship have been described as "empirical" or "post-positivist." Whatever the label, we suspect that many interpersonal scholars would concur with the epistemological and ontological assumptions of what Pavitt (1999, 2000, 2003) terms *scientific realism:*

- Interpersonal communication scholars have never adhered to extreme views associated with the labels "empiricism" or "positivism" such as claims that the only thing about which we can have knowledge is brute sense experience or that unobservable intervening variables should not be part of our theories.

- Observation is theory laden, but this does not necessitate complete "perspectivism" or the position that there is no basis for judging the probability of a knowledge claim independent of one's personal beliefs.

- People are volitional beings, and yet some degree of predictability can be achieved with regard to human action; people make choices, albeit from sets of options and circumstances not entirely of their own making.

- There is no single form that scientific theories or explanations must take; different questions (e.g., "How did X come about?" vs. "What purpose is served by X?") require different answers (i.e., causal vs. functional).

- Interpersonal communication research is influenced by the social and historical contexts in which it is conducted. Scholars need to be reflexive regarding how the questions they ask or the explanations they offer are shaped by cultural values.

- Social science theories of interpersonal communication can be of practical value when they offer general accounts of how desired outcomes can be achieved and hence provide actors with some sense of "control" (i.e., understanding about factors that will influence the probability of them achieving those outcomes, without which they likely will experience feelings of confusion or hopelessness).

Other elements of Pavitt's view (e.g., whether scientific explanations must be "reductive" in the sense he argues) are more controversial, but the preceding points describe the assumptive base for a good deal of interpersonal communication theory and research.

Apart from this dominant perspective, interpersonal communication from its early roots also has included alternative voices who challenged these assumptions. Barnett Pearce presented the Coordinated Management of Meaning in the first chapter of the 1976 volume, a rules-based perspective that rejected the notion that most interpersonal communication was amenable to causal explanation (for a reply, see Miller & Berger, 1978). Bochner (1985, 1994, 2002) has published a "perspectives" chapter in each edition of the *Handbook of Interpersonal Communication Research,* where he initially argued that there is more than one legitimate view about the goals that should underlie interpersonal communication research (also see Braithwaite & Baxter, 2008) and more recently has discussed the value and challenges in doing narrative inquiry on interpersonal communication. Over time, those advocating "social" (e.g., Leeds-Hurwitz, 1995; Shepherd, 1998) and "feminist" (e.g., Wood, 1993) perspectives also have challenged many of the aforementioned assumptions.

Interpersonal communication also has been the subject of ideological critiques, where scholars working within (e.g., Parks, 1982) and outside (e.g., Lannamann, 1991) of the dominant perspective have explored how taken-for-granted assumptions about interpersonal communication reflect cultural and historical forces. Based on this work, Lannamann advocates a critical perspective on interpersonal communication that moves analyses of power away from only interpersonal or dyadic levels to consider societal forces that shape taken-for-granted meanings. In contrast, Parks (1995) draws on the metaphor of an "intellectual commons" to propose guidelines for how scholars working from different perspectives might productively engage each other's work.

We expect that the study of interpersonal communication will continue to feature dominant and alternative metatheoretical voices, a trend that we personally view as healthy. Although most contributors to this volume adopt what has been the dominant voice in interpersonal communication scholarship, contributors working from dialectical (Baxter & Braithwaite), ethnographic (Fitch), and social constructionist (Myers) views reject at least some of the assumptive base that has guided interpersonal research.

Focus on Applied and Funded Scholarship

The focus in our field on applied scholarship is long standing. In fact, the Applied Communication Division of what is now the National Communication Association (NCA) began in 1976, the year that the first Miller volume was published. The division had a focus on organizational and governmental applications at that time. NCA documents of that year contained a statement that the organization would assist members in writing grants and that this was seen as a desirable, but peripheral, service to their other missions. In 1991, NCA officially took over the publication of *The Journal of Applied Communication Research,* although it had been published for some years previously. At MSU in 1973–1975 and 1976–1978, G. R. Miller was heading up a grant funded by the National Science Foundation on videotape in the legal environment (VILE). This grant served as the focus of many theses and dissertations, and the book that resulted won the NCA Golden Anniversary Award. The Hawes and Foley work on Group Decisions in the 1976 book was funded by the Department of Education. Clearly, then, applied and funded research has been a priority in the field of interpersonal communication for quite some time, but today the focus is even stronger. NCA has continued this focus by engaging in a mission to promote funded research in our field (Morgan & Brashers, 2008).

There is a current focus in interpersonal communication scholarship on conducting theoretically grounded research with applied value, and much of this scholarship is funded by grants from foundations and governmental agencies. In fact, two books, *Applied Interpersonal Communication Matters: Family, Health, and Community Relations* (Dailey & LePoire, 2006) and *Studies in Applied Interpersonal Communication* (Motley, 2008) summarize several programs of research that do just this. They highlight socially meaningful research with an interpersonal focus on issues such as substance abuse, violence, sexual intimacy, health problems, divorce, safety, and aging. Although applied research is not our sole focus in this volume, the work of the authors of the present volume and interpersonal communication researchers who are authors in the other two volumes presents strong evidence of the breadth of fine scholarship that is occurring in applied interpersonal communication research today.

Several reasons exist for this upturn in applied and funded research in interpersonal communication. First, granting agencies and scholars in other fields are realizing the importance of communication for their endeavors. Second, funded scholarship has great benefits for departments of communication, although there are some drawbacks as well. Finally, scholars of interpersonal communication are dedicated to conducting socially meaningful research that will benefit others.

Granting agencies are finding communication research increasingly attractive (Buller, 2002). Internally, as universities realize that interdisciplinary teams are beneficial for research, communication is becoming a more central focus on these teams (Harrington, 2002; Slater, 2002). As one example, translational research in health, often referred to as bringing findings from the bench to the bedside, involves communication at its core. Health communication scholars such as Teri Albrecht, Don Cegala, and Rick Street who have long studied doctor-patient communication, and the results from many health campaigns have documented that interpersonal communication is as central to positive outcomes as are mass communication campaigns. A communication team at Michigan State is part of a federally funded Breast Cancer and the Environment Research Center communication core that stands alongside the biology core.

The nature of funded research in communication was the topic of a special issue of *The Journal of Applied Communication Research* in 2002. The authors of the articles in that volume highlighted how funded, applied research has many benefits but some drawbacks as well. It is beneficial to the university at large, particularly if it comes with full indirect costs (Buller, 2002; Harrington, 2002; Slater, 2002). Our field benefits as it receives notice in the social sciences, and more broadly, we are increasingly called on to contribute to policy decisions (Slater, 2002). It is beneficial to colleges and departments because as their reputation within universities and in the field increases, universities are more willing to give seed funds to projects that they believe will later be grant supported; they are more willing to give money for research initiatives, support staff, equipment, and graduate students, and salary savings can be spent on departmental needs (Harrington, 2002). It is beneficial to researchers because they can do socially meaningful work that benefits others, they can think creatively as they apply and further theory that has the potential to solve social problems, their professional reputations are enhanced, and they have the opportunity to fund and mentor graduate students on their research projects (Buller, 2002; Slater, 2002). Some of the drawbacks for departments and researchers as they pursue funded research programs are the time that grant applications and grant management take away from their other duties, the tasks and skills that have to be mastered, the resources that are needed including staff support, and the void in filling departmental teaching slots that is left when faculty and graduate students spend most of their time on funded research.

As noted briefly above, one reason that interpersonal communication scholars have emphasized applied scholarship is their genuine desire to do work that is socially meaningful and that will help others. As one example, Walid Afifi's work with Susan Morgan applied his theory of motivated information management (TMIM) to better understand how family communication affects decisions about organ donation, research that was funded by the Department of Transplantation of the Health Resources and Services Administration (Afifi et al., 2006).

Both of us have worked on applied and funded research within the domain of interpersonal relationships. Sandi worked with Brad Greenberg to investigate interpersonal communication on TV talk shows in 1985, research that was funded by the Kaiser Family Foundation (Smith et al., 1999). Subsequently, she and Stacy Smith received two grants from the Fetzer Institute to conduct research on the portrayal of altruism on television (Smith, Smith, et al., 2006; Smith, Smith, et al., 2008). Currently, she is working on approaches to reduce extreme drinking on campus using the social norms approach and merging it with persuasion theory research, which is funded by the Social Norms Research Institute and the U.S. Department of Education (Smith, Atkin, Martell, Allen, & Hembroff, 2006). Sandi also works on the aforementioned Center Grant for Breast Cancer and the Environment at MSU that is funded by the National Cancer Institute and National Institute of Environmental Health Sciences. She and others, including Chuck Atkin, Kami Silk, Pam Whitten, and Cynthia Stohl, are investigating a variety of communication phenomena related to breast cancer, including memorable messages about breast cancer examining speech acts, emotions evoked, preferred sources, and types of those messages (Smith, Atkin, et al., in press; Smith, Munday, et al., in press).

Steve works as part of a team of academics and service providers evaluating the impact of a new community program designed to enhance children's healthy development and school readiness by providing high-quality early childhood education, parenting education, and home visits (funded by the Lilly Endowment) and also is part of a "Safe Schools/Healthy Students" grant submitted to the Departments of Education and Justice that would evaluate the impact of drug resistance and bullying curricula as they were implemented in middle/high schools in his community.

Several facts seem apparent in this climate of applied and funded scholarship. Graduate students who work on grants and are mentored in the process of acquiring and carrying out grant work in applied areas of interpersonal communication will have an advantage as they begin their academic careers if their institution encourages them to be grant active. Interpersonal communication scholars who can apply their work to help solve real-world problems will advance our field and will likely acquire funding to do so.

Technology

Technology may be the evolving trend that has the most marked difference from when the earlier books were published. Early research on the use of technology in interpersonal relationships claimed that use of "lean" media, such as e-mail, would lead to depersonalization in interpersonal relationships. In the 1980s, there were still scholars arguing that interpersonal communication could only occur between two individuals who were interacting face-to-face. However, even by that point, Gerald Miller's critique of this situational approach to defining interpersonal communication was well known.

Today, we see that interpersonal relationships can be initiated, escalated, maintained, and dissolved either wholly, or in part, through mediated technology. As the title of Walther's (1996) much-cited article claims, computer-mediated communication (CMC) can be impersonal, interpersonal, or even hyperpersonal. The hyperpersonal approach to communication examines how interactants experience affection and intimacy as they assess one another interpersonally through CMC and shows how this process can lead to higher levels of perceived affection and intimacy than can face-to-face interaction. Each person in the CMC relationship can engage in selective self-presentation, and they can, in turn, idealize one other to an extent not possible in face-to-face communication where impressions cannot be enhanced to the same extent.

CMC is now recognized as one of the most fertile venues for dynamics of self-presentation and discerning the veracity of impressions gleaned online (Smith, Yoo, & Walther, 2008, p. 4557). CMC favors strategic self-presentation because many messages can be carefully formed "backstage" and sent asynchronously. When interactants are going to meet or have met face-to-face, the messages need to strike a balance between what is real and what is desirable.

Social networking sites such as Facebook are becoming an increasingly popular means of relating to one another. In a recent study, Foregger (2008) conducted an analysis of uses and gratifications of Facebook. Eight factors emerged as uses for Facebook. Of them, five factors have direct implication for the establishment and maintenance of interpersonal relationships: *connection, sexual attraction, utilities and upkeep* (e.g., posting photos and news about the self for others to see), *establish or maintain social ties,* and *social comparison.* Only *channel use* (as a replacement for e-mail), *marketplace* (to buy and sell), and *pass time* uses were less related to the establishment and development of interpersonal communication.

As technology further evolves, the study of the establishment and maintenance of interpersonal relationships via CMC is an area that will thrive. The topics in the Miller and Roloff volume, such as reciprocity, uncertainty, self-concept, emotion, compliance-gaining, conflict, self-disclosure, information exchange, and methods to analyze interpersonal interaction, could all be profitably studied within the CMC domain of interpersonal relationships today. In that same light, the topics of the current volume are basic interpersonal communication processes and domains that should remain timeless in their use and importance. We now turn to highlight and preview those theories, processes, and domains.

Overview of Chapters

The text begins with Roloff's commentary and this opening chapter. Part I is on *Metatheoretical Approaches to Interpersonal Communication Research*. The chapters in this section present examples of two broad metatheoretical perspectives that underlie current interpersonal research. In Chapter 2, Ascan Koerner and Kory Floyd review the significance of the evolutionary approach to behavioral sciences, including interpersonal communication. Over the past decade, scholars in several disciplines (social psychology, child/family studies) have developed evolutionary perspectives to understand the dynamics of personal relationships. Although they have not collaborated before, Koerner and Floyd both are conducting cutting-edge programs of research in our own discipline based on evolutionary assumptions. Koerner discusses the importance of social instincts for interpersonal relationships and his research on relational schemata and a universal grammar of relationships. Floyd reviews his research on evolutionary explanations of family communication and affectionate behavior. They finish by offering guidelines for the future role of the evolutionary approach in interpersonal communication research.

In Chapter 3, Leslie Baxter and Dawn Braithwaite present the newest version of their relational dialectics theory (RDT), one of the best-known original metatheories of interpersonal communication. After clarifying the goals of dialectical research (and hence criteria appropriate for evaluating RDT), they summarize the core premise and key concepts of RDT. They employ the term *discursive struggles* rather than *contradictions* to highlight how oppositions inherent in relating arise from the broader culture in which relationships are embedded and not just the participants' psychological needs. They review research that applies RDT to understand how participants make sense of contradictions encountered as couples renew their marital vows, children live in stepfamilies, or older women have their husbands moved to a nursing home due to the onset of dementia. They also call for future research that moves beyond identifying competing discourses to explore how those discourses are embedded in the broader culture and the relationship's history, as well as the anticipated reactions of specific/generalized others and how they interanimate meanings created in the moment. These first two chapters work well in tandem (e.g., one stressing universal, the other stressing culturally situated elements of relating) and show how interpersonal communication as an area of study has moved beyond prior metatheoretical debates between the "laws, rules, and systems" or "empirical, interpretive, and critical" scholarly camps.

Part II covers *Basic Interpersonal Processes* such as uncertainty and information management, relationship turbulence, and membership negotiation. The chapters in this section explore processes that occur over time as relationships unfold and that are accomplished via interpersonal communication. In Chapter 4, Leanne Knobloch reviews her emerging program of research on relationship uncertainty. She provides a history of research in this area from Shannon and Weaver to the present. Although her own work builds on Berger's classic uncertainty reduction theory, she recasts uncertainty as a judgment made about relationships themselves (not simply conversational partners) and draws links between participants' judgments and what they say as well as how they interpret their partner's messages in close relationships. She provides an overview of work on sources, levels, themes, and outcomes of relational uncertainty research. She offers important lessons learned from her own research that new researchers can take to heart and more seasoned researchers can use as reminders for good practice in their own work. Finally, she provides some new directions for research in relational uncertainty.

In Chapter 5, Walid Afifi describes the process by which he has developed and tested TMIM, which attempts to explain when participants do (not) seek information from and disclose information to relational partners. TMIM asserts that uncertainty causes anxiety in some situations, and when anxiety arises, the desire to reduce it drives behavior. Interactants then evaluate the costs and benefits associated with information seeking and gaining, including assessments of efficacy. Finally, they either seek or avoid information or cognitively reappraise the situation. One unique feature of TMIM is the attempt to model information management at a dyadic level, exploring decision making by information seekers and providers. He provides a nice overview of all the work currently being done that features uncertainty in our field and shows how this work differs from traditional uncertainty reduction theory in three ways: Uncertainty is sometimes valued, people sometimes avoid information when they are uncertain, and self-efficacy has a role in information management. Future directions for research that highlight TMIM's applied value are embedded within each of these three sections.

In Chapter 6, Denise Solomon, Kirsten Weber, and Keli Steuber explore the challenges that emerge when couples experience changes in their relationship prompted by life transitions. The relational turbulence model is showcased as a theory that accounts for polarized emotions, cognitions, and communication by exploring how relational uncertainty and interdependence both must be renegotiated during transitional periods in romantic relationships. Although tests of the theory have focused on the transition from casual to serious involvement in dating relationships, the model may also provide insight into the impact of transitions confronted by partners within longer-term romantic associations. To develop this point, the authors discuss recent research on how couples experience relationship turning points created by receiving a breast cancer diagnosis and discovering infertility. The opportunities and obstacles for future research on turbulence and transitions beyond courtship are examined.

In Chapter 7, Karen Myers explores how workplace relationships developed between newcomers and organizational veterans can facilitate or impede newcomers' integration into the larger organization. Workplace relationships have important implications for employees, not the least of which is that they play an important role in the process of member negotiation—that is the process by which individuals come to view themselves as organizational members. After describing her development (with John Oetzel) of a six-dimensional model of member negotiation, Myers describes her recent research exploring how women and people of color may face challenges in member negotiation due to factors (e.g., perceived similarity and organizational commitment) that influence workplace relationships with more seasoned organizational members. Her chapter illustrates how interpersonal and organizational literatures can inform one another and also the importance of examining what Miller (1976b) would have termed non-interpersonal as well as interpersonal relationships.

Part III of the book, titled *The Light and Dark Sides of Interpersonal Communication* is composed of four chapters that discuss what people "do" with interpersonal communication. Interpersonal communication can be used to deceive or hurt others, to manage conflict, and to provide support. By focusing on purposes that may be more or less healthy for relationships as well as complex message effects, the chapters in this section highlight the recent trend toward studying the "dark side" of interpersonal communication as described above.

In Chapter 8, Brant Burleson presents his recently developed dual-process model for the reception of social support messages. He describes his 30-year program of research on social support, from early work describing the characteristics and documenting the effects of highly versus less person-centered (HPC vs. LPC) comforting messages to later work (with Daena Goldsmith) developing a theory of conversationally induced reappraisal that explains how HPC messages influence a recipient's appraisals and hence emotional reactions. Although HPC comforting messages typically are evaluated as much more sensitive and effective than LPC, research also has found smaller but reliable individual, situational, and cultural differences in the degree to which this is the case—differences that until recently had been largely ignored. Building on dual-process models of persuasion, the newest work by Burleson attempts to explain personality, gender, situational, and cultural differences in the degree to which people prefer HPC over LPC messages, arguing that a recipient's ability and motivation to process support messages will influence the degree to which what is said versus just being there matters. His chapter illustrates the evolution of a research program over time, including the variety of factors that influence the directions that one's research takes.

In Chapter 9, John Caughlin and Allison Scott present their program of research on demand-withdrawal sequences, a conflict pattern where one party complains or nags while the other avoids the issue. After describing how this pattern has been investigated over time as well as its association with aversive outcomes in marital and parent/child relationships, they highlight limitations in current explanations for the pattern. Although most explanations assume that demanding and withdrawing are enacted in pursuit of goals, they fail to recognize that communicators are responsive to multiple, conflicting goals. The authors then offer a new explanation grounded in the multiple goals literature: "Demanding" and "withdrawing" are behaviors that can be motivated by different combinations of goals, which suggests that they may take different forms. Going back to videotaped interactions from their earlier research, they tentatively identify four different patterns of demand-withdrawal sequences and speculate how these patterns may be differentially associated with relational satisfaction (a direction for future work).

Chapter 10 is authored by two scholars, Judee Burgoon and Tim Levine, who have engaged in vigorous scholarly debate about how and when individuals are able to detect when others (including close others) are deceiving them. The authors provide a foundation for their separate research by first delineating three widely accepted findings in deception detection research and the reasons why people exhibit only slightly better than chance accuracy as they detect truth and deception, why their confidence in their ability to detect deception does not lead to accuracy, and the fact that they have a truth bias, especially in face-to-face interactions and with close others. Burgoon lays out the basics of interpersonal deception theory and provides results from two selected studies that highlight various influences on receiver judgments of truth and deception. Levine provides more evidence for the truth bias, discusses that the results of deception laboratory experiments are a function of the proportion of truth and lies presented to respondents, and reports on a study that found that lie detection in interpersonal relationships outside the lab often occurred after the fact. They end their chapter with a discussion of six directions that are important for the future of deception detection research. Both Burgoon and Levine focus on the interpersonal nature of the dyad as a main factor in truth bias and deception detection, and show the points on which they agree and what types of future studies are needed to resolve important controversies.

In Chapter 11, Anita Vangelisti and Alexa Hampel discuss their ongoing program of research on "hurtful" communication, how it fits in with several other programs of research on hurt in close relationships, how it has developed over time, and where it is headed in the future. Hurt feelings typically arise in response to relational transgressions that imply relational devaluation and thus threaten one's sense of safety and security. The authors present a thorough review of individual and relational factors as well as family cultures that influence interpretations and reactions to hurtful behavior. Perhaps more than any other chapter in our book, this one illustrates the progress that can be made toward understanding an important phenomenon when research teams from multiple disciplines are focused on a common topic and directly engage one another's work.

The last section of the book (Part IV) concerns *Relationships, Media, and Culture*. All three chapters in this section look at intersections between interpersonal communication, new/traditional media, and/or cultural portrayals of close relationships. In Chapter 12, Kristine Fitch describes her ongoing program of research on the cultural grounding of personal relationships. She describes her extensive ethnographic fieldwork on personal relationships in Columbia and how this work helped illuminate theretofore unexamined cultural assumptions underlying traditional literatures on compliance gaining, politeness, and so on. Her newer work uses ethnographic and semiotic (e.g., analysis of media texts) methods to compare relational codes—systems of meaning developed within particular relationships—embedded in four cultures. She discusses challenges in doing ethnographic research on interpersonal communication as well as writing for diverse audiences (interpersonal but also cultural studies scholars).

In Chapter 13, Joe Walther and Art Ramirez trace the development of theories and research on how individuals form relationships online. Given the widespread adoption and normalization of many forms of CMC, they argue for an explanation of media choice that focuses on the fact that different media channels may be chosen depending on participants' interpersonal goals. Given their theoretical training as communication scientists with a focus on nonverbal communication, they adopt a functional perspective that assumes that communicators use whichever cues are at hand when they communicate with others for various reasons. That belief underpins the development and testing of social information processing theory and the hyperpersonal model of CMC. Their chapter leads the reader through various technological situations and their interpersonal communication implications, ranging from photographic and avatar image-based CMC; plain text CMC, where conditions are ripe for idealization of a communication partner; and online and off-line mixed modes and social networking sites to the Web 2.0, which is essentially relationally based. Throughout the chapter, they highlight opportunities for future research.

Finally, Stacy Smith and Amy Granados, in Chapter 14, explore how close relationships are portrayed on television, focusing on violence, gender, and sexuality aspects of interpersonal relationships. The authors examine television portrayals of interpersonal relationships because they can be powerful sources of social learning for adolescents and adults about romantic relationships, friendships, emotional displays, race relations, or even antisocial behaviors. They examine theory and research on the effects that media depictions of violence, gender, and sexuality may have on viewers. They offer important insights about how interpersonal communication scholarship can inform media research in the future and discuss other future directions for research that they hope will set an agenda for both media and interpersonal communication scholars interested in assessing portrayals of interpersonal exchanges. Taken together, the chapters in this final section respond to historical calls for greater convergence between interpersonal and media studies as well as greater scrutiny of how people's conceptions of personal relationships are influenced by their larger culture.

References

Afifi, W., Morgan, S. E., Stephenson, M., Morse, C., Harrison, T., Reichert, T., et al. (2006). Examining the decision to talk with family about organ donation: Applying the theory of motivated information management. *Communication Monographs, 73*, 188–215.

Berger, C. R. (2005). Interpersonal communication: Theoretical perspectives, future prospects. *Journal of Communication, 55*, 415–447.

Bochner, A. (1985). Perspectives on inquiry: Representation, conversation, and reflection. In M. L. Knapp & G. R. Miller (Eds.), *Handbook of interpersonal communication* (pp. 27–58). Beverly Hills, CA: Sage.

Bochner, A. (1994). Perspectives on inquiry II: Theories and stories. In M. L. Knapp & G. R. Miller (Eds.), *Handbook of interpersonal communication* (2nd ed., pp. 21–41). Thousand Oaks, CA: Sage.

Bochner, A. (2002). Perspectives on inquiry III: The moral of stories. In M. L. Knapp & J. A. Daly (Eds.), *Handbook of interpersonal communication* (3rd ed., pp. 73–101). Thousand Oaks, CA: Sage.

Bochner, A. (2008, January). The consequences of fragmentation: Is the NCA convention over-programmed? *Spectra*, 3–5.

Braithwaite, D. O., & Baxter, L. (Eds.). (2008). *Engaging theories in interpersonal communication: Multiple perspectives.* Thousand Oaks, CA: Sage.

Braithwaite, D. O., & Eckstein, N. J. (2003). How people with disabilities communicatively manage assistance: Helping as instrumental support. *Journal of Applied Communication Research, 31,* 1–26.

Buller, D. B. (2002). Final thoughts on funded communication research. *Journal of Applied Communication Research, 30,* 411–417.

Burleson, B. R. (1992). Taking communication seriously. *Communication Monographs, 59,* 79–86.

Burleson, B. R., & Mortenson, S. R. (2003). Explaining cultural differences in evaluations of emotional support behaviors: Exploring the mediating influences of value systems and interaction goals. *Communication Research, 30,* 113–146.

Cappella, J. N. (1987). Interpersonal communication: Definition and fundamental questions. In C. R. Berger & S. H. Chaffee (Eds.), *Handbook of communication science* (pp. 184–238). Newbury Park, CA: Sage.

Dailey, R. M., & LePoire, B. A. (2006). *Applied interpersonal communication matters: Family, health, and community relations.* New York: Peter Lang.

Fitch, K. L. (1998). *Speaking relationally: Culture, communication, and interpersonal connection.* New York: Guilford Press.

Foregger, S. (2008). *Uses and gratifications of Facebook.com.* Unpublished doctoral dissertation, Michigan State University.

Harrington, N. G. (2002). Funded research in communication: A chairperson's perspective. *Journal of Applied Communication Research, 30,* 393–401.

Harrison, R. P. (1976). The face in face-to-face interaction. In G. R. Miller (Ed.), *Explorations in interpersonal communication research* (pp. 217–236). Beverly Hills, CA: Sage.

Kim, M. S. (2002). *Non-Western perspectives on human communication: Implications for theory and practice.* Thousand Oaks, CA: Sage.

Knapp, M. L., & Daly, J. A. (Eds.). (2002). *Handbook of interpersonal communication* (3rd ed.). Thousand Oaks, CA: Sage.

Knapp, M. L., & Miller, G. R. (Eds.). (1985). *Handbook of interpersonal communication.* Newbury Park, CA: Sage.

Knapp, M. L., & Miller, G. R. (Eds.). (1994). *Handbook of interpersonal communication* (2nd ed.). Thousand Oaks, CA: Sage.

Lannamann, J. W. (1991). Interpersonal communication research as ideological practice. *Communication Theory, 1,* 179–203.

Lapinski, M. K., & Levine, T. (2000). Culture and information manipulation theory: The effects of self-construal and locus of benefit on information manipulation. *Communication Studies, 51,* 55–73.

Leeds-Hurwitz, W. (Ed.). (1995). *Social approaches to communication.* New York: Guilford Press.

Markus, H. R., & Kitayama, S. (1991). Culture and the self: Implications for cognition, emotion, and motivation. *Psychological Review, 98,* 224–252.

Miller, G. R. (Ed.). (1976a). *Explorations in interpersonal communication.* Beverly Hills, CA: Sage.

Miller, G. R. (1976b). Foreword. In G. R. Miller (Ed.), *Explorations in interpersonal communication* (pp. 9–16). Beverly Hills, CA: Sage.

Miller, G. R. (1981). "'Tis the season to be jolly": A yuletide assessment of communication research. *Human Communication Research, 7,* 317–377.

Miller, G. R., & Berger, C. R. (1978). On keeping the faith in matters scientific. *Western Journal of Communication, 42,* 44–57.

Miller, G. R., & Steinberg, M. (1975). *Between people: A new analysis of interpersonal communication.* Chicago: Science Research Associates.

Morgan, S. E., & Brashers, D. (2008, April). Research funding, Report from the research board. *Spectra,* 6–9.

Morton, T. L., Alexander, J. F., & Altman, I. (1976). Communication and relationship definition. In G. R. Miller (Ed.), *Explorations in interpersonal communication* (pp. 105–126). Beverly Hills, CA: Sage.

Motley, M. T. (2008). *Studies in applied interpersonal communication.* Thousand Oaks, CA: Sage.

Parks, M. (1982). Ideology in interpersonal communication: Off the couch and into the world. In M. Burgoon (Ed.), *Communication yearbook 5* (pp. 79–107). New Brunswick, NJ: Transaction Books.

Parks, M. (1995). Ideology in interpersonal communication research: Beyond the couches, talk shows, and bunkers. In B. R. Burleson (Ed.), *Communication yearbook 18* (pp. 480–497). Thousand Oaks, CA: Sage.

Pavitt, C. (1999). The third way: Scientific realism and communication theory. *Communication Theory, 9,* 162–188.

Pavitt, C. (2000). Answering questions requesting scientific explanations for communication. *Communication Theory, 10,* 379–404.

Pavitt, C. (2003). Theory-data interaction from the standpoint of scientific realism: A reaction to Bostrom. *Communication Monographs, 71,* 333–342.

Pearce, W. B. (1976). The coordinated management of meaning: A rules-based theory of interpersonal communication. In G. R. Miller (Ed.), *Explorations in interpersonal communication* (pp. 17–36). Beverly Hills, CA: Sage.

Roloff, M. E., & Anastasiou, L. (2000). Interpersonal communication research: An overview. In W. B. Gudykunst (Ed.), *Communication yearbook 24* (pp. 51–70). Thousand Oaks, CA: Sage.

Roloff, M. E. & Miller, G. R. (Eds.). (1987). *Interpersonal processes: New directions in communication research.* Newbury Park, CA: Sage.

Shepherd, G. J. (1998). The trouble with goals. *Communication Studies, 49,* 294–299.

Sillars, A. L., & Weisburg, J. (1987). Conflict as a social skill. In M. E. Roloff & G. R. Miller (Eds.), *Interpersonal processes: New directions in communication research* (pp. 140–171). Newbury Park, CA: Sage.

Slater, M. D. (2002). Communication research on a broader stage: An introduction to the special forum on funded research in communication. *Journal of Applied Communication Research, 30,* 315–320.

Smith, S. L., Smith, S. W., Pieper, K. M., Downs, E., Yoo, J., Ferris, A., et al. (2008). Conceptualizing altruism on American television: The development of a content coding scheme. In S. Sprecher, L. Underwood, & B. Fehr (Eds.), *The science of compassionate love: Research, theory, and applications* (pp. 53–79). Oxford, UK: Wiley-Blackwell.

Smith, S. W., Atkin, C. K., Martell, D., Allen, R., & Hembroff, L. (2006). A social judgment theory approach to conducting formative research in a social norms campaign. *Communication Theory, 16,* 141–152.

Smith, S. W., Atkin, C. K., Munday, S., Skubisz, C., & Stohl, C. (in press). The impact of personal and/or close relationship experience on memorable messages about breast cancer and the perceived speech acts of the sender. *Journal of Cancer Education.*

Smith, S. W., Mitchell, M., AhYun, J., Johnson, A., Orrego, V., & Greenberg, B. S. (1999). The nature of close relationships as presented in television talk shows. *Communication Studies, 50,* 175–187.

Smith, S. W., Munday, S., LaPlante, C., Kotowski, M. R., Atkin, C. K., Skubisz, C., et al. (in press). Topics and sources of memorable breast cancer messages: Their impact on prevention and detection behaviors. *Journal of Health Communication.*

Smith, S. W., Smith, S. L., Pieper, K. M., Yoo, J. H., Ferris, A., Downs, E., et al. (2006). Altruism on American television: Examining the prevalence of, and context surrounding, such acts. *Journal of Communication, 56,* 707–727.

Smith, S. W., Yoo, J. H., & Walther, J. (2008). Self presentation. In W. Donsbach (Ed.), *The international encyclopedia of communication* (Vol. 10, pp. 4555–4559). Oxford, UK: Wiley-Blackwell.

Spitzberg, B. H., & Cupach, W. R. (Eds.). (1994). *The dark side of interpersonal communication.* Hillsdale, NJ: Lawrence Erlbaum.

Spitzberg, B. H., & Cupach, W. R. (Eds.). (1998). *The dark side of close relationships.* Mahwah, NJ: Lawrence Erlbaum.

Spitzberg, B. H., & Cupach, W. R. (Eds.). (2007). *The dark side of interpersonal communication* (2nd ed.). Mahwah, NJ: Lawrence Erlbaum.

Walther, J. B. (1996). Computer-mediated communication: Impersonal, interpersonal, and hyperpersonal interaction. *Communication Research, 23,* 3–43.

Wilson, S. R., Morgan, W. M., Hayes, J., Bylund, C. E., & Herman, A. P. (2004). Mothers' child abuse potential as a predictor of maternal and child behaviors during playtime interactions. *Communication Monographs, 71,* 395–421.

Wood, J. T. (1993). Enlarging conceptual boundaries: A critique of research in interpersonal communication. In S. P. Bowen & N. J. Wyatt (Eds.), *Transforming visions: Feminist critiques of speech communication* (pp. 19–50). New Jersey: Ablex.

PART I

Metatheoretical Approaches to Interpersonal Communication Research

2

Evolutionary Perspectives on Interpersonal Relationships

Ascan F. Koerner

Kory Floyd

Interpersonal communication research is inherently interdisciplinary. Interpersonal communication scholars often integrate and synthesize the work of other disciplines, and their work is affected by developments in those disciplines. One such development is the (re)emergence of evolutionary approaches for studying human behavior. Although evolutionary theory is considered among humanity's crowning scientific-theoretical achievements ever since Darwin (1859), its early (mis)application to human behaviors had regrettable consequences such as justifications of colonialism, slavery, eugenics, and genocide. Partially due to these abuses, evolutionary explanations of human behavior have been discredited for most of the latter part of the 20th century. Recently, however, evolutionary explanations of human behavior have become more sophisticated in their descriptive and predictive ability and in their ethical awareness, and have regained currency in many of the social sciences. In fact, evolutionary theory is poised to become the standard explanatory framework for any scientific explanation of human behavior.

This change has taken place mainly in psychology. With a few exceptions, interpersonal communication researchers thus far have largely ignored these changes. This is unfortunate, because it means that our discipline ignores what we personally consider to be the most exciting new insights into human behavior, in general, and interpersonal communication, in particular. In this chapter, we will show why these insights are so exciting and how they have affected our own research and that of others. Ultimately, we hope to motivate interpersonal communication scholars to consider the relevance of evolutionary theory to their own investigations and to provoke a new dialogue among interpersonal communication scholars about the potential utility and consequences of adopting evolutionary principles as a guiding framework for inquiry. We believe that these efforts will ultimately contribute to the development of this important theoretic approach and help shape how it is used to explain human behavior rather than leaving this important task to other disciplines.

After a brief primer on evolutionary psychology, we review our own research in interpersonal communication that is informed by evolutionary theory. Then we discuss research by others both within and outside our discipline that has used evolutionary theory to address issues relevant to interpersonal communication. We will conclude with a short section on future developments that we foresee for the evolutionary approach to interpersonal communication.

Evolutionary Psychology: A Primer

Thus far, the most sophisticated accounts of how evolution affects human behavior have been provided by evolutionary psychologists. Because not all readers are familiar with it, we briefly review its key insights and concepts here. For more complete introductions, we refer the reader to Buss (2007) and Buss and Kenrick (1998).

Evolutionary psychology is based on Darwin's (1859) theory of evolution, which in its modern form proposes that species evolve because their genetic information is subject to random mutation and natural selection. In this process, selection favors those mutations, called adaptations, that increase the gene carrier's chance at reproduction and survival, which are more likely to be passed on to the next generation. Thus, selection affects both survival and reproductive strategies of the organism. An important clarification about selection is that it operates at the level of the gene, not at the level of the organism. Thus, adaptations are not necessarily best for the individual, but will best ensure the continuation of the individual's genes into subsequent generations. This feature of selection helps explain, for instance, why individuals invest resources in their children, nieces and nephews, or grandchildren, even at a cost to themselves (a topic we will take up in greater detail below). Another important insight of evolutionary theory is that for adaptations to occur, the mutation need not lead to perfection. All that is required for an adaptation is a comparative advantage over intra- and interspecies competitors, given the environmental conditions at the time.

A core concept in evolutionary psychology is *evolved psychological mechanism* (EPM), which is the cognitive equivalent to the physical adaptation in bodily evolution. EPMs are genetically based and therefore subject to evolution. They allow an organism to solve routine information processing problems of survival and reproduction efficiently and reliably. Examples of EPMs in humans related to survival include a preference for fatty and sugary foods (motivating sufficient calorie intake) and fear of heights (avoiding dangerous places). Examples of EPMs related to reproduction include a preference for mates exhibiting signs of genetic and physical health, because resulting offspring would have the best chances for survival.

Another core concept in evolutionary psychology is the *environment of evolutionary adaptedness* (EEA), which refers to the environmental conditions that promoted a specific adaptation. These are potentially at odds with the current environment that the organism inhabits. Examples in humans include again humans' preference for high-calorie foods, which in the industrialized world where food is plentiful may actually be maladaptive because it leads to obesity. Throughout human history, however, food supplies were unreliable and usually insufficient, and this adaptation ensured that humans at least attempted to ingest enough sugar and fat to survive. Considering the long time required for humans to go through enough generations for genetic changes to penetrate the gene pool, the EEA is particularly important, because it forces scholars to consider the conditions present when adaptations occurred rather than considering the conditions humans face today. The length of time required for adaptations to take place also suggests that the specific problem addressed by an EPM has to have been a historically stable aspect of the environment. Given that humans and their ancestors have lived in groups for millennia, the fundamental interpersonal challenges they face have not substantially changed over thousands of generations (such as finding and retaining mates, building coalitions, maintaining groups, influencing others, and coordinating activities) and, quite possibly, are subject to evolution.

Our Own Work: Using Evolutionary Theory in Interpersonal Communication

Here, we discuss how we use evolutionary theory researching important interpersonal processes. We both come from interpersonal communication programs emphasizing quantitative social science (Floyd at Arizona,

Koerner at Wisconsin), but neither had been trained in evolutionary explanations of communicative behaviors. Starting our own research programs, however, we soon realized that many of the communication phenomena we were interested in could be better understood when considering an evolutionary framework. Examples discussed below include Koerner's work on relational models and sharing social reality in families and Floyd's work on resource allocation in families and the effects of affectionate communication on personal health.

Relational Models

Research has shown that relational knowledge comes in two forms, declarative and procedural (Baldwin, 1992). Declarative knowledge defines what things are, whereas procedural knowledge defines how things work in the form of if-then contingencies. Both types of knowledge are not acquired by the brain in the passive and reflective manner, as if inscribed onto a tabula rasa (Pinker, 2002). Rather, the brain anticipates what it learns from interaction with the environment by having certain proto brain structures that, when exposed to the right stimuli, develop into the appropriate representations. For example, as social mammals, humans are inherently equipped with social instincts (EPMs related to relationships) that allow them to form and maintain interpersonal relationships. Like other EPMs, these have been subject to evolutionary pressures. Pinker (1994) has explicated a similar process with regard to language acquisition and shown that children will develop complete representations of language even when exposed to incomplete or inconsistent examples of language use in their speech communities, something he argues is only possible because of proto language structures in the developing brain.

Extending this idea, Koerner (2006) proposed that cognitive representations of relationships are based on an evolved "universal grammar of relationships." An important aspect of this grammar is fundamental forms of relating, which Koerner argued consist of relational models first identified by Fiske (1991, 1992, 2004): communal sharing, authority ranking, equality matching, and market pricing.

Communal sharing is similar to Mills and Clark's (1982) communal relationship. Relating according to this model means that partners are equivalent and undifferentiated and share values, beliefs, and goals. In communal sharing, no distinct individual identities exist; rather, the groups to which individuals belong are differentiated. Communal sharing is often based on perceptions of common bonds, such as familial or tribal relationships.

Authority ranking means persons are differentiated by social rank, and identity is equivalent to rank. Differences between individuals arise from their hierarchical positions with respect to one another. Each rank brings with it its own set of rights and responsibilities, which form the basis for expectations and evaluations of one's own and of others' behaviors.

Equality matching means equality between individuals. When using this model, persons maintain equality, and interactions and exchanges are balanced in direct one-for-one reciprocity, such as turn-taking or tit-for-tat retaliation. In equality matching, individuals are distinct social entities with the *exact* same rights and responsibilities. Imbalances are salient and need to be resolved because they violate the basis of the relationship.

Market pricing means interactions and social exchanges are similar to economic transactions. Relating according to this model is characterized by proportionality, which requires that different aspects of relationships are converted to a single currency or metric. Existing imbalances in certain domains of a relationship can be balanced by reverse imbalances in other domains of the same relationship. The market pricing relational model is roughly equivalent to social exchange theory (Roloff, 1981, 1987; Rusbult & Buunk, 1993) and to Mills and Clark's exchange relationship (Clark & Mills, 1979; Mills & Clark, 1982).

It is important to remember that relational models specify ways of relating; not relationships. That is, within interpersonal relationships, partners relate to each other using all four relational models at different times and in different relationship domains. Koerner (2006) demonstrated this by comparing relational model use across three relationship types (mother, friend, and acquaintance) and two cultures (the United States and Singapore). Results showed that in eight different relationship domains (exchange, distribution and use, working, decision making, influence, identity, relating, and relationship), participants used all four relational models to varying degrees in their three relationships. The relative use of relational models was affected by culture (i.e., horizontal and vertical individualism/collectivism, Triandis, 1995), by relationship type, and by relationship domain.

Regarding culture, Koerner found that horizontal collectivism was correlated with communal sharing, vertical collectivism with authority ranking, horizontal individualism with equality matching, and vertical individualism with market pricing. These correlations, however, were only modest ($.11 < r < .26$), indicating that while there is a main effect of culture on relational model use, it is a small one.

With respect to relationship types, results indicted that participants in their relationships with mothers most frequently used communal sharing, followed by authority ranking and equality matching, and finally market pricing. In friendships, communal sharing and equality matching were used most frequently, followed by market pricing, and authority ranking was used least. In acquaintanceships, equality matching and market pricing were used most frequently, and communal sharing and authority ranking were used least. Although the differences in model use explained by relationship type were statistically significant, the effects sizes again were modest ($\eta_p^2 = .04$ to $.11$).

Main effects were also obtained for relationship domains, reflecting that certain relational models are used more frequently in some domains regardless of relationship type. For example, in decision making, communal sharing was used frequently, but equality matching and authority ranking were not. More important than the main effects for relationship, culture, and domain, however, was that all possible two- and three-way interactions between culture, relationship type, and relationship domains were significant ($\eta_p^2 = .04$ to $.29$). This indicates that while the forms of relating defined by the relational models are stable, how they are used in relationships is dynamic and affected by culture, relationship type, relationship domains and how these variables interact. Rather than describing stable relationships, relational models constitute the building blocks of the combinatorial system that makes up the universal grammar of relationships. Discovering the rules by which these building blocks are combined, and particularly, how such rules are negotiated communicatively, still needs to be investigated. Because the cognitive mechanisms underlying these rules must have evolved, this discovery will only be possible if future research is informed by an evolutionary framework.

Family Communication and Shared Social Reality

Another area in which Koerner's research is informed by evolutionary theory is family communication patterns theory, which describes how habitual use of communication behaviors to achieve shared social reality leads to stable family communication patterns with predictable outcomes. Koerner and colleagues investigated how genetic relatedness affects family communication in the context of adoption and tested the hypothesis that different types of family communication patterns have different effects on adopted versus nonadopted children.

An initial study (Rueter & Koerner, 2008), using a sample of 592 family quartets (2 parents and 2 children) consisting of families with various configurations of biological and adopted children, produced results that suggest that family communication patterns are more influential on the adjustment and social competence of adopted than of biological children. Specifically, family communication that de-emphasizes conversation orientation put adopted children at a three to five times higher risk for maladaptation than biological children. In contrast, there are no differences in adjustment between biological and adopted children stemming from families emphasizing conversation orientation. Thus, whereas "good" communication benefits all children equally well, "poor" parent-child communication does create risk especially for adopted children, whereas biological children seem more resilient to it. Rueter and Koerner interpret these findings to mean that biologically related family members are less reliant on communication to establish a shared reality than nonrelated family members, because some of their social perception and thought processes are more similar than those of biologically unrelated family members. Clearly, this research program is just developing and these findings and explanations are preliminary at this point, but like Koerner's work on relational models, they do suggest an important contribution of social EPMs, which ultimately can only be understood within an evolutionary framework.

Resource Allocation in Family Relationships

One superordinate evolutionary goal is reproduction, but because selection operates at the level of genes rather than organisms, individuals need not reproduce for genes to achieve reproductive success. In his *theory of inclusive fitness,* Hamilton (1964) clarified that individuals can aid the reproductive success of their genes not only by procreation, but also by aiding other carriers of their genetic material such as siblings, nephews, or cousins. Relationships vary in terms of their level of genetic relatedness, that is, the proportion of genes that vary from person to person. For instance, monozygotic twins share 100% of their genes, whereas dizygotic twins, full biological siblings, and parents and children share 50%. Half-biological siblings and grandparents and grandchildren share 25%, first cousins share 12.5%, and individuals typically share none of their unique genetic material with steprelatives, adoptive relatives, in-laws, and spouses. Consequently, some personal relationships are more important than others in terms of their ability to contribute to reproductive success.

It is therefore adaptive with respect to reproductive success for individuals to contribute more of their resources to those who share their genes than to genetically unrelated others, other things being equal. This qualification—other things being equal—is consequential for two reasons. First, in apparent contradiction to Hamilton's (1964) argument, people routinely invest heavily in friends and romantic partners with whom they share no genetic material. Two observations resolve this ostensible contradiction. First, romantic partners often become sexual partners, enabling direct reproduction, and even platonic friends can contribute to one's reproductive success by facilitating introductions to potential romantic partners. Thus, even though friends and romantic partners often share none of an individual's genetic material, they can both contribute to the individual's reproductive success. Second, although reproduction is a superordinate goal, it is not one's only goal in life. More proximal goals, such as security or companionship, can motivate the formation of relationships even if they have no potential to contribute to reproductive success.

A second reason is that genetic relatedness alone does not determine how successful a relative is in propagating one's genes. Individual differences matter. For example, a menopausal aunt is less likely to propagate one's genes than a pregnant granddaughter, even though one shares an equal proportion of genes with each. Thus, we would expect adults to invest more heavily in younger relatives than in the older ones.

When all else is equal, however, genetic relatedness does determine investment. For example, Daly and Wilson (1980) argued that parents discriminate among children when investing resources, to maximize their own chances for reproductive success, a claim supported by Anderson, Kaplan, and Lancaster (1997), who found parents investing substantially more economic resources in biological children than in stepchildren.

Floyd (2006) has proposed that the communication of affection is a resource that contributes to survival via its health benefits and, therefore, to the ability to procreate. If Hamilton's (1964) and Daly and Wilson's (1980) theories are correct, it follows that certain relationships should be more affectionate than others. This hypothesis has been tested in family relationships that vary systematically in genetic relatedness. For instance, Floyd and Morman (2002) found that men gave more affection to biological sons than to stepsons. Similarly, Floyd and Morr (2003) reported that adults were more affectionate with siblings than siblings-in-law. Importantly, each of these findings would support alternative, nonevolutionary explanations. For instance, most people have known their biological relatives longer than their steprelatives or in-laws, and probably feel emotionally closer to their biological relatives; thus, variables such as closeness or relationship duration could account for the difference in affectionate behavior observed between relationship types. In both studies, however, the differences in affectionate behavior could not be accounted for by differences in closeness, relational duration, proximity, frequency of contact, or other plausible alternatives. Even with these variables controlled, the relationships still differed systematically in their levels of affectionate behavior in the manner that an evolutionary explanation predicts.

Daly and Wilson (1980) also suggested that parents discriminate even among their biological children, investing more resources in those who are most likely to produce offspring. Because parents have greater reproductive success when their children reproduce than when they do not, it is adaptive for them to invest more in children with greater reproductive potential. Several factors might inhibit reproductive probability, including sterility or the inability to attract a mate. Homosexuality also inhibits reproductive probability, and research has shown that fathers give more affection to heterosexual than homosexual sons, even with competing explanations controlled (Floyd, 2001).

Affectionate Communication and Health

A robust literature demonstrates that receiving affectionate behavior benefits health (Floyd, 2006), and recent research has illuminated the health benefits of expressing affection. Floyd's (2006) *affection exchange theory* (AET) argues that affectionate behavior is adaptive when received and also when expressed. Specifically, receiving and expressing affection reduces the body's susceptibility to stress and activates its hormonal reward systems, which have sedative and analgesic effects.

Several studies aimed to identify the health parameters most reliably associated with affectionate communication. For instance, Floyd (2002) demonstrated that highly affectionate people are happier, more self-assured, less stressed, less likely to be depressed, more likely to engage in regular social activity, less likely to experience social isolation, and more likely to be in good mental health. Similarly, Floyd, Hesse, and Haynes (2007) found that a higher trait affection level is associated with lower blood pressure.

Based on these associations, experiments have examined potential causal relationships between affection and health. For instance, Floyd, Mikkelson, Tafoya, et al. (2007) found that affectionate writing accelerates recovery from stress, and Floyd, Mikkelson, Hesse, and Pauley (2007) demonstrated that affectionate writing significantly reduced cholesterol. Current work in Floyd's laboratory is investigating outcomes such as C-reactive protein, Epstein-Barr virus antibodies, and serum glucose. If affectionate communication is adaptive for survival, as AET claims, then exploration of its health benefits can generate understanding about the connections between social behavior and well-being.

The Work of Others: Applications of Evolutionary Theory Relevant to Interpersonal Communication

We are far from the only scholars using the evolutionary perspective in ways that inform our understanding of interpersonal communication. Indeed, most relevant work is done in other disciplines, and it behooves interpersonal communication researchers to be aware of the implications of this research for the study of interpersonal communication. In this section, we take a brief look at three areas of research that are informed by evolutionary theories and relevant for interpersonal communication: attachment, physical attraction, and the interpersonal investments of mothers and fathers in their children.

Attachment

Few relationship theories rival attachment theory in terms of the attention it has received and the research it has inspired. Often overlooked is that attachment theory is firmly rooted in evolutionary theory. Influenced by the work of early ethologists such as Konrad Lorenz, who studied imprinting of birds, Bowlby investigated attachment bonds between infants and primary caregivers, based on the understanding that such bonds are required for infants to survive and therefore should be instinctive, that is, evolved.

Attachment is particularly relevant to applications of evolutionary informed interpersonal research because it illuminates the interdependence of innateness, EPMs, and the environment. Regardless of the specific model of attachment proposed, attachment theories (Ainsworth, Blehar, Waters, & Walls, 1978; Bartholomew, 1990; Bartholomew & Horowitz, 1991; Bowlby, 1969, 1972) propose that infant attachment develops based on care received from primary caregivers. Consistent and responsive care leads to secure attachment, consistent neglect leads to avoidant and/or dismissive attachment, and inconsistent or overinvolved care leads to anxious-ambivalent or preoccupied attachment. Thus, it is the combination of an EPM (i.e., the attachment system) with environmental stimuli (i.e., parental care) that leads to the socially relevant behavior (i.e., infant attachment). Thus, rather than describing a deterministic and inflexible process that excludes the social, attachment describes an evolved mechanism that is flexible and responsive to the environment.

Physical Attractiveness in Personal Relationships

From an evolutionary perspective, the principal reason physical attraction exists is to promote procreation. It follows that physical attributes humans find attractive should enhance the potential for producing healthy offspring. Thus, what physical features are generally considered attractive is neither due to chance nor the product of culture or media messages. Empirical research supports this view and shows that the notion "beauty is in the eye of the beholder," although pervasive, is largely untrue; humans show substantial agreement in what they find physically attractive about others. There is individual, cultural, and historical variation in judgments of attractiveness, but it is minimal compared with the level of consistency across individuals, cultures, and time periods (Buss, 1989).

One practically universal predictor of attractiveness is symmetry—the extent to which both sides of the body mirror each other. During fetal development, environmental stressors (e.g., pollutants) and genetic problems (e.g., recessive genes) cause an organism to deviate from symmetry, making symmetry a reliable marker of genetic fitness (Trivers, Manning, Thornhill, Singh, & McGuire, 1999). Thus, humans should find symmetry attractive, and multiple studies confirm this (Langlois et al., 2000).

Another practically universal aspect of attractiveness is a female's waist-to-hip ratio (WHR). Across cultures and historical periods, women have been considered most attractive when their WHR is approximately .70 (Singh, 1993). This is true regardless of the woman's absolute body dimensions; for instance, every single Miss America crowned between 1923 and 1987—during which time preferences for women's overall body type varied—had a WHR between .69 and .72 (Singh, 1993).

A WHR of .70 also maximizes fertility. In women, it corresponds to higher levels of estrogens (Tonkelaar, Seidell, van Noord, Baander-van Halewijn, & Ouwehand, 1990) and lower levels of androgens (Rebuffé-Scrive, Cullberg, Lundberg, Lindstedt, & Björntorp, 1989). These increase a woman's probability of getting pregnant and also of carrying a fetus to term. For example, Zaadstra et al. (1993) found that women with a WHR less than .80 were twice as likely to get pregnant following artificial insemination as were those with ratios greater than .80.

If perceptions of attractiveness have evolved to increase reproductive success, it follows that attractiveness should translate into reproductive success. Several studies have demonstrated this. For instance, body symmetry predicts the number of sexual partners for adults (e.g., Gangestad & Thornhill, 1997) and Thornhill, Gangestad, and Comer (1995) found that a man's body symmetry predicts his partner's likelihood of achieving orgasm during intercourse. This is significant for reproduction because the female orgasm increases retention of her partner's sperm in the reproductive tract, elevating her chances for pregnancy (Baxter & Bellis, 1993).

Women's and Men's Parental Care for Children

Mothers provide more parental care, on average, than do fathers. Feminist scholars have suggested that this division of labor results from patriarchal societies and the culturally sanctioned subjugation of women (Chodorow, 1978). It is not a uniquely human phenomenon, however; maternal care exceeds paternal care in a huge range of species, including species of birds, reptiles, fish, insects, and amphibia (Clutton-Brock, 1991). It is reasonable to argue, therefore, that this division of parental labor reflects motivations that are generalizable beyond *Homo sapiens,* making any human-specific explanation necessarily incomplete.

Evolutionary psychologists argue that a father's lesser investments results from *paternity certainty,* or a father's certainty that his mate's children are his biological offspring and not those of another man (Trivers, 1972). Maternity certainty is seldom in question, but because sexual fertilization in humans occurs internally, paternity certainty is more vulnerable. Sexual infidelity on the part of the mother, whether voluntary or involuntary, makes fertilization by a man other than her mate possible (Daly & Wilson, 1987).

Paternity certainty is significant for parental labor because, in an evolutionary sense, men hamper their reproductive success by investing in children who are not their biological offspring, because they do not carry the men's genetic material. Two caveats about this explanation are in order. First, men do not consciously calculate their paternity certainty and use it to make decisions about parental investment. According to evolutionary psychology, they do not have to; rather, the tendency to be attuned to paternity certainty would have been selected for, because it maximizes reproductive success. Second, this explanation does not suggest that men do (or should) invest nothing in nonbiological children. As Pinker (2002) noted, reproductive success is not the only thing that matters in the parent-child relationship; parents also have moral, ethical, and legal obligations to care for their children, whether those children will further their reproductive success or not.

Summary and Conclusion

We have reviewed principles relevant to Darwin's theories of natural and sexual selection and evolutionary psychology, discussed our own applications of these principles in communication research, and identified other provocative lines of research that are relevant for the study of human communication. To bring our discussion full circle, we focus in this section on some of the benefits and challenges of using evolutionary theories in the study of communication, and we offer three pragmatic suggestions for researchers wishing to do so.

Benefits and Challenges

Perhaps the greatest benefit to the evolutionary approach is the sheer breadth of human behavior it can explain. Whereas many communication theories focus on singular phenomena (e.g., adaptation, deception, uncertainty reduction), evolutionary psychology provides a basis for understanding and predicting a wide variety of social behaviors, including those related to conflict, emotion, intimacy, deception, attraction, pair bonding, infidelity, and coercion. Evolutionary psychology is not a "theory of everything," and other theories may be better suited to the task of predicting, for instance, moment-to-moment changes in behavioral adaptation (e.g., interaction adaptation theory; Burgoon, Stern, & Dillman, 1995). However, no theoretic approach used in the social sciences even approaches the evolutionary perspective in terms of the breadth of human behaviors it can explain. To the extent that theories used in the communication discipline get narrower and narrower in their focus (e.g., language expectancy theory, Burgoon, 1995; inconsistent nurturing as control theory, Le Poire, Hallett, & Erlandson, 2000), their practical utility diminishes even if their predictive power is great. In contrast, given the superordinate nature of survival and reproductive motives, principles of natural selection and evolutionary psychology provide a coherent, parsimonious, and powerfully predictive basis for explaining myriad social behaviors—at the individual, dyadic, familial, group, and social levels—under a single explanatory framework.

A second advantage of the evolutionary approach is that it explains some counterintuitive aspects of the human social experience. In the nonverbal communication literature, for instance, much attention has been paid to the *halo effect,* wherein people with one positive quality (usually physical attractiveness) are perceived as having other positive qualities as well (such as higher than average intelligence, honesty, or empathy; see Dion, 1986; Feingold, 1992). Social scientists have stressed that the halo effect is merely perceptual, and that attractive people are not *actually* more intelligent, honest, or empathic than average, but are only perceived to be. Evolutionary psychology provides a basis for predicting otherwise, however, at least with respect to intelligence. Kanazawa and Kovar (2004) offered four propositions that, if supported, logically imply that attractive people actually are more intelligent than average:

> (1) Men who are more intelligent are more likely to attain higher status than men who are less intelligent. (2) Higher-status men are more likely to mate with beautiful women than lower-status men. (3) Intelligence is heritable. (4) Beauty is heritable. (p. 227)

Considerable empirical evidence exists to support each of these propositions, and considered collectively, they provide a coherent and logically complete explanation for the counterintuitive notion that beautiful people are indeed more intelligent than less attractive people.

Chief among the challenges of using the evolutionary approach is that it is widely criticized (by academics and nonacademics alike) on the basis of misunderstanding. Perhaps the most common criticism leveled against evolutionary theory—and evolutionary psychology, in particular—is that it justifies social inequities by calling them "natural." For instance, some would say that the evolutionary explanation for the division of parental labor discussed earlier is untenable because it suggests that women's greater investment in children is natural, therefore justifying policies or social structures designed to keep women in the home and out of the workplace. A more extreme example comes from Thornhill and Palmer's (2000) explanation of rape, not as an exercise of men's power over women, but as an evolved strategy for men to further their reproductive success. Evolutionary explanations for social ills are understandably provocative and controversial—and unfortunately, researchers in the past have attempted to use evolutionary principles as justification for racist and sexist social policies.

Explaining a behavior is not the same thing as condoning it, however, and calling something *natural* does not imply that it is *good*. No contemporary evolutionary psychologist would argue that rape is justified or that women should not work simply because he or she understands the reasons why these patterns might have evolved. It must be recalled that evolutionary psychology locates the adaptive purpose behind a characteristic by referencing how the characteristic was advantageous in the EEA, which may or may not imply that the characteristic is still adaptive today. Explaining why behaviors such as rape or differential parental investment might have provided survival or reproductive advantages in the EEA in no way provides ammunition for justifying these behaviors today, nor does it prevent scientists or policymakers from working to alter them.

A related criticism is that evolutionary explanations for behavior portray people as slaves to their biology, negating not only the concept of free will but also the rich influences of culture, gender, class, media, and other social variables. This notion is so fundamentally contrary to many people's conscious experience that it is easy to dismiss evolutionary explanations on this basis. In fact, however, the premise was inaccurate to begin with, in two important ways. First, *suggesting that a behavior has an evolutionary cause does not imply that the behavior has no other causes.* A propensity for affection may be evolutionarily motivated, for instance, but affectionate behavior is also subject to norms of politeness (Erbert & Floyd, 2004), demand characteristics of the social environment (Floyd & Morman, 1997), and other variables. Few behaviors, if any, can reasonably be said to have a singular cause, so evolutionary explanations no more dismiss other potential causes than environmental explanations do. The second inaccuracy in the premise is the notion that a behavior that is evolutionarily motivated cannot be controlled, thereby releasing people from their liability for it ("my genes made me do it"). This, too, is a misunderstanding of evolutionary theory. Few would disagree, for instance, that behaviors such as eating and sleeping are biologically motivated; humans eat and sleep because we must do these things to survive, not because we were socialized into eating and sleeping. That does not imply that we cannot control these behaviors, however, only that there is an evolutionary motive for doing them in the first place. Consequently, it is a logical fallacy to conclude that people bear no responsibility for their behaviors if those behaviors were evolutionarily motivated, and *no one working in the field of evolutionary psychology suggests this* (see Alcock, 2001).

A third criticism often levied against evolutionary theory is that it is nonfalsifiable. Because its causal mechanisms are ultimate motivations (survival and procreation) rather than proximal states that can be readily manipulated (such as specific cognitions or emotions) and because the theoretic argument points to what was adaptive in the EEA rather than in contemporary contexts, it is easy to conclude that evolutionary theories are not falsifiable, and therefore, of limited scientific utility. This is an important concern for evolutionary scientists, one that should motivate careful attention to experimental design (as we detail below). It must be remembered, however, that falsifiability is a property of scientific *hypotheses,* not theories. Through the process of logical deduction, scientific theories give rise to hypotheses that are products of—and therefore, not part of—the theories from which they are derived. Hypotheses are directly testable and must be both verifiable and falsifiable to be of scientific value (Reynolds, 2006). The relevant concern, therefore, is *whether hypotheses derived from evolutionary theories are falsifiable,* and we submit that they are. In this chapter, for instance, we have discussed the hypotheses that women provide more parental care than men, that horizontal collectivism predicts communal sharing, and that physical symmetry predicts a person's attractiveness, among other predictions. Each of these hypotheses is verifiable and falsifiable because it can be either supported or unsupported on the basis of data, just as most hypotheses derived from social and cultural theories can be. Theories themselves (whether evolutionary or social) are never directly falsifiable because they are not directly testable; support for theories is always implied by support for hypotheses derived from them (see Suppe, 1977).

Areas of Opportunity for Future Work

One arena in which evolutionary principles are strongly explanatory is the study of family communication. According to evolutionary psychology, family relationships are distinct from all other human relationships because they involve reproductive processes and shared genetic material. As Floyd and Haynes (2005) detailed, the evolutionary approach provides a basis for understanding a host of variables relevant to family communication, including romantic love, jealousy, sexual infidelity, divorce, nepotism, parental care, and parent-child conflict. Instead of constructing different explanations for each of these relational characteristics, evolutionary psychology explains all of them as a function of the drive for reproductive success. This is an elegant, parsimonious explanation with extraordinary predictive power and the potential to unify a broad range of findings on family communication under a single explanatory framework.

Likewise, the study of emotion and emotional communication would benefit greatly by employing evolutionary principles. Emotions have both survival and reproductive benefit: Fear, for instance, motivates people to fight or flee from perceived threats, whereas jealousy promotes vigilance over the fidelity of one's romantic relationship. The same motivations can drive emotional expression: Conveying anger to a foe can derail an impending attack, and conveying interest and attraction can accelerate relational development. There is no question that the communication of emotion is subject to individual differences and cultural, social, and gender effects (see, e.g., Metts & Planalp, 2002). The functions served by an emotional expression may well be linked to the evolutionary motives that gave rise to the emotion in the first place, however, so a more thorough understanding of communicative behavior is facilitated by accounting for that.

Finally, explicating the constituent parts and delineating the rules of implementation of the universal grammar of relationships also provides a fruitful field for further investigations. Although relational models are good candidates to be at least some of the constituent parts, there certainly are more that await discovery. Moreover, the ways in which these constitute parts are combined and implemented in social cognition are almost entirely unknown, although culture probably plays a role (Fiske, 2004), as do individual differences in personality and experiences. In other words, we are only at the very beginning of understanding how a relational grammar may work. Because it holds the promise to provide a comprehensive account of how relationships are represented in cognition and how relational information is processed, its potential impact on the study of interpersonal communication is immense. For example, rather than pitting theories proposing communal, equity, or social exchange relationships against each other, by recognizing that individuals relate to each other according to the different relational models within the same relationship, relational grammar theory directs the researchers' focus to those variables that make one mode of relating more likely than others. In addition, a focus on communication is emphasized because the possibility at any given time to relate in various modes highlights the need for interactants to come to an agreement about what mode to employ in a given situation.

Practical Suggestions

For those researchers who wish to incorporate evolutionary principles into their own research, let us conclude this chapter by echoing three practical suggestions offered by Floyd and Haynes (2005). The first is to conceptualize variables of interest in terms of the survival and/or procreative benefits they would likely have conferred in the EEA. In what ways would a given characteristic (attractiveness, intelligence, propensity for aggression) have helped our evolutionary ancestors respond successfully to survival or reproductive challenges? For instance, attractiveness increases mating opportunities, intelligence provides problem-solving abilities, and a propensity for aggression can keep potential survival threats at bay. Whether the characteristic is adaptive in the modern environment is not relevant to whether it once served an adaptive function; as we noted above, for instance, the preference for sweets would have ensured that our ancestors consumed adequate sugar, which is necessary for survival, even though this preference is somewhat maladaptive today. To be subject to the laws of natural selection, however, the characteristic must be at least partially heritable, so purely learned behaviors (such as the language one speaks) cannot be selected for, even though the mechanisms that support them (such as the cognitive ability to acquire language) may be.

A second practical suggestion is to design hypothesis tests such that alternative explanations can be controlled for. This is a hallmark of the scientific process, but it is particularly important in this context because the same prediction can often be derived from both evolutionary and nonevolutionary explanations. As discussed earlier, for instance, Floyd and Morman's (2002) finding that men are more affectionate with biological sons than stepsons can be explained by the theory of discriminative parental solicitude, but it could also be explained as a function of differential levels of emotional closeness or relationship duration. If alternative explanations are not controlled for, then the predicted result will support all possible explanations equally; it was therefore imperative for Floyd and Morman to demonstrate that the hypothesized difference between biological and steprelationships held even when differences in closeness and relationship duration were held constant. Importantly, this does not mean that closeness and duration were *ruled out* as potential explanations—indeed, these accounted for significant variance in affectionate behavior—but only that the predicted difference was significant even after their influence was removed.

This observation gives rise to our final suggestion, which is to consider contextual influences carefully to avoid oversimplified hypotheses. On the basis of evolutionary principles, an unsophisticated researcher might predict that parents will invest no resources in their stepchildren because there is no reproductive benefit in doing so; finding this hypothesis to fail, then, the researcher may conclude that the evolutionary explanation is wrong. In fact, however, the hypothesis was untenable in the first place, because even if reproductive success is one influence on parental behavior, it is not the only influence. Proximal goals and imperatives are also operative, so parents may not invest in their stepchildren to further their reproductive success, but may do so out of love, ethical responsibility, and legal obligation.

Communication researchers are fortunate to have a broad array of theories from which to investigate interpersonal phenomena. Although theories of evolution and natural selection have not been widely used thus far by interpersonal communication scholars, we believe that they offer a logically complete system for explaining a wide range of human communicative behaviors. As such, they represent a parsimonious and provocative account of human communication to which interpersonal communication researchers can beneficially avail themselves.

References

Ainsworth, M. D., Blehar, M. C., Waters, E., & Walls, S. (1978). *Patterns of attachment: Assessed in the strange situation and at home.* Hillsdale, NJ: Erlbaum.

Alcock, J. (2001). *The triumph of sociobiology.* Oxford, UK: Oxford University Press.

Anderson, J. G., Kaplan, H. S., & Lancaster, J. B. (1997, June). *Paying for children's college: The paternal investment strategies of Albuquerque men.* Paper presented at the Ninth Annual Conference of the Human Behavior and Evolution Society, Tucson, AZ.

Baldwin, M. W. (1992). Relational schemas and the processing of social information. *Psychological Bulletin, 112,* 461–484.

Bartholomew, K. (1990). Avoidance of intimacy: An attachment perspective. *Journal of Social and Personal Relationships, 7,* 147–178.

Bartholomew, K., & Horowitz, L. M. (1991). Attachment styles among young adults: A test of a four-category model. *Journal of Personality and Social Psychology, 61,* 226–244.

Baxter, R. R., & Bellis, M. A. (1993). Human sperm competition: Ejaculate manipulation by females and a function for the female orgasm. *Animal Behavior, 46,* 887–909.

Bowlby, J. (1969). *Attachment and loss: Vol. 1. Attachment.* New York: Basic Books.

Bowlby, J. (1972). *Attachment and loss: Vol. 2. Separation: Anxiety and anger.* New York: Basic Books.

Burgoon, J. K., Stern, L. A., & Dillman, L. (1995). *Interpersonal adaptation: Dyadic interaction patterns.* New York: Cambridge University Press.

Burgoon, M. (1995). Language expectancy theory: Elaboration, explication and extension. In C. R. Berger & M. Burgoon (Eds.), *Communication and social influence processes* (pp. 29–51). East Lansing: Michigan State University Press.

Buss, D. M. (1989). Sex differences in human mate preferences: Evolutionary hypotheses tested in 37 cultures. *Behavioral and Brain Sciences, 12,* 1–49.

Buss, D. M. (2007). *Evolutionary psychology: The new science of the mind* (3rd ed.). Boston: Allyn & Bacon.

Buss, D. M., & Kenrick, D. T. (1998). Evolutionary social psychology. In D. T. Gilbert, S. T. Fiske, & G. Lindzey (Eds.), *The handbook of social psychology* (4th ed., Vol. 2, pp. 982–1026). Boston: McGraw-Hill.

Chodorow, N. (1978). *The reproduction of mothering.* Berkeley: University of California Press.

Clark, M. S., & Mills, J. (1979). Interpersonal attraction in exchange and communal relationships. *Journal of Personality & Social Psychology, 37,* 12–24.

Clutton-Brock, T. H. (1991). *The evolution of parental care.* Princeton, NJ: Princeton University Press.

Daly, M., & Wilson, M. (1980). Discriminative parental solicitude: A biological perspective. *Journal of Marriage and the Family, 42,* 277–288.

Daly, M., & Wilson, M. (1987). The Darwinian psychology of discriminative parental solicitude. *Nebraska Symposium on Motivation, 35,* 91–144.

Darwin, C. (1859). *On the origin of species.* London: John Murray.

Dion, K. K. (1986). Stereotyping based on physical attractiveness: Issues and conceptual perspectives. In C. P. Herman, M. P. Zanna, & E. T. Higgins (Eds.), *Physical appearance, stigma and social behavior: The Ontario Symposium* (Vol. 3, pp. 7–21). Hillsdale, NJ: Lawrence Erlbaum.

Erbert, L. A., & Floyd, K. (2004). Affectionate expressions as face-threatening acts: Receiver assessments. *Communication Studies, 55,* 230–246.

Feingold, A. (1992). Good-looking people are not what we think. *Psychological Bulletin, 111,* 304–341.

Fiske, A. P. (1991). *Structures of social life: The four elementary forms of human relations: Communal sharing, authority ranking, equality matching, market pricing.* New York: Free Press.

Fiske, A. P. (1992). The four elementary forms of sociality: Framework for a unified theory of social relations. *Psychological Review, 99,* 689–723.

Fiske, A. P. (2004). Relational models theory 2.0. In N. Haslam (Ed.), *Relational models theory: A contemporary overview* (pp. 3–25). Mahwah, NJ: Lawrence Erlbaum.

Floyd, K. (2001). Human affection exchange: I. Reproductive probability as a predictor of men's affection with their sons. *Journal of Men's Studies, 10,* 39–50.

Floyd, K. (2002). Human affection exchange: V. Attributes of the highly affectionate. *Communication Quarterly, 50,* 135–152.

Floyd, K. (2006). *Communicating affection: Interpersonal behavior and social context.* Cambridge, UK: Cambridge University Press.

Floyd, K., & Haynes, M. T. (2005). Applications of the theory of natural selection to the study of family communication. *Journal of Family Communication, 5,* 79–101.

Floyd, K., Hesse, C., & Haynes, M. T. (2007). Human affection exchange: XV. Metabolic and cardiovascular correlates of trait expressed affection. *Communication Quarterly, 55,* 79–94.

Floyd, K., Mikkelson, A. C., Hesse, C., & Pauley, P. M. (2007). Affectionate writing reduces total cholesterol: Two randomized, controlled trials. *Human Communication Research, 33,* 119–142.

Floyd, K., Mikkelson, A. C., Tafoya, M. A., Farinelli, L., La Valley, A. G., Judd, J., et al. (2007). Human affection exchange: XIII. Affectionate communication accelerates neuroendocrine stress recovery. *Health Communication, 22,* 123–132.

Floyd, K., & Morman, M. T. (1997). Affectionate communication in nonromantic relationships: Influences of communicator, relational, and contextual factors. *Western Journal of Communication, 61,* 279–298.

Floyd, K., & Morman, M. T. (2002). Human affection exchange: III. Discriminative parental solicitude in men's affectionate communication with their biological and nonbiological sons. *Communication Quarterly, 49,* 310–327.

Floyd, K., & Morr, M. C. (2003). Human affection exchange: VII. Affectionate communication in the sibling/spouse/sibling-in-law triad. *Communication Quarterly, 51,* 247–261.

Gangestad, S. W., & Thornhill, R. (1997). Human sexual selection and development stability. In J. A. Simpson & D. T. Kenrick (Eds.), *Evolutionary social psychology* (pp. 169–195). Mahwah, NJ: Lawrence Erlbaum.

Hamilton, W. D. (1964). The genetical evolution of social behavior. I & II. *Journal of Theoretical Biology, 7,* 1–52.

Kanazawa, S., & Kovar, J. L. (2004). Why beautiful people are more intelligent. *Intelligence, 32,* 227–243.

Koerner, A. F. (2006). Models of relating—not relationship models: Cognitive representations of relating across interpersonal relationship domains. *Journal of Social and Personal Relationships, 23,* 629–653.

Langlois, J. H., Kalakanis, L., Rubenstein, A. J., Larson, A., Hallam, M., & Smoot, M. (2000). Maxims or myths of beauty? A meta-analytic and theoretical review. *Psychological Bulletin, 126,* 390–423.

Le Poire, B. A., Hallett, J. S., & Erlandson, K. T. (2000). An initial test of inconsistent nurturing as control theory: How partners of drug abusers assist their partners' sobriety. *Human Communication Research, 26,* 432–457.

Metts, S., & Planalp, S. (2002). Emotional communication. In M. L. Knapp & J. A. Daly (Eds.), *Handbook of interpersonal communication* (pp. 339–373). Thousand Oaks, CA: Sage.

Mills, J., & Clark, M. S. (1982). Exchange and communal relationships. In L. Wheeler (Ed.), *Review of Personality and Social Psychology* (Vol. 3, pp. 121–144). Beverly Hills, CA: Sage.

Pinker, S. (1994). *The language instinct.* New York: HarperCollins.

Pinker, S. (2002). *The blank slate: The modern denial of human nature.* New York: Viking.

Rebuffé-Scrive, M., Cullberg, G., Lundberg, P. A., Lindstedt, G., & Björntorp, P. (1989). Anthropometric variables and metabolism in polycystic ovarian disease. *Hormone Metabolic Research, 21,* 391–397.

Reynolds, P. D. (2006). *A primer in theory construction.* Boston: Allyn & Bacon.

Roloff, M. (1981). *Interpersonal communication: The social exchange approach.* Beverly Hills, CA: Sage.

Roloff, M. (1987). Communication and reciprocity within intimate relationships. In M. E. Roloff & G. R. Miller (Eds.), *Interpersonal processes: New directions in communication research* (pp. 11–38). Newbury Park, CA: Sage.

Rueter, M. A., & Koerner, A. F. (2008). The effect of family communication patterns on adopted adolescent adjustment. *Journal of Marriage and Family, 70,* 715–727.

Rusbult, C. E., & Buunk, B. P. (1993). Commitment processes in close relationships: An interdependence analysis. *Journal of Social and Personal Relationships, 10,* 175–204.

Singh, D. (1993). Adaptive significance of waist-to-hip ratio and female physical attractiveness. *Journal of Personality and Social Psychology, 65,* 293–307.

Suppe, F. (1977). *The structure of scientific theories* (2nd ed.). Urbana-Champaign: University of Illinois Press.

Thornhill, R., Gangestad, S. W., & Comer, R. (1995). Human female orgasm and mate fluctuating asymmetry. *Animal Behavior, 50,* 1601–1615.

Thornhill, R., & Palmer, C. T. (2000). *A natural history of rape: Biological bases of sexual coercion.* Cambridge, MA: MIT Press.

Tonkelaar, I., Seidell, J. C., van Noord, P. A. H., Baander-van Halewijn, E. A., & Ouwehand, I. J. (1990). Fat distribution in relation to age, degree of obesity, smoking habits, parity and estrogen use: A cross-sectional study in 11,825 Dutch women participating in the DOM-Project. *International Journal of Obesity, 14,* 753–761.

Triandis, H. C. (1995). *Individualism and collectivism.* Boulder, CO: Westview.

Trivers, R. L. (1972). Parental investment and sexual selection. In B. Campbell (Ed.), *Sexual selection and the descent of man, 1871–1971* (pp. 136–179). Chicago: Aldine.

Trivers, R., Manning, J. T., Thornhill, R., Singh, D., & McGuire, M. (1999). Jamaican symmetry project: Long-term study of fluctuating symmetry in rural Jamaican children. *Human Biology, 71,* 417–430.

Zaadstra, B. M., Seidell, J. C., van Noord, P. A. H., te Velde, E. R., Habbema, J. D. F., Vrieswijk, B., et al. (1993). Fat and female fecundity: Prospective study of effect of body fat distribution on conception rates. *British Medical Journal, 306,* 484–487.

3

Relational Dialectics Theory, Applied

Leslie A. Baxter

Dawn O. Braithwaite

For over a decade a good portion of our individual and joint work has been focused on applying relational dialectics theory (RDT) to communication in close relationships, especially family communication. It's a separate story to address how two scholars end up collaborating—a story that is part serendipity, part complementarity, and part friendship. Intellectually speaking, Leslie developed RDT (with Barbara Montgomery; Baxter & Montgomery, 1996) and was seeking to apply it to as diverse an array of relational phenomena as possible in order to help the theory continue to evolve. Dawn, on the other hand, had a keen interest in seeing how communication theory could be applied to help us understand problematic relational-communication experiences that people find challenging in their everyday lives. A professional marriage of theory and application was thus launched, and the purpose of this chapter is to discuss the research that has resulted, directly and indirectly, from this union. The bulk of this work has been focused on family communication, and in this sense we are examples of what the editors are calling "boundary spanners."

The chapter will be organized into four main sections. First, we will discuss some of the main features of RDT. Second, we will discuss the methods appropriate to applications of RDT. Third, we will discuss the research findings of significance. Fourth, and last, we will reflect on the directions we plan to pursue in future research.

Relational Dialectics Theory

We referred above to the notion of a theory evolving because we think a good theory is not static but continues to grow through uses made of it. Elsewhere (Baxter, 2004a), the general evolution of RDT since its first formal articulation by Baxter and Montgomery in 1996 has been discussed. In a nutshell, RDT is a specific articulation of *dialogism* as it applies to communication in personal relationships; dialogism is the name Holquist (2002) has used to describe the focus of the 50-year-long scholarly work of the Russian philosopher of language and culture, Mikhail Bakhtin (1981, 1984, 1986, 1990; for an overview, see Baxter, 2007b). Although the 1996 articulation of RDT addressed a wide range of concepts drawn from dialogism, most applications of the theory latched onto only one of those concepts introduced in the opening chapters of the 1996 book— contradiction. Subsequent articulations of RDT (Baxter, 2004b, 2006, in press; Baxter & Braithwaite, 2008) have attempted to enrich applications of RDT by drawing attention to, and elaborating on, more nuanced features of the theory introduced in the 1996 articulation. Space limitations do not permit us to repeat this discussion of the theory's evolution; thus, in this chapter, we will emphasize the aspects of RDT that have informed our program of research.

To understand how to evaluate and use RDT, it is important to identify its paradigmatic location. Within the traditional paradigmatic triad of postpositivistic, interpretive, and critical perspectives, RDT comes closest to the assumptions of interpretivism. Like interpretive approaches, RDT eschews the postpositivistic assumptions that support much of the empirical work in interpersonal communication, favoring instead a focus on a local and situated understanding of meanings and meaning making. However, unlike in interpretive approaches, language rather than individual consciousness is regarded as central to experience, according to RDT. Furthermore, interpretive approaches tend to presuppose a consensual, unified conception of meaning and culture, in contrast to the dialogic focus in RDT on meaning making as a fragmented, tensional, and multi-vocal process. More recently, Deetz (2001) has proposed a fourth para-digmatic perspective to add to the traditional three—what he calls a dialogic perspective:

> Dialogic research emphasizes dissensus production and the local/situated nature of understanding. . . . Language replaces consciousness as central to experi-ence. . . . [T]he linguistic turn enabled a critique of normative [post-positivistic] research's claim of objectivity through examining the processes by which objects are socially constituted and the role of language in that process and simultaneously a critique of interpretive research through demonstrating the fragmentation of cultures and personal identities and removing the psycholog-ical subject from the center of experience. (pp. 31–32)

RDT sits within the dialogic fold as articulated by Deetz—hardly a surprise given the theory's grounding in Bakhtin's dialogism.

Given the paradigmatic location of RDT, how should we evaluate and use the theory? Much to our chagrin, many scholars in interpersonal communi-cation evaluate RDT against the standards of postpositivistic theory; that is, they assess the theory's ability to predict and causally explain empirical rela-tionships among variables. Instead, scholars should assess RDT by the stan-dard of heurism: Does the theory enable us to understand meaning making in an insightful way (Baxter & Babbie, 2004; Lindlof & Taylor, 2002)?

RDT uses the term *dialectical* rather than the term *dialogic* in the theory's label, although, for our purposes, the terms are interchangeable (Baxter & Montgomery, 1996). However, it is important to observe that not everyone uses the term *dialectical* in a way that is synonymous with Bakhtin's notion of dialogue. Bakhtin (1986) was, in fact, quite critical of the deployment of overly abstract and mechanistic conceptions of dialectics, such as those that he experienced in the Stalinist Russia of the 1920s when he began his schol-arly career. Bakhtin's sense of dialogism is quite close to our conception of dialectics as articulated by Murphy (1971): a general worldview "destructive of neat systems and ordered structures, and compatible with the notion of a social universe that has neither fixity nor solid boundaries" (p. 90). We resist efforts by some to regard all dialectical approaches as interchangeable and elsewhere have discussed fundamental differences in various dialectical approaches (Baxter & Braithwaite, 2006c; Montgomery & Baxter, 1998).

The core premise of dialogism, and of RDT, is that meaning making is a process that emerges from the struggle of different, often competing, *dis-courses*. Simply stated, a discourse is a worldview or a system of meaning. Bakhtin (1981) described discourses as "specific points of view on the world, forms for conceptualizing the world in words, specific world views, each characterized by its own objects, meanings, and values" (pp. 292–293). Bakhtin (1981) described all of language use as "a contradiction-ridden, tension-filled unity" of "verbal-ideological" tendencies (p. 272). Verbal-ideological tendencies are discourses. We now prefer the phrase *discursive struggle* over the term *contradiction* to underscore that the oppositions are discourses, not psychological needs or functions, as some have mistakenly thought.

But where do these discourses reside in language use? Key to answering this question is Bakhtin's conception of communication as intertextual; that is, his view that meaning making rests in the interdependence of messages (Baxter, 2007a). Bakhtin (1986) called this interdependence of messages the "chain of speech communion" (p. 93). Imagine any utterance as a link in a chain that extends outward to other links before it and to subsequent links after it. The meaning of the utterance is interdependent with these other links. Baxter and Montgomery (1996) have articulated four such kinds of links, which are places where discourses come into play with one another. First, some of the links in the chain of speech communion are quite distant in space and time; these *distal already-spokens* represent already-spoken utterances of the past that occurred prior to a given encounter between relationship partners. Some of these distal already-spoken links are quite local and situated in the history of the parties' relationship with each other. A relationship's history of interactions constitutes its discourse of the past, which interanimates with interactions of the present, creating a discursive struggle of the given with the new.

Other distal already-spokens reflect discourses uttered by others that already circulate in the broader culture in which the relationship parties are embedded. Relationships are not isolated, dyadic phenomena driven by the psychological states of the two parties. Rather, they are social processes that speak culture whenever the parties open their mouths in conversation (Baxter, 1997; Baxter & Montgomery, 1996). Various dialectical scholars have consistently noted that certain discursive struggles keep popping up in study after study (for an early review, see Werner & Baxter, 1994). Arguably foremost among these are the discursive struggles of *integration-separation* and *expression-nonexpression*. *Integration-separation* has been labeled in different ways—as *connection-autonomy, interdependence-independence, intimacy-autonomy, closeness-separateness,* to mention but a few examples. Relationship parties value connection to the partner yet at the same time value autonomy from the partner. Why does this discursive struggle keep appearing? The value attached to *integration* is a system of meaning that reflects a circulating discourse of community in the broader U.S. society: what Bellah, Madsen, Sullivan, Swidler, and Tipton (1985) referred to as the ideology of moral/social community. The value attached to *separation* is a system of meaning that reflects the competing discourse of utilitarian/expressive individualism that also circulates broadly in U.S. society (Bellah et al., 1985). When relationship parties talk in ways that value either or both of these discourses, they are talking culture; their talk is ideologically freighted. Similarly, the expression-nonexpression tension (whose labels vary from scholar to scholar and include *openness-closedness, candor-discretion,* and *disclosure-privacy,* among others) can be heard as the articulation of two competing cultural discourses that also circulate broadly in U.S. society. The value attached to expressive openness is understandable to those who are culturally steeped in the discourse of individualism, in which it is accepted as natural that individuals have the right to express their thoughts and to use self-disclosure as a means to grow as individuals. At the same time, nonexpression makes cultural sense to those steeped in the same discourse of individualism, which values the individual's right to privacy as much as it values an individual's freedom of expression.

We have used two frequently identified discursive struggles—integration-separation and expression-nonexpression—to illustrate how utterances are social in their articulation of circulating cultural discourses. However, other cultural discourses in competition might well be discussed as well. For example, in our stepfamily research discussed below, we hear competing discourses of the family—a discourse of the "real family," which values bonds of blood, and a discourse of the family as a system of mutual care. Our theoretical point is that it is problematic to draw the boundary of relational communication at the dyadic border, because relationships are sites of culture. Thus, at the level of theory, RDT functions as a boundary spanner that crosses cultural-communication and interpersonal-communication domains.

Proximal already-spokens represent chain links that are more immediate. The term refers to the utterances in the current interaction event (Baxter & Montgomery, 1996). Although meaning making is ultimately an indeterminate affair, always and ongoingly open to emergent new meanings, parties rarely settle in the interaction moment for such indeterminate chaos. Instead, different discourses jockey to occupy the dominant meaning-for-the-moment position. As Bakhtin (1981) stated it, "Every concrete utterance of a speaking subject serves as a point where centrifugal as well as centripetal forces are brought to bear" (p. 272). Different kinds of meaning can be constructed. Some constructions function to elide or skirt discursive struggles. For example, parties can jointly privilege one discourse over others, positioning it with centripetal dominance. If, over time, the same discourse is repeatedly privileged by relationship parties, it becomes what Bakhtin (1981) referred to as authoritative. Authoritative discourses are accepted as true, natural, and taken-for-granted meanings. However, Bakhtin (1981) argued that it is quite effortful for interactants to sustain authoritative discourses, because centrifugal discourses, while muted, are never eradicated and lurk as niggling semantic thorns with the potential to disrupt the taken-for-granted meanings of authoritative discourses.

Relationship parties also elide discursive struggles in the moment when, over time, their constructed meanings have inverted centripetal and centrifugal discourses. That is, at time A, one discourse is centered while competing discourses are muted, yet at time B, a muted discourse becomes centered and the formerly dominant discourse moves to the centrifugal margins. Alternatively, parties can segment by topic or situation which discourse will be centered and which will be marginalized: Topic/situation A thematizes one discourse, whereas Topic/situation B thematizes a competing discourse. These two forms of discursive avoidance—which are referred to as spiraling inversion and segmentation, respectively (Baxter & Montgomery, 1996)—appear to be quite commonly enacted by relationship parties.

Ambiguity, or equivocation, is yet another way relationship parties can skirt discursive struggles. The discursive beauty of an ambiguous meaning is that it is open to multiple interpretations, thereby avoiding the centripetal-centrifugal struggle entirely by giving the appearance of thematizing multiple competing discourses, which vary according to who is interpreting the meaning.

In contrast to the communicative work of discursive avoidance is communicative activity by parties that features a mixture of competing discourses in the same communicative moment (Baxter & Braithwaite, in press). A *hybrid meaning* (Bakhtin, 1981, p. 358) is the mixture of competing discourses to create a new meaning, more or less akin to the mixing of oil and vinegar to make a salad dressing. Another kind of discursive mixture is what Bakhtin (1990, p. 67) referred to as an *aesthetic moment;* that is, meaning making in which discourses are no longer framed as oppositional but instead merge in a way that profoundly alters each system of meaning. These mixtures are akin to chemical reactions—for example, the combination of hydrogen and oxygen to form an entirely new entity, water. Rituals are a particularly important communicative activity in which competing discourses are combined; when enacted successfully, they accomplish aesthetic moments for relationship parties (Baxter & Braithwaite, 2006a). We will return below to a discussion of rituals.

The third and fourth links in the chain of speech communion involve *addressivity* (Baxter & Montgomery, 1996). As Bakhtin (1986) indicated, "An essential (constitutive) marker of the utterance is its quality of being directed to someone, its addressivity" (p. 95). *Proximal not-yet-spokens* are the anticipated responses of the other(s) with whom a speaker is interacting at the moment. *Distal not-yet-spokens* are the anticipated responses of a generalized other, or superaddressee—for example, the anticipated responses of members of the social network who may subsequently hear about an interaction event through gossip or of others in general, including strangers. Through addressivity, we add the dimension of anticipated evaluation and judgment—what will others think of a speaker's utterance, especially with respect to moral discourses of the ideal? Speakers anticipate whether their utterances will be regarded as good or bad by proximal and distal addressees, and adapt accordingly. Addressivity is a feature of communication that makes it difficult for speakers to sustain an authoritative discourse. Others will always be different from us, bringing to an interaction "horizons of seeing" (Bakhtin, 1990, p. 22) that are to some extent different from our own. To the extent that we speak in ways that recognize potential differences in worldviews, our utterances will invariably be multivocal, even if other discourses are given only a token verbal nod. The moral accounts speakers provide to addressees—their reflexive self-evaluations, reason giving, justifications, disclaimers, and so forth—are particularly rich in insight into the discursive struggle of the "ideal" with and against the "real."

RDT is a social constructionist theory in that according to the theory, the joint communicative work of relationship parties creates meaning. Meanings are constructed with respect to partner identities and relationship identities. Unlike other social constructionist approaches, however, RDT conceptualizes discursive struggle as the generative engine through which meanings are wrought, however fluid and dynamic those might be.

How to Apply RDT: Contrapuntal Analysis

The analytic method best suited to applications of RDT is what Bakhtin (1984) labeled *contrapuntal analysis* (p. 221). Contrapuntal analysis is a specific kind of discourse analysis, one among many discourse-analytic approaches used by scholars to understand uttered talk. Contrapuntal analysis focuses on the interplay, that is, the "collision" (p. 184) or "counterpoint" (p. 221), of different discourses as they appear implicitly or explicitly in talk. Beyond this general discussion, however, Bakhtin (1984) failed to provide a detailed methodological primer on how to conduct a contrapuntal analysis, instead giving us only an illustrative analysis of the novels of his favorite author, Dostoevsky. Thus, we have had to develop over the years our own methodological how-to primer of how to conduct a contrapuntal analysis. Contrapuntal analysis, as we deploy it, is integrally tied to the chain of speech communion discussed above.

Regardless of the kind of textual data with which we work, the set of analytic questions is the same. Contrapuntal analysis interrogates textual data to find credible answers to these questions: (a) What are the discourses given voice in the text? (b) In what ways are these discourses linked to broader cultural already-spokens, the already-spokens of the parties' relational past, and anticipated not-yet-spokens represented by idealized or normative judgments? and (c) How do these discourses interanimate to create meanings-in-the-moment—do parties elide the discursive struggles or construct discursive mixtures? To date, our research program has focused the most attention on the first of these analytic questions, with secondary attention to the second and third questions. This analytic imbalance is one we hope to correct in our future research.

Our research program has used three primary types of textual data, characterized by different addressees. We have relied extensively on textual data in the form of interview transcripts with relationship parties, derived through qualitative, in-depth interviewing (see, e.g., Kvale, 1996; McCracken, 1988; Rubin & Rubin, 2004). We have framed these transcripts less as objective reports of our informants' relational communication experiences and more as written texts of the interviews as communication events in their own right, featuring an informant and his or her addressee—the interviewer (Mishler, 1986). Sensitive to the addressivity feature of talk, we interpret transcripts with an analytic eye toward the informant's anticipation of addressee evaluation. That is, we have attended in particular to how informants anticipate counterpoint views and provide the interviewer-addressee with accounts that suggest an awareness on the informant's part that what he or she says could be evaluated against a cultural backdrop of normative expectations of "good" or "appropriate" relating. Of course, our interviewers go out of their way not to evaluate informants, but informants nonetheless have an awareness that they are giving an account to a proximal addressee-stranger—the interviewer—as well as to imagined distal superaddressees in the form of unknown others who might someday read the transcripts or excerpts from them. These accounts often address multiple discourses and have provided us with particularly rich insights into the discursive struggles of the "ideal" and the "real" in informants' relational experiences.

Sometimes, informant talk is calcified with an authoritative discourse that displays itself in what White (2003) has referred to as dialogic contraction; that is, informants speak in absolutist ways sprinkled with words such as *always, never, naturally, obviously,* or *of course.* More commonly, informants swim in cultural streams steeped in the crosscurrents of competing discourses. Their talk reveals these discursive struggles, and how the informant invokes different discourses functions to position some as central and others as more marginalized.

Often, informants engage multiple discourses in highly implicit ways—with what Bakhtin (1984) referred to as the "sideward glance" (p. 208). Central to our analysis of "the sideward glance" is careful attention to White's (2003) work in dialogic expansion. When talk is dialogically expansive, it allows for more than one discursive possibility. A variety of discourse markers accomplish dialogic expansion, and we attend to them in informant talk as a way to locate the presence of multiple discourses in a text. For example, adversative discourse markers such as *but* or *however* (Schriffrin, 1996) function as linguistic markers by which the propositional content of two different discourses is contrasted, thereby creating clash or semantic struggle. Talk that is rich in adversative discourse markers can be unfolded into a hypothetical turn-taking dialogue, with each alternative discourse occupying a conversational turn (Bakhtin, 1984).

Many other discourse markers help us locate the presence of multiple discourses. For example, qualifiers such as *sort of, maybe,* and *a little* hint at struggle because they function with vagueness to indicate the possibility of alternative interpretations (White, 2003). Talk with a "halting quality"—with hesitations, dysfluencies, and reservations—also suggests discursive struggles (Bakhtin, 1984). Whenever an utterance hints "that alternative propositions are possible or even likely" (White, 2003, p. 267), a speaker engages multiple discourses. For example, in phrases such as *some think* or *I've heard that,* we are given verbal nods to alternative perspectives. However, not all discourses are necessarily treated equally in informant talk, and we attend analytically to the evaluative tone of speakers in order to discern which discourses are more or less valued. For example, an utterance such as "It would be better for everyone if we could always be open, but sometimes I find myself avoiding talk with my stepparent because I feel like I don't know him very well" clearly marks with the *but* the presence of two discourses—a discourse of openness and a discourse of nonexpression. However, openness is evaluatively positioned as the ideal, although it is breached in practice.

Although informants often mark discursive struggle in implicit ways, our interview protocols usually include questions designed to open up space for more explicit talk about discursive struggles. In particular, we often ask informants to tell us what they like and what they find challenging about some phenomenon of interest to us. In addition, we usually ask informants to tell us about their "ideal" and how their experiences do, and do not, realize this ideal. These questioning strategies provide us with complementary insight into the discursive struggles that informants implicitly mark for us in their talk.

We have also used, to a lesser extent, focus-group interviewing (Hedges, 1985; Krueger, 1988; Morgan, 1988, 1992). In particular, we opt for less structured formats, which maximize the opportunities for the participants to talk with one another about the topic at hand. The moderator generally asks a smaller number of questions, each quite general in nature. Participants talk with one another, rather than to the moderator, who attends to the group's process. Our interview protocols, like our dyadic interview protocols described above, often contain questions designed to reveal discursive struggles in an explicit manner. We have given the focus groups opportunity to create written documents as part of their interaction. In a focus-group study of young-adult stepchildren, Dawn and her colleagues asked the young-adult stepchildren to have a discussion and then to design brochures to give coparents in different households advice on communicating with each other. The focus groups produced main points and added drawings that captured what it meant to function communicatively in the middle between their parents. Written transcriptions of group discussions were then analyzed for both explicit and implicit evidence of discursive struggles.

We have also used transcripts of tape-recorded talk between relationship parties, although this method of data collection has been underused by us to date (a weakness in our research program that needs correction). Talk between relationship parties informs us about the joint communicative work of parties in a way that an interview with only one member of a relationship cannot.

Major Findings

In this section, we will describe the major findings that emerge from our joint empirical research employing RDT. This theory has been the centerpiece of our work across several different contexts. We will not report here on research we have done that does not use RDT; however, it is important to note that these other studies have been instrumental in informing our RDT work and have led us into new contexts that brought to light novel aspects of the discursive struggle among relating parties. In addition, we would be remiss if we did not acknowledge the profound influence of the scholarship of our many colleagues and students.

Our first study together was an examination of the contradictions of renewing marital vows (Braithwaite & Baxter, 1995). We began this study not long after we met and started discussing our shared interest in relational and family rituals and especially in rituals that occurred during or following family change. We had read about couples renewing their marital vows—for example, several couples in Hollywood had participated in this ritual—and we had witnessed these rituals occurring within our communities. Thus, we interviewed couples who had participated in marital-renewal ceremonies. We conducted many of these interviews in the participants' homes and, along with their discourse about the rituals, we were able to examine artifacts from the ceremonies such as invitations, photographs, videos, clothing, rings, cake decorations, guest books, music, and poems.

We noted that most previous RDT researchers had focused their studies at the level of dyads; yet we were very interested in the vow-renewal ceremony, as we found it ideal to study relationships as embedded and maintained in larger social webs (the distal already-spokens we referenced earlier in this chapter). We knew that most couples held vow renewals in the presence of family, friends, and officials (most often clergy). The vow-renewal ceremony represented a particularly powerful way to study how the couples and members of their social networks simultaneously addressed competing tendencies in relationships. Rituals are multivocal, as relational parties respond to competing demands and identities at once (Baxter & Braithwaite, 2006a). Thus, in this first study, we examined ways in which the vow-renewal ceremony allows married couples to manage opposing tendencies reflected in this ritual. We discovered that this celebration was responsive to three discursive struggles: (a) *public-private*—the celebration of marriage as simultaneously a personal/private relationship and, at the same time, a social/public relationship; (b) *stability-change*—the celebration of marriage as an arena for paying homage both to longevity and to the ability to preserve and adapt; and (c) *conventionality-uniqueness*—the celebration of marriage as a conventionalized social form and a uniquely constructed culture of two. We concluded that this vow ritual functioned to help couples maintain marital bonds; and for us, it represented an opportunity to study marriage in older adult life.

We subsequently reanalyzed the renewal-of-vows data in a second study to identify traces of sociocultural ideologies that circulate in mainstream U.S. society (Baxter & Braithwaite, 2002). We identified discursive links to the distal already-spokens of two competing ideologies of marriage: (a) marriage as an institution embedded within a dominant ideology of community and (b) marriage as a source of psychological gratification embedded within a more muted ideology of individualism.

Our attention remained in the stage of older adult life as we examined the communication of couples when the husband had moved to a nursing home due to the onset of adult dementia from Alzheimer's disease and related disorders (ADRD). Dawn had previously completed a study of three couple types resulting from the state of "married widowhood" (Rollins, Waterman, & Esmay, 1985) for the wives. We recognized that the concept of "married widowhood" is itself centered on discursive struggle, as the partners are married, with one partner in decline. The community-based partner is faced with disengaging from, and grieving the emotional and cognitive loss of, his or her partner—a liminal state of married and widowed and a contradictory relational experience. Thus, we encountered the discourse of these women using RDT, examining the knot of discursive struggles that represented their experiences. More specifically, we focused on the communication practices of these women as they managed these contradictions in interaction with their husbands (Baxter, Braithwaite, Golish, & Olson, 2002).

We found that the limited mental and communicative abilities of the husbands created a great struggle for the wives because they desperately wanted to communicate with the husband they once knew and, at the same time, they needed to redefine their marital relationship and their own identity. The primary discursive struggle that arose in the talk of these wives was what we labeled *presence-absence,* as the wives coped with the tension of interacting with a husband who was physically present but cognitively and emotionally absent. This dialectical tension animated the talk of these women, and we identified three additional interrelated discursive struggles of *certainty-uncertainty, openness-closedness,* and *past-present.* We highlighted the different communication practices that the wives used to manage each struggle.

During the time when we were working in these first two contexts, we began an extended series of studies of communication in stepfamilies, which we currently continue. While we have centered some of these studies on other theoretical perspectives, the bulk of our work has been guided by RDT, and we will discuss five projects here. In an initial study of stepfamily development, we saw in the discourse of stepfamily members the competing demands that arise in stepfamily life. In our first RDT-based study of stepfamily communication, we zeroed in on stepfamily rituals and examined how members of stepfamilies interact and develop their families through ritual enactments (Braithwaite, Baxter, & Harper, 1998).

We asked stepchildren, parents, and stepparents from different stepfamilies to discuss their stepfamily routines and traditions, focusing first on a routine or tradition from their "original" family that ended when they became a stepfamily, then on one that started in the original family and was carried over to the stepfamily, and finally on one that began in the stepfamily. As we analyzed these data, it became clear that a central feature of informants' discussions of their stepfamily rituals was the contradictory interplay of members' original, or "old," family with the "new" stepfamily. Employing RDT, we focused on the dialectic of *old-new* to understand the role rituals play in the transition to the stepfamily and how rituals help stepfamilies manage the interplay of the "old" and the "new" families.

When we examined the rituals that ceased in the stepfamily era, we saw that these rituals honored the old family yet were unable to speak meaningfully to the new family; thus they were not allowed into the stepfamily system. Old family rituals that were successfully imported into the stepfamily were those that celebrated both the old and the new families and, in many cases, also highlighted the contrast between life before the stepfamily and life within the stepfamily. Finally, rituals that were started in the stepfamily were those that highlighted the interplay of the old and the new families. These were consequential, as they created opportunities to gather together the members of both the old and the new families. We discussed the importance for stepfamilies of honoring both the old and the new families in their rituals and relationships.

In our second and third projects, we focused on dyadic relationships within the stepfamily. In the first of these, we looked at discursive struggles in the stepchild relationships in the stepfamily, especially in the children's communication with their stepparent. In the second study, we focused on discursive struggles in the child-nonresidential parent relationship. Much of the existing stepfamily research adopts the perspective of the adults in the family to the neglect of the perspective of children. We wanted to understand the contradictions perceived by stepchildren to characterize stepfamily communication; therefore, we engaged in interviews with young-adult stepchildren (Baxter, Braithwaite, Bryant, & Wagner, 2004).

We identified three contradictions in the discourse of these stepchildren, reflected in dialectics of integration, expression, and parental regulation. In the dialectic of integration, we identified a discursive struggle of *closeness-distance,* as the stepchildren expressed a strong desire for both contact and detachment simultaneously in the stepfamily. Many of the stepchildren perceived their stepparent as an outsider who disrupted the closeness of their "old" family. The stepparent functioned as a wedge; close communication with the stepparent often left stepchildren feeling disloyal to their old family, especially to the nonresidential parent. Thus, the stepchild experienced and wanted a type of communication with the stepparent that was emotionally distant. At the same time, the stepchildren expressed the desire for closeness and intimacy with their stepparent.

A second discursive struggle of parental authority was present in stepchildren's simultaneous desire for family authority to reside in their residential parent and desire for there to be joint authority shared by the residential parent and the stepparent, in a dialectic we labeled *one parent-two parent.* While most of the stepchildren we interviewed wanted both the residential parent and the stepparent to share parental authority, when the stepparent did enact authority, the stepchildren were often very resistant. The third discursive struggle involved a desire for informational *openness-closedness* with the stepparent. Although they prescribed total openness among stepfamily members, stepchildren reported engaging in communication that often lacked openness. We noted that this disjuncture between idealized openness and their practices of nonexpression were difficult for stepchildren.

The next move in our third project was to recognize the importance of expanding the stepfamily boundary to take into account communication and relationships with family members outside of the boundary of the stepfamily household. We have devoted several studies to this cause. We framed one of these in RDT to examine interactions of stepchildren with their non-residential parent (Braithwaite & Baxter, 2006), exploring the discursive struggles stepchildren face as they simultaneously seek to maintain a relationship with their nonresidential parent and form relationships within the new stepfamily.

In our analysis of interview data, we focused on discursive struggles perceived by college-age stepchildren to characterize communication with their nonresidential parent. We discovered that stepchildren's perceptions of communication were animated by two contradictions: *parenting-nonparenting* and *openness-closedness*. The parenting-nonparenting dialectic appears under the supradialectic of integration-separation. What we heard in the discourse of these stepchildren was a desire for a close, parental relationship with their nonresidential parent, and yet they found this relationship challenging because it took effort, it disrupted their everyday lives, and it caused them to experience conflict and loyalty concerns as they tried to maintain a relationship with both parents.

As in the previous study, we found openness-closedness to animate the communication and relationships between these children and their nonresidential parents. On the one hand, the stepchildren very much wanted open and intimate communication with their nonresidential parent; yet, at the same time, openness was often problematic. Stepchildren managed this contradiction via segmentation (Baxter, Braithwaite, et al., in press). The stepchildren we interviewed described being open about topics they considered safe and closed about those they perceived as sensitive or unsafe. Thus, stepchildren often kept the communication with their nonresidential parent at the level of safe, surface topics, and they limited discussions about the residential parent, life in the stepfamily, or the stepparent. This made it difficult for children to maintain a close relationship with their nonresidential father or mother and for this person to parent them.

The difficulties of managing openess-closedness between households led to the fourth study, which we designed to pursue this metaphor of children feeling caught in the middle between their parents in greater depth. Dawn and her students sought to better understand how stepchildren communicatively negotiate this center ground in stepfamily life (Braithwaite, Toller, Daas, Durham, & Jones, 2008). We wondered, if stepchildren do not want to be caught in the middle, metaphorically, where do they want to reside in stepfamilies? The research team used RDT to examine these issues.

The research team brought young-adult children together in focus groups to talk about their experiences in stepfamilies so as to examine how stepchildren experience and communicatively manage being caught in the middle between their parents as they live in different households. We asked each focus group to create text for a brochure for parents, and the groups added drawings to the process, which we found very useful in our analysis (two of these drawings are included in Braithwaite et al., 2008).

What we heard in the discourse of these stepchildren is that the children want to be *centered* on the family, while at the same time they want to avoid being caught in the middle. What emerged in these data was a dialectic of *freedom-constraint*. Stepchildren desired the liberty to communicatively negotiate and enact desired relationships with their parents. At the same time, these stepchildren had to manage the limitations resulting from parental patterns of communication, both when parents cooperated with one another and (especially) when they did not. We also identified the openness-closedness dialectic animating the discourse of these stepchildren, as they felt caught in the middle between their parents when parents were too open or too closed. Our central contribution in this study was a description of what it means for stepchildren to be centered; they want to be informed on issues that they need to know about and left out of issues that would result in their being caught in the middle. When parents negotiate this dialectic successfully, children in stepfamilies feel centered on what they perceive to be their rightful place in the stepfamily.

In the most recent chapter in our in stepfamily studies, our fifth study is a return to stepfamily rituals. We interviewed young-adult stepchildren about the origin of their stepfamily, particularly the marriage ceremony of their parent and stepparent. In our conclusions, we make note of an *individual-collective* dialectic that animates the experiences of stepchildren concerning the remarriage of their parents (Baxter, Braithwaite, et al., in press). This dialectic involves the discursive struggle between a privileging of the couple and their marriage, on the one hand, and a privileging of the whole stepfamily unit, on the other hand. We have discovered that most stepchildren find the remarriage of their parents to be an empty ritual when the stepfamily as a unit is marginalized. However, in the few instances when the ritual had meaning for the stepchildren we interviewed, they perceived that the ritual was enacted in a way that honored their role in the new stepfamily and also did not delegitimize their family of origin. Our advice to parents is that "it will be wise to be mindful of how their remarriage ceremony can simultaneously honor their marriage and at the same time explicitly celebrate the formation of the new family" (p. 31).

Directions for Future Research

Where are we going next? Joined by Betsy Bach and combining research teams at the universities of Iowa, Montana, and Nebraska, we have begun what we envision as the first of a series of studies in the communication of fictive kin. Fictive kin are those persons who are regarded as family but are not blood or legal kin. We are driven by our desire to understand what makes persons "family" to one another and the role of communication in this process. As mentioned earlier in this chapter, our studies in the step-family context lead us to want to understand the dialectical nature of what it means to be a "real" family. We are interested in how our sampled families negotiate the integration-separation and openness-closedness dialectics, among others. We have collected well over 100 interviews with members of fictive families and are analyzing these data.

Other family relationships that set competing discourses in bold relief strike us as natural candidates for future study. For example, sibling relationships are often experienced as competitive yet affiliative relationships. Adoptive relationships provide opportunities to study the interplay of two conceptions of family—the concept of the family of the heart with and against a biological conception of the family. Relationships between adult children and their elderly parents afford an opportunity to study the competing discourses that may surround the role reversal of offspring who function as caregivers for parents.

More generally, scholars interested in RDT need to focus more concertedly on the second and third questions implicated in a contrapuntal analysis. To date, RDT-based research (ours as well as others) has tended to focus primarily on the first analytic question: that of identifying the competing discourses that are present in communicative texts. It is no longer sufficient merely to identify competing discourses. Two additional issues remain understudied. These discourses need to be located in the chain of speech communion: Are they voices from the broader culture? From the relationship's history? From anticipated evaluative judgments of fellow relationship parties or generalized others? Second, the details of language use need to be studied to examine how competing discourses interanimate to create meanings in the moment. Bakhtin (1984) urges scholars to pay attention to the micropractices of talk, for the interplay of discourses usually unfolds at the fine-grained level. Leslie has begun this level of work in a study of romantic and friendship dyads (Baxter, Foley, & Thatcher, 2008), but much additional work is needed to identify the ways in which discourses are jockeyed in the prosaics of talk.

Because centripetal and centrifugal discourses are not on an equal playing field, RDT-based research creates a space for a more critical approach to family communication (Baxter & Braithwaite, 2006b). Scholars need to understand how dominant, centripetal discourses end up being reproduced in family relationships, and how centrifugal discourses are ongoingly marginalized. A dialogic perspective is optimistic that centripetal discourses can be dislodged as new meanings emerge in the discursive struggles of communicative practices. However, as a scholarly community, interpersonal and family scholars have not chosen to emphasize communication as inventive (Baxter & Braithwaite, 2007).

References

Bakhtin, M. M. (1981). *The dialogic imagination: Four essays by M. M. Bakhtin* (M. Holquist, Ed.; C. Emerson & M. Holquist, Trans.). Austin: University of Texas Press.

Bakhtin, M. M. (1984). *Problems of Dostoevsky's poetics* (C. Emerson, Ed. & Trans.). Minneapolis: University of Minnesota Press. (Original work published 1979)

Bakhtin, M. M. (1986). *Speech genres and other late essays* (C. Emerson & M. Holquist, Eds.; V. McGee, Trans.). Austin: University of Texas Press.

Bakhtin, M. M. (1990). *Art and answerability: Early philosophical essays by M. M. Bakhtin* (M. Holquist & V. Liapunov, Eds.; V. Liapunov & K. Brostrom, Trans.). Austin: University of Texas Press.

Baxter, L. A. (1997). Locating the social in interpersonal communication. In J. S. Trent (Ed.), *Communication: Views from the helm for the 21st century* (pp. 60–65). Boston: Allyn & Bacon.

Baxter, L. A. (2004a). A tale of two voices. *Journal of Family Communication, 4,* 181–192.

Baxter, L. A. (2004b). Distinguished Scholar article: Relationships as dialogues. *Personal Relationships, 11,* 1–22.

Baxter, L. A. (2006). Relational dialectics theory: Multivocal dialogues of family communication. In D. O. Braithwaite & L. A. Baxter (Eds.), *Engaging theories in family communication: Multiple perspectives* (pp. 130–145). Thousand Oaks, CA: Sage.

Baxter, L. A. (2007a). *The distinctiveness of communication research: A dialogic perspective.* Unpublished manuscript, University of Iowa.

Baxter, L. A. (2007b). Mikhail Bakhtin and the philosophy of dialogism. In P. Arneson (Ed.), *Perspectives on philosophy of communication* (pp. 247–268). West Lafayette, IN: Purdue University Press.

Baxter, L. A. (in press). Relational dialectics theory. In W. Donsback (Ed.), *The international encyclopedia of communication*. London: Blackwell.

Baxter, L. A., & Babbie, E. (2004). *The basics of communication research*. Belmont, CA: Wadsworth.

Baxter, L. A., & Braithwaite, D. O. (2002). Performing marriage: The marriage renewal ritual as cultural performance. *Southern Communication Journal, 67,* 94–109.

Baxter, L. A., & Braithwaite, D. O. (2006a). Family rituals. In L. H. Turner & R. West (Eds.), *The family communication sourcebook* (pp. 259–280). Thousand Oaks, CA: Sage.

Baxter, L. A., & Braithwaite, D. O. (2006b). Introduction. In D. O. Braithwaite & L. A. Baxter (Eds.), *Family communication theories* (pp. 1–16). Thousand Oaks, CA: Sage.

Baxter, L. A., & Braithwaite, D. O. (2006c). Social dialectics: The contradictions of relating. In B. Whaley & W. Samter (Eds.), *Contemporary communication theories and exemplars* (pp. 275–292). Mahwah, NJ: Erlbaum.

Baxter, L. A., & Braithwaite, D. O. (2007). *Reclaiming uncertainty: The formation of new meanings*. Unpublished manuscript, University of Iowa.

Baxter, L. A., & Braithwaite, D. O. (2008). Relational dialectics theory: Crafting meaning from competing discourses. In L. A. Baxter & D. O. Braithwaite (Eds.), *Engaging theories in interpersonal communication* (pp. 349–362). Thousand Oaks, CA: Sage.

Baxter, L. A., Braithwaite, D. O., Bryant, L., & Wagner, A. (2004). Stepchildren's perceptions of the contradictions of communication with stepparents. *Journal of Social and Personal Relationships, 21,* 447–467.

Baxter, L. A., Braithwaite, D. O., Golish, T. D., & Olson, L. N. (2002). Contradictions of interaction for wives of elderly husbands with adult dementia. *Journal of Applied Communication Research, 30,* 1–16.

Baxter, L. A., Braithwaite, D. O., Koenig Kellas, J., LeClair-Underberg, C., Lamb-Normand, E., Routsong, T., et al. (in press). Empty ritual: Young-adult stepchildren's perceptions of the remarriage ceremony. *Journal of Social and Personal Relationships.*

Baxter, L. A., Foley, M., & Thatcher, M. (2008). Marginalizing difference in personal relationships: A dialogic analysis of how partners talk about their differences. *Journal of Communication Studies, 1,* 33–55.

Baxter, L. A., & Montgomery, B. M. (1996). *Relating: Dialogues and dialectics*. New York: Guilford Press.

Bellah, R. N., Madsen, R., Sullivan, W. M., Swidler, A., & Tipton, S. M. (1985). *Habits of the heart: Individualism and commitment in American life*. Berkeley: University of California Press.

Braithwaite, D. O., & Baxter, L. A. (1995). "I do" again: The relational dialectics of renewing marriage vows. *Journal of Social and Personal Relationships, 12,* 177–198.

Braithwaite, D. O., & Baxter, L. A. (2006). "You're my parent, but you're not": Dialectical tensions in stepchildren's perceptions about communication with the nonresidential parent. *Journal of Applied Communication Research, 34,* 30–48.

Braithwaite, D. O., Baxter, L. A., & Harper, A. M. (1998). The role of rituals in the management of the dialectical tension of "old" and "new" in blended families. *Communication Studies, 48,* 101–120.

Braithwaite, D. O., Toller, P., Daas, K., Durham, W., & Jones, A. (2008). Centered, but not caught in the middle: Stepchildren's perceptions of contradictions of communication of co-parents. *Journal of Applied Communication Research, 36,* 33–55.

Deetz, S. (2001). Conceptual foundations. In F. M. Jablin & L. L. Putnam (Eds.), *The new handbook of organizational communication* (pp. 3–46). Thousand Oaks, CA: Sage.

Hedges, A. (1985). Group interviewing. In R. Walker (Ed.), *Applied qualitative research* (pp. 71–91). Brookfield, VT: Gower.

Holquist, M. (2002). *Dialogism* (2nd ed.). New York: Routledge.

Kvale, S. (1996). *InterViews: An introduction to qualitative research interviewing.* Thousand Oaks, CA: Sage.

Krueger, R. A. (1988). *Focus groups: A practical guide for applied research.* Newbury Park, CA: Sage.

Lindlof, T. R., & Taylor, B. C. (2002). *Qualitative communication research methods* (2nd ed.). Thousand Oaks, CA: Sage.

McCracken, G. (1988). *The long interview.* Newbury Park, CA: Sage.

Mishler, E. G. (1986). *Research interviewing: Context and narrative.* Cambridge, MA: Harvard University Press.

Montgomery, B. M., & Baxter, L. A. (Eds.). (1998). *Dialectical approaches to studying personal relationships.* Hillsdale, NJ: Erlbaum.

Morgan, D. L. (1988). *Focus groups as qualitative research.* Newbury Park, CA: Sage.

Morgan, D. L. (1992). Designing focus group research. In M. Stewart (Ed.), *Tools for primary care research* (pp. 177–193). Thousand Oaks, CA: Sage.

Murphy, R. (1971). *The dialectics of social life.* New York: Basic Books.

Rollins, D., Waterman, D., & Esmay, D. (1985). Married widowhood. *Activities, Adaptation, and Aging, 7,* 67–71.

Rubin, H. J., & Rubin, I. S. (2004). *Qualitative interviewing: The art of hearing data.* Thousand Oaks, CA: Sage.

Schriffrin, D. (1996). *Discourse markers.* Cambridge, UK: Cambridge University Press.

Werner, C., & Baxter, L. A. (1994). Temporal qualities of relationships: Organismic, transactional, and dialectical views. In M. L. Knapp & G. R. Miller (Eds.), *Handbook of interpersonal communication* (2nd ed., pp. 323–379). Thousand Oaks, CA: Sage.

White, P. R. R. (2003). Beyond modality and hedging: A dialogic view of the language of intersubjective stance. *Text, 23,* 259–284.

PART II

Basic Interpersonal Processes

4

Relational Uncertainty and Interpersonal Communication

Leanne K. Knobloch

Uncertainty is a pervasive part of human interaction (Berger & Gudykunst, 1991; Brashers, 2001; Kramer, 2004). It echoes through the hallways of hospitals, corporate headquarters, and shopping malls. It softens the claims of meteorologists who forecast the weather on the television news. It surrounds expectant mothers and fathers who assemble to learn about the birthing process. It envelops the trading frenzy on the floor of the stock exchange. It permeates the faces of teachers and students on the first day of school. It blankets airport travelers in their quest to clear security checkpoints, board flights, and retrieve luggage. It pervades negotiations between foreign diplomats. It fills casinos and racetracks with excitement. It qualifies the predictions of pollsters on Election Day. It even penetrates day-to-day interactions between friends, siblings, and spouses.

Perhaps because uncertainty is such a fundamental part of relating to others, it occupies a central place in the study of interpersonal communication. Uncertainty has received systematic attention for its role in shaping communication between acquaintances (Sunnafrank, 1990; Tidwell & Walther, 2002), doctors and patients (Brashers, 2001; Gordon, Joos, & Byrne, 2000; Mishel, 1999), employers and employees (Kramer, 2004), and strangers hailing from different cultural backgrounds (Berger & Gudykunst, 1991). Work on close relationships has investigated uncertainty between parents and children

(T. D. Afifi & Schrodt, 2003), siblings (Bevan, Stetzenbach, Batson, & Bullo, 2006), friends (W. A. Afifi & Burgoon, 1998; Planalp & Honeycutt, 1985), dating partners (Knobloch, 2005, 2006), and spouses (Knobloch, Miller, Bond, & Mannone, 2007; Turner, 1990).

My program of research examines how people communicate when they are grappling with questions about the nature of a close relationship. I believe that this topic is important to understand for two reasons. First, relational uncertainty predicts the well-being of relationships (Knobloch, 2008; Knobloch, Miller, & Carpenter, 2007; Solomon & Knobloch, 2004). Perhaps more notably, how people communicate under conditions of relational uncertainty predicts whether relationships succeed or fail (Planalp, Rutherford, & Honeycutt, 1988). Both reasons suggest that relational uncertainty merits study because it is closely tied to the health of intimate associations.

I devote this chapter to telling the story of the relational uncertainty construct. By describing how scholarship has unfolded, I hope to accomplish three objectives. One is to organize the literature. A second is to describe the lessons I have learned while conducting research on relational uncertainty. A third is to identify how recent conceptual advances may inform future research. I begin the story by explaining the origins of the uncertainty construct within the field.

The Roots of Uncertainty Within Interpersonal Communication

Uncertainty occurs when people are unsure about their environment (Berger & Bradac, 1982; Berger & Calabrese, 1975). More specifically, uncertainty arises from the quantity of possible outcomes and the probability that each outcome may transpire (Shannon & Weaver, 1949). Uncertainty is low when only one alternative is likely to happen; it is high when several alternatives are equally likely to happen. Uncertainty exists when individuals lack confidence in their ability to predict future outcomes and explain past outcomes (Berger & Bradac, 1982). People have difficulty predicting future outcomes when they are unsure which possibility is most likely to occur. Individuals have difficulty explaining past outcomes when they are unsure why an event happened. In short, uncertainty denotes people's confidence in their predictive power and explanatory power (Berger & Calabrese, 1975).

The construct possesses a storied history in the field of interpersonal communication (Bradac, 2001). Over half a century ago, information theory first considered the role of uncertainty in the transmission of messages (Shannon

& Weaver, 1949). The theory employed a mathematical model to specify how much information messages can carry with minimal distortion. Messages containing unique information are most effective for reducing uncertainty. Because noise limits the amount of information messages can convey, messages optimize signal transmission by balancing predictable redundancy with unpredictable data. Information theory laid a foundation for scholars to explicate uncertainty in dyadic interaction.

Theories of attribution also paved the way for conceptualizing uncertainty. Heider (1958) characterized people as "naïve scientists" who are motivated to make sense of the world around them. He proposed that individuals discern the causes of behavior to render their surroundings predictable. Other scholars extended Heider's (1958) ideas by claiming that people make attributions for behavior in terms of locus, stability, control, and globality (e.g., Kelley, 1971; Manusov & Harvey, 2001; Weiner, 1986). Attribution theories shed light on uncertainty by arguing that individuals are motivated to generate explanations for behavior.

Uncertainty reduction theory (URT) examined uncertainty in the domain of acquaintance (Berger & Calabrese, 1975; Berger & Gudykunst, 1991). URT built on information theory and attribution theories to explicate how strangers behave in initial interaction. From information theory (Shannon & Weaver, 1949), URT borrowed the idea that uncertainty stems from the number and likelihood of alternatives that may occur. From attribution theories (Heider, 1958; Kelley, 1971), URT derived the premise that individuals are motivated to predict and explain their surroundings. URT argued that uncertainty is salient in acquaintance because strangers lack information about each other's attitudes, values, and characteristics. The theory also proposed axioms linking uncertainty with five features of message production (verbal communication, nonverbal expressiveness, information seeking, intimacy of communication content, and reciprocity) and two features of message processing (judgments of similarity and liking).

After a decade that saw an explosion of research on uncertainty (for reviews, see Berger, 1987, 1988), predicted outcome value theory (POV) reformulated the axioms of URT by arguing that individuals seek to maximize rewards and minimize costs (Sunnafrank, 1986, 1990). Whereas URT suggested that principles of uncertainty reduction are superior to principles of resource exchange for predicting people's behavior in initial interaction (Berger & Calabrese, 1975), POV embraced the opposite position. POV employed a social exchange perspective to derive competing predictions about how individuals communicate with acquaintances (e.g., Altman & Taylor, 1973; Kelley & Thibaut, 1978; Thibaut & Kelley, 1959). POV proposed that reducing uncertainty helps individuals decide whether additional interaction with a stranger will be rewarding or costly. Consequently, POV posited that people's motivation to dispel uncertainty is subordinate to the goal of anticipating the advantages and disadvantages of relationship development. Berger (1986) defended URT by claiming that uncertainty reduction must occur before individuals can forecast the rewards and costs of subsequent interaction.

The Emergence of Relational Uncertainty

As the debate about the relative merits of URT and POV raged on (e.g., Grove & Werkman, 1991; Kellermann & Reynolds, 1990; Sunnafrank, 1990), some scholars discarded the acquaintance context in favor of examining uncertainty within intimate associations (e.g., Berger & Bradac, 1982; Prisbell & Andersen, 1980). For example, Parks and Adelman (1983) found that individuals are particularly uncertain when they have limited contact with a dating partner's friends and family members. Gudykunst (1985) observed that uncertainty is negatively correlated with similarity and liking between friends. In a pair of studies, Planalp and Honeycutt (1985) and Planalp et al. (1988) discovered that people experience events that cause them to question some aspect of a friendship or dating relationship. These investigations provided empirical evidence that uncertainty is salient beyond the bounds of relationship formation.

Vestiges of URT and POV were apparent in the early forays into the context of close relationships (Knobloch & Solomon, 2002a). Perhaps the most notable holdover was a focus on questions about partners. URT and POV emphasized partners as the most relevant source of uncertainty within acquaintance (Berger & Gudykunst, 1991; Sunnafrank, 1990), and scholars continued to privilege doubts about partners in the first studies of intimate associations. All of the investigations employed a version of the Clatterbuck Uncertainty Evaluation Scale (CLUES) (Clatterbuck, 1979), the instrument prominent in research on URT and POV. The CLUES items gauge uncertainty by asking people how confident they are in their ability to make attributions for a partner's behavior. Sample items include the following: (a) How confident are you of your general ability to predict how your partner will behave? (b) How accurate are you at predicting the values your partner holds? (c) How well do you know your partner? The conceptual and operational definitions of uncertainty in early work on close relationships mirrored the partner predictability issues foregrounded by URT and POV.

Over time, scholars began to consider how uncertainty may be different within established relationships versus acquaintances. Turner (1990) conducted a pioneering but unheralded study in which she worked to tailor the uncertainty construct to the context of marriage. She developed a relationship-focused measure of attributional confidence (RECLUES) modeled after Clatterbuck's (1979) scale. Sample items include the following: (a) How confident are you of your general ability to predict the future of your relationship? (b) How sure are you about the closeness of your relationship? (c) How confident are you in your ability to explain the events in your relationship? Six years later, W. A. Afifi and Reichert (1996) created a scale measuring people's uncertainty about their partner's commitment to a courtship (e.g., "If you were asked about what this person envisions for your relationship, how certain would you be with your answer?"). Both investigations marked initial attempts to examine the themes of uncertainty in established relationships.

I began my program of research with the goal of reconceptualizing uncertainty within the domain of close relationships. A first task was explication. To that end, Denise Solomon and I defined *relational uncertainty* as the questions people have about involvement within close relationships (Knobloch & Solomon, 1999). We crafted the construct to possess a more narrow scope than the one spotlighted by URT and POV. Whereas relational uncertainty refers to the doubts individuals have about participating in a relationship (Knobloch & Solomon, 2002a), uncertainty in URT and POV encompasses any issue that could spark doubts about another person.

Sources of Relational Uncertainty

A next step was to identify the sources of relational uncertainty. We trained a research assistant to interview individuals about their experiences of uncertainty within courtship (Knobloch & Solomon, 1999). Participants discussed partner and relationship predictability issues, but they also identified another source of doubt. Most participants mentioned uncertainty about their *own* involvement in the relationship ("Do I really like this person?" "I'm not sure if I want to get involved in a relationship." "I don't know how much I am willing to commit to this relationship."). At first, we were struck by the novelty of people's focus on their own doubts. A careful rereading of Berger and Bradac's (1982) seminal book, however, revealed that they had anticipated this insight years earlier: "In fact, we would argue that in order for a relationship to continue, it is important that the persons involved in the relationship consistently update their fund of knowledge about themselves, their relational partner, and their relationship" (pp. 12–13).

We proceeded to conceptualize relational uncertainty as an umbrella term that refers to questions arising from self, partner, and relationship sources (Knobloch & Solomon, 1999, 2002a). *Self uncertainty* involves the doubts people have about their own involvement in a relationship ("How certain am I about my feelings for my partner?"). *Partner uncertainty* encompasses the questions individuals have about their partner's involvement in a relationship ("How certain am I about my partner's feelings for me?"). *Relationship uncertainty* includes the doubts people have about the relationship as a whole ("How certain am I about where this relationship is going?"). Whereas self and partner uncertainty focus on individuals, relationship uncertainty exists at a higher level of abstraction because it considers the dyad as a unit (Berger & Bradac, 1982).

Self, partner, and relationship uncertainty are interrelated yet distinct constructs (Knobloch, 2007a). Although their bivariate correlations typically range from $r = .60$ to $r = .85$ (Knobloch & Carpenter-Theune, 2004; Knobloch & Donovan-Kicken, 2006; Knobloch & Solomon, 1999, 2002b, 2005), the strong positive zero-order correlations mask more complex associations. Self and partner uncertainty are *negatively* associated when relationship uncertainty is partialled out (Knobloch & Solomon, 1999), which implies that people tend to experience either self uncertainty or partner uncertainty when relationship uncertainty is held constant. Moreover, the three sources diverge in their associations with people's appraisals of interference from partners (Solomon & Knobloch, 2004), their perceptions of how much social network members hinder their courtship (Knobloch & Donovan-Kicken, 2006), the directness of their communication about irritations (Theiss & Solomon, 2006b), their feelings of jealousy (Theiss & Solomon, 2006a), and their reports of how much time they spend thinking about their courtship (Knobloch, 2007b). Not surprisingly, then, the sources of relational uncertainty do not form a unidimensional first-order or second-order factor (Knobloch & Carpenter-Theune, 2004; Knobloch & Solomon, 1999, 2002b; Knobloch, Solomon, & Cruz, 2001; Solomon & Knobloch, 2004).

Levels of Relational Uncertainty

Relational uncertainty occurs on both global and episodic levels (Knobloch, 2007a). Relational uncertainty on a global level encompasses people's general doubts about the nature of a relationship (Knobloch & Solomon, 1999, 2002a). It can be assessed by asking individuals to report their overall perceptions of self uncertainty ("How certain am I about how much I want to pursue this relationship?"), partner uncertainty ("How certain am I about how much my partner wants to pursue this relationship?"), and relationship uncertainty ("How certain am I about the future of this relationship?").

Global relational uncertainty is useful for predicting message production and processing under routine circumstances (Knobloch, 2006; Knobloch & Solomon, 2005). Perhaps for this reason, most research has examined relational uncertainty on a global level (Knobloch, 2007a).

Relational uncertainty on an episodic level refers to the questions people experience due to a discrete event (Knobloch, 2005; Knobloch & Solomon, 2003; Planalp et al., 1988). Scholars have documented the kinds of events that spark episodic relational uncertainty within friendships and dating relationships (W. A. Afifi & Metts, 1998; Emmers & Canary, 1996; Planalp & Honeycutt, 1985; Planalp et al., 1988), within cross-cultural relationships (Sodetani & Gudykunst, 1987), and within marriages (Turner, 1990). According to this work, relational uncertainty increasing events often involve deception, competing relationships, and surprising changes in a partner's behavior (Emmers & Canary, 1996; Planalp et al., 1988; Turner, 1990).

Episodic relational uncertainty can be measured in two ways. One option is to ask participants to report on an event they have experienced recently ("How much did this event increase my uncertainty about my view of this relationship?"). A second alternative is to solicit participants' appraisals of a hypothetical event ("How much would this event increase my uncertainty about my partner's view of this relationship?"). Episodic relational uncertainty is valuable for documenting the strategies people use to communicate about unexpected events (Knobloch, 2005; Knobloch & Solomon, 2002b, 2003).

Themes of Relational Uncertainty

Whereas the sources and levels of relational uncertainty are relevant across interpersonal associations, the themes of relational uncertainty vary by dyadic context (Knobloch, 2008). Dating partners tend to experience relational uncertainty about issues internal to their courtship, including questions about their desire for the relationship, their goals for its development, and the mutuality of feelings between partners (Knobloch & Solomon, 1999). Spouses usually grapple with relational uncertainty about external forces that may affect their marriage, including questions about children, finances, extended family, household chores, and career trajectories (Knobloch, 2008). Within the context of illness, people often contend with relational uncertainty tied to their diagnosis, including questions about how to disclose their illness, seek social support, and set boundaries for interaction (Brashers, Neidig, & Goldsmith, 2004; Brashers et al., 2003). These nuances demonstrate that the themes of relational uncertainty are linked to the dyadic context under investigation (Knobloch & Solomon, 2002a).

In sum, scholars recognized the relevance of relational uncertainty to intimate associations very shortly after the birth of URT (Berger & Bradac, 1982; Prisbell & Andersen, 1980). Initial investigations followed URT's lead by emphasizing questions about partners (Gudykunst, 1985; Parks & Adelman, 1983), but later work accentuated self, partner, and relationship sources of doubt (Knobloch & Solomon, 1999). Other research provided a more nuanced view of the levels (Planalp & Honeycutt, 1985; Turner, 1990) and themes (Knobloch, 2008; Knobloch & Solomon, 2002a) of relational uncertainty. This explication laid a foundation for investigating the outcomes of relational uncertainty. I turn to that chapter of the story next.

Outcomes of Relational Uncertainty

Scholarship on the outcomes of relational uncertainty implies that relating is difficult when people are unsure about involvement (Knobloch, 2007a). This finding is consistent across investigations of cognitive appraisals, emotional reactions, message production, and message processing. I describe the research on each outcome in the following subsections.

Cognition

Work on cognitive outcomes suggests that relational uncertainty corresponds with a pessimistic outlook. Relational uncertainty is positively correlated with people's appraisals of the severity of irritating partner behavior (Solomon & Knobloch, 2004; Theiss & Solomon, 2006b) and the severity of unexpected events (Knobloch & Solomon, 2002b) within courtship. It also is positively associated with people's perceptions that conversations with their spouse are threatening to themselves and to their marriage (Knobloch, Miller, Bond, et al., 2007). Relational uncertainty is negatively correlated with individuals' reports of the stability of their courtship (Knobloch, 2007b). Similarly, it is negatively associated with people's perceptions that their friends and family members are supportive of their courtship (Knobloch & Donovan-Kicken, 2006). In sum, individuals experiencing relational uncertainty may unfavorably evaluate their partner, their relationship, and even members of their social network.

Emotion

Research on emotional outcomes hints at similar negativity. Relational uncertainty on a global level is positively correlated with dating partners' feelings of anger, sadness, and fear (Knobloch, Miller, & Carpenter, 2007).

Similarly, global relational uncertainty is positively associated with jealousy according to both cross-sectional (Dainton & Aylor, 2001; Knobloch et al., 2001) and longitudinal (Theiss & Solomon, 2006a) research. Episodic relational uncertainty is positively correlated with dating partners' reports of anger, sadness, and fear in conjunction with unexpected events (Knobloch & Solomon, 2002b). These results suggest that people grappling with relational uncertainty may feel more negative emotion.

Message Production

Communicating with a partner can be hazardous when people lack information about the nature of a relationship (W. A. Afifi & Burgoon, 1998; Knobloch, 2006; Knobloch & Carpenter-Theune, 2004). Myriad embarrassing outcomes can transpire: Individuals may damage their image, appear needy or clumsy, make the other person uncomfortable, discover that partners are mismatched in their feelings, and/or jeopardize the relationship (W. A. Afifi & Burgoon, 1998; Baxter & Wilmot, 1985; Knobloch & Carpenter-Theune, 2004). Because people experiencing relational uncertainty do not possess the contextual information they need to rule out potential pitfalls, they may have to attend to every possible face threat (Knobloch, 2006). Accordingly, communicating with a partner may be more risky under conditions of relational uncertainty.

Data imply that individuals are more reluctant to talk about face-threatening episodes when they are experiencing relational uncertainty. In fact, relational uncertainty is negatively correlated with people's propensity to discuss jealousy with their partner (Theiss & Solomon, 2006a) and their willingness to confront their partner about unexpected incidents (Knobloch & Solomon, 2002b). Similarly, partner and relationship uncertainty are negatively associated with direct communication about irritating partner behavior (Theiss & Solomon, 2006b). These results suggest that people may evade communicating about embarrassing events under conditions of relational uncertainty.

If individuals experiencing relational uncertainty are reticent about specific episodes, then they may hesitate to communicate about a host of face-threatening topics. My colleague and I worked to identify the breadth of issues that may be off-limits under conditions of relational uncertainty (Knobloch & Carpenter-Theune, 2004). We asked 216 participants in dating relationships to identify the topics they avoid discussing with their partner. Consistent with previous research (Baxter & Wilmot, 1985), individuals reported avoiding issues such as (a) the state of the relationship, (b) norms for appropriate behavior, (c) extradyadic activity, (d) prior romantic relationships, (e) conflict-inducing topics, and (f) negative life experiences.

Relational uncertainty was positively associated with the number of avoided topics participants identified. Also as we predicted, relational uncertainty was positively associated with people's appraisals of how much talking about the avoided topics would damage their image and harm their courtship. Our results cohere with similar studies documenting a positive correlation between relational uncertainty and topic avoidance within cross-sex friendships (W. A. Afifi & Burgoon, 1998) and family relationships (T. D. Afifi & Schrodt, 2003; Bevan et al., 2006).

A similar propensity for avoidance may be apparent in characteristics of messages. In a recent study (Knobloch, 2006), I hypothesized that individuals experiencing relational uncertainty may be reluctant to assert a definition of their courtship that may not be shared by their partner. I tested my logic by asking 248 participants to simulate leaving a date request voice mail message for their partner. Then, I trained research assistants to rate the messages along several dimensions. Findings indicated that relational uncertainty was negatively associated with the affiliativeness, relationship focus, and explicitness of the messages. Accordingly, people's hesitation to go on record with an explicit characterization of their relationship may extend to features of messages.

Message Processing

Perhaps because URT and POV emphasized uncertainty as a predictor of message production, limited work has examined relational uncertainty as a predictor of message processing. Ample theorizing from other domains, however, implies that people draw on information about their surroundings to make sense of utterances (Dillard, Solomon, & Samp, 1996; Honeycutt, Cantrill, Kelly, & Lambkin, 1998; Planalp & Rivers, 1996). By extension, individuals who lack knowledge about their relationship may have difficulty interpreting their partner's messages.

Within the context of courtship, the challenges of message processing may be manifest in a *tentativeness bias* such that people experiencing relational uncertainty may have difficulty drawing firm conclusions from conversation. Denise Solomon and I conducted a study to evaluate this reasoning (Knobloch & Solomon, 2005). We asked 120 dating couples to (a) complete measures of relational uncertainty, (b) engage in a videotaped conversation, and (c) report their thoughts and feelings about the conversation. We also trained research assistants to identify the relationship-focused speaking turns in the conversation. Relational uncertainty was negatively associated with people's reports of relationship talk after covarying the perceptions of the coders. In other words, individuals may have trouble recognizing relationship talk under conditions of relational uncertainty. Relational uncertainty also was negatively associated with the extremity of people's judgments of the intimacy of their partner's messages. Hence, people grappling with relational uncertainty may have problems drawing definitive conclusions about how much intimacy their partner displayed. Both findings suggest that dating partners may interpret messages tentatively under conditions of relational uncertainty (see also Hewes, Graham, Doelger, & Pavitt, 1985).

Within the context of marriage, the challenges of message processing may be apparent in a *pessimism bias* such that spouses who are unsure about their marriage may evaluate conversation negatively. My colleagues and I collected self-report and observational data from 125 married couples who engaged in two videotaped conversations (Knobloch, Miller, Bond, et al., 2007). As we predicted, individuals experiencing relational uncertainty interpreted their spouse's messages as less affiliative, more dominant, and less involved. Notably, however, relational uncertainty did not predict coders' perceptions of affiliation, dominance, or involvement. We interpreted these findings to be consistent with a pessimism bias: Spouses grappling with relational uncertainty had negative reactions to conversations that seemed normal to outside observers.

An intriguing implication is that people may experience relational uncertainty differently in courtship versus marriage. Courtship is a period of discernment in which individuals may expect to experience doubts as a diagnostic byproduct of the mate selection process (e.g., Baxter & Bullis, 1986; Baxter & Wilmot, 1985), so they may be cautious in interpreting their partner's messages under conditions of relational uncertainty (Knobloch & Solomon, 2005). In contrast, marriage entails a legal contract that carries personal, moral, and structural obstacles to termination. Marriage is considered a long-term commitment, it requires bureaucratic action to dissolve, and it yields joint assets such as property, children, pets, and memories that are impossible to divide (e.g., Johnson, Caughlin, & Huston, 1999). Doubts about the future of a marriage could be a precursor to divorce, so spouses experiencing relational uncertainty may be pessimistic in interpreting their partner's relational messages. Thus, relational uncertainty may correspond with a tentativeness bias within courtship but a pessimism bias within marriage. More broadly, these findings underscore the importance of attending to the dyadic domain when theorizing about relational uncertainty (e.g., Knobloch & Solomon, 2002a).

In total, research suggests that relating is more complicated under conditions of relational uncertainty. People experiencing relational uncertainty tend to draw negatively valenced cognitions and feel negatively valenced emotions (Knobloch & Solomon, 2002b). Perhaps because of elevated face threats, individuals grappling with questions about the nature of their relationship may avoid communicating openly with their partner about sensitive topics (T. D. Afifi & Schrodt, 2003; Knobloch & Carpenter-Theune, 2004). Moreover, people confronted with relational uncertainty may be susceptible to message processing biases (Knobloch & Solomon, 2005). Irony exists in the latter pair of findings: Those who most need insight into their relationship are least likely to discuss the issue with their partner and to interpret their partner's messages accurately.

Lessons Learned About Relational Uncertainty

While investigating the cognitive, emotional, and communicative outcomes of relational uncertainty, I have learned several lessons about how to study the construct. I gleaned some of these insights from designing studies, mulling over data, and working to reconcile competing findings. Other insights emerged from feedback that colleagues, editors, and reviewers provided on my work. I describe these lessons in the hopes that other scholars can profit from them.

Lesson 1: Do Not Overlook the Benefits of Relational Uncertainty

One insight is to attend to the rewards (as well as the costs) of relational uncertainty. To date, most empirical results suggest that relational uncertainty is detrimental to intimate associations. Relational uncertainty may spark pessimistic cognitions and negative emotions (Knobloch, Miller, & Carpenter, 2007; Theiss & Solomon, 2006b). It also may elevate the complexity of message production and processing (Knobloch, 2006; Knobloch & Solomon, 2005). In a recent study that offers the most direct test of this logic, I found that relational uncertainty was negatively associated with spouses' reports of marital quality (Knobloch, 2008). Ample findings imply that relational uncertainty is an obstacle to maintaining satisfying relationships.

Although the benefits of relational uncertainty are easy to ignore, neglecting them would be a mistake. Relational uncertainty may be rewarding in at least three ways. First, it may add spice to a languishing partnership (Baxter & Montgomery, 1996). If too much certainty dampens excitement (Livingston, 1980), then relational uncertainty may be valuable for inciting passion, alleviating boredom, and offering occasions to reaffirm devotion (Baxter & Montgomery, 1996; Knobloch & Solomon, 2002a). Second, relational uncertainty may shield individuals from face-threatening blunders when relationships are fragile. If ambiguity increases the salience of identity threats (Knobloch & Carpenter-Theune, 2004), then relational uncertainty may play a protective role by encouraging people to produce messages mindfully, cautiously, and prudently (Knobloch, 2006). Third, relational uncertainty may prevent individuals from learning bad news. If questions about involvement make people reluctant to engage in direct information seeking (T. D. Afifi & Schrodt, 2003; W. A. Afifi & Burgoon, 1998), then relational uncertainty may insulate them from disappointment, at least temporarily (e.g., W. A. Afifi & Weiner, 2006; Knobloch & Solomon, 2005). A danger in disregarding the rewards of relational uncertainty is that it fosters a simplistic view of the construct.

Lesson 2: Attend to the Salience of Relational Uncertainty

A second lesson is that relational uncertainty varies in intensity across populations. This principle is illustrated by the heterogeneous mean values observed in recent research. In the context of courtship (N = 525), Knobloch, Miller, and Carpenter (2007) observed midrange mean scores for self uncertainty (M = 2.74, SD = 1.20), partner uncertainty (M = 3.07, SD = 1.57), and relationship uncertainty (M = 2.93, SD = 1.28; 6-point scale). T. D. Afifi and Schrodt (2003) asked individuals to complete a variation of the CLUES scale about their family members (N = 601 adolescents and young adults); they documented a mean of 1.91 (SD = 0.68; 7-point scale). Bevan et al. (2006) solicited data on siblings' uncertainty about behavioral norms (N = 212); they reported a mean of 1.37 (SD = 1.09; 7-point scale). Knobloch, Miller, Bond, et al. (2007) collected observations from 125 married couples; they obtained very low mean values for self uncertainty (M = 1.40, SD = 0.54), partner uncertainty (M = 1.51, SD = 0.69), and relationship uncertainty (M = 1.48, SD = 0.62; 6-point scale). These descriptive statistics suggest that the magnitude of relational uncertainty may vary across types of relationships.

Although all four studies identified an association between relational uncertainty and a communication variable, the latter three investigations were likely plagued by floor effects. Would those studies have documented larger effect sizes if more variance in relational uncertainty was free to covary with the dependent variables? One way to answer that question would be to target individuals grappling with more acute doubts about the nature of their relationship. Collecting data from people who are questioning their relationship intensely (e.g., couples seeking counseling, families in transition, spouses contemplating divorce, friends negotiating major life changes) would shed light on the predictive power of relational uncertainty when doubts are particularly salient. Another strategy would be to evaluate whether employing convenience samples underestimates the magnitude of relational uncertainty experienced in the population. All four studies gathered observations from individuals who volunteered for a study of communication in relationships, which may have artificially restricted the mean levels of relational uncertainty. The general challenge is to design research in ways that solicit ample variation in relational uncertainty.

Lesson 3: Recognize That Both Insiders and Outsiders Experience Relational Uncertainty

A third insight concerns the link between relational uncertainty and message processing. As previously noted, studies have documented evidence of both a tentativeness bias (Knobloch & Solomon, 2005) and a pessimism bias (Knobloch, Miller, Bond, et al., 2007) when individuals process messages under conditions of relational uncertainty. How did my colleagues and I identify bias? In both studies, we examined how people's perceptions of relational uncertainty predicted their own views of the conversation versus independent judges' views of the conversation. Dating partners experiencing relational uncertainty perceived the conversation to contain less relationship-focused talk after controlling for the judgments made by outside observers (Knobloch & Solomon, 2005). Spouses experiencing relational uncertainty felt that their partner behaved less constructively in conversation, but relational uncertainty did not predict judges' ratings of behavior (Knobloch, Miller, Bond, et al., 2007). Hence, we concluded that biases were present because relational uncertainty predicted the perceptions of participants but not coders.

This interpretation is not wholly straightforward. Of course, outsiders are blind to the nuances of dyadic history, so their judgments should be free of the biases that may cloud insiders' perceptions under conditions of relational uncertainty. At the same time, outsiders possess no information about the nature of the relationship, so their judgments may be swayed by questions of their own. Perhaps observers hesitate to draw firm conclusions about conversation because they are not completely confident in their interpretations (e.g., Knobloch, Miller, Bond, et al., 2007). If so, then scholars who evaluate message processing under conditions of relational uncertainty are faced with a dilemma: Where does the bias lie? If the vantage point of observers is deemed accurate, then any divergence is attributed to the bias of insiders. If the vantage point of insiders is accepted at face value, then scholars forfeit the ability to gauge the bias of insiders experiencing relational uncertainty.

My overarching advice is to carefully consider what view to privilege when investigating the link between relational uncertainty and message processing (e.g., Cappella, 1991).

Lesson 4: Use Multiple Methods to Investigate Relational Uncertainty

A fourth lesson is a fundamental principle of social scientific inquiry: Employ multiple methods to triangulate findings (Kerlinger & Lee, 2000). A notable advancement in this regard involves episodic relational uncertainty. Early work asked individuals to describe a relational uncertainty–increasing event they had experienced recently (Emmers & Canary, 1996; Knobloch & Solomon, 2003; Planalp & Honeycutt, 1985; Turner, 1990). A variation on this strategy involves training participants to recognize unexpected episodes and instructing them to complete a questionnaire after they have encountered one (Planalp et al., 1988). More recently, scholars have solicited people's appraisals of hypothetical events (Knobloch & Solomon, 2002b).

Both strategies have strengths and weaknesses. An advantage of self-reported episodes is that they are germane, authentic, and noteworthy to participants. A disadvantage is that people's retrospective descriptions are subject to memory biases. Fortunately, individuals' recall should be fairly accurate because unexpected events tend to be salient (Knobloch, 2005; Planalp et al., 1988). One advantage of hypothetical scenarios is that they allow the content of the episodes to be standardized across participants. They also provide insight into people's immediate cognitive appraisals, emotional reactions, and behavioral intentions. On the other hand, hypothetical scenarios may not be believable to participants. Researchers have sought to circumvent this weakness by crafting scenarios that participants see as realistic (e.g., Knobloch & Solomon, 2002b). The majority of studies have examined either self-reported events or hypothetical scenarios in isolation (cf. W. A. Afifi & Metts, 1998; Emmers & Canary, 1996; Knobloch & Solomon, 2002b, 2003; Planalp et al., 1988), which limits the capacity to identify differences between the two methods.

I conducted an investigation to shed light on this issue (Knobloch, 2005). I recruited 278 individuals involved in a dating relationship to (a) report on a recent unexpected event and (b) appraise a hypothetical unexpected event. The order of tasks was counterbalanced across participants. Results indicated that the associations between the independent variables (intimacy, cognitive appraisals of the event, emotional reactions to the event) and the dependent variables (behavioral responses) did not differ for the self-reported versus hypothetical episodes. Hence, the method of data collection did not moderate the substantive findings. Notable mean differences were apparent between the two data collection strategies, however. The self-reported events evoked (a) more episodic self and relationship uncertainty, (b) more negatively valenced cognitions, (c) more anger and sadness but less happiness, and (d) more destructive behaviors. Thus, participants viewed the self-reported episodes to be more detrimental than the hypothetical episodes.

What explains the divergence? One possibility is that the self-report strategy solicits the most striking unexpected event individuals have experienced. Another explanation is that the hypothetical strategy allows people to forecast their potential reactions more optimistically than their actual reactions. A third possibility is that the self-report strategy favors volatility but the hypothetical strategy privileges the realism of the event. Gauging the validity of these explanations will require additional data. Other methods also await investigation. A laboratory study would illuminate people's proximal responses to episodic relational uncertainty, but it may not generalize to how individuals experience unexpected events in their daily lives. A diary study would shed light on how people respond to unexpected events over time, but if participants become sensitized to episodic relational uncertainty, then their perceptions may be tainted. All four strategies have unique strengths and weaknesses, so scholars should employ multiple methods to disentangle the true variance from the method variance.

New Directions for Research on Relational Uncertainty

Echoing this volume's focus on new directions for interpersonal communication, I nominate avenues for future work on relational uncertainty along both theoretical and applied lines. I begin by considering directions for additional research that arise from recent theoretical advances within the field of interpersonal communication. Then, I discuss avenues for further scholarship that fall outside the dyadic context of interpersonal communication.

Inside the Domain of Interpersonal Communication

For decades, scholars turned to URT (Berger & Calabrese, 1975) and POV (Sunnafrank, 1990) to conceptualize the link between uncertainty and interpersonal communication. Remnants of URT and POV are still apparent in the literature on relational uncertainty (Knobloch & Miller, 2008; Knobloch & Solomon, 2002a), but three emerging theories have begun to alter the conceptual landscape of work in this area. In the following paragraphs, I identify directions for future research that stem from relational dialectics theory, the relational turbulence model, and uncertainty management theory.

Relational Dialectics Theory

Whereas URT and POV suggest that individuals prefer predictability (Berger & Calabrese, 1975; Sunnafrank, 1990), relational dialectics theory argues that individuals possess competing desires for certainty and uncertainty in their relationships (Baxter, 2004, 2006; Baxter & Montgomery, 1996; Baxter & Braithwaite, Chapter 3, this volume). It proposes that the tension between certainty and uncertainty stems from a dialectic interplay between unified but opposite forces. Predictability may be comfortable, but it also may lead to stagnation and monotony (Baxter & Erbert, 1999; Livingston, 1980). Novelty may be exciting, but it also may foster anxiety and vulnerability (Berger, 1987). Hence, relational dialectics theory underscores the importance of examining people's needs for both certainty *and* uncertainty.

This insight implies a new direction for the study of relational uncertainty. Most work has assumed that individuals eschew relational uncertainty (Knobloch, 2007a, 2008), but relational dialectics theory suggests that people's desire for predictability versus novelty may depend on the situation. Consequently, scholars should identify the conditions under which relational certainty and uncertainty are valuable for individuals within close relationships. Do people gravitate toward excitement during early stages of relationship development but toward predictability during later stages? Do couples prefer to be uncertain about occasional breaks from daily routines but certain about their long-term commitment to the relationship? Do repeated attempts at novel activities (e.g., spur-of-the-moment getaways, surprise gifts) become monotonous over time? Do people's personality characteristics, socioeconomic status, and cultural background shape the relational uncertainty issues they find exciting versus worrisome? Recent conceptual advances by relational dialectics theory raise these questions as agenda items for future research.

Relational Turbulence Model

URT and POV imply that uncertainty recedes as relationships develop over time (Berger & Calabrese, 1975; Sunnafrank, 1990), but the relational turbulence model proposes that relational uncertainty is prominent during times of transition (Knobloch, 2007b; Solomon & Knobloch, 2004; Solomon,

Weber, & Steuber, Chapter 6, this volume). The model argues that relational uncertainty leads people to be cognitively, emotionally, and behaviorally reactive when relationships are in flux (Knobloch & Donovan-Kicken, 2006). Accordingly, the model implies that relational uncertainty shapes how individuals communicate during times of transition. It advances the current understanding of relational uncertainty by emphasizing that people's doubts about involvement may ebb and flow as relationships progress (e.g., Knobloch & Solomon, 2002b).

Although tests of the relational turbulence model have focused on the transition from casual dating to serious involvement within courtship, the model is designed to be more broadly applicable to other kinds of transitions (Knobloch, 2007b). Thus, a direction for future expansion is to evaluate the role of relational uncertainty in transitions across the life span of close relationships. Does relational uncertainty heighten reactivity between friends when they negotiate the transition from a geographically close to a geographically distant relationship? What questions are partners unsure about when they become first-time parents? How does relational uncertainty shape people's communication as their children leave home and they transition to an empty nest? What part does relational uncertainty play when individuals adjust to retirement? All of these questions stemming from the relational turbulence model await future research.

Uncertainty Management Theory

URT suggests that individuals are fundamentally motivated to reduce uncertainty (Berger & Calabrese, 1975); POV proposes that people seek to dispel uncertainty when they anticipate receiving rewards (Sunnafrank, 1990). In contrast, uncertainty management theory identifies uncertainty reduction as only one of several options for dealing with ambiguous situations (Brashers, 2001). Individuals also may choose to (a) seek information to preserve uncertainty, (b) discount information, (c) cling to inaccurate information, or (d) avoid information altogether (Brashers, 2001; Brashers, Goldsmith, & Hsieh, 2002). According to uncertainty management theory, people select these latter communication strategies to foster hope, maintain optimism, circumvent fear, cultivate self-efficacy, and avoid feeling overwhelmed (Brashers et al., 2000). This theory offers a more nuanced portrayal of the association between uncertainty and information seeking.

Uncertainty management theory has informed investigations of how individuals manage uncertainty about illness (Brashers et al., 2000), but it has implications for uncertainty about relationships as well. For example, Brashers et al. (2003) found that people living with HIV have questions about how others will respond to them, how to prevent social isolation, how to initiate new relationships, and how to maintain current relationships with family, friends, and romantic partners. These findings suggest that relational uncertainty is relevant to the ways in which individuals seek and avoid health information. Accordingly, a direction for future research is to examine how doubts about involvement intersect with people's experience of illness. Does relational uncertainty predict how friends communicate when one partner is suffering from depression? Does it play a role in how spouses interact when one person is grappling with a cancer diagnosis? Does it govern the choices partners make when one individual is battling an addiction to nicotine, alcohol, narcotics, or gambling? A next generation of research on relational uncertainty is poised to tackle these questions sparked by uncertainty management theory.

Outside the Domain of Interpersonal Communication

Other directions for future research involve broadening the relational uncertainty construct beyond the dyadic boundaries of interpersonal communication. One possibility is to conceptualize relational uncertainty as a family-level construct as well as a dyadic-level construct. In a recent pioneering study, T. D. Afifi and Schrodt (2003) verified that individuals experience uncertainty about their family as a whole. Findings indicated that participants in postdivorce single families and stepfamilies felt more uncertain about their family than those in first-marriage families. T. D. Afifi and Schrodt's (2003) work is innovative because it implies that relational uncertainty may be relevant to groups of people as well as individuals. An avenue for additional work is to capitalize on this idea by documenting the content, predictors, and outcomes of relational uncertainty at the level of the family.

Relational uncertainty may be relevant to organizations as well. Of course, individuals may experience dyadic-level relational uncertainty about their associations with supervisors and colleagues (e.g., Kramer, 1999; Morrison, 2002). Moreover, they may grapple with dyadic-level questions about how to manage the professional versus personal interactions they have with coworkers who also are friends and romantic partners (e.g., Bridge & Baxter, 1992; Kramer, 1999). At a more macro unit of analysis, people may be unsure about their loyalty to an organization, their role within an organization, and their value to an organization (Heath & Gay, 1997; Kramer, 2004; Kramer, Dougherty, & Pierce, 2004). This research implies that relational uncertainty may have utility as an organization-level construct. Hence, an agenda item for future research is to document the themes, causes, and consequences of relational uncertainty at the organization level (Kramer, 1999).

Perhaps the broader task is to integrate but demarcate findings across contexts. The themes of relational uncertainty may vary within acquaintance (Berger & Calabrese, 1975; Sunnafrank, 1990), courtship (Knobloch & Solomon, 1999, 2002a), marriage (Knobloch, Miller, Bond, et al., 2007; Turner, 1990), family (T. D. Afifi & Schrodt, 2003), and coworker (Kramer, 1999, 2004) relationships. Each of these domains may foster doubts about different kinds of issues. On one hand, tailoring the relational uncertainty construct to the context under investigation is vital for capturing the ambiguity salient to people (Knobloch, 2008). On the other hand, failing to assimilate findings across contexts leads to fragmentation in the literature. Advancing universal claims is impossible if scholars conceptualize and operationalize relational uncertainty in idiosyncratic ways. This issue poses two challenges for scholars. First, they must be mindful of the domain under investigation while seeking generalizable conclusions. Second, they must be willing to collaborate with scholars working in related subdisciplines such as family communication and organizational communication. It is a complex assignment, to be sure, but an essential one.

Conclusion

In this chapter, I have chronicled how scholarship on relational uncertainty has unfolded. Although I have emphasized the theoretical and empirical implications of the literature, I would be remiss not to return to the pragmatic examples of uncertainty that opened the chapter. Questions abound in the interactions individuals have with strangers, acquaintances, coworkers, family members, friends, and romantic partners (Berger & Bradac, 1982; Knobloch & Solomon, 2002a; Kramer, 2004). Clearly, relational uncertainty matters in people's lives (e.g., Berger & Gudykunst, 1991; Mishel, 1999). For that reason, scholars should continue to accumulate knowledge about how individuals negotiate relational uncertainty.

References

Afifi, T. D., & Schrodt, P. (2003). Uncertainty and the avoidance of the state of one's family in stepfamilies, post divorce single-parent families, and first-marriage families. *Human Communication Research, 29,* 516–532.

Afifi, W. A., & Burgoon, J. K. (1998). "We never talk about that": A comparison of cross-sex friendships and dating relationships on uncertainty and topic avoidance. *Personal Relationships, 5,* 255–272.

Afifi, W. A., & Metts, S. (1998). Characteristics and consequences of expectation violations in close relationships. *Journal of Social and Personal Relationships, 15,* 365–393.

Afifi, W. A., & Reichert, T. (1996). Understanding the role of uncertainty in jealousy experience and expression. *Communication Reports, 9,* 93–103.

Afifi, W. A., & Weiner, J. L. (2006). Seeking information about sexual health: Applying the theory of motivated information management. *Human Communication Research, 32,* 35–57.

Altman, I., & Taylor, D. A. (1973). *Social penetration: The development of interpersonal relationships.* New York: Holt, Rinehart, & Winston.

Baxter, L. A. (2004). Distinguished scholar article: Relationships as dialogues. *Personal Relationships, 11,* 1–22.

Baxter, L. A. (2006). Relational dialectics theory: Multivocal dialogues of family communication. In D. O. Braithwaite & L. A. Baxter (Eds.), *Engaging theories in family communication: Multiple perspectives* (pp. 130–145). Thousand Oaks, CA: Sage.

Baxter, L. A., & Bullis, C. (1986). Turning points in developing romantic relationships. *Human Communication Research, 12,* 469–493.

Baxter, L. A., & Erbert, L. A. (1999). Perceptions of dialectical contradictions in turning points of development in heterosexual romantic relationships. *Journal of Social and Personal Relationships, 16,* 547–569.

Baxter, L. A., & Montgomery, B. M. (1996). *Relating: Dialogues and dialectics.* New York: Guilford Press.

Baxter, L. A., & Wilmot, W. W. (1985). Taboo topics in close relationships. *Journal of Social and Personal Relationships, 2,* 253–269.

Berger, C. R. (1986). Uncertain outcome values in predicted relationships: Uncertainty reduction theory then and now. *Human Communication Research, 13,* 34–38.

Berger, C. R. (1987). Communicating under uncertainty. In M. E. Roloff & G. R. Miller (Eds.), *Interpersonal processes* (pp. 39–62). Newbury Park, CA: Sage.

Berger, C. R. (1988). Uncertainty and information exchange in developing relationships. In S. W. Duck (Ed.), *Handbook of personal relationships* (pp. 239–255). New York: Wiley.

Berger, C. R., & Bradac, J. J. (1982). *Language and social knowledge: Uncertainty in interpersonal relationships.* London: Edward Arnold.

Berger, C. R., & Calabrese, R. J. (1975). Some explorations in initial interaction and beyond: Toward a developmental theory of interpersonal communication. *Human Communication Research, 1,* 99–112.

Berger, C. R., & Gudykunst, W. B. (1991). Uncertainty and communication. In B. Dervin & M. J. Voight (Eds.), *Progress in communication sciences* (Vol. 10, pp. 21–66). Norwood, NJ: Ablex.

Bevan, J. L., Stetzenbach, K. A., Batson, E., & Bullo, K. (2006). Factors associated with general partner uncertainty and relational uncertainty within early adulthood sibling relationships. *Communication Quarterly, 54,* 367–381.

Bradac, J. J. (2001). Theory comparison: Uncertainty reduction, problematic integration, uncertainty management, and other curious constructs. *Journal of Communication, 51,* 456–476.

Brashers, D. E. (2001). Communication and uncertainty management. *Journal of Communication, 51,* 477–497.

Brashers, D. E., Goldsmith, D. J., & Hsieh, E. (2002). Information seeking and avoiding in health contexts. *Human Communication Research, 28,* 258–271.

Brashers, D. E., Neidig, J. L., & Goldsmith, D. J. (2004). Social support and the management of uncertainty for people living with HIV. *Health Communication, 16,* 305–331.

Brashers, D. E., Neidig, J. L., Haas, S. M., Dobbs, L. K., Cardillo, L. W., & Russell, J. A. (2000). Communication in the management of uncertainty: The case of persons living with HIV or AIDS. *Communication Monographs, 67,* 63–84.

Brashers, D. E., Neidig, J. L., Russell, J. A., Cardillo, L. W., Haas, S. M., Dobbs, L. K., et al. (2003). The medical, personal, and social causes of uncertainty in HIV illness. *Issues in Mental Health Nursing, 24,* 497–522.

Bridge, K., & Baxter, L. A. (1992). Blended friendships: Friends as work associates. *Western Journal of Communication, 56,* 200–225.

Cappella, J. N. (1991). Mutual adaptation and relativity of measurement. In B. M. Montgomery & S. Duck (Eds.), *Studying interpersonal interaction* (pp. 103–117). New York: Guilford Press.

Clatterbuck, G. W. (1979). Attributional confidence and uncertainty in initial interaction. *Human Communication Research, 5,* 147–157.

Dainton, M., & Aylor, B. (2001). A relational uncertainty analysis of jealousy, trust, and maintenance in long-distance versus geographically close relationships. *Communication Quarterly, 49,* 172–188.

Dillard, J. P., Solomon, D. H., & Samp, J. A. (1996). Framing social reality: The relevance of relational judgments. *Communication Research, 23,* 703–723.

Emmers, T. M., & Canary, D. J. (1996). The effect of uncertainty reducing strategies on young couples' relational repair and intimacy. *Communication Quarterly, 44,* 166–182.

Gordon, G. H., Joos, S. K., & Byrne, J. (2000). Physician expressions of uncertainty during patient encounters. *Patient Education and Counseling, 40,* 59–65.

Grove, T. G., & Werkman, D. L. (1991). Conversations with able-bodied and visibly disabled strangers: An adversarial test of predicted outcome value and uncertainty reduction theories. *Human Communication Research, 17,* 507–534.

Gudykunst, W. B. (1985). The influence of similarity, type of relationship, and self-monitoring on uncertainty reduction processes. *Communication Monographs, 52,* 203–217.

Heath, R. L., & Gay, C. D. (1997). Risk communication: Involvement, uncertainty, and control's effect on information scanning and monitoring by expert stakeholders. *Management Communication Quarterly, 10,* 342–372.

Heider, F. (1958). *The psychology of interpersonal relations.* New York: Wiley.

Hewes, D. E., Graham, M. L., Doelger, J., & Pavitt, C. (1985). "Second-guessing": Message interpretation in social networks. *Human Communication Research, 11,* 299–334.

Honeycutt, J. M., Cantrill, J. G., Kelly, P., & Lambkin, D. (1998). How do I love thee? Let me consider my options: Cognitions, verbal strategies, and the escalation of intimacy. *Human Communication Research, 25,* 39–63.

Johnson, M. P., Caughlin, J. P., & Huston, T. L. (1999). The tripartite nature of marital commitment: Personal, moral, and structural reasons to stay married. *Journal of Marriage and the Family, 61,* 160–177.

Kellermann, K., & Reynolds, R. (1990). When ignorance is bliss: The role of motivation to reduce uncertainty in uncertainty reduction theory. *Human Communication Research, 17,* 5–75.

Kelley, H. H. (1971). *Attribution in social interaction.* Morristown, NJ: General Learning Press.

Kelley, H. H., & Thibaut, J. W. (1978). *Interpersonal relations: A theory of interdependence.* New York: Wiley.

Kerlinger, F. N., & Lee, H. B. (2000). *Foundations of behavioral research* (4th ed.). Belmont, CA: Wadsworth.

Knobloch, L. K. (2005). Evaluating a contextual model of responses to relational uncertainty increasing events: The role of intimacy, appraisals, and emotions. *Human Communication Research, 31,* 60–101.

Knobloch, L. K. (2006). Relational uncertainty and message production within courtship: Features of date request messages. *Human Communication Research, 32,* 244–273.

Knobloch, L. K. (2007a). The dark side of relational uncertainty: Obstacle or opportunity? In B. H. Spitzberg & W. R. Cupach (Eds.), *The dark side of interpersonal communication* (2nd ed., pp. 31–59). Mahwah, NJ: Lawrence Erlbaum.

Knobloch, L. K. (2007b). Perceptions of turmoil within courtship: Associations with intimacy, relational uncertainty, and interference from partners. *Journal of Social and Personal Relationships, 24,* 363–384.

Knobloch, L. K. (2008). The content of relational uncertainty within marriage. *Journal of Social and Personal Relationships, 25,* 467–495.

Knobloch, L. K., & Carpenter-Theune, K. E. (2004). Topic avoidance in developing romantic relationships: Associations with intimacy and relational uncertainty. *Communication Research, 31,* 173–205.

Knobloch, L. K., & Donovan-Kicken, E. (2006). Perceived involvement of network members in courtships: A test of the relational turbulence model. *Personal Relationships, 13,* 281–302.

Knobloch, L. K., & Miller, L. E. (2008). Uncertainty and relationship initiation. In S. Sprecher, A. Wenzel, & J. Harvey (Eds.), *The handbook of relationship initiation* (pp. 121–134). New York: Psychology Press.

Knobloch, L. K., Miller, L. E., Bond, B. J., & Mannone, S. E. (2007). Relational uncertainty and message processing in marriage. *Communication Monographs, 74,* 154–180.

Knobloch, L. K., Miller, L. E., & Carpenter, K. E. (2007). Using the relational turbulence model to understand negative emotion within courtship. *Personal Relationships, 14,* 91–112.

Knobloch, L. K., & Solomon, D. H. (1999). Measuring the sources and content of relational uncertainty. *Communication Studies, 50,* 261–278.

Knobloch, L. K., & Solomon, D. H. (2002a). Information seeking beyond initial inter-action: Negotiating relational uncertainty within close relationships. *Human Communication Research, 28,* 243–257.

Knobloch, L. K., & Solomon, D. H. (2002b). Intimacy and the magnitude and expe-rience of episodic relational uncertainty within romantic relationships. *Personal Relationships, 9,* 457–478.

Knobloch, L. K., & Solomon, D. H. (2003). Responses to changes in relational uncer-tainty within dating relationships: Emotions and communication strategies. *Communication Studies, 54,* 282–305.

Knobloch, L. K., & Solomon, D. H. (2005). Relational uncertainty and relational information processing: Questions without answers? *Communication Research, 32,* 349–388.

Knobloch, L. K., Solomon, D. H., & Cruz, M. G. (2001). The role of relationship development and attachment in the experience of romantic jealousy. *Personal Relationships, 8,* 205–224.

Kramer, M. W. (1999). Motivation to reduce uncertainty: A reconceptualization of uncertainty reduction theory. *Management Communication Quarterly, 13,* 305–316.

Kramer, M. W. (2004). *Managing uncertainty in organizational communication.* Mahwah, NJ: Erlbaum.

Kramer, M. W., Dougherty, D. S., & Pierce, T. A. (2004). Managing uncertainty dur-ing corporate acquisition: A longitudinal study of communication during an air-line acquisition. *Human Communication Research, 30,* 71–101.

Livingston, K. R. (1980). Love as a process of reducing uncertainty: Cognitive theory. In K. S. Pope (Ed.), *On love and loving* (pp. 133–151). San Francisco: Jossey-Bass.

Manusov, V., & Harvey, J. H. (Eds.). (2001). *Attribution, communication behavior, and close relationships.* New York: Cambridge University Press.

Mishel, M. H. (1999). Uncertainty in chronic illness. In J. J. Fitzpatrick (Ed.), *Annual review of nursing research* (Vol. 17, pp. 269–294). New York: Springer.

Morrison, E. W. (2002). Information seeking within organizations. *Human Communication Research, 28,* 229–242.

Parks, M. R., & Adelman, M. B. (1983). Communication networks and the develop-ment of romantic relationships: An expansion of uncertainty reduction theory. *Human Communication Research, 10,* 55–79.

Planalp, S., & Honeycutt, J. M. (1985). Events that increase uncertainty in personal relationships. *Human Communication Research, 11,* 593–604.

Planalp, S., & Rivers, M. (1996). Changes in knowledge of personal relationships. In G. J. O. Fletcher & J. Fitness (Eds.), *Knowledge structures in close relationships: A social psychological approach* (pp. 299–324). Mahwah, NJ: Erlbaum.

Planalp, S., Rutherford, D. K., & Honeycutt, J. M. (1988). Events that increase uncer-tainty in personal relationships II: Replication and extension. *Human Communication Research, 14,* 516–547.

Prisbell, M., & Andersen, J. F. (1980). The importance of perceived homophily, level of uncertainty, feeling good, safety, and self-disclosure in interpersonal relationships. *Communication Quarterly, 28,* 22–33.

Shannon, C. E., & Weaver, W. (1949). *The mathematical theory of communication.* Champaign: University of Illinois.

Sodetani, L. L., & Gudykunst, W. B. (1987). The effects of surprising events on intercultural relationships. *Communication Research Reports, 4,* 1–6.

Solomon, D. H., & Knobloch, L. K. (2004). A model of relational turbulence: The role of intimacy, relational uncertainty, and interference from partners in appraisals of irritations. *Journal of Social and Personal Relationships, 21,* 795–816.

Sunnafrank, M. (1986). Predicted outcome value during initial interactions: A reformulation of uncertainty reduction theory. *Human Communication Research, 13,* 3–33.

Sunnafrank, M. (1990). Predicted outcome value and uncertainty reduction theories: A test of competing perspectives. *Human Communication Research, 17,* 76–103.

Theiss, J. A., & Solomon, D. H. (2006a). Coupling longitudinal data and multilevel modeling to examine the antecedents and consequences of jealousy experiences in romantic relationships: A test of the relational turbulence model. *Human Communication Research, 32,* 469–503.

Theiss, J. A., & Solomon, D. H. (2006b). A relational turbulence model of communication about irritations in romantic relationships. *Communication Research, 33,* 391–418.

Thibaut, J. W., & Kelley, H. H. (1959). *The social psychology of groups.* New York: Wiley.

Tidwell, L. C., & Walther, J. B. (2002). Computer-mediated communication effects on disclosure, impressions, and interpersonal evaluations: Getting to know one another a bit at a time. *Human Communication Research, 28,* 317–348.

Turner, L. H. (1990). The relationship between communication and marital uncertainty: Is "her" marriage different from "his" marriage? *Women's Studies in Communication, 13,* 57–83.

Weiner, B. (1986). An attributional theory of motivation and emotion. New York: Springer-Verlag.

5

Uncertainty and Information Management in Interpersonal Contexts

Walid A. Afifi

In many ways, the "story" of the uncertainty area in the communication discipline provides insight into the workings of scientific inquiry, generally, and interpersonal communication scholarship, specifically. The introduction of Berger and Calabrese's *uncertainty reduction theory* (URT) in 1975 brought attention to the construct of uncertainty among interpersonal communication scholars and served to shape the landscape of that area for years. Generations of students, myself included, were introduced to the theory as one of the few original theories developed by interpersonal communication scholars and were intrigued by its precision and heuristic utility. The theory was primarily founded on two principles: (1) individuals react negatively to uncertainty and (2) information reduces uncertainty. So one of the essential predictions was that individuals responded to uncertainty by seeking information.

With one notable exception (see Sunnafrank, 1986), that ideological lens to uncertainty and its behavioral outcomes dominated interpersonal communication research for nearly two decades. In fact, Johnson, Case, Andrews, and Allard (2005), in their review of this research area, referenced the long-held idea of a universal desire for uncertainty reduction as a one-time "shibboleth" (i.e., defining belief) of the communication discipline. However, the 1990s produced calls for scholars to challenge URT's essential principles (see, e.g., Babrow, 1992). Those calls ultimately led to a second phase of research on uncertainty in the discipline, a new wave of enthusiasm about the construct, and the introduction of several theoretical alternatives. The result has been that the ideology of *uncertainty reduction* has been mostly replaced by that of *uncertainty management.*

The past 15 years have seen a remarkable surge in scholarly interest in the areas of uncertainty management and information seeking. In fact, during this period, communication scholars have advanced at least nine models or theoretical perspectives with direct relevance to these processes (for a review of a similar growth of interest within other disciplines, see Case, 2002; Vakkari, 1998). Listed in order of original publication, they are the *problematic integration theory* (Babrow, 1992), *comprehensive model of information seeking* (Johnson & Meischke, 1993), *theory of uncertainty management* (Brashers et al., 2000), *normative approach to uncertainty* (Goldsmith, 2001), *model of social information seeking via CMC* (Ramirez, Walther, Burgoon, & Sunnafrank, 2002), *risk perception attitude framework* (Rimal & Real, 2003), *theory of managing uncertainty* (Kramer, 2004), *relational turbulence model* (Solomon & Knobloch, 2004; Solomon, Weber, & Steuber, Chapter 6, this volume), and *theory of motivated information management* (Afifi & Weiner, 2004).

In addition, one of the most productive efforts to examine uncertainty in interpersonal contexts to appear in the past decade is Knobloch's work on relational uncertainty (for a review, see Knobloch, Chapter 4, this volume). It is worth noting that this theoretical growth has been accompanied by equally impressive attention on the part of these scholars to socially important questions. These frameworks have been applied to topics in organizational (Kramer, 2004) and family communication (Afifi & Schrodt, 2003), to aspects of the experience of HIV sufferers (Brashers et al., 2000) and cancer patients (Babrow, 2001; Johnson, 1997), to other health topics, including organ donation (Afifi et al., 2006), dialysis (Hines, Babrow, Badzek, & Moss, 1997), sexual health (Afifi & Weiner, 2006), family planning (Mookerjee & Babrow, 2002), genetic testing (Dillard & Carson, 2005), diabetes risk (Turner, Rimal, Morrison, & Kim, 2006), and physical therapy (Babrow & Dinn, 2005), and to many other important life events.

The goal of this chapter is to summarize what we have learned in the past 15 years about uncertainty management processes in applied interpersonal settings and to offer directions for future work in this domain. I will begin with an overview of the theory of motivated information management (TMIM; Afifi & Weiner, 2004)—the most recent of the new approaches. I then review some of the controversies that challenged assumptions of the uncertainty reduction paradigm and laid the ground for TMIM, focusing especially on work in applied settings. Throughout, I outline possible directions for advancing the area, generally, and TMIM, specifically.

The Theory of Motivated Information Management

We (Afifi & Weiner, 2004) developed TMIM to accomplish three goals: (1) to bring together the diverse findings related to uncertainty management in interpersonal encounters, (2) to explicate the role of efficacy in the process, and (3) to offer a framework that explicitly recognizes both the information seeker and the information provider in the exchange. The theory explicitly limits its scope to the consideration of uncertainty management in *interpersonal* encounters. Figure 5.1 presents a visual overview of TMIM's key concepts and predictions, reflecting the broader inclusions of emotion, as put forth by Afifi and Morse (in press).

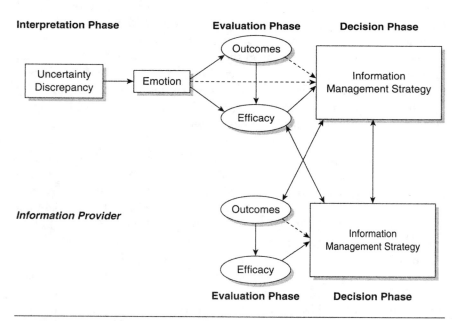

Figure 5.1   The Information Management Process as Proposed in TMIM

Note: The figure is intended as a visual simplification of the general theoretical framework. The dashed paths represent paths that are partly mediated by other variables with which the relevant variable has associations.

The Information Seeker

The theory argues that potential information seekers go through three phases in deciding whether to and/or how to gather information from an individual. The first phase—labeled the *interpretation phase*—starts with awareness about an *uncertainty discrepancy* on an important issue. Individuals hold an uncertainty discrepancy when they determine that the amount of uncertainty they *have* about an issue or person is different from the amount of uncertainty they *want*. The greater that difference (regardless of whether it reflects a desire for more or less uncertainty), the larger the discrepancy. Our reliance on this construct acknowledged the calls by Babrow (1992) and Brashers et al. (2000) to shift the ideology that scholars applied to uncertainty. That ideology, popularized by URT (Berger & Calabrese, 1975), assumed that individuals almost universally (a) experienced uncertainty as detrimental and (b) sought to reduce it. In contrast, Babrow (2001) and Brashers's (2001) work brought to light cases in which individuals (a) were satisfied with high levels of uncertainty (or, in some cases, sought more uncertainty than they had) and/or (b) avoided uncertainty reduction. Both types of situation will occupy much of this chapter's attention.

The next noteworthy position that we took was to argue that uncertainty discrepancy caused anxiety—an anxiety produced by disequilibrium between actual and desired states (Afifi & Weiner, 2004; but see Afifi & Morse, in press, for recent extension to emotions beyond anxiety). Consistent with most cybernetic models (see Carver & Scheier, 1998), the purpose of the information management process, according to TMIM, is to recalibrate the gap between actual and desired levels of uncertainty.

To understand the next phase of the process, we turned to Bandura's (1986) social cognitive theory. We (Afifi & Weiner, 2004) predicted that the path which individuals adopt in service of the recalibration goal is dependent on two cognitive assessments made in what we labeled the *evaluation phase*. Individuals first assess "the benefits and costs of a particular information-seeking strategy" (p. 176), that is, make outcome assessments, and second, make various efficacy assessments related to each option.

The outcome assessments are defined as being of two kinds: process- and results-based expectancies. The former captures the expected outcomes associated with the action of seeking information (e.g., the mere act of asking the boss about your performance comes with benefits and costs unrelated to what he or she might say about the performance itself), while the latter addresses the expected benefits and costs associated with the information gained (e.g., the boss might tell you that your performance is subpar). Both these outcome assessments go into individuals' general perception of the benefits and costs that would come from taking a particular information-seeking approach with a specific target. That expectation, we argued, is partly mediated in its impact on strategy choice by three efficacy assessments.

Despite the rich history of scholarship on efficacy (see Bandura, 1997), TMIM's inclusion of efficacy as a central feature of the uncertainty management process is one aspect that makes it unique from other interpersonal theories of uncertainty. We (Afifi & Weiner, 2004) argued that individuals make three types of efficacy assessments in this context. They assess their

1. *communication* efficacy—whether they "possess the skills to complete successfully the communication tasks involved in the information-management process" (p. 178),

2. *coping* efficacy—whether they "have the emotional, instrumental, and other resources (e.g., network support) to manage the process- and results-based outcomes they expect from the information-management strategy under consideration" (p. 178), and

3. *target* efficacy—whether "the information target is able and willing to provide complete information" (p. 178).

These assessments work in concert with one another and have the greatest direct impact on individuals' choice of strategies. That choice is made in the final phase (labeled the *decision* phase).

The decision phase involves selection among three general strategies: (a) seeking information, (b) avoiding information, and (c) cognitively reappraising the situation (Afifi & Weiner, 2004). Each of these general strategies has subcomponents. Information-seeking tactics vary, at the most general level, on dimensions of efficiency and appropriateness (see Douglas, 1987). Avoidance strategies vary on a passive-to-active continuum. Finally, cognitive reappraisals involve reassessment of the actual level of uncertainty, the desired level of uncertainty, or the importance of the issue. TMIM predicts that individuals choose strategies that they deem likely to reduce their uncertainty discrepancy but that are also consistent with their evaluation-phase assessments.

The Information Provider

An important aspect of TMIM is its explicit recognition that the information management process in interpersonal encounters is a dyadic one. Once an actor engages a target, the process immediately involves another person. As a result, we (Afifi & Weiner, 2004) proposed an evaluation and a decision phase for information providers (IPs) that closely resemble those of information seekers (ISs). Specifically, we proposed that IPs immediately assess the outcomes that they expect to come from disclosing information to the seeker, then make related efficacy judgments. Like ISs, IPs make efficacy assessments about *communication* efficacy (their ability to skillfully communicate the information to the seeker) and *coping* efficacy (their ability to cope with the consequences of revealing the information) as well as about *target* efficacy (the target's ability and willingness to manage the information). Together, these outcome and efficacy assessments predict the IP's selection of information provision strategies. In the case of IPs, the strategies may differ in completeness, directness, channel selection (e.g., face-to-face or e-mail), and location of disclosure (private vs. public), among other dimensions. The IP's response has immediate implications for the IS's information management decisions, either by affecting the seeker's level of uncertainty or his or her assessments of outcomes and efficacy levels. That influence, in turn, affects the IP's decision, and the interactive nature of the process starts over. As we noted in the original development of the theory, "even subtle cues from providers may lead seekers to make adjustments across all phases of the model, including shifts in their level of uncertainty, anxiety, outcome assessments and efficacy assessments, ultimately leading to mid-exchange shifts in information-seeking behavior" (pp. 184–185).

This overview of the TMIM framework articulates the theoretical positions we took in advancing the theory, but fails to offer the background of controversies that situate it. The remainder of the chapter does so, while also addressing TMIM's contribution to these issues and reflecting on directions for future research.

Assumptions of Contemporary Theories of Uncertainty and Information Management

Consistent with contemporary theories of uncertainty, TMIM, shifts the claims originally provided by URT in two ways: (1) It questions the claim that uncertainty is (almost) always undesirable, and explicitly acknowledges important cases in which uncertainty is valued, and (2) it challenges the supposition that individuals (almost) always seek information when faced with uncertainty, and proposes that individuals often avoid information in response to uncertainty. TMIM also advances a third claim to the theoretical landscape. It includes the concept of efficacy as a mediator of the link between uncertainty management needs (and the chosen uncertainty management strategy). Each of these positions will be discussed in turn.

Uncertainty Is Sometimes Valued

Central to the ideological shift that was made in this second phase of research on uncertainty is the argument that maintaining or even increasing uncertainty is sometimes preferred to its reduction. Those in the medical field reflected on that position several decades ago (e.g., Davis, 1960), and again very recently, when Whitmarsh, Davis, Skinner, and Bailey (2007, p. 1083) noted the ways in which parents and physicians "open a space for uncertainty in the diagnosis, symptoms, and prognosis" in pediatric genetic illness. Mishel (1988; Mishel & Clayton, 2003), in his development of the *uncertainty in illness perspective,* was among the first social scientists to formalize that view of uncertainty. Consistent with this ideology, Babrow and Kline (2000) claimed that "the ideology of uncertainty reduction is a weak, limited, and potentially dangerous general understanding" of health-related decisions (p. 1810), and Brashers (2001) argued that the "fundamental challenge of refining theories of communication and uncertainty is to abandon the assumption that uncertainty will produce anxiety" (p. 477).

The evidence for the utility of this ideological shift is strong. For example, several studies have shown that uncertainty for the terminally ill or their family sometimes means hope, a feeling that is crucial for individuals facing seemingly damning futures (see, e.g., Babrow, 1992; Brashers et al., 2000, 2003; Gill & Babrow, 2007). In contrast to this focus on uncertainty about negative life events, Wilson, Centerbar, Kermer, and Gilbert (2005) reported three experiments that tested what they called the "pleasure paradox." Their data showed that reducing uncertainty about pleasurable future events has the paradoxical result of more quickly ending the pleasure associated with those events. Although participants consistently believed that *reducing their uncertainty* would bring more pleasure than not doing so, it in fact ended that pleasure. In other words, individuals' erroneous belief that uncertainty reduction would prolong pleasure in particular situations ultimately led to an early end to that experience—a finding not predictable from an uncertainty reduction paradigm. Evidence that uncertainty is beneficial when anticipating *positive events,* together with the relatively voluminous data showing the benefits of uncertainty in the face of *negative events,* stretches the breadth of situations in which scholars have challenged the premise that uncertainty is always detrimental.

TMIM's Contribution

In developing TMIM, we searched for an uncertainty construct that would allow us flexibility in capturing uncertainty-related states and motivations, while still recognizing the anxiety that results from particular uncertainty states (see Afifi & Morse, in press, for discussion of broader emotional impacts). As noted earlier, those efforts led us to the notion of uncertainty discrepancy (Afifi & Weiner, 2004). The construct first struck us when reading Chaiken, Giner-Sorolla, and Chen's (1996) reference to the "sufficiency" notion. They argued that individuals' motivation to process information systematically was a function of the distance between their actual and desired levels of confidence on the issue at hand. As it turns out, the "sufficiency principle" is a central feature of the *heuristic-systematic model of information processing* (see, e.g., Chaiken, 1987). Although this model applies to information *processing* more than to uncertainty management or information seeking, the suggestion that individuals respond to a *gap* between desired and actual states, as opposed to the particular states themselves, fit perfectly into the emergent uncertainty management ideology. Moreover, the idea is based on well-established evidence about system activation (Ursin, 1988), is a central tenet of *control theory* (for a review, see Carver & Scheier, 1998), and allows for cases in which individuals have high uncertainty and are comfortable with it as well as cases in which they have low uncertainty and are uncomfortable with it—situations that cannot be accounted for by an uncertainty reduction paradigm.

Unpublished data from three TMIM studies speak directly to the utility of this ideological shift (see Table 5.1). The first study (Afifi, Dillow, & Morse, 2004) involved college students' uncertainty about something their romantic partner did or said (often relatively benign). The second study (Afifi & Weiner, 2006) tested the theory with a similar population and relationship type (romantic relationships) but focused on sexual health. The third study (Afifi & Afifi, in press) examined adolescents' uncertainty regarding the strength of their parents' relationship. Despite differences in the populations being examined, the relational context in which the uncertainty is playing out, and the issue at hand, two findings are relatively consistent.

First, in all three studies, a number of individuals (the percentage in the first column of the table) reported wanting to be *more* uncertain than they were about the issue at hand. While the sizes of these groups were consistently small, this finding speaks to the utility of an uncertainty management paradigm as against one that assumes a constant desire for uncertainty reduction. Second, and perhaps most notably, a high percentage of individuals who reported having *no discrepancy* on the issue (i.e., having no desire to decrease or increase their uncertainty) also had something less than complete certainty on it. In other words, people were comfortable with being less than completely certain about the issue.

In sum, the data unequivocally demonstrate that uncertainty is sometimes beneficial, thus seemingly challenging the validity of the uncertainty reduction paradigm. *But* note that the data from TMIM studies also suggest that only

Table 5.1   Uncertainty Discrepancy Scores Across Three TMIM Studies

	Want More Uncertainty		Not Discrepant	
	T1	T2	T1	T2
Relational information[a]	7	11	21 (35/7)	26 (53/14)
Sexual health[b]	4	4	37 (26/10)	47 (36/17)
Parents' relationship[c]	6	na	57 (52/30)	na

Notes: The data reflect percentages of the sample. The numbers in parentheses to the left of the slash represent the percentage of nondiscrepant participants who had something less than complete certainty on the issue (i.e., who were comfortable with less than complete certainty on the issue). The number to the right of the slash represents that subsample's percentage in the overall sample (e.g., Study 1/Time 1: 35% of the nondiscrepant group in that study, and 7% of the entire sample in that study, were comfortable with something less than complete certainty).

a. *n* = 222. Uncertainty discrepancy was measured by subtracting the response to "How confident are you [about the issue in question]?" from the response to "How confident do you want to be [about the issue in question]?" with the scale ranging from "Not at all" to "Completely."

b. *n* = 142. Uncertainty discrepancy was measured by subtracting the response to "How much do you know [about the issue in question]?" from the response to "How much do you want to know [about the issue in question]?" with the scale ranging from "Nothing" to "Everything."

c. *n* = 112. Uncertainty discrepancy was measured by subtracting the response to "How confident are you [about the issue in question]?" from the response to "How confident do you want to be about the issue in question]?" with the scale ranging from "Not at all" to "Completely."

between 4% and 11% of individuals want more uncertainty and only between 7% and 30% of individuals are comfortable with something other than complete certainty. In other words, the uncertainty-related motivations of a clear majority of participants in those studies, at least, *would be* captured by the uncertainty reduction paradigm. Thus, it seems worthwhile to more closely examine the conditions under which individuals are motivated by something other than the need for uncertainty reduction.

Where Do We Go From Here?

Although scholars have appropriately been struck by evidence in favor of the uncertainty management paradigm, their enthusiasm may reflect an overemphasis on the benefits of uncertainty vis-à-vis its detriments (see Woodgate & Degner, 2002). Current communication approaches leave us with the understanding that individuals sometimes value uncertainty (e.g., when uncertainty is viewed as hope) but do not offer an adequate theoretical account of when such a view prevails.

Evolutionary drives (see Koerner & Floyd, Chapter 2, this volume) may be an explanatory frame that could advance scholarship in this domain. Curiously, the few proponents of that perspective who have addressed the role of uncertainty land squarely on the side of the uncertainty reduction paradigm. For example, Inglis (2000) cites uncertainty reduction as "an ever-present necessity for survival" (p. 1568) and notes that "the ability to adapt to unfamiliar and novel situations is a fundamental requirement for animals living in complex and stochastic environments" (p. 1568). In other words, the survival of the species *relies on* the evolutionary promotion of an internal drive to reduce uncertainty (an argument that Berger, 1987, too, has implied). But how might we reconcile this evolutionary argument with clear evidence of cases where individuals find value in elevated levels of uncertainty?

Let us take a closer look at the function of uncertainty reduction as a feature of survival. The assumption is that uncertainty reduction allows us to exercise control over our fate by revealing potential threats and thereby allowing us to protect ourselves. But what if the drive to reduce uncertainty led us to the conclusion that we are fated to death and can do nothing about it? Would uncertainty reduction still hold its evolutionary utility? I argue that it would not. In fact, believing in an inevitable death would likely result in behaviors (e.g., surrender) that encouraged one's rapid demise. It is only by challenging the perceived inevitability of death that individuals are encouraged to expend resources and energy to persevere. Perseverance requires shaking off the original sense of the inevitability of doom. In other words, individuals *must* increase their level of uncertainty in these contexts to produce the optimism necessary to protect against surrender and guaranteed demise. So when inevitable death is perceived, survival may suddenly rely on an uncertainty-related drive that is opposite from that which dominates the motivational system under typical circumstances (see also Inglis, 2000).

Much more work needs to be done before we can conclude that this explanation or a revised form accounts for the variance in uncertainty motivations. For one, the analysis must be able to stretch beyond cases in which death is the perceived outcome of uncertainty reduction. However, a revised form of the perspective does seem to offer promise for better predictability for when the now-proven drive to maintain elevated uncertainty overtakes the more typical drive to reduce it.

Individuals Sometimes Avoid Information in Response to Uncertainty

As noted above, a second bulwark of the uncertainty reduction paradigm was that individuals seek information when faced with uncertainty. While there is considerable support for that prediction, there is also a good deal of evidence in the past three decades which challenges that claim. The context of genetic testing perhaps most vividly brings out the difficult issues that individuals face when deciding whether to seek information under conditions of high uncertainty. Indeed, Johnson et al. (2005) dubbed genomics the "perfect information-seeking research problem" (p. 323) because it so consistently challenges long-held beliefs about individuals' motivation to seek information.

The essence of what makes genetic testing such a difficult decision is that it sometimes puts individuals in an acute conundrum. They could discover that they (or their offspring) have a debilitating condition or terminal illness, or they could remain "blissfully" ignorant (see Case, Andrews, Johnson, & Allard, 2005, for a review). Testing for Huntington's disease (HD) makes that choice particularly stark. The disease is hereditary, therefore identifiable through genetic testing and placing certain individuals at high risk. The disease typically produces severe physical and mental deterioration, and there is no known cure or even adequate treatment. So those identified as having HD appear destined to experience a gradual and painful death. However, HD symptoms only start appearing in later adult life; younger adults with the disease show no ill effects. Although knowing one's HD status should be a priority, even if only for the sake of contributing to the decision about whether to have children, the vast majority of at-risk adults (i.e., those with a genetic link to the disease) choose to avoid testing (Robins Wahlin, 2007). In fact, Robins Wahlin's (2007) summary of studies in this area revealed that only 3% to 21% of at-risk individuals across the globe decide to get tested for the disease. Studies of such decisions in other domains of genetic testing reveal a somewhat higher willingness to seek information, but still show several illnesses for which the majority of individuals avoid testing (see Gaff, Cowan, Meiser, & Lindeman, 2006; Lerman, Croyle, Tercyak, & Hamann, 2002).

This evidence points to *situational* aspects that challenge the uncertainty reduction paradigm's suggestion that we are voracious information seekers. Other challenges to the uncertainty reduction paradigm have come from personality theorists. These scholars have found predictable individual differences in the desire to seek information. Central among these approaches has been Miller's identification of two styles of information processing: "monitors," "who typically scan for threat-relevant information" (Miller, Brody, & Summerton, 1988, p. 142), and "blunters," who, in contrast, "typically ignore threat-relevant information" (p. 142). This framework has produced voluminous data, both in medical and lab settings, and has consistently revealed differences in the way that these two personality types react to uncertainty. Monitors seek information about potential health threats while blunters avoid it (Miller, 1995). Other scholars have shown similar personality-based patterns outside the health domain (e.g., Ickes, Dugosh, Simpson, & Wilson, 2003; Kruglanski & Webster, 1996).

TMIM's Contribution

Given all this evidence, and the fact that data from an investigation relatively early in my career led us (Afifi & Burgoon, 1998) to conclude that "certainty about undesired information is itself undesirable" (p. 267), it should come as no surprise that we explicitly recognized multiple information management options in our development of TMIM. We did so by noting three general strategy decisions facing individuals with an uncertainty discrepancy: to seek information, to avoid information, or to engage in cognitive reappraisal (Afifi & Weiner, 2004). To date, the theory's tests have primarily measured its ability to predict direct information seeking (for exceptions, see Afifi & Afifi, in press; Afifi et al., 2004). However, I again turn to unpublished data from these studies—this time to lend insight into the relative commonality of avoidance as a strategy selected in the face of uncertainty discrepancy.

As noted earlier, Afifi et al. (2004) were interested in examining individuals' search for relationally relevant information from romantic partners. In the follow-up survey (3 weeks after the TMIM predictor variables were assessed), participants were asked whether they had "made any effort to seek information about the issue since the first survey" and whether they had "made any effort to avoid information about the issue since the first survey." Narrowing the analysis to those who reported an uncertainty discrepancy at Time 1, 47% claimed to have made no effort to seek information and 11% indicated making active efforts to avoid seeking information. Unpublished data from Afifi and Afifi (in press) show somewhat similar patterns. Specifically, 77% of adolescents who reported an uncertainty discrepancy about the strength of their parents' relationship during the entry survey also reported engaging in at least some avoidance in the interaction that followed (as assessed through an average score higher than 1 on a 7-point avoidance measure), and 17% reported significant amounts of avoidance (as assessed through an average score on that measure that exceeded the scale midpoint). In other words, even in cases much less severe than terminal illness, we see a good number of people who engage in either active or passive avoidance in the face of uncertainty discrepancy.

In sum, the data unequivocally show that individuals do not always respond to uncertainty by seeking information. But should they? Surprisingly, we know relatively little about the consequences of information seeking as a response to uncertainty discrepancy.

Where Do We Go From Here?

Scholars have not adequately addressed the supposition that searching for information is actually something we should recommend. In fact, a review of the literature offers good reasons to question that long-held assumption.

One of the assumptions of most research in this area is that knowledge translates to informed (i.e., better) decisions. In the words of late 16th- and early 17th-century British philosopher Francis Bacon, "Knowledge is power." Indeed, studies repeatedly show that information seeking is associated with positive psychological and physiological responses, including a reduction in stress and anxiety and a general improvement in overall well-being (for a review, see Czaja, Manfredi, & Price, 2003). That makes sense—after all, what could be detrimental about seeking information?

Actually, a review of the literature suggests quite a few negative outcomes of information seeking. For example, the discovery of negative health information has been shown to increase psychological distress, negatively affect general health, produce suicidal ideation, lead to poor health decisions, and harm family relations (e.g., Decruyenaere et al., 2003; Johnson, et al., 2005; Rosen, Knäuper, & Sammut, 2007). Other negative outcomes from information seeking in this context include survivor's guilt, harm to familial bonds, social stigma, workplace discrimination, and loss of insurance (Johnson et al., 2005; Robins Wahlin, 2007). In fact, Baum, Friedman, and Zakowski's (1997) review of literature on stress and genetic testing, led them to conclude that "learning that one will likely develop a life-threatening illness is stressful and may outweigh beneficial effects of uncertainty reduction" (p. 15).

Of course, another danger of information seeking is the possibility that one may discover, and then trust, incorrect information. In the medical context, that possibility may work in two ways. First, individuals who seek information about a medical condition may be misled into believing that they have an illness that they, in fact, do not (Jepson, Hewison, Thompson, & Weller, 2007; Kalichman et al., 2006). Second, individuals who seek information may be misled into believing that they do not have an illness when they, in fact, do. In either case, the discovered information may lead individuals to confidently engage in behaviors that unknowingly lead to a more rapid drop in health. A recent study we conducted (Afifi & Weiner, 2006) showed the consequences of these possibilities in relational contexts. Specifically, only 2% of college participants believed that their partner had a sexually transmitted infection (STI)—a number far below the 30% to 40% of college students who government reports estimate have an STI (Academy for Educational Development, 2000). But perhaps the most troubling aspect of that study emerged from a follow-up analysis we conducted (Afifi & Lucas, 2008), which showed that the respondents' confidence in the negative status of their partners came from relatively voracious information seeking on the matter. In other words, their search for information led many of them to incorrectly believe that their partner was not infected. Might they have been better off not seeking information?

The preliminary analysis (Afifi & Weiner, 2006) suggested that this was not the case, but the follow-up information reintroduces doubt. Might the continued uncertainty have led to safer sexual behaviors? We do not know. What we do know from prior literature is that searches for information are guided by motivational forces that bias the information we find (see Forgas, 2001). Relational contexts are especially prone to biased information searching and processing (Murray, 1999), with considerable consequences for well-being.

In the end, it is difficult to know what to recommend. On the one hand, seeking information has clear benefits. Without knowing about a medical condition, individuals cannot engage in actions that can address it. On the other hand, seeking information also has clear risks. Discovering a medical condition that is debilitating or terminal, or reacting to incorrect information that stemmed from a well-intentioned search for information, has well-chronicled consequences. The literature in this domain is woefully incomplete. We need more guidance to help health professionals advise and individuals decide. One variable that might help direct research efforts in this domain is efficacy.

The Role of Self-Efficacy in Uncertainty Management

Bandura (1995) defined (perceived) self-efficacy as "beliefs in one's capabilities to organize and execute the courses of action required to manage prospective situations" (p. 2). The construct has been a force in social scientific inquiry for three decades and has been a consistent predictor of both thought and action (for a review, see Bandura, 1997). It is certainly one of the most important constructs we have for predicting behavior. Unexplainably, though, references to efficacy have been almost entirely absent from the literature on uncertainty management and/or information seeking in interpersonal settings. Addressing that limitation was one of our main goals in advancing TMIM.

TMIM's Contribution

A summary of the findings on the role of efficacy in this process speaks to its importance but also to the need for much greater attention to the ways in which the various types of efficacy operate in various information management contexts. Notably, the only efficacy component to significantly influence information-seeking strategies across all four tests of the theory has been *communication* efficacy (for a review, see Afifi & Afifi, in press). Perceptions of the target's efficacy to honestly provide information has been the second most consistent efficacy component, appearing as a significant predictor in three of the four tests. The other proposed efficacy assessments (coping efficacy and perceptions of the target's efficacy vis-à-vis access to information) have each significantly accounted for variance in the information management choice in only one of the four studies.

Where Do We Go From Here?

Two issues in relation to efficacy's performance in tests of TMIM will be briefly addressed. The first is the consistent role of communication efficacy and target honesty and the second is the inconsistent role of coping efficacy and target information access.

Communication efficacy and the perceived honesty subcomponent of target efficacy have served as mediators of individuals' information-seeking decisions across several contexts. As such, their absence from prior frameworks of uncertainty management within interpersonal encounters undoubtedly slowed progress within that domain. Yet the application of these assessments in the domain of uncertainty or information management remains in its infancy. Much work still needs to be done on both measurement and predictive precision. These constructs also need to be compared with other variables to which they have close conceptual ties. Specifically, the construct of perceived interpersonal competence (see Spitzberg & Cupach, 1984) should share considerable variance with perceived communication efficacy. Moreover, since perceived honesty is a dimension of credibility (see McCroskey & Young, 1981), the honesty subcomponent of target efficacy likely operates in ways similar to assessments of source credibility. We need to know more about both the overlap and the unique contributions that each of these related constructs makes to TMIM's success as a predictive framework.

While communication efficacy and perceived target honesty have done well as predictors, coping efficacy and the target's perceived access to information have not. In the most recent investigation, we argued that the surprising failure of coping efficacy may reflect a combination of a restricted measure and the limited relevance of coping assessments to situations involving negative outcome expectancies (Afifi & Afifi, in press). Given what we know about the role that perceived coping efficacy (or related constructs) plays in decisions to seek information in health contexts (e.g., genetics, HIV), it is premature to give up on its utility as a predictor of information management decisions. However, considerable effort must go into improving both measurement and testing situations so that we can best understand the impact of coping efficacy on this process.

The relative failure of the access subcomponent of target efficacy is also likely due to methodological aspects of past investigations. Specifically, all tests to date have asked individuals to consider targeting others who naturally have access to the information being sought. As such, variance on that dimension is likely too small to allow fair testing of its role. Indeed, the only investigation that did find target access to be a significant predictor of information seeking was our study of partner's sexual health (Afifi & Weiner, 2006). In a context such as that, it is certainly plausible that a partner is unaware of his or her infection status (symptoms often do not appear at all, appear months after original infection, or go unnoticed). Consistent with the theory, the study showed that individuals were less likely to seek information from their partners to the extent that they perceived them to be unaware of their infection status. So, again, it seems premature to write off the influence of perceived target access to the information without more complete measurement work and more rigorous testing situations.

Summary and Future Directions

In this chapter, I have summarized the status of two of the primary premises underlying the uncertainty reduction paradigm and discussed the need to incorporate efficacy into our understanding of uncertainty management decisions. In doing so, I have offered possible explanations for still-lingering questions and have recommended directions for future research. This area of research is still ripe for additional investigation. Despite decades of research attention, there is still much that we do not know. In fact, besides pursuing the suggestions I have advanced in this chapter, three other goals will occupy my research energies in the near future. First, TMIM must be subjected to experimental designs that will allow testing of the proposed causal structure imbedded in the framework. Although every test to date has minimally included an over-time design, all have essentially been correlational in nature. That must change before the framework can start to hold its own as a valuable contribution to our knowledge about the information management process. Second, future investigations using TMIM must begin to clarify the role of the IP. The interpersonal information management process is an interactive one, but no studies to date have adequately examined the interactive nature of the process during conversations. Doing so will force more precision into our theorizing about the role of the IP (an area in this literature that is weak) and will help us more fully understand the process. Finally, we must more closely attend to the role that emotions play in the selection of information management strategies. Babrow (2001) and Brashers (2001) explicitly recognize emotional appraisals as a foundational part of the uncertainty management process, but we do not yet adequately know how emotions affect the assessments that mediate the choice of strategies. We recognized the need to do so in our original theoretical treatise (Afifi & Weiner, 2004). Time has further emphasized the importance of doing so. Encouraged by methodological advances and new theoretical lenses, the literature on emotions and their influence on cognition and behavior is experiencing a drastic resurgence of attention (see Peters, Västfjäll, Gärling, & Slovic, 2006). The current work has direct and clear application to our knowledge about how people respond to uncertainty.

Shaped by Berger's model of scholarship, the area continues to be theory generating and theory driven. The work also triangulates methodologies and is heavy on application to important real-world issues. In sum, the ongoing research on uncertainty and information management in interpersonal contexts is one reason for the current excitement about interpersonal communication scholarship.

References

Academy for Educational Development. (2000, May). *Sexually transmitted diseases: An overview*. Report prepared by the Center for Community-Based Health Strategies (now the Center on AIDS and Community Health). Washington, DC: Author.

Afifi, T. D., & Schrodt, P. (2003). Uncertainty and the avoidance of the state of one's family in stepfamilies, postdivorce single-parent families, and first-marriage families. *Human Communication Research, 29*, 516–532.

Afifi, W. A., & Afifi, T. D. (in press). Adolescents' avoidance tendencies and physiological reactions to discussions about their parents' relationship: Implications for post-divorce and non-divorced families. *Journal of Social and Personal Relationships*.

Afifi, W. A., & Burgoon, J. K. (1998). "We never talk about that:" A comparison of cross-sex friendships and dating relationships on uncertainty and topic avoidance. *Personal Relationships, 5*, 255–272.

Afifi, W. A., Dillow, M., & Morse, C. (2004). Seeking information in relational contexts: A test of the theory of motivated information management. *Personal Relationships, 11*, 429–450.

Afifi, W. A., & Lucas, A. (2008). Information seeking in initial stages of relationship development. In S. Sprecher, A. Wenzel, & J. Harvey (Eds.), *Handbook of relationship initiation* (pp. 135–152). New York: Psychology Press.

Afifi, W. A., Morgan, S. E., Stephenson, M., Morse, C., Harrison, T., Reichert, T., et al. (2006). Examining the decision to talk with family about organ donation: Applying the theory of motivated information management. *Communication Monographs, 73*, 188–215.

Afifi, W. A., & Morse, C. R. (in press). Expanding the role of emotion in the theory of motivated information management. In T. D. Afifi & W. A. Afifi (Eds.), *Uncertainty, information management, and disclosure decisions: Theories and applications.* New York: Routledge.

Afifi, W. A., & Weiner, J. L. (2004). Toward a theory of motivated information management. *Communication Theory, 14,* 167–190.

Afifi, W. A., & Weiner, J. L. (2006). Seeking information about sexual health: Applying the theory of motivated information management. *Human Communication Research, 32,* 35–57.

Babrow, A. S. (1992). Communication and problematic integration: Understanding diverging probability and value, ambiguity, ambivalence, and impossibility. *Communication Theory, 2,* 95–130.

Babrow, A. S. (2001). Uncertainty, value, communication, and problematic integration. *Journal of Communication, 51,* 553–573.

Babrow, A. S., & Dinn, D. (2005). Problematic discharge from physical therapy: Communicating about uncertainty and profound values. In E. B. Ray (Ed.), *Health communication in practice: A case study approach* (2nd ed., pp. 27–38). Hillsdale, NJ: Erlbaum.

Babrow, A. S., & Kline, K. N. (2000). From "reducing" to "coping with" uncertainty: Reconceptualizing the central challenge in breast self-exams. *Social Science & Medicine, 51,* 1805–1816.

Bandura, A. (1986). *Social foundations of thought and action: A social cognitive theory.* Englewood Cliffs, NJ: Prentice Hall.

Bandura, A. (Ed.). (1995). *Self-efficacy in changing societies.* Cambridge, UK: Cambridge University Press.

Bandura, A. (1997). *Self-efficacy: The exercise of control.* New York: Freeman.

Baum, A., Friedman, A. L., & Zakowski, S. G. (1997). Stress and genetic testing for disease risk. *Health Psychology, 16,* 8–19.

Berger, C. R. (1987). Communicating under uncertainty. In M. E. Roloff & G. R. Miller (Eds.), *Interpersonal processes: New directions in communication research* (pp. 39–62). Newbury Park, CA: Sage.

Berger, C. R., & Calabrese, R. J. (1975). Some explorations in initial interactions and beyond: Toward a developmental theory of interpersonal communication. *Human Communication Research, 1,* 99–112.

Brashers, D. E. (2001). Communication and uncertainty management. *Journal of Communication, 51,* 477–497.

Brashers, D. E., Neidig, J. L., Haas, S. M., Dobbs, L. K., Cardillo, L. W., & Russell, J. A. (2000). Communication in the management of uncertainty: The case of persons living with HIV or AIDS. *Communication Monographs, 67,* 63–84.

Brashers, D. E., Neidig, J. L., Russell, J. A., Cardillo, L. W., Haas, S. M., Dobbs, L. K., et al. (2003). The medical, personal, and social causes of uncertainty in HIV illness. *Issues in Mental Health Nursing, 24,* 497–522.

Carver, C. S., & Scheier, M. F. (1998). *On the self-regulation of behavior.* New York: Cambridge University Press.

Case, D. O. (2002). *Looking for information: A survey of research on information seeking, needs, and behavior*. Amsterdam: Academic Press.

Case, D. O., Andrews, J. E., Johnson, D. J., & Allard, S. L. (2005). Avoiding versus seeking: The relationship of information seeking to avoidance, blunting, coping, dissonance, and related concepts. *Journal of the Medical Library Association, 93*, 353–362.

Chaiken, S. (1987). The heuristic model of persuasion. In M. P. Zanna, J. M. Olson, & C. P. Herman (Eds.), *Social influence: The Ontario symposium* (Vol. 5, pp. 3–39). Hillsdale, NJ: Erlbaum.

Chaiken, S., Giner-Sorolla, R., & Chen, S. (1996). Beyond accuracy: Defense and impression motives in heuristic and systematic information processing. In P. M. Gollwitzer & J. A. Bargh (Eds.), *The psychology of action: Linking cognition and motivation to behavior* (pp. 553–578). New York: Guilford Press.

Czaja, R., Manfredi, C., & Price, J. (2003). The determinants and consequences of information seeking among cancer patients. *Journal of Health Communication, 8*, 529–562.

Davis, F. (1960). Uncertainty in medical prognosis: Clinical and functional. *American Journal of Sociology, 66*, 41–47.

Decruyenaere, M., Evers-Kiebooms, G., Cloostermans, T., Boogaerts, A., Demyttenaere, K., Dom, R., et al. (2003). Psychological distress in the 5-year period after predictive testing for Huntington's disease. *European Journal of Human Genetics, 11*, 30–38.

Dillard, J. P., & Carson, C. L. (2005). Uncertainty management following a positive newborn screening for cystic fibrosis. *Journal of Health Communication, 10*, 57–76.

Douglas, W. (1987). Affinity testing in initial interactions. *Journal of Social and Personal Relationships, 4*, 3–15.

Forgas, J. P. (Ed.). (2001). *Handbook of affect and social cognition*. Mahwah, NJ: Lawrence Erlbaum.

Gaff, C. L., Cowan, R., Meiser, B., & Lindeman, G. (2006). Genetic services for men: The preferences of men with a family history of prostate cancer. *Genetics in Medicine, 8*, 771–778.

Gill, E. A., & Babrow, A. S. (2007). To hope or to know: Coping with uncertainty and ambivalence in women's magazine breast cancer articles. *Journal of Applied Communication Research, 35*, 133–155.

Goldsmith, D. J. (2001). A normative approach to the study of uncertainty and communication. *Journal of Communication, 51*, 514–533.

Hines, S. C., Babrow, A. S., Badzek, L., & Moss, A. H. (1997). Communication and problematic integration in end-of-life decisions: Dialysis decisions among the elderly. *Health Communication, 9*, 199–217.

Ickes, W., Dugosh, J. W., Simpson, J. A., & Wilson, C. L. (2003). Suspicious minds: The motive to acquire relationship-threatening information. *Personal Relationships, 10*, 131–148.

Inglis, I. R. (2000). The central role of uncertainty reduction in determining behaviour. *Behaviour, 137*, 1567–1599.

Jepson, R. G., Hewison, J., Thompson, A., & Weller, D. (2007). Patient perspectives on information and choice in cancer screening: A qualitative study in the UK. *Social Science & Medicine, 65*, 890–899.

Johnson, J. D. (1997). *Cancer-related information seeking.* Cresskill, NJ: Hampton Press.

Johnson, J. D., Case, D. O., Andrews, J. E., & Allard, S. L. (2005). Genomics: The perfect information-seeking research problem. *Journal of Health Communication, 10*, 323–329.

Johnson, J. D., & Meischke, H. (1993). A comprehensive model of cancer-related information seeking applied to magazines. *Human Communication Research, 19*, 343–367.

Kalichman, S. C., Cherry, C., Cain, D., Weinhardt, L. S., Benotsch, E., Pope, H., et al. (2006). Health information on the Internet and people living with HIV/AIDS: Information evaluation and coping styles. *Health Psychology, 25*, 205–210.

Kramer, M. W. (2004). *Managing uncertainty in organizational communication.* Mahwah, NJ: Lawrence Erlbaum.

Kruglanski, A. W., & Webster, D. M. (1996). Motivated closing of the mind: "Seizing" and "freezing." *Psychological Review, 103*, 263–283.

Lerman, C., Croyle, R. T., Tercyak, K. P., & Hamann, H. (2002). Genetic testing: Psychological aspects and implications. *Journal of Consulting and Clinical Psychology, 70*, 784–797.

McCroskey, J. C., & Young, T. J. (1981). Ethos and credibility: The construct and its measurements after three decades. *Central States Speech Journal, 32*, 24–34.

Miller, S. M. (1995). Monitoring versus blunting styles of coping with cancer influence the information patients want and need about their disease: Implications for cancer screening and management. *Cancer, 76*, 167–177.

Miller, S. M., Brody, D. S., & Summerton, J. (1988). Styles of coping with threat: Implications for health. *Journal of Personality and Social Psychology, 54*, 142–148.

Mishel, M. H. (1988). Uncertainty in illness. *Image: The Journal of Nursing Scholarship, 20*, 225–232.

Mishel, M. H., & Clayton, M. F. (2003). Theories of uncertainty in illness. In M. J. Smith & P. Liehr (Eds.), *Middle range theory for nursing* (pp. 55–84). New York: Springer.

Mookerjee, D., & Babrow, A. S. (2002, November). *Information seeking in family planning: What women say about their experiences in West Bengal, India.* Paper presented at the annual conference of the National Communication Association, Chicago.

Murray, S. L. (1999). The quest for conviction: Motivated cognition in romantic relationships. *Psychological Inquiry, 10*, 23–34.

Peters, E., Västfjäll, D., Gärling, T., & Slovic, P. (2006). Affect and decision making: A "hot" topic. *Journal of Behavioral Decision Making, 19*, 79–85.

Ramirez, A., Jr., Walther, J. B., Burgoon, J. K., & Sunnafrank, M. (2002). Information-seeking strategies, uncertainty, and computer-mediated communication. *Human Communication Research, 28*, 213–228.

Rimal, R. N., & Real, K. (2003). Perceived risks and efficacy beliefs as motivators of change: Use of the risk perception attitude (RPA) framework to understand health behaviors. *Human Communication Research, 29,* 370–399.

Robins Wahlin, T.-B. (2007). To know or not to know: A review of behaviour and suicidal ideation in preclinical Huntington's disease. *Patient Education and Counseling, 65,* 279–287.

Rosen, N. O., Knäuper, B., & Sammut, J. (2007). Do individual differences in intolerance of uncertainty affect health monitoring? *Psychology and Health, 22,* 413–430.

Solomon, D. H., & Knobloch, L. K. (2004). A model of relational turbulence: The role of intimacy, relational uncertainty, and interference from partners in appraisals of irritations. *Journal of Social and Personal Relationships, 21,* 795–816.

Spitzberg, B. H., & Cupach, W. R. (1984). *Interpersonal communication competence.* Beverly Hills, CA: Sage.

Sunnafrank, M. (1986). Predicted outcome value during initial interactions: A reformulation of uncertainty reduction theory. *Human Communication Research, 13,* 3–33.

Turner, M. M., Rimal, R. N., Morrison, D., & Kim, H. (2006). The role of anxiety in seeking and retaining risk information: Testing the risk perceptions attitude framework in two studies. *Human Communication Research, 32,* 130–156.

Ursin, H. (1988). Expectancy and activation: An attempt to systematize stress theory. In D. H. Hellhammer, I. Florin, & H. Weiner (Eds.), *Neurobiological approaches to human disease* (pp. 313–334). Toronto, Ontario, Canada: Huber.

Vakkari, P. (1998). Growth of theories on information seeking: An analysis of growth of a theoretical research program on the relation between task complexity and information seeking. *Information Processing and Management, 34,* 361–382.

Whitmarsh, I., Davis, A. M., Skinner, D., & Bailey, D. B., Jr. (2007). A place for genetic uncertainty: Parents valuing an unknown in the meaning of disease. *Social Science & Medicine, 65,* 1082–1093.

Wilson, T. D., Centerbar, D. B., Kermer, D. A., & Gilbert, D. T. (2005). The pleasures of uncertainty: Prolonging positive moods in ways people do not anticipate. *Journal of Personality and Social Psychology, 88,* 5–21.

Woodgate, R. L., & Degner, L. F. (2002). "Nothing is carved in stone!" Uncertainty in children with cancer and their families. *European Journal of Oncology Nursing, 6,* 191–202.

6

Turbulence in Relational Transitions

Denise Haunani Solomon

Kirsten M. Weber

Keli Ryan Steuber

T he rise and fall of close relationships is a subject that has been embraced by novelists, songwriters, and authors of self-help books. Research on personal relationships also occupies an important position within the study of interpersonal communication. In its infancy, personal relationships research was dominated by a focus on people's traits and perceptions as forces behind attraction, relationship escalation, and the stability of interpersonal associations (see Huston, Surra, Fitzgerald, & Cate, 1981; Morton & Douglas, 1981). Pioneering communication scholars recognized the limits of a psychological perspective on intimacy, and they positioned communication processes at the heart of interpersonal relationships (see, e.g., Miller, 1976). The study of personal relationships and interpersonal communication

Authors' Note: The authors are grateful to Jennifer Priem and Stephanie Gookin, who helped with the breast cancer and infertility projects, respectively; to Dr. Leanne Knobloch, Dr. Jennifer Theiss, and Dr. Rachel McLaren, who participated in the development of the relational turbulence model; and to Dr. Michael Roloff, for laying the foundation for this endeavor.

scholarship now embrace multiple disciplinary perspectives, but this early work forged a union between research on interpersonal communication and the study of personal relationships that remains in place today. And although this marriage has borne many offspring, the central issue continues to inspire scholarly work: What is the role of interpersonal communication as personal relationships develop, decay, persist, and falter?

Over the years, many answers to this question have been offered. Knapp (1984) suggested that communication is the vehicle that propels interpersonal relationships through stages of increasing and decreasing intimacy. Berger and Calabrese (1975) emphasized the role of communication in reducing uncertainty as the foundation for interpersonal relationships. Baxter and Bullis (1986) highlighted the turning points that occur as relationships develop, as well as the ways in which communication participates in those events. Relationship dynamics were elaborated within Baxter's (1988) relational dialectics perspective, which characterizes communication as interwoven in people's experience of relationship tensions (see also Baxter & Braithwaite, Chapter 3, this volume; Baxter & Montgomery, 1996). Research on relational communication (e.g., Burgoon & Hale, 1984, 1987) emphasizes how messages inherently create and modify the association between interaction partners. As these contributions illustrate, conceptions of the link between interpersonal communication and personal relationships have focused on both global processes that evolve within developing associations and local features of messages.

The aforementioned perspectives on communication in personal relationships have yielded many insights, yet each has limitations. Stage models of relationship development ignore the nuance, complexity, and uniqueness of the paths that relationship partners travel (e.g., Surra, 1985). Likewise, uncertainty reduction theory's emphasis on the drive to reduce uncertainty has been criticized (Brashers, 2001). Research on turning points typically involves describing the experience of change in close relationships (e.g., Bullis, Clark, & Sline, 1993; Graham, 1997), rather than advancing a theoretical framework to explain those experiences. Similarly, a relational dialectics perspective is designed to sensitize scholars to features of close relationships, rather than explain or predict dialectical tensions (Baxter & Montgomery, 1996, p. 6). Finally, a focus on relational communication captures the fluid nature of relationships, but it seems to ignore the fact that perceptions of relationships are largely stable from week to week (see, e.g., Solomon & Theiss, 2008).

When we consider these limitations in concert, two general issues emerge. First, efforts to understand how communication participates in the rise and fall of close relationships needs to grapple with the substantial variability that exists within these associations. Specifically, a perspective is needed that does justice to the fact that people are sometimes thinking about relational intimacy and sometimes not, and that communication sometimes matters a lot to relationships and sometimes it does not. Second, the theoretical architecture needs to clarify the mechanisms that underlie variability within interpersonal associations. What conditions provoke escalations in closeness, a state of uncertainty and the desire to reduce it, the perception of an event as a critical turning point, the emergence or resolution of dialectical tension, or attention to relational messages? In our view, understanding the role of interpersonal communication within personal relationships involves clarifying the mechanisms that shape communication experiences and make communication salient to the development, decay, persistence, or faltering of personal relationships.

Our contribution to these efforts is the *relational turbulence model,* a theory that focuses on transitions within close relationships as moments that make interpersonal communication relevant to relationship outcomes. *Transitions* can be understood as responses to change (Marineau, 2005) in which there are varying degrees of instability during the adaptive process (Walker, 2001). Transitions are complex and multidimensional (George, 1993), and these consequential moments are both embedded within and shaped by their social context (Elmberger, Bolund, & Lützén, 2000; Tomlinson, 1996). In particular, transitions create change that involves the reorganization and reintegration of identities, roles, relationships, or behaviors, which may require people to alter their current conduct or the way in which they define themselves or their relationships. In other words, when people move from the known to the unknown, the social context within which they live also changes.

We conceive of transitions as the changes in circumstances that create the *potential* for relationships to change, rather than as the changes in relationships themselves. We reserve the term *turbulence* to label the tumultuous experiences that might occur within relationships in response to a transition. Consider the metaphor of turbulence during flight. At a particular altitude and speed, an aircraft moves smoothly through the air, and the pilots have limited sensation of movement. When air pressure or wind speed outside the plane change, the pilots may be jostled or feel the plane speed up or change altitude. Depending on how quickly the plane adjusts or moves through the conditions, the impact on the pilots can range from minimal to extreme. And if conditions persist, pilots might have to make more dramatic adjustments to regain a smooth and level flight. Our conception of transitions aligns with the changes in conditions outside the aircraft; turbulence encompasses the sensations of bumpiness, acceleration, or altitude change that are experienced by the pilots.

In this chapter, we recount the path we have followed in our efforts to understand what happens during relational transitions. We begin with the genesis of the research program in the first author's work with her PhD advisor, Michael Roloff, and the development of the theory in collaboration with Leanne Knobloch and Jennifer Theiss. Then we discuss efforts by the coauthors that have extended the program of research to address socially significant and contemporary research questions.

The Development of the Relational Turbulence Model

Denise Solomon

In the 1990s, Michael Roloff and I collaborated on a series of studies of conflict in personal relationships. Our focus was on why people sometimes keep complaints about a relationship partner to themselves (Cloven & Roloff, 1993a; Roloff & Cloven, 1990), as well as the cognitive biases that are introduced when people brood about their conflicts (Cloven & Roloff, 1991, 1993b). Underlying these studies, however, was a deeper question about how relationship qualities suppress or enable communication about dissatisfying experiences and how communication, or a lack thereof, might promote or undermine intimacy. We began, therefore, to consider how intimacy corresponds with the incidence of conflict avoidance, as well as the motives for withholding irritations from a dating partner (Cloven & Roloff, 1994). In a complementary study, I examined how intimacy is associated with the directness of messages that people craft to solicit a date with a romantic partner (Solomon, 1997). Our findings revealed that nonlinear associations between intimacy and either conflict avoidance or the directness of date requests were modestly better fits to the data than were linear trends.

As Mike and I sought to locate our findings within the literature, we noted a recurrent pattern in the empirical record. Across numerous studies with dating samples, something anomalous happened at moderate levels of intimacy within dating relationships (however intimacy was operationalized).[1] Billingham and Sack (1987) documented the highest level of verbal aggression in a relationship stage defined as "in love and would like to marry, but have never discussed marriage." In another study, people's experiences of negative emotions varied across relationships of short, medium, and long duration, with the highest levels evident in relationships of medium length (Aune, Aune, & Buller, 1994). Another investigation, which used retrospective accounts to map the development of courtships, found that open conflict increases in frequency as relationships progress from casual to serious dating, but then tapers off (Huston et al., 1981). On a more positive note, Emmers and Dindia (1995) observed that intimate touch increases from low to moderate levels of intimacy, and levels off once partners have formed a committed relationship.

Because intimacy was operationalized in various ways and these studies were focused on different relationship experiences, the symmetry of the findings was especially striking.

An empirical pattern of this sort invites theory, which I pursued with Leanne Knobloch. Leanne and I queried the unique qualities of dating relationships at moderate levels of intimacy, and we proposed two answers. As detailed elsewhere in this volume, Leanne's research highlights the ambiguity people confront as they move a relationship from noncommittal to mutually committed. *Relational uncertainty* is the degree of confidence individuals have in their perceptions of involvement within a relationship; it encompasses questions people have about their own involvement in a relationship, their partner's level of involvement, and the nature of the dyadic unit (Berger & Bradac, 1982; Knobloch & Solomon, 1999, 2002a). Thus, relational uncertainty captures an intrapersonal phenomenon that may be evoked when individuals perceive a change from familiar to unfamiliar circumstances.

In Solomon and Knobloch (2001), we reasoned that relational uncertainty increases during the transition from casual to serious dating. Within nonintimate relationships, dating partners can rely on scripts for first dates and casual romances to guide their behavior (see, e.g., Honeycutt, 1993; Honeycutt & Cantrill, 2001). Likewise, formalizing commitment can resolve questions about involvement in the relationship (Baxter & Bullis, 1986). When relationships have progressed beyond the initial phase, yet lack a clear and mutual commitment, individuals may question what they want out of the relationship, how invested their partner is, and the nature of the relationship (Baxter, 1988). In the same way that flying from warm air into a cold front might cause a pilot to wonder what is happening, escalation beyond casual dating sparks uncertainty about involvement in the relationship.

My training with Michael Roloff emphasized principles of social exchange, so I nominated interdependence processes as a second mechanism underlying the nonlinear patterns we had observed. The development of interdependence requires that partners allow each other to influence or shape their activities. A partner's influence in activities is experienced as facilitation when it allows routines to be more effective or increases the likelihood that goals will be achieved (Berscheid, 1983; Knobloch & Solomon, 2004). When a partner's influence disrupts routines, the result is the experience of *interference from a partner* (Berscheid, 1983; Knobloch & Solomon, 2004). This explication highlights how experiences of interference are an interpersonal phenomenon that results when partners struggle to coordinate their actions following a change in their circumstances.

Our thinking about how experiences of interference might vary with relationship development was elaborated in Solomon and Knobloch (2001; Knobloch & Solomon, 2004). Within nonintimate relationships, partners have few opportunities to affect each other's experiences, and interference is correspondingly low. As partners become more intimate, however, they allow each other to participate in previously autonomous routines. Eventually, everything from eating meals to visiting families can become dependent on a partner's behavior. When people first allow a partner to affect their activities, that partner often disrupts well-established routines. For example, you have dinner late because your partner is working over-time, and your family might criticize you for spending your vacation with your partner's relatives. Over time, a couple forms a joint routine that allows them to achieve their goals more effectively. To continue the example, you might go exercise when your partner works late and forego family obligations to enjoy a romantic vacation. Just as a change in flying condi-tions might require copilots to figure out who will take the controls and who will monitor the radio, partners merging their routines must integrate previously independent behaviors and priorities.

With relational uncertainty and interference from a partner answering the "what happens during transitions" question, we turned our attention to their consequences. Recall that turbulence encompasses amplified experi-ences within relationships, such as polarized cognitions, stronger emotions, and more extreme communication behavior (see also Knobloch, 2007). To return to our airplane example, consider the greater awareness, stronger emotions, and heightened reflexes pilots might experience following a large and sudden change in altitude. In general, then, the relational turbulence model describes how relational uncertainty and interference from a partner induce a state of reactivity.

In a series of studies, Leanne Knobloch, Jennifer Theiss, and I docu-mented the consequences of relational uncertainty, and we noted relevant findings reported by other researchers. For example, doubts about a rela-tionship correspond with cognitive outcomes, ranging from an inability to draw relationship inferences (Knobloch & Solomon, 2005) to a tendency to appraise irritations as more serious (Solomon & Knobloch, 2004; Theiss & Solomon, 2006b). Relational uncertainty is also linked to more extreme emotional reactions to surprising events (Knobloch & Solomon, 2003), jealousy threats (Knobloch, Solomon, & Cruz, 2001; Theiss & Solomon, 2006a), and changes in sexual intimacy (Theiss & Solomon, 2007). With regard to communication, relational uncertainty has been implicated in a tendency to avoid conversations about the relationship (Baxter & Wilmot, 1985), to engage in topic avoidance or withhold private information (Afifi & Burgoon, 1998; Afifi & Guerrero, 2000; Knobloch & Carpenter-Theune, 2004), and to evade discussions of surprising relationship events (Knobloch & Solomon, 2002b). Thus, a variety of polarized cognitions, emotions, and communication behaviors correlate with relational uncertainty.

Theory and research suggest that a partner's interference in activities also increases reactivity to relationship events. Berscheid (1983) argued that disruptions to action sequences correspond with heightened emotional reactivity. Likewise, Berkowitz's (1989) frustration-aggression hypothesis suggests that goal interference drives negative reactions. In addition, empirical evidence shows that interference from a partner is positively correlated with the perceived severity of irritations (Solomon & Knobloch, 2004; Theiss & Solomon, 2006b), the intensity of emotional jealousy (Knobloch et al., 2001; Theiss & Solomon, 2006a), negative evaluations of social networks (Knobloch & Donovan-Kicken, 2006), perceptions of relational turbulence (Knobloch, 2007), and indirectness of communication about relationship problems (Theiss & Solomon, 2006b). This body of work links experiences of goal interference to polarized cognitions, emotions, and communication.

At this point in the research program, we had growing confidence in the relevance of relational uncertainty and interference from a partner as qualities that shape reactions to a variety of episodes that unfold in close relationships. At about this time, Kirsten Weber and I began to think about transitions that occur beyond the initial development of romantic relationships. Relational uncertainty might recur whenever changes in the circumstances of the relationship prompt people to revisit questions about their own involvement in the relationship, their partner's involvement, and the relationship itself. Likewise, couples are susceptible to goal interference whenever a couple has reason to modify pre-existing routines. Accordingly, we began to pay less attention to the development of intimacy in courtships, and we focused on relational uncertainty and interference from a partner as mechanisms shaping people's experiences in ongoing close relationships. In the remaining two sections of the chapter, coauthors Kirsten Weber and Keli Steuber describe our efforts to use the relational turbulence model to shed light on two significant transitions within established romantic relationships.

Relational Turbulence and Experiences of Breast Cancer

Kirsten Weber

Women have a 1 in 8 lifetime risk of being diagnosed with breast cancer. Roughly 178,480 new cases of invasive breast cancer were expected in 2007 in the United States (American Cancer Society [ACS], 2007). Moreover, 3% of women in the United States are likely to die from breast cancer, including an estimated 40,460 deaths in 2007 (ACS, 2007). Many researchers have documented how breast cancer can cause distress both in general (Given &

Given, 1993; Northouse, Laten, & Reddy, 1995) and about specific topics, such as mortality or medical procedures (Hilton, 1988). Far less research has considered how the diagnosis of breast cancer sparks a relationship transition. Denise and I hoped that by applying the relational turbulence model to the experience of breast cancer, we might contribute to efforts to alleviate the distress experienced by women and their families.

To begin our exploration of breast cancer as a transition that produces turbulence, Denise and I conducted a theme analysis focused on the sources of distress voiced by contributors to 33 Web logs and 87 discussion board strings devoted to breast cancer topics (see Weber & Solomon, in press). Six themes emerged from the analysis. *Integrating old and new identities* encompasses the struggle women face as they try to reconcile who they were before cancer with their sense of self as a cancer patient and survivor. *Managing information* identifies how women negotiate their own and others' needs as information is shared, received, and interpreted. *Co-owning the disease* describes the struggle over who owns the disease and, therefore, who has a right to make treatment decisions, control information sharing, or grieve. *Managing threats to intersubjectivity* embodies the overwhelming feeling that no one can really understand how it feels to be a breast cancer patient, unless they themselves have been diagnosed. *Symbolizing self* captures the worry caused by changes to a breast cancer patient's body and how other individuals react to those changes. A final theme, *going on with life's tasks,* includes experiences that coincide with breast cancer, ranging from normal daily activities to major events like the death of a loved one.

Relational uncertainty permeated the themes we identified in this analysis. In particular, women expressed concern about how relationship partners would react to the diagnosis, how they would cope with the news, and how it would affect their relationships. One woman expressed concerns about how her cancer affected her relationship with her family: "I felt that I had let my family down. I hated knowing that they would have to go through this because of me" (32).[2] Another woman disclosed, "I find that exposing myself even to my boyfriend is difficult even though he has been awesome. The problem in my head is that he saw the 'before'; now there is this 'after'" (59). This woman also wondered about future romances and asked, "Can someone out there tell me when and what to tell people when u date, what to expect as far as reactions and how am I ever going to get naked again with someone new?" (59). As these quotations illustrate, telling others they have the disease, experiencing the before and after of the disease with a partner, living with side effects that are visible to self and others, and anticipating future interactions all stimulated feelings of uncertainty about a woman's own involvement in her relationships, her partner's involvement within the relationship, or about the future of personal relationships more generally.

The discourse we examined also revealed experiences of goal interference, especially as women tried to cope with their disease or find room for cancer in their lives. For example, one woman disclosed, "I assumed that my family would not plan activities that involved me for two or three days after chemo. I was wrong" (29). Another breast cancer patient expressed frustration with the interactions she had with her friends:

> You really find out who your friends are when you go through something like this. I know I had some so called friends who acted like they were going to catch my breast cancer from me if they got near me. Then again, Sally, there are those people that just don't know what to say or do and avoid keeping in touch with you. Then there are those people that act like you just have a little cold. (61)

A husband also explained how cancer changed the life he and his wife shared:

> Unfortunately, there is no going back to "normal" and forgetting that this ever happened; Maggie's omnipresent lymphedema is a daily reminder and it places real limits on our lives. But, these are limits that we are gradually coming to understand, accept, and work within. (20)

As these examples illustrate, patients expressed discontent with how friends and other loved ones reacted to their diagnosis, violated their expectations for emotional and instrumental support, and undermined their ability to cope. The husband's comment also reveals how adjusting to the changes imposed by breast cancer required changes in the daily operations of the relational system. In these ways, relationship partners were a source of interference for women with breast cancer as circumstances required changes to activities and patterns of interdependence.

After documenting the relevance of relational uncertainty and interference from a partner within the breast cancer experience, Denise and I examined whether these relationship qualities amplified the distress experienced by breast cancer patients. Based on the relational turbulence model, we predicted that relational uncertainty and interference from a partner exacerbate cognitive, affective, and communicative reactions to the stressors that confront breast cancer survivors. As detailed elsewhere (Weber & Solomon, 2007), we conducted a Web-based survey in which breast cancer survivors in committed romantic relationships ($N = 53$) provided information on that relationship, as well as on stressful experiences associated with their breast cancer. In particular, women identified specific stressors that they had experienced in the past 2 weeks, and then reported their cognitive, emotional, and communicative reactions to those stressors.

The results indicated that relational uncertainty and interference from a partner were positively associated with the intensity of negative feelings about stressors associated with breast cancer. In addition, we observed a negative association between relational uncertainty and the positivity of communication with a partner about sources of distress. Also, women who reported more goal interference from a partner tended to describe communication about recent stressors as less positive and more direct. These findings are consistent with the relational turbulence model because they suggest that breast cancer survivors who have relational uncertainty or experience interference from a partner have more negative and pronounced emotional and communicative reactions.

This study also revealed patterns that were contrary to our predictions; in particular, women who reported more doubts about their partner and the relationship also communicated more directly about stressors with their partner. In previous studies focused on college dating relationships, people who experienced relational uncertainty tended to avoid communication with their partners or to use more indirect communication strategies (see, e.g., Knobloch & Carpenter-Theune, 2004; Theiss & Solomon, 2006b). Our sample of breast cancer survivors was in a very different stage of life, and the majority estimated the likelihood of remaining in their romantic relationship for the rest of their life at 100%. Perhaps when doubts emerge within relationships that are perceived as permanent, people are more compelled to address stressful experiences or concerns with a partner. Although our interpretation of these findings is speculative, it coheres with evidence that people are more likely to express relational irritations when romantic partners are unlikely to exit the relationship (Roloff & Cloven, 1990; Solomon, Knobloch, & Fitzpatrick, 2004).

Although Denise and I have only scratched the surface in this line of inquiry, we are encouraged that the parameters highlighted by the relational turbulence model can shed light on the experiences of breast cancer survivors. Viewed through the lens of the theory, breast cancer is certainly more than a disease, and it is more than a relational crisis. Just like pilots coordinating their reactions to pressure changes, breast cancer patients can use communication to negotiate experiences of relational uncertainty or interference from a partner. Our goal for the future is to identify the communication behaviors that help partners transcend the challenges imposed by breast cancer and forge bonds that will sustain them throughout survivorship.

Relational Turbulence and the Experience of Infertility

Keli Steuber

Although most couples in marital or domestic partnerships assume that they will have children (Greil, 1991), 1 in 6 couples will experience infertility. Thousands of couples attempt to treat their condition by charting their reproductive cycle or taking ovulation-inducing hormones. Other partners experiment with more advanced treatments, despite the fact that these procedures have only a 25% success rate and can cost the same as a new car or a down payment on a home (Centers for Disease Control and Prevention, 2007). Being diagnosed with infertility is often the beginning of a major shift in the life course of an individual and a relationship—a shift that can prompt couples to seek counseling for myriad issues (see Greil, Leitko, & Porter, 1988; Leiblum, 1997; Schneider & Forthofer, 2005). For example, spouses may experience conflict about whether to undergo medical treatment and for how long (Epstein & Rosenberg, 1997). When couples do pursue treatment, they can be overwhelmed by disruptions to their work schedules, social life, and daily routines. Emotionally, the roller coaster of hope and disappointment inherent in each treatment cycle keeps partners in an exhausting and chronic indefinite state. Thus, infertility forces couples to confront emotionally laden and life-changing decisions about whether to pursue treatments that, while time-consuming, costly, and probably unsuccessful, might fulfill a dream of parenthood.

Viewing infertility through the framework provided by the relational turbulence model highlights how difficulty in conceiving a child sparks a transitional period in which couples question or renegotiate aspects of their relationship. As in the Weber and Solomon (in press) study, we turned to online discourse to gain insight into the relationship issues that emerge when couples experience infertility. Specifically, we located a sample of 49 discussion boards and 31 Web logs and conducted a theme analysis of the discourse (see Steuber & Solomon, 2008). Using the parameters of the relational turbulence model as a guide, we identified six themes. *Relational invalidation* captures people's concern that their relationship is no longer a priority for either themselves or their partner. *Implications of blame* refers to the tensions that emerge when people blame either themselves or their partner for the infertility. *Supremacy of the pregnancy goal* encompasses the many ways in which treating infertility (e.g., keeping medical appointments and performing prescribed sexual activities) overwhelms the partnership. *Violated treatment expectations* embodies the frustrations people feel when their partners focus too much or too little on overcoming infertility. Two final themes reflect the potentially positive implications of infertility for relational or personal identities. *Strengthened relational identity* is revealed by discourse about how experiences of infertility enhanced emotional intimacy and forged a deeper bond between partners. Likewise, some people discussed a *personal identity shift,* or an emotionally charged moment, in which they reframed their infertility experience or decided to stop treatment.

Relational uncertainty was highlighted in the themes that addressed *relational invalidation* and *implications of blame*. These aspects of the infertility experience show how difficulties having a baby can cause people to question their relationship, especially their partner's current and future involvement in the partnership. For example, one woman wrote of her husband, "He is bailing on our doctor's appointment today because he forgot to ask for the time off . . . apparently his priorities are his job, his immediate family, then me" (20). Another contributor questioned his wife's view of their association because "her intensity at this makes me feel that all I am to her is a sperm donor" (52). One woman's inability to produce a child made her question her husband's commitment to her; she wrote, "My husband wants another so bad . . . we have been trying for 7 yrs. I sometimes feel he doesn't want to be with me but just doesn't know how to tell me" (40). The experience of infertility includes many opportunities to invalidate the relationship by focusing too much or too little on treatment, and placing blame for the infertility can prompt either partner to question their union. In other words, discovering and coping with infertility can ignite questions and doubts about an ongoing relationship.

The discourse also revealed many opportunities for goal interference, which were encompassed in the themes focused on the *supremacy of the pregnancy goal* and *violated expectations for treatment involvement*. One woman wrote about how infertility consumed her, "I cannot continue to allow shots, hormones, and surgeries to rule my life. . . . My body cannot take any more. My marriage cannot take any more. My emotions cannot take anymore" (53).

Many individuals reported frustrations at sex that had become "routine" (37), "mechanical" (73), or "almost like a scheduled event" (67). One man wrote, "I can't stand sex anymore. I'm under so much stress about it that it's hard for me to maintain an erection, even with medication. Forget about having sex 'for fun.' It stopped being that a long time ago" (52). Another contributor expressed irritation at her "very open minded, enlightened, supportive, educated" husband when he discounted her desire to pursue adoption because, "Basically if it's not 'his' child he won't consider it" (32). Whether goal interference occurs when treatment overrides daily routines and sexual intimacy or when individuals perceive their spouses to be impeding the treatment process, infertility can wreak havoc on a couple's everyday routines and overall lifestyle.

In addition to the relational turbulence themes, our analysis revealed themes related to identity, including *strengthened relational identity* and *personal identity shift*. In particular, some couples adopted a team mentality as they worked together toward the goal of a baby. People also wrote of new personal insights, often stemming from an infertility-related epiphany. To illustrate, one woman struggled with the sudden realization that she may never be a biological mother: "And the startling truth came to me then . . . it's not that God CAN'T make me pregnant, that's absurd, of course. It's that He won't" (29). These experiences mark not only a shift in the infertility experience, but also in perceptions of self as an individual and a member of a family.

The study summarized here is just the beginning of our efforts to illuminate the experience of infertility using the relational turbulence model. We have seen that a diagnosis of infertility sparks a relationship transition during which family plans are challenged, reproductive goals are adapted, and identities are in flux. The arduous task of treating infertility can also cause partners to question each other's commitment to the relationship, and it requires substantial changes in routines if partners hope to achieve parenthood. The turbulence seems to end only when a child is brought into the family or when a couple wholeheartedly commits to a decision to end treatment. Until either outcome occurs, their infertile status strips couples of control, teases them with hope, and pains them with frustration. Not unlike the crisis that unfolds when pilots encounter engine trouble, surviving infertility with their relationship intact requires that partners resolve their doubts and coordinate their actions to meet considerable demands. Our goal in future research is to identify the communication processes that allow partners to make this significant transition with as little turbulence as possible.

Looking Ahead

In this chapter, we have recounted the development of the relational turbulence model through the first author's collaborations with other scholars and in our recent investigations of people coping with breast cancer and infertility. Over the period in which this research was conducted, the theory evolved from an effort to account for unusual activity at moderate levels of intimacy in premarital romantic relationships to a framework that is focused more generally on relationship characteristics that might emerge when people's circumstances change. As we look to the future, we see several directions for developing this line of research.

First, empirical studies to date are consistent with the idea that relational uncertainty and interference from a partner amplify relationship experiences; however, the data are generally less favorable to the prediction that these mechanisms peak at moderate levels of intimacy within premarital romantic relationships. One limitation to this program of research is that "moderate" intimacy has been defined relative to the distribution of the intimacy variable within each study. As a result, we lack a consistent test of how the transition from casual to serious involvement increases both doubts about the relationship and goal interference. In addition, the variety of operationalizations of intimacy in studies conducted by the broader field of scholars complicates efforts to use tools such as meta-analysis to synthesize previous findings. Moreover, only one study to date has tracked intimacy and experiences of relational uncertainty and interference from a partner longitudinally (Solomon & Theiss, 2008). The limitations of prior research call for further investigation of relational uncertainty and interference from a partner over the course of developing romantic relationships.

A second unresolved question concerns the nature of events that spark transitions. In the language of our airplane metaphor, what kinds of changes in flying conditions are most likely to catch the attention of the pilots? We can think of several other transitions, such as becoming parents, being laid off from work, moving out of state, or launching children from the family home, that can reorganize both involvement in a relationship and the partners' goals and routines. What about seemingly lesser changes— sending children to school for the first time, getting a new puppy, trying a new diet, or buying a second car? The events we featured in this chapter also highlight how transitions might be initiated by changes in one partner's circumstances, as in the case of illness, or by changes in the relational system, as when family plans are altered. Transitions can also stem from external causes—such as losing a job or the death of a parent—that affect a couple's circumstances or from changes originating within the relationship itself, such as deciding to start a family or redefining commitments to each other. As we look to future research, we hope to clarify the qualities of events that prompt partners to rethink and reorganize their relationship.

We also wonder about how differences among people, relationships, and social contexts affect the processes described in the relational turbulence model. For example, personal traits, such as sensation seeking, need for certainty, or love style, might affect the degree of fluctuation in circumstances that people tolerate without experiencing changes to their relationship. At a broader level of analysis, the types of events that constitute relationship transitions are embedded within cultural norms and values. For example, breast cancer raises concerns about the "ideal" female body, and infertility raises questions about whether the "dream" of parenthood is attainable. Episodes such as these are imbued with cultural notions about identity and relationships that affect what couples experience and must manage.

Fourth, we note the need to incorporate personal and relational identities as another location for change during relationship transitions. In the discourse of women with breast cancer, we saw that this disease affects a woman's sense of self in sometimes dramatic ways. One woman, for example, described coming to terms with her loss of hair:

> The very second I have even a quarter inch on my head I'll be ditching this wig. . . . I don't care if people think I'm gay or a skinhead or both. Maybe on

the weekend I'll even ditch the scarf as well, and watch people react to me. Should be interesting. (25)

Likewise, part of coping with infertility involves accepting a revised image of oneself as a parent. For example, a woman acknowledged that she would never be a mother to a biological child:

> I need to accept that it's not going to happen for me. . . . I am not giving up on my dream of becoming a mother, but I am letting go of my dream of a successful pregnancy. We are going to move on. . . . It is time." (80)

Although the relational turbulence model has developed around a focus on people's perceptions of their relationships, the projects described in this chapter point to people's self-conceptions as another important facet of life transitions.

To understand why some couples confronted by breast cancer, infertility, or other turbulent transitions emerge with a stronger sense of their priorities, more conviction to their principles, and a fortified relational bond, we consider the identity implications of transitions to be an important direction for future research. The altered identities that develop as people experience novel circumstances might contribute to the relationship doubts and disrupted patterns of interdependence that sometimes follow from those changes. Alternatively, relationship qualities that can surface during transitions might prompt individuals and their partners to forge new conceptions of themselves and their relationships. Clarifying the role of identity changes during life transitions might help us understand when identity shifts initiate turbulent processes or when they represent the adaptive evolution of personal and relational identities.

Finally, we see a need to delve into the processes that link relational uncertainty and experiences of goal interference with heightened reactivity to relationship events. Knobloch and Solomon (2005) found that relational uncertainty corresponds with perceiving conversations with a partner as more difficult, but why? We have also seen that experiences of goal interference are associated with greater emotional reactivity (see, e.g., Knobloch et al., 2001; Knobloch, Miller, & Carpenter, 2007); again, we wonder what processes underlie this association. One possibility is that people process relational information differently when they are experiencing relational uncertainty, goal interference, or turbulence more generally (McLaren, 2007). Or, perhaps, these relationship qualities exacerbate physiological stress reactions (Priem, 2007). As these alternatives imply, we intend to look further into the mind and the body to understand the variability of experiences as people communicate with partners in personal relationships.

Conclusion

In its present configuration, the relational turbulence model emphasizes how changes in people's circumstances can raise questions about their romantic relationships and disrupt their everyday routines. In turn, the theory specifies that relational uncertainty and goal disruption make people more reactive to the variety of irritations, suspicions, and surprises that might occur in a romantic relationship. Importantly, the experience of turbulence is not wholly negative. As partners resolve doubts about the relationship and find ways to help each other achieve goals, they may reaffirm their commitment, clarify ambiguities, and witness their ability to work through challenges together (Knobloch & Solomon, 2002a). Thus, the relational turbulence model highlights how transitions require couples to establish or revisit the foundations of their intimacy in ways that can either create ongoing distress or promote relational well-being.

Notes

1. Although many of these studies neither tested the significance of nonlinear effects nor discussed the nonlinear trend, informed readers will recognize Michael Roloff's trademark attention to detail in discerning these patterns.
2. The numbers following quotes identify the discussion board or blog from which the quote was drawn. Although this information has no direct interpretation, we provide it to clarify the variety of units represented in the quoted material. Except for the substitution of pseudonyms, direct quotes are exact representations of the original texts.

References

Afifi, W. A., & Burgoon, J. K. (1998). "We never talk about that": A comparison of cross-sex friendships and dating relationships on uncertainty and topic avoidance. *Personal Relationships, 5,* 255–272.

Afifi, W. A., & Guerrero, L. K. (2000). Motivations underlying topic avoidance in close relationships. In S. Petronio (Ed.), *Balancing the secrets of private disclosures* (pp. 165–179). Mahwah, NJ: Lawrence Erlbaum.

American Cancer Society. (2007). *How many women get breast cancer?* Retrieved January 30, 2007, from www.Cancer.Org/docroot/cri/content/cri_2_2_1x_how_many_people_get_breast_cancer_5.Asp?Sitearea=

Aune, K. S., Aune, R. K., & Buller, D. B. (1994). The experience, expression and perceived appropriateness of emotions across levels of relationship development. *Journal of Social Psychology, 134,* 141–150.

Baxter, L. A. (1988). A dialectical perspective on communication strategies in relationship development. In S. Duck, D. F. Hay, S. E. Hobfoll, W. Ickes, & B. M. Montgomery (Eds.), *Handbook of personal relationships: Theory, research, and interventions* (pp. 257–273). Oxford, UK: Wiley.

Baxter, L. A., & Bullis, C. (1986). Turning points in developing romantic relationships. *Human Communication Research, 12*, 469–493.

Baxter, L. A., & Montgomery, B. M. (1996). *Relating: Dialogues & dialectics.* New York: Guilford Press.

Baxter, L. A., & Wilmot, W. W. (1985). Taboo topics in close relationships. *Journal of Social and Personal Relationships, 2*, 253–269.

Berger, C. R., & Bradac, J. J. (1982). *Language and social knowledge: Uncertainty in interpersonal relationships.* London: Edward Arnold.

Berger, C. R., & Calabrese, R. J. (1975). Some explorations in initial interaction and beyond: Toward a developmental theory of interpersonal communication. *Human Communication Research, 1*, 99–112.

Berkowitz, L. (1989). Frustration-aggression hypothesis: Examination and reformation. *Psychological Bulletin, 106*, 59–73.

Berscheid, E. (1983). Emotion. In H. H. Kelley, E. Berscheid, A. Christensen, J. Harvey, T. L. Huston, G. Levinger, et al. (Eds.), *Close relationships* (pp. 110–168). San Francisco: Freeman.

Billingham, R. E., & Sack, A. R. (1987). Conflict tactics and the level of emotional commitment among unmarrieds. *Human Relations, 40*, 59–74.

Brashers, D. (2001). Communication and uncertainty management. *Journal of Communication, 51*, 477–497.

Bullis, C., Clark, C., & Sline, R. (1993). From passion to commitment: Turning points in romantic relationships. In P. Kalbfleisch (Ed.), *Interpersonal communication: Evolving interpersonal relationships* (pp. 213–236). Hillsdale, NJ: Lawrence Erlbaum.

Burgoon, J. K., & Hale, J. L. (1984). The fundamental topoi of relational communication. *Communication Monographs, 51*, 193–214.

Burgoon, J. K., & Hale, J. L. (1987). Validation and measurement of the fundamental themes of relational communication. *Communication Monographs, 54*, 19–41.

Centers for Disease Control and Prevention. (2007). *2004 assisted reproductive technology report.* Retrieved August 1, 2007, from www.cdc.gov/art/ART2004/index.htm

Cloven, D. H., & Roloff, M. E. (1991). Sense-making activities and interpersonal conflict: Communicative cures for the mulling blues. *Western Journal of Speech Communication, 55*, 134–158.

Cloven, D. H., & Roloff, M. E. (1993a). The chilling effect of aggressive potential on the expression of complaints in intimate relationships. *Communication Monographs, 60*, 199–219.

Cloven, D. H., & Roloff, M. E. (1993b). Sense-making activities and interpersonal conflict, II: The effects of communicative intentions on internal dialogue. *Western Journal of Communication, 57*, 309–329.

Cloven, D. H., & Roloff, M. E. (1994). A developmental model of decisions to withhold relational irritations in romantic relationships. *Personal Relationships, 1*, 143–164.

Elmberger, E., Bolund, C., & Lützén, K. (2000). Transforming the exhausting to energizing process of being a good parent in the face of cancer. *Health Care for Women International, 21*, 485–499.

Emmers, T. M., & Dindia, K. (1995). The effect of relational stage and intimacy on touch: An extension of Guerrero and Andersen. *Personal Relationships, 2*, 225–226.

Epstein, Y. M., & Rosenberg, H. S. (1997). He does, she doesn't; she does, he doesn't: Couple conflicts about infertility. In S. R. Leiblum (Ed.), *Infertility: Psychological issues and counseling strategies* (pp. 129–148). Oxford, UK: Wiley.

George, L. (1993). Sociological perspectives on life transitions. *Annual Review of Sociology, 19*, 353–373.

Given, B., & Given, C. W. (1993). Patient and family caregiver reaction to new and recurrent breast cancer. *Journal of the American Medical Women's Association, 47*, 201–206.

Graham, E. E. (1997). Turning points and commitment in post-divorce relationships. *Communication Monographs, 64*, 350–368.

Greil, A. L. (1991). *Not yet pregnant: Infertile couples in contemporary America.* New Brunswick, NJ: Rutgers University Press.

Greil, A. L., Leitko, T. A., & Porter, K. L. (1988). Infertility: His and hers. *Gender and Society, 2*, 172–199.

Hilton, B. A. (1988). The phenomenon of uncertainty in women with breast cancer. *Mental Health Nursing, 9*, 217–238.

Honeycutt, J. M. (1993). Memory structures for the rise and fall of personal relationships. In S. Duck (Ed.), *Individuals in relationships* (pp. 60–80). Newbury Park, CA: Sage.

Honeycutt, J. M., & Cantrill, J. G. (2001). *Cognition, communication, and romantic relationships.* Mahwah, NJ: Lawrence Erlbaum.

Huston, T. L., Surra, C. A., Fitzgerald, N. M., & Cate, R. M. (1981). From courtship to marriage: Mate selection as an interpersonal process. In S. Duck & R. Gilmour (Eds.), *Personal relationships 2: Developing personal relationships* (pp. 53–88). New York: Academic Press.

Knapp, M. L. (1984). *Interpersonal communication and human relationships.* Boston: Allyn & Bacon.

Knobloch, L. K. (2007). Perceptions of turmoil within courtship: Associations with intimacy, relational uncertainty, and interference from partners. *Journal of Social and Personal Relationships, 24*, 363–384.

Knobloch, L. K., & Carpenter-Theune, K. E. (2004). Topic avoidance in developing romantic relationships: Associations with intimacy and relational uncertainty. *Communication Research, 31*, 173–205.

Knobloch, L. K., & Donovan-Kicken, E. (2006). Perceived involvement of network members in courtships: A test of the relational turbulence model. *Personal Relationships, 13*, 281–302.

Knobloch, L. K., Miller, L. E., & Carpenter, K. E. (2007). Using the relational turbulence model to understand negative emotion within courtship. *Personal Relationships, 14,* 91–112.

Knobloch, L. K., & Solomon, D. H. (1999). Measuring the sources and content of relational uncertainty. *Communication Studies, 50,* 261–278.

Knobloch, L. K., & Solomon, D. H. (2002a). Information-seeking beyond initial interaction: Managing relational uncertainty within close relationships. *Human Communication Research, 28,* 243–257.

Knobloch, L. K., & Solomon, D. H. (2002b). Intimacy and the magnitude and experience of episodic relational uncertainty within romantic relationships. *Personal Relationships, 9,* 457–478.

Knobloch, L. K., & Solomon, D. H. (2003). Responses to changes in relational uncertainty within dating relationships: Emotions and communication strategies. *Communication Studies, 54,* 282–305.

Knobloch, L. K., & Solomon, D. H. (2004). Interference and facilitation from partners in the development of interdependence within romantic relationships. *Personal Relationships, 11,* 115–130.

Knobloch, L. K., & Solomon, D. H. (2005). Relational uncertainty and relational information processing: Questions without answers? *Communication Research, 32,* 349–388.

Knobloch, L. K., Solomon, D. H., & Cruz, M. G. (2001). The role of relationship development and attachment in the experience of romantic jealousy. *Personal Relationships, 8,* 205–224.

Leiblum, S. R. (1997). Love, sex, and infertility: The impact of infertility on couples. In S. R. Leiblum (Ed.), *Infertility: Psychological issues and counseling strategies.* (pp. 149–166). Oxford, UK: Wiley.

Marineau, M. (2005). Health/illness transition and telehealth: A concept analysis using the evolutionary method. *Nursing Forum, 40,* 96–106.

McLaren, R. M. (2007, October). *Relational framing during relationship transitions.* Paper presented at the annual meeting of the Pennsylvania Speech Communication Association, State College, PA.

Miller, G. R. (1976). Foreword. In G. R. Miller (Ed.), *Explorations in interpersonal communication.* Beverly Hills, CA: Sage.

Morton, T. L., & Douglas, M. A. (1981). Growth of relationships. In S. Duck & R. Gilmour (Eds.), *Personal relationships 2: Developing personal relationships* (pp. 3–26). New York: Academic Press.

Northouse, L., Laten, D., & Reddy, P. (1995). Adjustment of women and their husbands to recurrent breast cancer. *Research in Nursing & Health, 18,* 515–524.

Priem, J. S. (2007, October). *The physiology of turbulence.* Paper presented at the annual meeting of the Pennsylvania Speech Communication Association, State College, PA.

Roloff, M. E., & Cloven, D. H. (1990). The chilling effect in interpersonal relationships: The reluctance to speak one's mind. In D. D. Cahn (Ed.), *Intimates in conflict: A communication perspective* (pp. 49–76). Hillsdale, NJ: Lawrence Erlbaum.

Schneider, M. G., & Forthofer, M. S. (2005). Associations of psychosocial factors with the stress of infertility treatment. *Health and Social Work, 30*(3), 183–191.

Solomon, D. H. (1997). A developmental model of intimacy and date request explicitness. *Communication Monographs, 64,* 99–118.

Solomon, D. H., & Knobloch, L. K. (2001). Relationship uncertainty, partner interference, and intimacy within dating relationships. *Journal of Social and Personal Relationships, 18,* 804–820.

Solomon, D. H., & Knobloch, L. K. (2004). A model of relational turbulence: The role of intimacy, relational uncertainty, and interference from partners in appraisals of irritations. *Journal of Social and Personal Relationships, 21,* 795–816.

Solomon, D. H., Knobloch, L. K., & Fitzpatrick, M. A. (2004). Relational power, marital schema, and decisions to withhold complaints: An investigation of the chilling effect on confrontation in marriage. *Communication Studies, 55,* 146–167.

Solomon, D. H., & Theiss, J. A. (2008). A longitudinal test of the relational turbulence model. *Personal Relationships, 15,* 339–357.

Steuber, K. R., & Solomon, D. H. (2008). Relational uncertainty, partner interference, and infertility: A qualitative study of discourse within online forums. *Journal of Social and Personal Relationships, 25,* 831–855.

Surra, C. A. (1985). Courtship types: Variations in interdependence between partners and social networks. *Journal of Personality and Social Psychology, 49,* 357–375.

Theiss, J. A., & Solomon, D. H. (2006a). Coupling longitudinal data and multi-level modeling to examine the antecedents and consequences of jealousy experiences in romantic relationships: A test of the relational turbulence model. *Human Communication Research, 32,* 469–503.

Theiss, J. A., & Solomon, D. H. (2006b). A relational turbulence model of communication about irritations in romantic relationships. *Communication Research, 33,* 391–418.

Theiss, J. A., & Solomon, D. H. (2007). Communication and the emotional, cognitive, and relational consequences of first sexual encounters in heterosexual dyads. *Communication Quarterly, 55,* 179–206.

Tomlinson, P. (1996). Marital relationship change in the transition to parenthood: A re-examination as interpreted through transition theory. *Journal of Family Nursing, 2,* 286–305.

Walker, A. (2001). Trajectory, transition and vulnerability in adult medical-surgical patients: A framework for understanding in-hospital convalescence. *Contemporary Nursing, 11,* 206–216.

Weber, K. M., & Solomon, D. H. (2007, November). *A relational turbulence model of distress and communication associated with breast cancer.* Paper presented at the annual meeting of the National Communication Association, Chicago.

Weber, K. M., & Solomon, D. H. (in press). Locating relationship and communication issues among stressors associated with breast cancer. *Health Communication.*

7

Workplace Relationships and Membership Negotiation

Karen K. Myers

The workplace is a source of many types of relationships: demanding supervisors, unpredictable subordinates, competitive coworkers, and challenging clients, as well as friendships with individuals who are not only proximal, but with whom we may share considerable interests (Fritz & Omdahl, 2006). The latter relationships can enhance work life; research suggests that close friendships in the workplace boost job satisfaction by nearly 50% (Rath, 2006). They also promote productivity because much of what we do in our organizational roles can only be accomplished through our relationships. Workplace relationships also may be the source of anguish. For example, 10% of American employees report that they have felt the pressure of a bully in their places of work (Lutgen-Sandvik, Tracy, & Alberts, 2007).

Workplace relationships can be multiplex, intense, interdependent, and complicated (Waldron, 2003), but they are especially significant because of the amount of time Americans spend at work and the frequency with which workers change jobs and form new relationships. In 2005, the average American worker spent 1,758 hours working (U.S. Bureau of Labor Statistics, 2007), which translates to more than 35 hours per week, including both full- and part-time employees. For most, this means more time spent with coworkers than with family. Americans also change jobs at ever-increasing rates, with the average employment tenure now at an average of 4 years (U.S. Bureau of Labor Statistics, 2006). Whether as the newcomer or the veteran adapting to new coworkers, developing working relationships is a foundational, continuous aspect of organizational life.

Workplace relationships initially are formed and redefined throughout members' association with an organization, but relationship development is germane as workers are socialized and assimilated into new organizations and units. In this chapter, I call attention to the links between organizational or workgroup integration and forging workplace relationships. Although informed by research on organizational socialization and assimilation, this chapter does not merely focus on newcomers as focal points of change during their integration but also on relationships that are mutually constructed between newcomers and more seasoned veterans. Thus I use the term *membership negotiation,* a construct borrowed from McPhee and Zaug (2000), to indicate the process of transforming individuals to organizational members. It is the ongoing communicative exchange that results in acceptance or marginalization on behalf of other members (both old and new) as they mutually evaluate each other (Scott & Myers, 2007).

I draw connections between traditional interpersonal research on relationships and the study of organizational integration processes, traditionally the realm of organizational scholars. I begin by describing organizations—social entities created through human interaction which become consequential environments for interpersonal interactions and the development of relationships. Next, I present a brief review of previous research on workplace relationships and a survey of research on assimilation, the process by which individuals become a part of an organization or workgroup. I then describe my own research linking assimilation processes to the development of workplace relationships. In the last section, I pose questions for the future study of workplace relationships and membership negotiation, arguing that research grounded in interpersonal interaction can contribute toward understanding the organizational experience.

Relationships in the Workplace

Setting the Scene

It is tempting to construe workplace relational communication simply as interaction that takes place within a given context—an organization. However, as Dillard and Solomon (2000) argue, context is foundational and greatly influences interaction. Workplace communication and organizational interactions, in general, have many of the relational qualities described above but are influenced by structural elements of the organizing process. Through micro-/macrocommunication practices, members constitute the structure and the culture that is the essence of the organization (Giddens, 1984; McPhee & Zaug, 2000). Structures created in interaction, in turn, constrain and guide communication associated with organizational membership (Seibold & Myers, 2005). For example, some organizational cultures encourage friendliness and informality, others contribute to the creation of formal, uniplex relationships, and still others foster competitiveness and secrecy. These differing environments become the foundation for workplace interaction. Thus, workplace communication has far-reaching consequences not just for the communicative partners but for the development and sustainability of the organization as well as for others who interact within this social system.

Investigating Relationships in the Workplace

Workplace relationships share characteristics with nonwork friendships. They are based on the presumption of progression and continuity (Rawlins, 1981; Sroufe & Fleeson, 1986), they imply certain role expectations (Knobloch & Solomon, 2003; Planalp, 1985), and they can be multidimensional (Reis, Collins, & Berscheild, 2000; Sroufe & Fleeson, 1986). But workplace relationships also differ from friendships in many ways. First, they can be formed and dissolved without mutual choice of the members. Those who work in our closest proximity—teammates and supervisors, for example—may be selected (and deselected) by others in the organization with little or no input from the focal members. Second, workplace relationships can be crucial for workers' financial livelihood. Third, when relationships are successful, they can facilitate cooperation and the development of networks leading to opportunities that may not otherwise occur. Strained relationships can inhibit growth, leading to fewer partnerships and fewer occasions for new opportunities. Those relationships may be complicated by interdependency as well as group identity and can be overtly or covertly competitive in nature. Fourth, workplace relationships often carry the expectation of task performance and productivity. While this may draw members closer together, personality clashes and role conflicts can also lead to negative consequences for individuals and the organization.

Most investigations into organizational membership issues are conducted by researchers in the fields of organizational communication, management, and social psychology (e.g., Anderson & Thomas, 1996; Ashforth & Mael, 1998; Fairhurst, 1993; Fix & Sias, 2006; Olufowote, Miller, & Wilson, 2005), but interpersonal researchers also have explored the complex relational dynamics that occur in the workplace. Bridge and Baxter (1992) reported five dialectical tensions associated with organizational features and membership variables stemming from blended relationships (relationships that are both personal and work-related). They found that tensions arising from person-work relationships are related to organizational formalization and relationship closeness. Strategies workers use to manage these tensions are related to status equality, workgroup cohesion, and the amount of dual-role tension felt by the participants. Other interpersonal research has examined provocative topics such as the effects of romantic relationships on coworkers and workplace performance, finding that illicit relationships can have negative effects on the workgroup, while most romantic workplace relationships have benign effects on partners or coworkers (e.g., Dillard, Hale, & Segrin, 1994). Sexual harassment (Bingham & Battey, 2005; Buzzanell, 2004; Dougherty & Smythe, 2004; Lee & Guerrero, 2001), communication accommodation (Hecht & Krieger, 2006; McCann & Giles, 2006), and differences in response related to inequity between American and Korean coworkers (Westerman, Park, & Lee, 2007) reflect interpersonal and organizational interests informed by both literatures.

Developing and maintaining workplace relationships involves evaluating other members for their potential value toward meeting organizational goals and predicting their social contributions. As members interact with coworkers, they ask themselves, "Is this individual helping us make our quota?" "Is this worker doing her fair share?" "How will the new coworker compare to me?" Judging coworkers' potential social contributions provokes questions such as "Is he a complainer?" "Will I enjoy conversations with her?" "Could this be a new lunch buddy?" Occurring consciously or subconsciously, these judgments lead to varying degrees of member acceptance (or nonacceptance) as individuals work together. They are especially apparent in *workplace integration,* as newcomers enter and negotiate their place in the workgroup and/or organization.

Workplace Integration

Organizational researchers investigate the process of newcomers entering and becoming a part of organizations within the rubric of organizational *socialization* or *assimilation.* Moreland and Levine (2001) define socialization as "a process of mutual adjustment that produces changes over time in the relationship between a person and a group" (p. 69). A closely related process, assimilation, entails learning about and learning how to function in an organizational environment (Jablin, 1987, 2001). As newcomers assimilate they learn about the organization and develop a common framework described as "a kind of knowledge shared by experienced organizational members" that guides them in organizational interaction and decision making (Van Maanen & Schein, 1979, p. 212). Newcomers also learn about normative rules of conduct in the organization, which is important because what might be perfectly acceptable in one organization, such as missing a meeting or arriving a few minutes late for work, may not be accepted in another.

Assimilation and socialization research reveals how groups and organizations attempt to shape individuals into productive members using various tactics (Jones, 1986; Van Maanen & Schein, 1979), how newcomers proactively seek out information (Miller & Jablin, 1991; Morrison, 1993), and how they adapt (Ashforth, Saks, & Lee, 1998), negotiate, and individualize their roles (e.g., Ashforth, 2001; Ashford & Taylor, 1990; Graen, 1976). Most socialization and assimilation studies acknowledge but do not focus on the relationships that develop between organizational members as a result of socialization.

Moreland and Levine (1982, 2001) describe the process of socialization (which I will be reconceptualizing as membership negotiation) as reciprocal interactions between newcomers and old-timers. Implicated in their theory are the *relationships* that members develop in small, close-knit groups of members who communicate regularly. Their model depicts three group-socialization processes: mutual evaluation, commitment, and role transition. As members demonstrate their ability to adhere to normative rules of behavior and contribute to workgroup goals, others *evaluate* each member's ability to function effectively in the group. With positive evaluation, members may develop *commitment* toward each other, the workgroup, and the organization. Mowday and Steers (1979) explain that commitment is associated with an individual's identification with a target and willingness to work on its behalf. Commitment toward the organization and other members is not guaranteed and not fixed, often fluctuating throughout membership. Moreland and Levine (1982) suggest that "consequences of group commitment include acceptance" (pp. 148–149). The attainment or nonattainment of commitment and acceptance causes members to *transition*, which can involve acceptance of the person as a participating member, marginalization of the member, or turnover. Moreland and Levine propose that these processes are not time limited but are reoccurring cycles of evaluation, commitment, and transition that continue until members exit the group or organization. Thus, members' relationships with supervisors and coworkers may evolve over time (Hess, Omdahl, & Fritz, 2006).

Elements of this model, and much of the social interaction between organizational members, can be further illuminated by interpersonal communication perspectives. Expectancy violation theory (see, e.g., Burgoon, 1993; Burgoon, Berger, & Waldron, 2000) may explain why some workgroup members are negatively or positively evaluated and eventually marginalized or accepted by coworkers. According to expectancy violation theory, individuals are judged based on contextual norms and beliefs about appropriate behaviors in particular circumstances. When members violate others' expectations of appropriate behavior, others' future attributions and responses toward the actor are affected (Leets, 2001). Behaviors that are negatively assessed because they violate expectations cause the actor to be judged more negatively than if he or she had met standard expectations (Burgoon, 1993). The actor's ability to reward or punish also influences whether others judge the behavior negatively or positively. For example, powerful, popular, or physically attractive persons offer reward power because they can grant resources or desirous friendships. They are more likely to receive positive valence (or at least neutral valence) when violating expectations than violators who do not have an ability to reward (Floyd & Voloudakis, 1999). Consequently, when newcomers' behaviors violate existing organizational and workgroup norms, coworkers make attributions about those behaviors that may cause fellow employees to welcome or exclude the newcomers. Newcomers, especially at lower levels in the organization, are likely to wield less reward power than more tenured members, which may explain why they often find themselves adjusting to accommodate to their new organizational situation (Cooper-Thomas & Anderson, 2002; Jablin & Kramer, 1998).

Another interpersonal theory that can help in understanding the development of workplace relationships, but has received little attention from organizational communication researchers, is social exchange theory. Social exchange theory proposes that, given a choice between two alternatives, individuals choose the one that is more rewarding (Cox & Kramer, 1995; Roloff, 1981). In organizational settings, coworkers, and especially newcomers, are similarly evaluated and selected by their colleagues. Selections may be made according to the member's task capability, or just as commonly, the individual's social desirability. Those who are routinely left out— not selected for promotion, chosen to be part of a team, or asked to join others for coffee breaks or lunch—do not become central to the workgroup and organization.

Other studies on interpersonal constructs and related topics offer additional understanding into membership negotiation: studies on personal attraction (Burleson, 1998; Hogg & Hardie, 1991), yielding insights into why some newcomers may be accepted into the workgroup more readily based on their physical and social attractiveness; studies on envy and jealousy (Guerrero & Afifi, 1999; Guerrero & Andersen, 1998; Patient, Lawrence, & Maitlis, 2003); and studies on *relationship framing*, or how organizational members conceptualize and talk about their relationships with coworkers, with supervisors, and in direct reports (Dillard, Solomon, & Samp, 1996; Knobloch & Solomon, 2003). Interpersonal research thus affords insight into competitiveness, evaluation, and feedback among organizational members as they attempt to discursively position themselves in their workgroups.

Developing Workplace Relationships

Most early investigations of organizational assimilation focused on micropractices that occur during the first few weeks and months of organizational entry. While informative, this focus caused early studies to take a narrow view of assimilation, typically examining only management's efforts to socialize recruits or, conversely, newcomer adaptation. Most contemporary researchers take a more expansive view of membership negotiation processes that includes how agents interact to negotiate their relationships within the social system. Thus, many researchers (including me) use social constructivist theory to incorporate the organization's culture and mutual interaction in investigations of member integration. Values and the meanings assigned to practices are culturally specific, derived from interaction with social actors in a specific time and place (Harré, 1979; Penman, 1992). Social constructivism is a move away from functional views, which focus primarily on cause and effect. Instead, this perspective specifies that social relations create meanings that shape human cognition and behavior (Harré, 1979), and thus yields a more complete picture of workers' organizational experience.

In the next section, I describe some of my own research, emphasizing how investigations in membership negotiation can be informed by and provide insights into workplace relationships. The section ends with some suggestions for future research linking membership negotiation with interpersonal theories, constructs, and research.

Membership Negotiation and Diversity

The overarching purpose of my research is to examine the interpersonal dynamics involved in membership negotiation. Toward that end, I have sought to redress problems of the assimilation approach by taking a nonlinear, relational perspective, reconceptualizing socialization and assimilation as processes of negotiation involving recursivity between newcomers and others in the organization (Myers, 2006), offering a theoretical framework rooted in structuration theory (Scott & Myers, 2007; Seibold & Myers, 2005) and sensitive to occupation (Myers & McPhee, 2006) and diversity (Myers & Shenoy, 2006) as well as to the precursors of vocational socialization (Myers, Stoltzfus, Gailliard, & Jahn, 2008).

The basis of my investigations in membership negotiation is a six-dimensional model and associated measurement instrument that I developed with John Oetzel to depict and operationalize the *processes* of becoming a part of an organization (Myers & Oetzel, 2003). Our study of organizational members from several industries was conducted in two phases. Interviews in Phase 1 resulted in a model depicting membership negotiation (which we were then calling organizational assimilation) that included the following processes: *becoming familiar with others (supervisors in particular), acculturating and adapting, becoming involved, feeling recognized, learning job skills,* and *role negotiating. Becoming familiar with others,* part of developing workplace relationships, was mentioned by all but one of the participants. Many of the five other processes also necessarily involve modes of relating to others in the workplace, such as demonstrating involvement and receiving recognition as contributing members.

The Myers and Oetzel (2003) study spawned a follow-up project (Myers, 2005) that tested the model among *high-reliability workers*—workers who work in situations that are dangerous for themselves and/or others (Weick, 1993; Weick, Sutcliffe, & Obstfeld, 1999). The purpose was to reevaluate the six dimensions in a high-reliability context with municipal firefighters. I found that the nature of the firefighters' work and the culture of the organization influenced their membership-negotiation experience. Absolute conformity was the norm in this paramilitary organization, so it was not surprising to find that firefighters did not role-negotiate. Due to the dangerous nature of their work, it simply would not be feasible for firefighters to individually change their jobs. Also interesting was the essential function of trust among the members of the crew. In most occupations, trust is an outcome of membership negotiation; in high-reliability organizations, the development of trusting relationships is a foundational element of the integration process, as much so as learning how to complete tasks.

A third project with roots in the Myers and Oetzel (2003) model, and a second study including municipal firefighters, was conducted with Bob McPhee (Myers & McPhee, 2006). We explored individual-level assimilation and group-level communicative processes in highly interdependent workgroups. We used hierarchical linear modeling to examine individual- and crew-level influence on four assimilation outcomes: involvement, trustworthiness, commitment, and acceptance. Individual-level predictors of these outcomes were proactivity, tenure, acculturation, and job competency. We also predicted a linear progression of the four assimilation outcomes as a way of testing a modified version of the Moreland and Levine model (1982, 2001) discussed earlier. Specifically, we theorized that involvement would precede the development of trustworthiness within the crew, paving the way for commitment to the group and potentially leading to feeling acceptance among crew members. Although we did not confirm the model, we found that individual-level acculturation (learning about and adapting to the crew's culture) predicted each of the four assimilation outcomes. In addition, involvement was a predictor of commitment and acceptance. The group-level variable in the study—crew performance proficiency—modified the influence of tenure, proactivity, involvement, acculturation, and trust on members' commitment. This study underscores the effect of a member's interaction with fellow crew members on the development of organizational and workgroup attachments as well as on the ability of groups to develop efficiency as highly interdependent crews.

My continuing research builds on these studies of membership negotiation and workplace interaction that enables individuals to adopt workgroup, organizational, and occupational roles. Next, I introduce two studies in progress that are designed to contribute to knowledge about membership negotiation and to offer meaningful implications for workplace relationships.

Research in Progress: Diverse Experiences in Membership Negotiation

Soon after the Myers and Oetzel (2003) organizational assimilation model was published, intercultural researchers began to ask us about how the model and the associated measurement instrument apply to women and men who are traditionally underrepresented (i.e., to people who are not white and/or not male). We affirmed the model's generalizability, citing a nearly equal number of men and women in the qualitative study (6 men and 7 women) and the large number of members of both sexes (114 men and 219 women) in the quantitative validation study. A closer examination of the quantitative phase of the study revealed a potential lack of ethnic diversity. Of the 342 participants, 45% were Caucasian and 43% were Hispanic. Furthermore, most of the nonwhite workers were clustered in nonsupervisory positions. Could systematic variance in assimilation based on differences such as participant sex, ethnicity, and country of origin be revealed with a deeper examination of their membership experiences?

Extant diversity literature strongly suggests that differences in values and life experiences can affect nonwhite members' and women's entry experiences (Allen, 1995; Ashcraft & Allen, 2003). One potentially mediating variable is institutional bias—the organizational preference for culturally prescribed values and behaviors (Khoo, 1988). According to Loden and Rosener (1991), many modern organizations are vestiges of a system originally created in colonial America and based on the values, perspectives, and culture of Western European white men but not aligning with those of nondominant groups. People of color and women can be disadvantaged—expected to adapt to a system of values that may not easily mesh with their own.

Cox (1994) defined 13 common organizational practices that create institutional bias against workers who are not a part of the white male cultural identity group. For example, policies that require workers to separate home from work life may present additional role conflict for nonwhite and/or nonmale employees with outside obligations such as family or religious commitments. Another institutional bias cited by Cox is "the tendency to define effective leadership in terms that reflect traits typical of the dominant group" (p. 209). Several studies investigating workers' perceptions of leadership qualities demonstrate masculine biases (e.g., Lord & Maher, 1993; Vecchio & Brazil, 2007). In most cases, the bias is unintentional—because many of these practices are a long-ingrained part of the society's and organization's culture, the assumptions associated with these policies and perceptions are often nearly invisible to dominant group members. The purpose of our study, therefore, is to compare the membership-negotiation experiences of women and people of color with the experiences of white men.

Suchitra Shenoy, a doctoral student at Purdue University, joined me in a project focusing on the membership-negotiation experiences of women and people of color (Myers & Shenoy, 2006). Diversity research demonstrates that life experiences related to cultural differences make a difference in values, perceptions, and communication style (e.g., Allen, 1995; Cox, Lobel, & McLeod, 1991; Kikoski & Kikoski, 1996). We began with the Myers and Oetzel (2003) model and theorized about how the experiences of women and people of color might differ from those of white males. We reviewed intercultural literature to consider how diversity of *identity groups* may influence membership negotiation relative to those six processes. Alderfer (1982) defines an identity group as a group "whose members share some biological characteristic (such as race), have participated in equivalent historical experiences (such as migration), are currently subjected to certain social forces (such as unemployment), and as a result have similar world views" (p. 138). In the workplace, their "otherness" relative to race or gender may affect how members of other identity groups perceive and accept them and their shared worldviews.

Cultural differences affect who newcomers approach for working relationships (Allen, 1996), which influences relationships throughout their organizational tenures (Cox, 1994). Automatic preferences for interacting with individuals from similar identity cultures affect the development of social networks (Ibarra, 1992, 1993; McPherson, Smith-Lovin, & Cook, 2001) and of mentoring relationships (Thomas, 1990; Fitt & Newton, 1981) as well as the selection of individuals for leadership positions (Lord & Maher, 1993). Membership in a nondominant identity group related to race (e.g., Nkomo, 1992; Ragins, 1995) or gender (Ibarra, 1992) often results in less power, prestige, and status.

We proposed that three of the processes found in the Myers and Oetzel model (2003)—*becoming familiar with others, demonstrating involvement,* and *receiving recognition*—could differ for identity groups comprised of white women and men and women of color. To test these propositions, we interviewed a group of ethnically diverse workers and compared their experiences. Although we were sensitized to potential communicative processes of membership negotiation that might be more challenging for nonwhite males and women, we used a grounded approach, asking interview participants to reflect on and describe their perceptions of their organization's behavioral expectations and how they learned about those expectations. The 23 interviewees included 11 African Americans, 9 Caucasians, 2 Latino Americans, and 2 Asians. Twelve were females. Ages ranged from 20 to 58 years (mean = 37). Tenures in the workgroups and organizations ranged from 1 week to 35 years (mean = 7.63 years, median = 4 years). The participants worked in organizations of varying size in the Midwest and in the western United States.

Among our findings was that women and people of color had fewer opportunities to establish meaningful working relationships than white men. For example, when the women entered jobs or workgroups that were traditionally held by men, they were not welcomed by male coworkers, who seemed to fear that their presence in the workgroup might affect the group's climate. An airline pilot admitted that he did not think that women belong in the cockpit. Women and people of color were expected to adapt to norms of behavior more commonly exhibited by white males, but at the same time they found themselves penalized for violating expectations for their given identity group. Nonnative English speakers said that they found that inclusion and recognition could be more difficult when native-English-speaking Americans paid less attention to their ideas. Coworkers appeared less willing to make the effort to understand members who spoke with accents or did not speak English with proficiency. Most women and nonwhite workers reported that white men were the only probable leaders in their organizations. White males did not report these types of experiences and reported that they were unaware of the differences for nonwhites and women.

Overall, workers from the dominant culture (white and typically male) were less willing to be accepting of their coworkers' differences, and less likely to see that these differences could translate into meaningful contributions toward group and organizational goals. At an interpersonal level, they also were less willing to invest in relationships with members who were perceived as "different." These actions could be demonstrations of homophily—indications that individuals prefer to associate with people who are similar to themselves (Ibarra, 1992; McCroskey, McCroskey, & Richmond, 2006; McPherson et al., 2001). Although these differences were concerning, even upsetting, for some participants, some women and nonwhite males felt that their definitions of success were different from those of white men. Many were not concerned about developing close relationships with everyone in the workplace and had career expectations that may not involve formal leadership positions.

The Myers and Shenoy (2006) study serves to extend understanding about membership negotiation by highlighting the importance of positive coworker evaluation and of having the ability to forge productive working relationships. My commitment to broaden understanding about the processes of membership negotiation continues in another project designed largely based on findings from Myers and McPhee (2006). In this newest project, I will examine another type of high-reliability team—the health care team.

Communication in Health Care Teams

This study is still in the design stage and links the development of workplace relationships and membership negotiation with another high-reliability occupation: membership in a surgical team consisting of physicians, registered nurses, and patient care assistants. Apker, Propp, and Zabava Ford (2005) focused on nurses as part of health care teams, and used role theory and dialectic theory (Baxter & Montgomery, 1996) to reveal three types of role tensions experienced by the nurses. Differences in hierarchy and status as well as changing perceptions of their profession and professional identity created role tension and affected the nurses' ability to communicate with others in the team. Their study highlights the foundational nature of negotiating relationships to create and maintain effective teams. Although my planned study will investigate issues related to status and professional identity, the overarching purpose of the investigation is to examine communication among all members of the team and to test the modified membership-negotiation model developed in Myers and McPhee (2006).

Surgical teams have occupational similarities to municipal firefighting crews. Like surgical teams, firefighters spend up to 70% of their time on emergency medical response. In addition, both occupations include the provision of medical care members who are part of copresent, highly coupled teams (Myers & McPhee, 2006). Thus, members of both groups must communicate with teammates and work with efficient precision in high risk situations for the well-being of their patients (Lammers & Krikorian, 1997). Other similarities between the two professions include the prestige of their professions and the hierarchical structure of their teams.

However, differences between the occupations and cultures are likely to result in contrasting outcomes. First, firefighting crews are relatively stable (in Myers & McPhee, 2006, members had worked together on average for more than a year), whereas the makeup of surgical teams may vary from day to day. Second, members of surgical teams are more heterogeneous than firefighting crews. Within surgical teams, members have differing educational backgrounds, career paths, prestige, and presumed power. Third, the occupational identities of surgeons, anesthesiologists, surgical nurses, and surgical assistants also affect how the individual members of surgical teams view themselves, the other members of the workgroup, and their working relationships. Fourth, the strong, paramilitary culture of firefighting also mandates deference to more senior members. Regardless of rank, firefighters who have more time on the job are given considerable respect, even by their captain (the senior-ranking member of a crew). As a result, most new firefighters are acutely aware of their low status in the organizational hierarchy. This clearly defined pecking order (quasi-hierarchy) works to structure conduct both inside and outside the station walls.

A fifth potentially important distinction is related to differences in setting. Firefighters' work sites are varied (e.g., house fires in the suburbs, office buildings in city centers, traffic accidents on streets and freeways), and their work is often viewed by the public. In contrast, surgical teams work in the setting of a hospital where interactions are limited to a specific locale, for the most part, in surgical suites out of the public gaze. This contrast between public and private location is likely to influence members' behaviors. Goffman (1980) argued that individuals are aware of the need to perform differently when they are in public view (*frontstage*). *Backstage performances* (out of the public view) are likely to be less restrained by self-monitoring because individuals are less concerned about public perceptions.

This is in sharp contrast to firefighters, who often work surrounded by members of the community. Like the Myers and McPhee (2006) study, the thrust of this research is to explore how surgical team members coordinate their work and to discern whether trust and group cohesion influence their performance.

In the planned study, I anticipate that differences in work setting and organizational culture will mean that tenure and proactivity of surgical team members will not predict team members' trust. While firefighters must demonstrate their proactivity so as to be positively evaluated by fellow crew members, it seems likely that members of surgical teams are less concerned with their coworkers' commitment to their superiors and the organization and primarily concerned with their teammates' task competency. Myers and McPhee (2006) also found that involvement and the development of trust led to crew commitment and crew acceptance. In surgical teams, I predict task competency and professionalism will be related to commitment and acceptance.

Contributions to Organizational and Interpersonal Research

The research highlighted here demonstrates the integral relationship of membership negotiation and workplace relationships, underscoring the value of interpersonal research in organizational membership-related investigations. Although organizational communication research certainly has used interpersonal theories to examine workplace issue such as job satisfaction (e.g., Fix & Sias, 2006), job uncertainty (e.g., Kramer, 1994; Sias, 2005), and *leader-member exchange*—whether a member is considered part of their supervisor's in-group or out-group (e.g., Fairhurst, 1993; Fix & Sias, 2006; Olufowote et al., 2005), additional opportunities abound. Future studies should investigate factors that influence interpersonal attraction and affect decision making in employee selection interviews as well as who is befriended and who rises in the hierarchy. Does the desire to reduce uncertainty cause some individuals to proactively seek out organizational and work-related information, which, in turn, causes them to become involved in the job and in relationships with others? How do interpersonal interaction and expectancy violation influence the development of trust among workgroup members, especially in high-risk occupations? These are just some of the questions involved in membership negotiation, the answers to which may be informed by interpersonal theories and research.

It also is intriguing to consider the effect that workplace relationships have on members' trust and attachment to their workgroup and organization. Little research has investigated antecedents to trust in face-to-face workgroups (see Peterson & Albrecht, 1996, for one exception). For example, what is the role of trust in developing relationships in non-high-reliability contexts? Can interpersonal research that has explored predictors of romantic trust in online relationships (see Anderson & Emmers-Sommer, 2006) or relationship maintenance behaviors and their effect on marital trust (Kline & Stafford, 2004) be applied to workplace relationships? Studies outside the field of communication have examined members' relational embeddedness and its influence on whether the members choose to leave their organizations (Moran, 2005; Wijayanto, Kimono, & Gadjah, 2004) as well as how members' relational attachments to their coworkers and supervisors generalize to positive attachments to organizations (Ashforth & Johnson, 2001).

Workplace relationships are likely to change as a result of changing work situations. Research is emerging that asks how the lack of face-to-face interaction influences workers' attachments with coworkers and organizations. How are such attachments affected when telecommuters rarely or never see their coworkers (Hylmö, 2006; Zucchermaglio & Talamo, 2003; also see Walther & Ramirez, Chapter 13, this volume)? The situation surrounding temporary workers also is intriguing. Some research suggests that temporary workers are less concerned about reducing uncertainty with information seeking and impression management (Sias, Kramer, & Jenkins, 1997). Because they are in the organization temporarily, they are much less likely to make social connections with other members and are much more likely to be communicatively isolated. This presents challenges not only for temporary workers, but also for managers who must motivate workers who have little or no connection to the organization (Gossett, 2001).

Traditionally, organizational socialization and assimilation are viewed by scholars as a managerial topic concerned with how to mold individuals into productive organizational members (Merton, 1968). Research into socialization (and certainly personal experience) tells us that adjustment into the workplace is more than developing job competency. The social dimensions of integration can be more difficult than the technical aspects of work (Myers, 2005). Entering and becoming a part of organizations also involves making interpersonal connections that enable and perhaps improve performance, enhance the quality of our work life, and become foundational in the organizing process. The relationships we develop with others in the workplace can have substantial influence on how we feel about the work we do and how we spend a large portion of our time. Thus, the investigation of how individuals communicate with others to become functionally and socially included members of the workgroup and organization is valuable for theorists, organizations, and members.

References

Alderfer, C. P. (1982). Problems of changing white males' behaviors and beliefs concerning race relations. In P. S. Goodman (Ed.), *Change in organizations: New perspectives on theory* (pp. 122–165). San Francisco: Jossey-Bass.

Allen, B. J. (1995). "Diversity" and organizational communication. *Journal of Applied Communication Research, 23,* 143–155.

Allen, B. J. (1996). Feminist standpoint theory: A black woman's (re)view of organizational socialization. *Communication Studies, 47,* 257–271.

Anderson, N., & Thomas, H. D. C. (1996). Work group socialization. In M. A. West (Ed.), *Handbook of work group psychology* (pp. 423–450). Chichester, UK: Wiley.

Anderson, T. L., & Emmers-Sommers, T. M. (2006). Predictors of relationship satisfaction in online romantic relationships. *Communication Studies, 57*(2), 153–172.

Apker, J., Propp, K. M., & Zabava Ford, W. S. (2005). Negotiating status and identity tensions in healthcare team interactions: An exploration of nurse role dialectics. *Journal of Applied Communication Research, 33,* 93–115.

Ashcraft, K. L., & Allen, B. J. (2003). The racial foundation of organizational communication. *Communication Theory, 13,* 5–38.

Ashford, S., & Taylor, M. (1990). Adaptation to work transitions: An integrative approach. In K. M. Rowland (Ed.), *Research in personnel and human resource management* (Vol. 8, pp. 1–39). Greenwich, CT: JAI Press.

Ashforth, B. (2001). *Role transitions in organizational life: An identity perspective.* Mahwah, NJ: Lawrence Erlbaum.

Ashforth, B. E., & Johnson, S. A. (2001). Which hat to wear? The relative salience of multiple identities in organizational contexts. In M. A. Hogg & D. J. Terry (Eds.), *Social identity processes in organizational contexts* (pp. 31–48). Philadelphia: Psychology Press.

Ashforth, B. E., & Mael, F. A. (1998). The power of resistance: Sustaining valued identities. In R. M. Kramer & M. A. Neale (Eds.), *Power and influence in organizations* (pp. 89–119). Thousand Oaks, CA: Sage.

Ashforth, B., Saks, A. M., & Lee, R. T. (1998). Socialization and newcomer adjustment: The role of organizational context. *Human Relations, 51,* 897–926.

Baxter, L. A., & Montgomery, B. M. (1996). *Relating: Dialogues and dialectics.* New York: Guilford Press.

Bingham, S. G., & Battey, K. M. (2005). Communication of social support to sexual harassment victims: Professors' responses to a student's narrative of unwanted sexual attention. *Communication Studies, 56,* 131–155.

Bridge, K., & Baxter, L. A. (1992). Blended relationships: Friends as work associates. *Western Journal of Communication, 56*, 200–225.

Burgoon, J. K. (1993). Interpersonal expectations, expectancy violations, and emotional communication. *Journal of Language and Social Psychology, 12*, 30–48.

Burgoon, J. K., Berger, C. R., & Waldron, V. R. (2000). Mindfulness and interpersonal communication. *Journal of Social Issues, 56*(1), 105–127.

Burleson, B. R. (1998). Similarities in social skills, interpersonal attraction, and the development of personal relationships. In J. S. Trent (Ed.), *Communication: Views from the helm for the twenty-first century* (pp. 77–84). Boston: Allyn & Bacon.

Buzzanell, P. M. (2004). Revisiting sexual harassment in academe: Using feminist ethical and sense-making approaches to analyze macrodiscourses and micropractices of sexual harassment. In P. M. Buzzanell, H. Sterk, & L. H. Turner (Eds.), *Gender in applied communication contexts* (pp. 25–46). Thousand Oaks, CA: Sage.

Cooper-Thomas, H., & Anderson, N. (2002). Newcomer adjustment: The relationship between organizational socialization tactics, information acquisition, and attitudes. *Journal of Occupational and Organizational Psychology, 75*, 423–437.

Cox, S. A., & Kramer, M. W. (1995). Communication during employee dismissals: Social exchange principles and group influences on employee exit. *Management Communication Quarterly, 9*, 156–190.

Cox, T. H. (1994). *Cultural diversity in organizations*. San Francisco: Berrett-Koehler.

Cox, T. H., Lobel, S., & McLeod, P. (1991). Effects of ethnic group cultural difference on cooperative versus competitive behavior in a group task. *Academy of Management Journal, 34*, 827–847.

Dillard, J. P., Hale, J. L., & Segrin, C. (1994). Close relationships in task environments: Perceptions of relational types, illicitness, and power. *Management Communication Quarterly, 7*, 227–255.

Dillard, J. P., & Solomon, D. H. (2000). Conceptualizing context in message-production research. *Communication Theory, 10*, 167–175.

Dillard, J. P., Solomon, D. H., & Samp, J. A. (1996). Framing social reality: The relevance of relational judgments. *Communication Research, 23*, 703–723.

Dougherty, D. S., & Smythe, M. J. (2004). Sensemaking, organizational culture, and sexual harassment. *Journal of Applied Communication Research, 32*, 293–317.

Fairhurst, G. T. (1993). The leader-member exchange patterns of women leaders in industry: A discourse analysis. *Communication Monographs, 60*, 321–351.

Fitt, L. W., & Newton, D. A. (1981). When the mentor is a man and the protege a woman. *Harvard Business Review, 59*, 56–60.

Fix, B., & Sias, P. M. (2006). Person-centered communication, leader-member exchange, and employee job satisfaction. *Communication Research Reports, 23*, 35–44.

Floyd, K., & Voloudakis, M. (1999). Affectionate behavior in adult platonic friendships. *Human Communication Research, 25*, 341–369.

Fritz, H. M. H., & Omdahl, B. L. (2006). *Problematic relationships in the workplace*. New York: Peter Lang.

Giddens, A. (1984). *The constitution of society: Outline of the theory of structuration.* Berkeley: University of California Press.

Goffman, E. (1980). *Behavior in public places.* New York: Free Press. (Original work published 1963)

Gossett, L. (2001). The long-term impact of short-term workers: The work life concerns posed by the growth of the contingent workforce. *Management Communication Quarterly, 15,* 115–120.

Graen, G. (1976). Role-making processes within complex organizations. In M. D. Dunnette (Ed.), *Handbook of industrial and organizational psychology* (pp. 1201–1245). Chicago: Rand McNally.

Guerrero, L. K., & Afifi, W. A. (1999). Toward a goal-oriented approach for understanding strategic communicative responses to jealousy. *Western Journal of Communication, 63,* 216–248.

Guerrero, L. K., & Andersen, P. A. (1998). The dark side of jealousy and envy: Desire, delusion, desperation, and destructive communication. In B. H. Spitzberg & W. R. Cupach (Eds.), *The dark side of relationships* (pp. 33–70). Mahwah, NJ: Erlbaum.

Harré, R. (1979). *Social being: A theory for social psychology.* Oxford, UK: Blackwell.

Hecht, M. L., & Krieger, J. L. (2006). The principle of cultural grounding in school-based substance abuse prevention: The Drug Resistance Strategies Project. *Journal of Language and Social Psychology, 25,* 301–319.

Hess, J. A., Omdahl, B. L., & Fritz, J. M. H. (2006). Turning points in relationships with disliked coworkers. In J. M. H. Fritz & B. L. Omdahl (Eds.), *Problematic relationships in the workplace* (pp. 205–232). New York: Peter Lang.

Hogg, M. A., & Hardie, E. A. (1991). Social attraction, personal attraction, and self-categorization: A field study. *Personality and Social Psychology Bulletin, 17,* 175–180.

Hylmö, A. (2006). Telecommuting and the contestability of choice: Employee strategies to legitimize personal decisions to work in a preferred location. *Management Communication Quarterly, 19,* 541–569.

Ibarra, H. (1992). Homophily and differential returns: Sex differences in network structure and access in an advertising firm. *Administrative Science Quarterly, 37,* 422–447.

Ibarra, H. (1993). Personal networks of women and minorities in management: A conceptual framework. *Academy of Management Review, 18*(1), 56–87.

Jablin, F. M. (1987). Organizational entry, assimilation, and exit. In L. Putnam, F. M. Jablin, K. Roberts, & L. Porter (Eds.), *Handbook of organizational communication* (pp. 679–740). Newbury Park, CA: Sage.

Jablin, F. M. (2001). Organizational entry, assimilation, and exit. In F. M. Jablin & L. Putnam (Eds.), *The new handbook of organizational communication* (pp. 732–818). Thousand Oaks, CA: Sage.

Jablin, F. M., & Kramer, M. W. (1998). Communication-related sense-making and adjustment during job transfers. *Management Communication Quarterly, 12,* 155–182.

Jones, G. (1986). Socialization tactics, self-efficacy, and newcomers' adjustments to organizations. *Academy of Management Journal, 29,* 262–279.

Khoo, G. P. S. (1988). *Asian Americans with power and authority in the corporate world: An exploratory investigation.* Unpublished doctoral dissertation, University of California, Santa Cruz.

Kikoski, J. F., & Kikoski, C. K. (1996). *Reflexive communication in the culturally diverse workplace.* Westport, CT: Praeger.

Kline, S. L., & Stafford, L. (2004). A comparison of interaction rules and interaction frequency in relation to marital quality. *Communication Reports, 17*(1), 11–26.

Knobloch, L. K., & Solomon, D. H. (2003). Manifestations of relationship conceptualizations in conversation. *Human Communication Research, 29,* 482–515.

Kramer, M. W. (1994). Uncertainty reduction during job transitions: An exploratory study of the communication experiences of newcomers and transferees. *Management Communication Quarterly, 7,* 384–412.

Lammers, J. C., & Krikorian, D. (1997). Surgical teams as bona fide groups: Exploration and operationalization of a construct. *Journal of Applied Communication Research, 25,* 17–38.

Lee, J. W., & Guerrero, L. K. (2001). Types of touch in cross-sex relationships between coworkers: Perceptions of relational and emotional messages, inappropriateness, and sexual harassment. *Journal of Applied Communication Research, 29,* 197–220.

Leets, L. (2001). Explaining perceptions of racist speech. *Communication Research, 28,* 676–706.

Loden, M., & Rosener, J. B. (1991). *Workforce America! Managing employee diversity as a vital resource.* Homewood, IL: Business One Irwin.

Lord, R. G., & Maher, K. J. (1993). *Leadership and information processing: Linking perceptions and performance.* New York: Routledge.

Lutgen-Sandvik, P., Tracy, S. J., & Alberts, J. K. (2007). Burned by bullying in the American workplace: Prevalence, perception, degree, and impact. *Journal of Management Studies, 44*(6), 835–860.

McCann, R. M., & Giles, H. (2006). Communication with people of different ages in the workplace: Thai and American data. *Human Communication Research, 32,* 74–108.

McCroskey, L. L., McCroskey, J. C., & Richmond, V. P. (2006). Analysis and improvement of the measurement of interpersonal attraction and homophily. *Communication Quarterly, 54*(1), 1–32.

McPhee, R. D., & Zaug, P. (2000). The communicative constitution of organizations: A framework for explanation [Online]. *Electronic Journal of Communication/La Revue Electronique de Communication, 10*(1–2).

McPherson, M., Smith-Lovin, L., & Cook, J. M. (2001). Birds of a feather: Homophily in social networks. *Annual Review of Sociology, 27,* 415–444.

Merton, R. (1968). *Social theory and social structure.* New York: Free Press.

Miller, V., & Jablin, F. (1991). Information seeking during organizational entry: Influences, tactics, and a model of the process. *Academy of Management Review, 16,* 92–120.

Moran, P. (2005). Structural vs. relational embeddedness: Social capital and managerial performance. *Strategic Management Journal, 26,* 1129–1151.

Moreland, R. L., & Levine, J. M. (1982). Socialization in small groups: Temporal changes in individual-group relations. In L. Berkowitz (Ed.), *Advances in experimental social psychology* (Vol. 15, pp. 137–192). New York: Academic Press.

Moreland, R. L., & Levine, J. M. (2001). Socialization in organizations and work groups. In M. E. Turner (Ed.), *Groups at work: Theories and research* (pp. 69–112). Mahwah, NJ: Lawrence Erlbaum.

Morrison, E. (1993). Longitudinal study of the effects of information seeking on newcomer socialization. *Journal of Applied Psychology, 77,* 173–183.

Mowday, R. T., & Steers, R. M. (1979). The measurement of organizational commitment. *Journal of Vocational Behavior, 14,* 224–247.

Myers, K. K. (2005). A burning desire: Assimilation into a fire department. *Management Communication Quarterly, 18,* 344–384.

Myers, K. K. (2006). Assimilation and mutual acceptance. In J. Greenhaus & G. Callanan (Eds.), *Encyclopedia of career development* (pp. 31–32). Thousand Oaks, CA: Sage.

Myers, K. K., & McPhee, R. D. (2006). Influences on member assimilation in workgroups in high reliability organizations: A multilevel analysis. *Human Communication Research, 32,* 440–468.

Myers, K. K., & Oetzel, J. G. (2003). Exploring the dimensions of organizational assimilation: Creating and validating a measure. *Communication Quarterly, 51,* 438–457.

Myers, K. K., & Shenoy, S. (2006, November). *Workplace diversity, institutional bias, and organizational assimilation.* Paper presented at the annual meeting of the National Communication Association, San Antonio, TX.

Myers, K. K., Stoltzfus, K., Gailliard, B., & Jahn, J. (2008, November). *Exploring girls' and women's propensity to study and enter careers in STEM disciplines: Vocational anticipatory socialization and communication research opportunities.* Paper to be presented to the Organizational Communication Division of the National Communication Association, San Diego, CA.

Nkomo, S. M. (1992). The emperor has no clothes: Rewriting "race" in organizations. *Academy of Management Review, 17,* 487–513.

Olufowote, J. O., Miller, V. D., Wilson, S. R. (2005). The interactive effects of role change goals and relational exchanges on employee upward influence tactics. *Management Communication Quarterly, 18,* 385–403.

Patient, D., Lawrence, T. B., & Maitlis, S. (2003). Understanding workplace envy through narrative fiction. *Organization Studies, 24,* 1015–1044.

Penman, R. (1992). Good theory and good practice: An argument in progress. *Communication Theory, 2,* 234–250.

Peterson, L. W., & Albrecht, T. L. (1996). Message design logic, social support, and mixed-status relationships. *Western Journal of Communication, 60,* 291–309.

Planalp, S. S. (1985). Relational schemata: A test of alternative forms of relational knowledge as guides to communication. *Human Communication Research, 12,* 3–29.

Ragins, B. R. (1995). Diversity, power, and mentorship in organizations: A cultural, structural, and behavioral perspective. In M. M. Chemers, S. Oskamp, & M. A. Costanzo (Eds.), *Diversity in organizations: New perspectives for a changing workplace* (pp. 91–132). Thousand Oaks, CA: Sage.

Rath, T. (2006). *Vital friends: The people you can't afford to live without.* New York: Gallup Press.

Rawlins, W. K. (1981). *Friendship as a communicative achievement: A theory and an interpretive analysis of verbal reports.* Unpublished doctoral dissertation, Temple University, Philadelphia.

Reis, H. T., Collins, W. A., & Berscheild, E. (2000). The relationship context of human behavior and development. *Psychological Bulletin, 126,* 844–872.

Roloff, M. E. (1981). *Interpersonal communication: The social exchange approach.* Beverly Hills, CA: Sage.

Scott, C. W., & Myers, K. K. (2007, November). *Toward an integrative theory of membership negotiations: A structurational view of socialization, assimilation, and the duality of structure.* Paper presented at the annual meeting of the National Communication Association, Chicago.

Seibold, D. R., & Myers, K. K. (2005). Communication as structuring. In G. J. Shepherd, J. St. John, & T. Striphas (Eds.), *Communication as . . . perspectives on theory* (pp. 143–152). Thousand Oaks, CA: Sage.

Sias, P. M. (2005). Narratives of workplace friendship deterioration. *Journal of Social and Personal Relationships, 21,* 321–340.

Sias, P. M., Kramer, M. W., & Jenkins, E. (1997). A comparison of the communication behaviors of temporary employees and new hires. *Communication Research, 24,* 731–754.

Sroufe, L. A., & Fleeson, J. (1986). Attachment and the construction of relationships. In W. W. Hartup & Z. Rubin (Eds.), *Relationships and development* (pp. 51–71). Hillsdale, NJ: Erlbaum.

Thomas, D. A. (1990). The impact of race on managers' experiences of developmental relationships (mentoring and sponsorship): An intra-organizational study. *Journal of Organizational Behavior, 11*(6), 479–492.

U.S. Bureau of Labor Statistics. (2006). *Employee tenure in 2006.* Retrieved December 12, 2006, from www.bls.gov/news.release/tenure.nr0.htm

U.S. Bureau of Labor Statistics. (2007). *Employment, hours, and earnings from the current employment statistics survey.* Retrieved March 1, 2007, from http://data.bls.gov/PDQ/servlet/SurveyOutputServlet

Van Maanen, J., & Schein, E. (1979). Toward a theory of organizational socialization. *Research in Organizational Behavior, 1,* 209–264.

Vecchio, R. P., & Brazil, D. M. (2007). Leadership and sex-similarity: A comparison in a military setting. *Personnel Psychology, 60,* 303–335.

Waldron, V. R. (2003). Relationship maintenance in organizational settings. In D. J. Canary & M. Dainton (Eds.), *Maintaining relationships through communication* (pp. 163–184). Mahwah, NJ: Lawrence Erlbaum.

Weick, K. (1993). The collapse of sensemaking in organizations: The Mann Gulch disaster. *Administrative Science Quarterly, 38,* 628–652.

Weick, K., Sutcliffe, K., & Obstfeld, D. (1999). Organizing for high reliability: Processes of collective mindfulness. In B. M. Staw & R. Sutton (Eds.), *Research in organizational behavior* (Vol. 23, pp. 81–123). Greenwich, CT: JAI Press.

Westerman, C. Y. K., Park, H. S., & Lee, H. E. (2007). A test of equity theory in multi-dimensional friendships: A comparison of the U.S. and Korea. *Journal of Communication, 57,* 576–598.

Wijayanto, B. R., Kimono, G., & Gadjah, M. (2004). The effect of job embeddedness on organizational behavior. *International Journal of Business, 6,* 335–354.

Zucchermaglio, C., & Talamo, A. (2003). The development of a virtual community of practices using electronic mail and communicative genres. *Journal of Business and Technical Communication, 17,* 259–284.

PART III

The Light and Dark Sides of Interpersonal Communication

8

Explaining Recipient Responses to Supportive Messages

Development and Tests of a Dual-Process Theory

Brant R. Burleson

I have spent much of the last 30 years engaged in the study of *comforting communication,* which I define as messages having the goal of alleviating or lessening the emotional distresses experienced by others (Burleson, 1985). Comforting is closely related to *emotional support,* which has been defined as specific lines of communicative behavior enacted by one party with the intent of helping another cope effectively with emotional distress (Burleson, 2003a). Both comforting and emotional support are subsets of the broader construct of *supportive communication*—verbal and nonverbal behavior produced with the intention of providing assistance to others perceived as needing that aid (Burleson & MacGeorge, 2002).

Some especially important questions about comforting messages include how, when, and why these messages have positive or negative effects on recipients. In the past few years, several of my students and I have been developing a new theory that seeks to explain the diverse outcomes of comforting messages. In this chapter, I share the current version of this theory and summarize some of the recent research we've conducted to test it. First, though, I provide some background information about the nature and significance of comforting communication.

Supportive Communication: Its Significance and Features

The Significance of Comforting Communication

You might wonder how someone can spend the better part of 30 years studying any one thing, especially comforting communication. As a matter of fact, I find comforting a more intriguing subject matter today than when I first began studying it in the late 1970s; indeed, the more I study this phenomenon, the more fascinated I become with it.

One question that captures my attention is, "How can one person affect the emotional states of another—sometimes profoundly—just by talking to that other person?" For me, this question goes to the heart of the comforting phenomenon: Comforting aims to change the feelings of someone who appears to be angry, anxious, despondent, sad, or otherwise upset. When effective, the recipient of comforting efforts feels better about things, at least to some extent for some period of time. So how does this happen? How is it possible for one person to change the feelings of another? This is a fundamental theoretical question, and one that I continue to find absorbing. Answering this question requires not only a deep understanding of communication but also a full appreciation of emotions and how they work.

Beyond this fundamental theoretical question, there are a host of good reasons to study comforting. Most obviously, comforting communication can really help someone who is upset to feel better (Burleson, 1994). Comforting can also promote more effective coping behavior, helping people think more clearly about the problems they face and assisting them with the formulation of more effective plans for managing these problems (Thoits, 1986).

Less obviously, the comfort that we receive from others can protect our health and may even help us live longer. A growing body of research indicates that the stress that accompanies emotional upset can be harmful to our health, particularly if that emotional stress is frequent and/or enduring (Dougall & Baum, 2001). By reducing emotional upset, effective comforting can diminish the health-harming effects of stress on the cardiovascular system, the neuroendocrine system, and the immune system (Wills & Fegan, 2001).

Effective comforting also contributes to the "health" of our interpersonal relationships and our satisfaction with those relationships. People value the comforting skills of those in their social network, and they expect their friends, family members, and other intimates to "be there" for them in times of trouble and to offer sensitive expressions of sympathy, care, and support (Burleson, 2003b). Thus, it should come as little surprise that people who are skilled at providing emotional support are more popular, better liked, and have more lasting friendships and intimate relationships than those who are less skilled (Burleson, 2003a). These are some of the many reasons why I believe that comforting communication is important and merits study (for additional reasons, see Burleson & MacGeorge, 2002).

One of the things we know about comforting (that you can verify from your own experience) is that some messages intended to provide comfort are more effective than others. Some messages do a really good job of helping people feel better in a lot of different situations, other messages are only somewhat helpful, still other messages may not do much of anything, and some messages actually lead the recipient to feel a little—or a lot—worse about things. Indeed, there is a considerable body of research that shows that although many of the things that people say in the effort to make distressed others feel better are at least somewhat helpful, other things people say are ineffective and even downright hurtful (see Goldsmith, 2004). One implication of these findings is that effectiveness as a comforter requires more than good intentions (i.e., the intention to provide comfort and support); rather, effectiveness as a comforter generally requires several kinds of knowledge or skill, including knowledge of the comforting strategies that are more and less likely to improve negative emotional states.

Characteristics of Better and Worse Comforting Messages and How These Messages Work

If some of the things that people say in the effort to provide comfort are helpful and others are not, a relevant question is, "What are the characteristics or properties of more and less helpful comforting messages?" Several researchers, including me, have sought to answer this question (for reviews, see Burleson, 2003a; Goldsmith, 2004). My answer to this question makes use of the concept of *person-centered communication*. In the context of emotional support, person centeredness pertains to the extent to which messages explicitly acknowledge, elaborate, legitimize, and contextualize the feelings and perspective of a distressed other (Burleson, 1994). Thus, messages that exhibit low person centeredness (LPC) deny the other's feelings and perspective by criticizing or challenging their legitimacy, or by telling the other how he or she should act and feel. Moderately person-centered (MPC) comforting messages afford an implicit recognition of the other's feelings by attempting to distract the other's attention from the troubling situation, offering expressions of sympathy and condolence, or presenting explanations of the situation that are intended to reduce the other's distress. Highly person-centered (HPC) comforting messages explicitly recognize and legitimize the other's feelings by helping the other articulate those feelings, elaborate reasons why those feelings might be felt, and explore how those feelings fit in a broader context.

Originally, we only claimed that HPC comforting messages were more developmentally advanced and were more sophisticated forms of behavior than MPC or LPC messages. And we were very successful in showing that HPC messages are, in fact, more developmentally advanced; these messages are generated more often and are better understood by older adolescents and adults than by children and younger adolescents (Burleson, 1982; Clinton & Hancock, 1991). We were also successful in showing that, compared with less person-centered alternatives, HPC comforting messages are more sophisticated forms of behavior: HPC messages pursue more complex sets of interactional goals than less person-centered alternatives, and the ability to produce these messages depends on advanced social-cognitive abilities (see Burleson, 1985). These findings are important for numerous theoretical reasons (Coopman, 1997). But if HPC comforting messages aren't also *functionally* more effective than LPC messages (i.e., if they don't do a better job of reducing upset), then the theory of person-centered comforting would have little practical utility.

So, beginning in 1985, colleagues and I initiated a series of studies aimed at determining if HPC comforting messages are evaluated more positively than LPC messages and actually do a better job of improving the emotional states of recipients (Burleson & Samter, 1985). These studies were highly successful in demonstrating that people evaluate HPC comforting messages more positively than MPC and LPC messages and that HPC messages produce more desirable outcomes than MPC and, especially, LPC messages. Indeed, we were able to demonstrate the comparative effectiveness of HPC comforting messages for diverse message recipients under diverse sets of conditions (see review in Burleson et al., 2005). These findings clearly supported the claim that HPC comforting messages generally represent more effective strategies for providing emotional support than MPC or LPC messages.

In addition to finding strong effects for the person-centered quality of comforting messages, we also found differences in people's responses to comforting messages as a function of numerous source, recipient, and contextual variables. Typically, the effect sizes for these variables were small in comparison with the large effects observed for quality of the message (i.e., level of person centeredness). For example, in several studies, we found that men responded somewhat more positively than women to LPC comforting messages, whereas women responded somewhat more positively than men to HPC comforting messages; however, even with these differences, both men and women responded *much* more positively to HPC messages than to LPC messages (Kunkel & Burleson, 1999). Similar patterns of small differences existing within large similarities were found for several variables, including culture of the recipient (Burleson & Mortenson, 2003), personality of the recipient (Jones, 2005), and perceptions of recipient responsibility for the problem situation (Jones & Burleson, 1997). The small effects associated with these source, recipient, and contextual factors, as well as the challenge of explaining their influence, often led us to discount the effects of these variables or to provide only brief (and frequently ad hoc) accounts for their impact.

The theory of message person centeredness is an analysis of message features or message design. That is, the theory of message person centeredness provides a typology of messages, identifies important distinguishing features of messages, and makes claims about what are better and worse message forms with regard to both formal and functional criteria (i.e., message sophistication and message effectiveness). However, the theory of message person centeredness does *not* explain how and why certain messages (e.g., HPC strategies) affect the emotional states of others in the ways they do. That is, the theory of message person centeredness does not specify the underlying mechanisms through which various comforting messages influence the thoughts, feelings, and behaviors of recipients. This is a limitation I did not fully appreciate for several years.

Eventually, however, a colleague and I offered a theoretical account explaining why HPC comforting messages produced greater and more lasting changes in emotion than LPC messages (Burleson & Goldsmith, 1998). We argued that HPC messages (and similar message forms) do a better job than LPC messages of facilitating the recipient's cognitive reappraisal of the upsetting circumstance. Appraisal theories of emotion (e.g., Lazarus, 1991) maintain that people's appraisals of events (their cognitive representations and judgments about the personal significance of events) produce emotional reactions. Thus, in our *theory of conversationally induced reappraisals,* we argued that to help someone change their feelings about an upsetting situation, helpers need to foster the recipient's cognitive reappraisal of that situation, and we suggested HPC comforting messages do this better than alternative messages. HPC messages, in particular, encourage the distressed person to reflect on, explore, and seek understanding of their feelings. Experimental research (Jones & Wirtz, 2006) has recently provided direct support for this theoretical account of the causal mechanism through which HPC messages facilitate positive emotional change.

There is an important limitation in our theory of conversationally induced reappraisals, which was not evident to us when we developed this theory, but has become increasingly apparent. Specifically, this theory does not offer much, if any, explanation about how comforting messages that are moderate or low in person centeredness affect the emotional states of their recipients. Although MPC and LPC messages generally are not as effective as HPC messages at facilitating positive emotional change, and at least some LPC messages may make recipients feel worse rather than better, these messages *do* affect the emotional states of recipients and, at least for MPC messages, these effects are largely positive. However it is that MPC and LPC messages influence recipients, they don't appear to do so by fostering reappraisals of the problematic situation. So the mechanisms through which these less-than-optimal messages influence the emotional states of recipients also need to be explained.

As I considered this limitation of our reappraisal theory, it occurred to me that other theories that seek to explain the effects of supportive messages (e.g., Cutrona, 1990; Rogers, 1975) share this limitation. That is, most theories of supportive message effects focus on explaining how "optimal" message forms (however these may be defined) work, and frequently do not explain how suboptimal messages work. Reflection on this limitation suggested that a complete theory of supportive message effects needs to specify *multiple* distinct mechanisms through which various comforting messages influence the emotions of recipients. Thus, although HPC messages may foster reappraisals of the problematic situation, perhaps the MPC messages that express sympathy, care, and concern (e.g., "Gee, I'm really sorry this is happening to you; is there anything I can do? I really care") help the recipient feel better by bolstering his or her sense of social acceptance and self-worth, whereas the MPC messages that suggest a compensating activity (e.g., "Hey, Ben is having a party tonight; let's go over there for a while") help by getting recipients to refocus attention on a different (and presumably happier) circumstance. LPC messages that minimize the recipient's feelings (e.g., "Look, it's just not that big of a deal; do yourself a favor and just forget about it") might even provide some temporary relief by motivating recipients to suppress or ignore their feelings for some period, although intense scrutiny of this message might also result in recipients feeling criticized and rejected. A comprehensive theory needs to identify *all* the mechanisms through which different supportive messages produce their effects, as well as consider the magnitude and stability of the changes in recipient emotions typically achieved through each of these mechanisms.

A Conceptual Problem and a Path to a Potential Solution

Despite the limitations in our theories and research, by the late 1990s, I was pretty satisfied with our understanding of comforting skill, especially which messages worked best. Early in this decade (about 2001–2003), however, I worked on several projects that, collectively, led me to raise fundamental questions about *how* comforting messages work—and sometimes don't work.

First, I researched and wrote several articles during this period that provided extensive reviews of the supportive communication literature (Burleson, 2003a, 2003b; Burleson & MacGeorge, 2002). Doing the research for these articles made me better appreciate that variation in responses to supportive messages was common and sometimes pronounced. As noted above, research from our laboratory had found that responses to more and less person-centered comforting messages varied as a function of several demographic, personality, and situational variables. I noticed that many other researchers were reporting similar results: Effects for message types were often moderated by several characteristics of the recipient, helper, or communication situation (see reviews by Lakey & Cohen, 2000). However, the moderating effects for several of these variables were not consistent across studies; sometimes a particular variable (e.g., sex of recipient) had one effect, sometimes a different effect, and sometimes no effect (see MacGeorge, Graves, Feng, Gillihan, & Burleson, 2004). Moreover, because the moderating effects for source, recipient, and contextual variables on supportive message outcomes were rarely the focus of sustained research, explanations for them usually considered only the findings obtained in a particular study, which resulted in a disconnected set of microaccounts. Further complicating the picture, some studies found that aspects of supportive messages sometimes had little or no effect on recipients, even though other studies had found these aspects of messages exerted sizable effects (e.g., Uno, Uchino, & Smith, 2002). Other studies indicated that factors such as the quality of the interpersonal relationship between the helper and the recipient sometimes had significant effects on the outcomes of supportive interactions even when aspects of supportive messages did not (e.g., Clark et al., 1998). Thus, it became increasingly evident that there were some important inconsistencies in the literature on supportive message effects, and that these were not being addressed in a comprehensive or integrative manner.

There are numerous reasons why these variations and inconsistencies in findings about the effects of supportive messages are nontrivial and call for a comprehensive explanation. These variations are nontrivial theoretically because they indicate that the outcomes of supportive messages are influenced by more than just the message. Thus, the variations in message effects suggested that we had an incomplete understanding of the factors that influenced people's responses to supportive messages. Variation in message effects is nontrivial pragmatically because it indicates that helpers need to understand how and when various factors moderate the effects of comforting strategies and how to accommodate to these factors.

A second set of experiences during this period shaped my thinking about how variations in supportive message outcomes might be explained. With one of my colleagues at Purdue, I edited a large handbook focused on communication and social interaction skills (Greene & Burleson, 2003). As we worked on this project, I was impressed by how much we had come to know in the past 20 years about message production, the process of generating symbolic behavior designed to convey an internal state to another in the effort to realize some goal. But I was also struck by how little we knew about message reception, the process of interpreting the intentional symbolic behavior of another in the effort to understand the meaning and implications of that behavior. Research on and theorizing about the message production process really took off in the 1980s, and this continues to be a very active area for communication scholars (e.g., Greene, 1997). In contrast, there is comparatively little theory and research addressing the message reception process in interpersonal interaction. Despite the paucity of theory and research on the message reception process, the available work on this topic suggested to me that most variations in responses to supportive messages could be explained in terms of how people processed these messages. This insight was partially suggested by a fundamental postulate that informs virtually all my thinking about human behavior: People's actions (including their responses to messages) are a function of the ways in which they interpret or make sense of events. This postulate is a core tenet of the constructivist approach to communication (Delia, O'Keefe, & O'Keefe, 1982), a perspective to which I had been exposed to as a graduate student and which I subsequently used in most of my research on communication (Burleson, 2007). Applying this postulate to supportive messages implies that distinct responses to these messages are a function of differences in how these messages are interpreted or processed by recipients. Thus, a good theory of message reception should comprehensively explain both consistencies and variations in responses to supportive messages.

A third set of experiences during this period provided some clues about the form of a message reception theory that might successfully explain variations in responses to comforting messages. Beginning in 2000, I returned to teaching both undergraduate and graduate courses in persuasion. I had taught courses in persuasion early in my career, but other teaching demands led me away from the persuasion area for nearly two decades. A lot can happen in two decades! In fact, there had been a revolution in persuasion theory and research beginning in the late 1970s, and by the 1990s, the landscape of persuasion scholarship had been thoroughly transformed.

This revolution was generated by the introduction of what came to be called *dual-process* theories of persuasion, the best known of which are Petty and Cacioppo's (1986) Elaboration Likelihood Model (ELM) and Chaiken's (1980) Heuristic-Systematic Model (HSM). These (and related) dual-process models maintain that (a) multiple factors influence the amount of scrutiny or thought that people give to the messages they receive on particular occasions; (b) the effects of messages vary as a function of the amount of scrutiny they are given by recipients, with message content having the strongest effect on outcomes when messages are scrutinized extensively; and (c) when message content receives little scrutiny, other factors (such as cognitive heuristics tied to certain environmental cues) may substantially influence recipient outcomes. Dual-process theories of persuasion were developed in the effort to explain several troubling inconsistencies in persuasion research (e.g., sometimes argument quality influenced attitude change and sometimes it didn't; sometimes source credibility influenced attitude change and sometimes it didn't). Models such as the ELM and HSM explained these inconsistencies in terms of the amount of processing messages received (e.g., argument quality influenced attitudes most when messages were processed extensively, whereas source credibility had the strongest influence on attitudes when messages were processed less extensively).

The success of dual-process models in explaining inconsistencies in persuasion research suggested to me that some version of a dual-process model might successfully explain variations in the outcomes of supportive messages. It was apparent, however, that the existing dual-process models such as the ELM and HSM could not be directly applied to supportive communication. Dual-process models of persuasion focus on attitude change, whereas research on supportive communication focuses on change in emotional states and related outcomes. In addition, attitudes and emotions are changed through different mechanisms; persuasive messages differ from supportive messages in their goals, features, effects, and mechanisms of change; the factors that influence the amount of scrutiny messages receive are likely to differ in persuasion *versus* support contexts; the environmental factors that influence recipient responses when messages receive little scrutiny probably differ in persuasion and support contexts; and so on. Thus, although the general logic of the dual-process approach might provide an abstract framework for a theory of supportive message processing and outcomes, any substantive theory pertaining to supportive messages could not be "imported," but instead would need to be developed carefully in a manner that respected the unique qualities of this communicative genre.

By the summer of 2003, the broad elements of a theory were beginning to fall into place that might explain, among other things,[1] variations in responses to supportive messages. Unfortunately, I was unable to work on elaborating this prototheory for the next year due to other commitments. In fall 2004, however, I began working with a very talented group of graduate students on several projects directed at developing and testing this theory. Graham Bodie had a special interest in listening and message processing; Jessica Rack was initially interested in family communication but subsequently developed an interest in grief management for the bereaved; and Amanda Holmstrom had a special interest in emotional and esteem support. Throughout the 2004–2005 academic year, we discussed aspects of supportive communication, message reception, dual-process models, and related topics. In fall 2005, the four of us began meeting regularly to design a set of studies to test aspects of the theoretical model that we were gradually elaborating; we initiated data collection in spring 2006. Since then, we have completed a major research review, some theoretical papers, and several reports of empirical studies (Bodie & Burleson, 2008; Burleson, 2008; Burleson et al., 2007, 2008; Rack, Burleson, Bodie, Holmstrom, & Servaty-Seib, 2008; Servaty-Seib & Burleson, 2007). Several additional graduate students subsequently joined our research team (including Jennie Gill, Lisa Hanasono, and Jennifer McCullough), and we continue to analyze and report the data we have collected. Moreover, as I complete writing this chapter in spring 2008, both Graham and Jessica are engaged in dissertation projects focused on further refining and testing aspects of our model (Bodie, 2008; Rack, 2008). I next present the current version of our theory and describe some of our tests of it.

A Dual-Process Theory of Supportive Message Processing and Outcomes

The Theory

We have yet to present a formal statement of our theory, though we plan to do so in the near future (Burleson & Bodie, 2008). Elements of our theory are currently scattered in several different papers; thus, I abstract from those in describing our most recent thinking. Figure 8.1 presents a diagram (taken from Bodie & Burleson, 2008) that displays critical elements of our theory and how we think these elements may be connected.

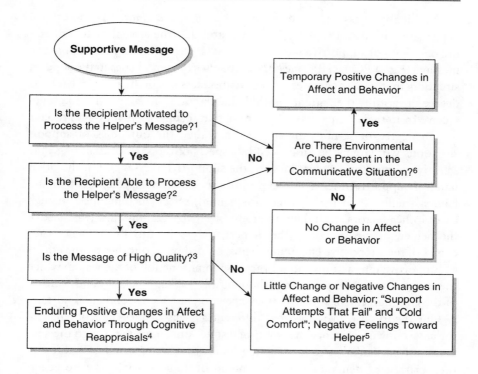

Figure 8.1   A Dual-Process Model for the Processing and Outcomes of
Supportive Messages

Source: Bodie and Burleson (2008).

Notes:

1. Motivation to process supportive messages is influenced by both situational factors (e.g., severity of problem, timing of message, message content) and individual-difference factors (e.g., perceived support availability, attachment style, affiliative need, locus of control).

2. Ability to process supportive messages is influenced by both situational factors (e.g., presence/absence of attention distracters) and individual-difference factors (e.g., age, cognitive complexity, communicative competence).

3. Quality of supportive messages is influenced by factors such as the explicit statement of helping intentions, verbal person centeredness, facework or politeness, and nonverbal immediacy, among others.

4. Mechanisms through which cognitive reappraisals effect enduring positive changes in affect and behavior are described by Burleson and Goldsmith (1998).

5. The harmful consequences of poor quality supportive messages that receive thoughtful processing are detailed in Burleson (2003a).

6. Environmental cues that can activate low elaboration affect change mechanisms include sex and attractiveness of the helper and type of the relationship between the helper and recipient.

Our dual-process theory maintains that *affective change* is the critical dependent variable in support contexts,[2] and that the crucial factors affecting outcomes of supportive interactions are (a) the content of the supportive message (e.g., LPC vs. HPC messages), (b) environmental cues in the support situation that can trigger responses to the message or helper, and (c) the degree of scrutiny (i.e., attention, thought, elaboration) supportive messages receive from their recipients. We propose that if supportive messages receive a high degree of scrutiny from recipients, then the outcomes of support situations will largely be influenced by aspects of message content (e.g., the sensitivity or person centeredness of the supportive message). On the other hand, if supportive messages receive little scrutiny, message content should have a smaller (and perhaps inconsequential) effect on outcomes; in such cases, other factors, including a variety of environmental cues (e.g., sex of the helper, attractiveness of the helper), may substantially influence outcomes of the supportive encounter. Thus, according to our theory, the effects of supportive interactions should vary as a joint function of the way in which these interactions are processed (thoughtfully vs. superficially) and features of the communicative situation (message content vs. environmental cues).

Our theory also proposes that different aspects of message content and the environment influence the emotional states of recipients through the activation of particular affect change mechanisms. These mechanisms differ in their processing demands (i.e., the amount of thinking each takes to generate some degree of affect change), as well as in the magnitude, speed, and stability of the changes they produce. For example, shifting the recipient's attention away from the troubling situation to something more pleasant (which might be accomplished through a variety of message features and/or environmental cues) may quickly and easily produce moderate to substantial changes in the feelings and behaviors of a distressed recipient. However, these changes are likely to be temporary, especially in the case of serious upsets; refocusing attention does nothing to alter the fundamental cause of emotional distress (a person's appraisals of a problematic situation), so a recipient's attention is likely to return the situation, regenerating the emotional upset (Nolen-Hoeksema & Morrow, 1993). In contrast, prompting reappraisals of the troubling situation through HPC messages is cognitively more demanding and may yield changes in emotions and behaviors rather slowly, but these changes are likely to be large and lasting once achieved since the underlying cause of the upset (the recipient's appraisals) has been modified (Donnelly & Murray, 1991).

Our theory also identifies numerous factors that influence the recipient's ability and motivation to process supportive messages (for a review of these, see Bodie & Burleson, 2008). Both aspects of the person (i.e., the individual differences) and the context (i.e., the situational factors) likely influence the capacity (ability) to process message content in a given situation and the desire and/or willingness (motivation) to process that content.

We recognize that our theory needs a good deal more conceptual work (more about this in the conclusion to this chapter). But in addition to generating refinements in theory through additional conceptual analyses, we believe that researchers can develop theory through empirical efforts designed to test aspects of the theory. Thus, I discuss some of our recent empirical studies next.

Testing Our Dual-Process Theory of Supportive Message Outcomes

As I hope is apparent, our theory is capable of generating numerous predictions about the processing and effects of supportive messages. In our initial empirical work, we focused on directly testing hypotheses about how the ability and motivation to process supportive messages influence some outcomes of these messages. We started here since our theory clearly predicts that supportive messages should have different outcomes as a function of the degree of processing they receive; if these predictions aren't supported, then there would be serious doubt about the theory as a whole.

We recently conducted two somewhat similar studies that focused on how factors that are supposed to influence processing ability and motivation affected people's evaluations of supportive messages.[3] One study examined recently bereaved adults' responses to grief management messages (Burleson et al., 2007). Participants in this study had experienced the death of someone personally known to them in the previous 2 years; they answered a brief questionnaire about that loss and the degree of upset they experienced. They then listed their thoughts about that situation; thought listing is a common way of measuring degree or depth of processing (see Cacioppo & Petty, 1981). Participants next evaluated the helpfulness of 64 different messages that are often used by people when seeking to comfort the bereaved; these messages were subsequently classified as exhibiting a low, moderate, or high level of person centeredness. The participants also completed measures of several cognitive abilities and personality traits.

A second study examined college students' evaluations of comforting messages that might be used by peers to help them cope with one of several upsetting problems (Burleson et al., 2008). Participants in this study received a scenario that described either a mildly severe problem (e.g., receiving a $20 parking ticket) or a moderately severe problem (e.g., getting one's car "booted" and having to pay $350 in fines and fees to get the car released). After having time to read and consider this situation, participants were asked to list their thoughts about it and to indicate how upsetting they found the situation. Participants were then asked to imagine they ran into a peer helper (either a male or female acquaintance) with whom they discussed the upsetting situation; they subsequently read and evaluated the helpfulness of six different messages that this helper might use "to make you feel better." These messages varied in level of person centeredness (2 low, 2 moderate, and 2 high). Again, participants also completed measures of several cognitive abilities and personality traits.

Both studies examined how message evaluations were influenced by *interpersonal cognitive complexity* (an individual difference that should influence the ability to process supportive messages) and degree of emotional upset (a situational factor that should influence the motivation to process supportive messages). Measures of cognitive complexity essentially tap social information processing capacity (Burleson et al., 2008; Burleson & Caplan, 1998); thus, if highly complex people are better able to process supportive messages, they should distinguish more sharply among messages that vary in person centeredness than less complex people. Because emotional distress is unpleasant, people experiencing greater distress should be more motivated than those experiencing less distress to reduce their degree of upset, and therefore may give greater attention to the content of helpers' supportive messages. Thus, if more upset people are more motivated to process supportive messages, they should distinguish more sharply among messages that vary in person centeredness than less upset people.

Both studies found support for the predicted effects of cognitive complexity and emotional upset on message evaluations. That is, in both studies, people who were cognitively complex and relatively upset discriminated more sharply between LPC and HPC messages in their evaluations of the helpfulness of these messages. Moreover, there was some indication that people who were *both* cognitively complex *and* comparatively upset discriminated the most sharply between LPC and HPC messages in their helpfulness ratings. In other words, and just as our theory predicts, the people who were both able and motivated to scrutinize supportive messages evaluated these messages more critically, judging LPC messages as less helpful and HPC messages as more helpful than people with lesser levels of ability and motivation. In addition, our studies found that the number of thoughts that people had about the upsetting situation, which presumably measures extent of processing, (a) was positively associated with the measures of cognitive complexity and emotional upset and (b) partially mediated the effects of the ability and motivation factors on message evaluations. These latter findings underscore that cognitive complexity and emotional upset partially influence message evaluations by influencing the degree of scrutiny those messages receive.

These studies obtained several other interesting findings. For example, in both studies there was evidence that very high levels of emotional upset undermined the ability to carefully process supportive messages. This finding is theoretically interesting because it suggests that a single variable (emotional upset) can, at different levels, both positively influence processing motivation and negatively influence processing ability; dual-process theories often emphasize that a particular variable can serve multiple roles with respect to message outcomes (see Petty & Wegener, 1998). This finding is pragmatically important in suggesting that even the most helpful and sensitive supportive messages (i.e., HPC strategies) will have suboptimal outcomes for recipients suffering from extreme upset; thus, helpers should probably seek to reduce the disruptively high upset of these recipients, perhaps through repeatedly offering simple condolences and expressions of sympathy (Greenberg, Rice, & Elliott, 1993), before using HPC messages.

Perhaps even more interesting, our comforting study found that when the motivation to process was low (due to low emotional upset), an aspect of the environment—sex of helper—influenced message evaluations. Specifically, we found that when processing motivation was low, male participants evaluated comforting messages attributed to female sources as more helpful than when those same messages were attributed to male sources. However, when participants were more motivated to scrutinize messages to reduce a somewhat greater degree of assumed upset, the effect for sex of helper disappeared. We interpret these results as indicating that our male participants used a "women provide good support" heuristic in evaluating messages when the motivation to scrutinize message content was low; women may be less inclined to use this heuristic than men since they appear to be both more motivated and able to process supportive messages than men (see Bodie & Burleson, 2008).

Conclusion

We are excited about our dual-process theory of supportive message processing and outcomes. This framework appears capable of explaining both variations and consistencies in the effects of supportive messages, doing so in a way that informs both theory and practice. Our theory allows us to explain parsimoniously most existing findings about factors moderating the effects of supportive messages and generates a host of new predictions that can be examined in empirical research. Our theory also holds considerable pragmatic potential; it provides an empirically sound basis for prescribing the types of support strategies to be used on various occasions with various recipients.

We have made some progress in specifying each of the major elements of our theory, but much work remains to be done in this regard. In particular, we need to give a great deal more attention to detailing the nature and operation of what we term *the social mechanisms of affect change,* the underlying processes through which message content and environmental cues promote modifications in the feelings and behaviors of support recipients. There surely are a host of such mechanisms, and we have only begun to identify them and how they work. Furthermore, research needs to determine the specific aspects of message content or the environment that typically activate a particular mechanism (or set of mechanisms).

Much more thinking is needed about the aspects of supportive interaction environments (i.e., cues) that can elicit changes in the thoughts, feelings, and behaviors of support recipients, especially when processing motivation and/or ability are low. In addition, research needs to determine whether message content and environmental cues can jointly influence the outcomes of supportive interactions and, if so, just how content and cues can work cooperatively or antagonistically. As some persuasion researchers suggest (e.g., Todorov, Chaiken, & Henderson, 2002), we suspect that cues can add to the effects of message content on some occasions, be overridden by message content on other occasions, and bias the impact of message content on still other occasions. But these suspicions need to be formulated precisely and then subjected to testing.

Another critical matter that requires additional conceptual and empirical work pertains to the fundamental nature of "elaboration" or "information processing" in the context of supportive situations. Exactly what is it that people do when they elaborate on (think about) supportive messages, what are the most important aspects of the elaboration concept that must be captured in a theory, and what are the most reliable and valid measures of elaboration with respect to supportive interactions? Conversely, what is the specific nature of low elaboration in support situations? This latter question is particularly important because, unlike persuasion contexts, all support contexts will have some relevance to the recipients of supportive efforts; after all, it is the helper's perception that the recipient is upset and needs assistance that prompts supportive efforts. This suggests that, in support situations, message recipients will almost always have *some* motivation to attend to a helper's supportive efforts. Thus, "low elaboration" processing in support situations may be more active and involved than in persuasion situations, and this difference in what counts as *relatively* low elaboration may have important implications for the processing and outcomes of both environmental cues and message content. In particular, our two studies found that message quality (i.e., message person centeredness) had a strong effect even for participants who had lower degrees of processing motivation and ability—just not as strong an effect as for participants who had higher degrees of processing motivation and ability. So the nature and consequences of low elaboration processing in support situations needs a good deal more conceptual and empirical analysis.

The results of our two recent studies testing hypotheses derived from our dual-process theory are encouraging; these studies show that both message content and environmental cues affect outcomes of supportive communication in predicted ways under various processing conditions. Of course, our studies also exhibit several limitations, including small effect sizes for many of the variables examined; these small effects may stem from the use of assessments based on recall (the bereavement study) or projection (the comforting study). I believe that we can learn a lot from people's recollections of what they found helpful in the past (the bereavement study), as well as from people's projections of what they think would be helpful in certain situations, were they to occur (the comforting study); previous research (Burleson & Samter, 1985; Jones, 2004) has found that these recollections and projections closely correspond with what actually helps people feel better. Still, examining recollections and projections is not the same as finding out what actually helps people feel better when they experience upsetting emotions as a result of some stressor.

Thus, our theory needs to be tested and refined through studies that examine how message quality, environmental cues, and factors that influence message processing jointly influence people's emotional states in "real-world" situations, both immediately and over time. We also need to conduct research that enables us to examine the processes (i.e., the affect change mechanisms) through which message content and/or environmental cues bring about emotional change, as well as the magnitude and stability of these changes. As a matter of fact, Graham Bodie is currently conducting a pair of studies for his dissertation research that address just these issues (Bodie, 2008).

In sum, the two studies we have thus far conducted leave a host of important questions unanswered; clearly, these studies need to be replicated and extended by research that examines other variables through more realistic and engaging designs. Still, we believe that our results to date suggest that a comprehensive dual-process approach to supportive communication can be developed and will have important insights for both theorists and practitioners.

Notes

1. One exciting additional implication of this developing theory was the insight that explaining variations in responses to comforting messages requires a much more general explanation of how people process and respond to supportive communication.

2. Our theory also provides analyses of several other dependent variables that are often of interest in studies of social support and supportive communication, including aspects of well-being such as stress, physical health, mental health, coping behavior, and relationship satisfaction and stability. In the context of research on emotional support, all these additional outcomes are generally viewed as influenced by affect change, which is why we regard affect change as the critical variable in studies of emotional support.

3. Petty and Wegener (1998, p. 328) observe that "perhaps the most popular procedure . . . to gauge the extent of message processing" involves varying the quality of experimental messages and then assessing the size of the message quality effect on dependent variables; larger message effects signal more extensive processing. Thus, in research on supportive messages, larger effects for the factor of person centeredness (i.e., message quality) on evaluations of message helpfulness signal more extensive processing of those messages.

References

Bodie, G. D. (2008). *Explication and tests of a dual-process theory of supportive message outcomes.* Unpublished doctoral dissertation, Purdue University, West Lafayette, IN.

Bodie, G. D., & Burleson, B. R. (2008). Explaining variations in the effects of supportive messages: A dual-process framework. In C. Beck (Ed.), *Communication yearbook 32* (pp. 354–398). New York: Routledge.

Burleson, B. R. (1982). The development of comforting communication skills in childhood and adolescence. *Child Development, 53,* 1578–1588.

Burleson, B. R. (1985). The production of comforting messages: Social-cognitive foundations. *Journal of Language and Social Psychology, 4,* 253–273.

Burleson, B. R. (1994). Comforting messages: Features, functions, and outcomes. In J. A. Daly & J. M. Wiemann (Eds.), *Strategic interpersonal communication* (pp. 135–161). Hillsdale, NJ: Erlbaum.

Burleson, B. R. (2003a). Emotional support skills. In J. O. Greene & B. R. Burleson (Eds.), *Handbook of communication and social interaction skills* (pp. 551–594). Mahwah, NJ: Erlbaum.

Burleson, B. R. (2003b). The experience and effects of emotional support: What the study of cultural and gender differences can tell us about close relationships, emotion, and interpersonal communication. *Personal Relationships, 10,* 1–23.

Burleson, B. R. (2007). Constructivism: A general theory of communication skill. In B. B. Whaley & W. Samter (Eds.), *Explaining communication: Contemporary theories and exemplars* (pp. 105–128). Mahwah, NJ: Erlbaum.

Burleson, B. R. (2008). What counts as effective emotional support? Explorations of individual and situation differences. In M. T. Motley (Ed.), *Studies in applied interpersonal communication* (pp. 207–227). Thousand Oaks, CA: Sage.

Burleson, B. R., & Bodie, G. D. (2008). *A dual-process theory of supportive message outcomes.* Manuscript in preparation.

Burleson, B. R., Bodie, G. D., Rack, J. J., Holmstrom, A. J., Hanasono, L., & Gill, J. N. (2007, November). *Good grief: Testing a dual-process model of responses to grief-management messages.* Paper presented at the annual meeting of the National Communication Association, Chicago.

Burleson, B. R., & Caplan, S. E. (1998). Cognitive complexity. In J. C. McCroskey, J. A. Daly, M. M. Martin, & M. J. Beatty (Eds.), *Communication and personality: Trait perspectives* (pp. 230–286). Cresskill, NJ: Hampton Press.

Burleson, B. R., & Goldsmith, D. J. (1998). How the comforting process works: Alleviating emotional distress through conversationally induced reappraisals. In P. A. Andersen & L. K. Guerrero (Eds.), *Handbook of communication and emotion: Research, theory, applications, and contexts* (pp. 245–280). San Diego, CA: Academic Press.

Burleson, B. R., & MacGeorge, E. L. (2002). Supportive communication. In M. L. Knapp & J. A. Daly (Eds.), *Handbook of interpersonal communication* (3rd ed., pp. 374–424). Thousand Oaks, CA: Sage.

Burleson, B. R., McCullough, J. D., Bodie, G. D., Rack, J. J., Holmstrom, A. J., Hanasono, L. K., et al. (2008). *It's how you think about it: Effects of ability and motivation on recipient processing of and responses to comforting messages.* Paper presented at the annual meeting of the International Communication Association, Montreal, Quebec, Canada.

Burleson, B. R., & Mortenson, S. R. (2003). Explaining cultural differences in evaluations of emotional support behaviors: Exploring the mediating influences of value systems and interaction goals. *Communication Research, 30,* 113–146.

Burleson, B. R., & Samter, W. (1985). Consistencies in theoretical and naive evaluations of comforting messages. *Communication Monographs, 52,* 103–123.

Burleson, B. R., Samter, W., Jones, S. M., Kunkel, A. W., Holmstrom, A. J., Mortenson, S. T., et al. (2005). Which comforting messages *really* work best? A different perspective on Lemieux and Tighe's "receiver perspective." *Communication Research Reports, 22,* 87–100.

Cacioppo, J. T., & Petty, R. E. (1981). Social psychological procedures for cognitive response assessment: The thought-listing technique. In T. V. Merluzzi, C. R. Glass, & M. Genest (Eds.), *Cognitive assessment* (pp. 309–342). New York: Guilford Press.

Chaiken, S. (1980). Heuristic versus systematic information processing and the use of source versus message cues in persuasion. *Journal of Personality and Social Psychology, 39,* 752–766.

Clark, R. A., Pierce, A. J., Finn, K., Hsu, K., Toosley, A., & Williams, L. (1998). The impact of alternative approaches to comforting, closeness of relationship, and gender on multiple measures of effectiveness. *Communication Studies, 49,* 224–239.

Clinton, B. L., & Hancock, G. R. (1991). The development of an understanding of comforting messages. *Communication Reports, 4,* 54–63.

Coopman, S. Z. (1997). Personal constructs and communication in interpersonal and organizational contexts. In G. Neimeyer & R. Neimeyer (Eds.), *Advances in personal construct psychology* (Vol. 4, pp. 101–147). Greenwich, CT: JAI Press.

Cutrona, C. E. (1990). Stress and social support: In search of optimal matching. *Journal of Social and Clinical Psychology, 9*, 3–14.

Delia, J. G., O'Keefe, B. J., & O'Keefe, D. J. (1982). The constructivist approach to communication. In F. E. X. Dance (Ed.), *Human communication theory: Comparative essays* (pp. 147–191). New York: Harper & Row.

Donnelly, D. A., & Murray, E. J. (1991). Cognitive and emotional changes in written essays and therapy interviews. *Journal of Social and Clinical Psychology, 10*, 334–350.

Dougall, A. L., & Baum, A. (2001). Stress, health, and illness. In A. Baum, T. A. Revenson, & J. E. Singer (Eds.), *Handbook of health psychology* (pp. 321–337). Mahwah, NJ: Erlbaum.

Goldsmith, D. J. (2004). *Communicating social support.* New York: Cambridge University Press.

Greenberg, L. S., Rice, L. N., & Elliott, R. (1993). *Facilitating emotional change: The moment-by-moment process.* New York: Guilford Press.

Greene, J. O. (Ed.). (1997). *Message production: Advances in communication theory.* Mahwah, NJ: Erlbaum.

Greene, J. O., & Burleson, B. R. (Eds.). (2003). *Handbook of communication and social interaction skills.* Mahwah, NJ: Erlbaum.

Jones, S. M. (2004). Putting the person into person-centered and immediate emotional support: Emotional change and perceived helper competence as outcomes of comforting in helping situations. *Communication Research, 31*, 338–360.

Jones, S. M. (2005). Attachment style differences and similarities in evaluations of affectively oriented communication skills and person-centered comforting messages. *Western Journal of Communication, 69*, 233–249.

Jones, S. M., & Burleson, B. R. (1997). The impact of situational variables on helpers' perceptions of comforting messages: An attributional analysis. *Communication Research, 24*, 530–555.

Jones, S. M., & Wirtz, J. (2006). How *does* the comforting process work? An empirical test of an appraisal-based model of comforting. *Human Communication Research, 32*, 217–243.

Kunkel, A. W., & Burleson, B. R. (1999). Assessing explanations for sex differences in emotional support: A test of the different cultures and skill specialization accounts. *Human Communication Research, 25*, 307–340.

Lakey, B., & Cohen, S. (2000). Social support theory and measurement. In S. Cohen, L. G. Underwood, & B. H. Gottlieb (Eds.), *Social support measurement and intervention* (pp. 29–52). New York: Oxford University Press.

Lazarus, R. S. (1991). *Emotion and adaptation.* New York: Oxford University Press.

MacGeorge, E. L., Graves, A. R., Feng, B., Gillihan, S. J., & Burleson, B. R. (2004). The myth of gender cultures: Similarities outweigh differences in men's and women's provision of and responses to supportive communication. *Sex Roles, 50*, 143–175.

Nolen-Hoeksema, S., & Morrow, J. (1993). Effects of rumination and distraction on naturally occurring depressed mood. *Cognition and Emotion, 7,* 561–570.

Petty, R. E., & Cacioppo, J. T. (1986). *Communication and persuasion: Central and peripheral routes to attitude change.* New York: Springer.

Petty, R. E., & Wegener, D. T. (1998). Attitude change: Multiple roles for persuasion variables. In D. Gilbert, S. Fiske, & G. Lindzey (Eds.), *The handbook of social psychology* (4th ed., pp. 323–390). New York: McGraw-Hill.

Rack, J. J. (2008). *Losses associated with grief and the evaluation of grief management messages.* Manuscript in preparation.

Rack, J. J., Burleson, B. R., Bodie, G. D., Holmstrom, A. J., & Servaty-Seib, H. L. (2008). Bereaved adults' evaluations of grief management messages: Effects of message person centeredness, recipient individual differences, and contextual factors. *Death Studies, 32,* 399–427.

Rogers, C. R. (1975). Empathic: An unappreciated way of being. *Counseling Psychologist, 5*(2), 2–10.

Servaty-Seib, H. L., & Burleson, B. R. (2007). Bereaved adolescents' evaluations of the helpfulness of support-intended statements: Associations with person centeredness and demographic, personality, and contextual factors. *Journal of Social and Personal Relationships, 24,* 207–223.

Thoits, P. A. (1986). Social support as coping assistance. *Journal of Counseling and Clinical Psychology, 54,* 416–423.

Todorov, A., Chaiken, S., & Henderson, M. D. (2002). The heuristic-systematic model of social information processing. In J. P. Dillard & M. Pfau (Eds.), *The persuasion handbook: Developments in theory and practice* (pp. 195–211). Thousand Oaks, CA: Sage.

Uno, D., Uchino, B. N., & Smith, T. W. (2002). Relationship quality moderates the effect of social support given by close friends on cardiovascular reactivity in women. *International Journal of Behavioral Medicine, 9,* 243–262.

Wills, T. A., & Fegan, M. F. (2001). Social networks and social support. In A. Baum, T. A. Revenson, & J. E. Singer (Eds.), *Handbook of health psychology* (pp. 209–234). Mahwah, NJ: Erlbaum.

9

Toward a Communication Theory of the Demand/Withdraw Pattern of Interaction in Interpersonal Relationships

John P. Caughlin

Allison M. Scott

D emand/withdraw is a pattern of communication in which one person complains or nags, while the relational partner avoids. It is usually thought of as occurring within a particular conflict episode, but demand/ withdraw also refers to repeated encounters in which one person raises an issue and the other physically leaves (see, e.g., Christensen & Heavey, 1993). In this chapter, we describe the scholarly roots of the construct, outline some of the major outcomes associated with demand/withdraw, and summarize the most prominent theoretical explanations for why demand/withdraw occurs. We also discuss our research program on demand/withdraw. Because this research program has involved a number of different collaborators, phrases like "our research" refer to the entire collective of researchers, not just the authors of this chapter. We argue that a multiple goals perspective of communication can provide a useful model for understanding demand/withdraw. We conclude with a discussion of how this rich framework can inform future research.

Scholarly Roots of the Construct

The stereotype of a demanding wife and withdrawn husband has persisted since the earliest systematic research on marriage. Terman, Buttenwieser, Ferguson, Johnson, and Wilson (1938), for example, reported that the most common marital grievance among husbands was a nagging wife. Terman et al. also suggested that unhappy husbands often avoid their partner by being "the gadabout rather than the stay-at-home type" (p. 164). Since Terman, numerous marital therapists have described patterns similar to demand/withdraw in maladjusted marriages (e.g., Fogarty, 1976; Napier, 1978). Since 1990, the number of systematic studies of demand/withdraw has increased. This heightened interest was inspired largely by Christensen (1988), who developed the two primary ways in which demand/withdraw has been assessed. First, Christensen's Communication Patterns Questionnaire (Christensen & Heavey, 1993) self-report measure assesses individuals' behaviors simultaneously (e.g., "Wife nags and demands while husband withdraws, becomes silent, or refuses to discuss the matter further"). The other common measure of demand/withdraw involves observers making global ratings of spouses' demanding and withdrawing behaviors during sample conversations (Christensen & Heavey, 1993).

Outcomes Associated
With Demand/Withdraw

In general, demand/withdraw is related to a variety of undesirable outcomes. Demand/withdraw is associated with concurrent marital dissatisfaction (see, e.g., Caughlin & Huston, 2002; Heavey, Layne, & Christensen, 1993), it predicts declines in marital satisfaction over time (Heavey, Christensen, & Malamuth, 1995), and it can portend divorce (Gottman & Levenson, 2000). Additionally, demand/withdraw is associated with physical abuse (Feldman & Ridley, 2000) as well as raised cortisol levels during conflict (Heffner et al., 2006), and couples high in demand/withdraw appear prone to depression (Byrne, Carr, & Clark, 2004).

Moreover, the correlates of demand/withdraw in marriage are not confined to the spouses. Noller, Feeney, Sheehan, and Peterson (2000) found that demand/withdraw between parents is associated with poor conflict management between parents and adolescents, suggesting that demand/withdraw between parents may adversely affect the parent-child relationship. Also, Afifi and Schrodt's (2003) findings suggest that demand/withdraw between divorced parents may be a stronger predictor of children's unhappiness than the divorce itself.

While most research on demand/withdraw has examined the pattern in marriage, demand/withdraw is also important in other relationships. Malis and Roloff (2006), for example, found that demand/withdraw in dating relationships is related to stress, intrusive thoughts, and hyperarousal. In a study of parent-adolescent dyads, we found that demand/withdraw is associated with low relational satisfaction, low self-esteem, and high adolescent drug use (Caughlin & Malis, 2004a, 2004b).

Explanations of Demand/Withdraw

Given the important outcomes associated with demand/withdraw, it is not surprising that scholars have been interested in explaining why demand/withdraw happens. There are a number of different theoretical models of demand/withdraw (for a review, see Eldridge & Christensen, 2002). While there are variations on the extant models, the majority of explanations focus on explaining why one person takes the role of demander and the other takes the role of withdrawer. In marriage, such explanations usually center on the tendency of wives to demand and husbands to withdraw (Christensen & Shenk, 1991). For example, the *gender difference perspective* (Eldridge & Christensen, 2002) suggests that stable differences between men and women explain why wife-demand/husband-withdraw (WDHW) occurs more than husband-demand/wife-withdraw (HDWW). Some scholars, for instance, have proposed that women are socialized to be more oriented toward relationships than are men (Napier, 1978).

Proponents of the *social structure perspective* suggest that the behavioral differences between men and women can be attributed to the relative power in relationships (Vogel & Karney, 2002). According to this perspective, men generally have more power and status than do women in North American culture, and this power discrepancy leads relationships to be arranged to comport more with men's preferences than with women's (Klein & Johnson, 1997). Such arrangements are thought to compel wives to seek changes in the relationship by demanding, whereas husbands seek to maintain the favorable status quo by avoiding issues.

The *conflict structure perspective* suggests that individuals' positions regarding specific conflict issues influence whether they tend to demand or withdraw. When spouses desire to change their partner, they are more likely to demand, and when spouses favor the status quo, they are more likely to withdraw (Eldridge & Christensen, 2002). Experimental studies that manipulate the topic of discussion generally support this view. Indeed, when couples discuss issues about which husbands want change and wives do not, the usual pattern of WDHW occurring more frequently than HDWW is not evident (Heavey et al., 1993).

Our Research on Demand/Withdraw

Our earliest research on demand/withdraw (Caughlin & Vangelisti, 1999) was influenced by the social structure and conflict structure perspectives. In this study, we examined the connection between spouses' desire for change on common conflict issues and their demanding and withdrawing behaviors. One difference between our study and previous studies was that, rather than picking topics so that one spouse wanted change and the other wanted to maintain the status quo, we had spouses discuss a standardized list of topics; thus, the extent to which spouses desired change varied considerably across couples—not just within dyads. The most interesting finding was that both spouses' desire for change was positively related to HDWW and WDHW. That is, individuals' desire for change was not only associated with their individual behavior, it was associated with the amount of demand/withdraw that the couple engaged in.

We also found in that first study that HDWW and WDHW were positively correlated within couples. We later confirmed this correlation in a separate sample of married couples (Caughlin & Huston, 2002). Also, our research on demand/withdraw in parent-adolescent dyads (Caughlin & Malis, 2004a) indicated a positive association between parent-demand/adolescent-withdraw (PDAW) and adolescent-demand/parent-withdraw (ADPW). Such findings suggest that some dyads develop a style in which individuals alternate in the demanding role but neither listens when the other demands. Note how such findings are not easily explained by previous perspectives of demand/withdraw, which focus on predicting which roles husbands and wives enact. That is, previous explanations were missing an important question: Why do some dyads engage in demand/withdraw more than others?

Obviously, our initial work on desire for change provided a partial answer to this question, but there was clearly more involved. Thus, we conducted two studies focusing on an *individual differences perspective* (Caughlin & Huston, 2006; Caughlin & Vangelisti, 2000). There had been previous attempts to link individual differences with demand/withdraw, but all of them involved what we call *self-influence models,* which posit that individuals' attributes primarily affect their own behavior (Caughlin & Vangelisti, 2000). For example, the gender differences perspective of demand/withdraw suggests that being male (and being socialized to desire independence in relationships) predisposes one to withdraw, and being female (and desiring relational closeness) predisposes one to demand. We pointed out that individual differences may shape the overall quality of relationships, and we labeled this possibility *relationship-influence models*. Consistent with this possibility, we found that spouses who are high in neuroticism, low in agreeableness, and low in conscientiousness are more likely than other spouses to have frequent HDWW and WDHW in their marriages (Caughlin & Huston, 2006; Caughlin & Vangelisti, 2000).

Like the previous findings showing that HDWW and WDHW are positively related within dyads, our research on relationship-influence models departed significantly from early work on demand/withdraw. We did find some similarities with previous research; for example, we found that demand/withdraw was inversely correlated with concurrent marital satisfaction (Caughlin, 2002; Caughlin & Huston, 2002). However, like a small number of other studies, we found that among some couples, demand/withdraw actually seemed to predict increases in satisfaction over time. On the surface, this finding appears to contradict other research suggesting that demand/withdraw foreshadows negative outcomes like divorce (Gottman & Levenson, 2000), but we proposed that the seemingly disparate findings could be explained if there are actually multiple distinct ways of engaging in demand/withdraw (Caughlin, 2002).

To this point, we had some good indications that the extant perspectives for explaining demand/withdraw were not entirely adequate. For various reasons, however, it was difficult to fully evaluate the extant models. One challenge in evaluating previous research on demand/withdraw in marriage is that gender and power are confounded in marital relationships. The social structure and gender differences explanations both aimed at explaining why WDHW occurred more frequently than did HDWW, but it is impossible to know whether this finding is better explained by inherent differences between sexes or power differences between men and women. Because one cannot assign men and women randomly to different levels of normative power, one cannot really separate those two explanations in intact marriages.

This problem was one reason we studied demand/withdraw in parent-adolescent dyads (Caughlin & Ramey, 2005). In terms of relative normative power, parents clearly have more than adolescents. Because both parents and adolescents can be either biological sex, examining demand/withdraw in such dyads allowed us to examine whether demanding is really linked to low normative power (as the social structure explanation would suggest) or sex.

The study found a small amount of support for gender differences; for example, mother-demand/adolescent-withdraw occurred slightly more often than did father-demand/adolescent-withdraw. However, there were much bigger effects for family role: Demand/withdraw involving the parent demanding and the adolescent withdrawing was much more common than the reverse pattern. Note that this runs counter to what one would expect if lack of normative power led to demanding. We argued that the social structure's link to normative power is incorrect; who tends to demand and who tends to withdraw has little to do with who is the most normatively powerful person in an objective sense. Instead, because parent-adolescent conflicts typically revolve around the parent trying to change the adolescent's behavior, parents need their child to cooperate to meet their goals. Trying to control the other's behavior, rather than being in a position of relative power, appears to be linked to demanding.

In sum, our research on demand/withdraw has suggested a number of ways in which the explanation of the pattern could be improved or elaborated. We argued that more research needs to examine variation across dyads in demand/withdraw rather than focus only on differences between husbands and wives. We showed that the variation across dyads is linked to the extent to which partners want change and to various individual differences. Moreover, it appears that attempting to control the other person's behavior is a more important predictor of demanding than is one's general level of normative power. Our research also suggested that there likely are multiple ways of engaging in demand/withdraw. Such results imply a level of complexity in demand/withdraw that is not sufficiently captured in previous models (or by existing ways of assessing demand/withdraw). To address this, we propose that a multiple goals perspective of communication provides a useful way of conceptualizing why demand/withdraw occurs.

A Multiple Goals Perspective of Demand/Withdraw

Overview

Much of the demand/withdraw literature implicitly assumes that people's goals during interaction can explain their behaviors; for example, the goal of desiring change is seen as leading to demanding, and wanting to keep the status quo is thought to lead to withdrawing. Many interpersonal communication scholars agree that communication is often aimed at addressing goals (e.g., Dillard, 1990; Wilson, 2002), but communication scholars note that "individuals generally pursue multiple goals simultaneously during their interactions with others" (Berger, 2005, p. 422). There are a number of distinct multiple goals theories, and a thorough discussion of multiple goals perspectives is beyond the scope of the current chapter (for a review, see Wilson & Feng, 2007). Instead, we focus on some common assumptions that are pertinent to explaining demand/withdraw.

Obviously, multiple goals perspectives posit that people attempt to accomplish multiple purposes simultaneously. The number of possible communication goals is infinite, and there are numerous useful ways of classifying goals. One common distinction is between primary and secondary goals (e.g., Dillard, Segrin, & Harden, 1989; Wilson, 2002). The primary goal is a person's main objective (i.e., what motivates the person to act), and it (at least partially) constitutes what that interaction is about. Secondary goals are additional goals that are relevant to the situation; these are often conceptualized as influencing or constraining how primary goals are pursued. Another useful way to classify goals is based on broad types of concerns that are relevant across interactions. Scholars often consider goals such as (a) instrumental goals, which describe the communicator's primary task (e.g., persuasion, support); (b) identity goals, which concern acting in ways that create and maintain desirable images for oneself and other interactants; and (c) relational goals, which describe people's desires pertaining to their relationships (Clark & Delia, 1979).

Unlike explanations of demand/withdraw that equate particular goals with particular behaviors (e.g., desiring change leads to demanding), a multiple goals explanation of demanding and withdrawing behaviors requires consideration of more than a single objective. To illustrate, imagine a scenario in which one person wants change on an issue. As suggested by existing models of demand/withdraw, this desire may impel the person toward raising the issue; thus, the goal of influencing the other to change is a potential primary goal. However, potentially relevant secondary goals could lead the person not to raise the issue. A person fearing relational upheaval might forego raising an issue, or a person worried about seeming dictatorial might censor certain demands.

Even if secondary goals do not prevent a person from raising an issue, they may shape how the issue is raised. Caughlin and Vangelisti (2006) argued that a number of secondary goals could lead a person raising a conflict issue to do so in a positive or integrative way rather than by nagging or demanding. Some secondary goals that could constrain a person from demanding include wanting to maintain a harmonious relationship, wanting to seem like a reasonable or caring individual (i.e., maintaining a positive identity), being sensitive to the potential for nagging to imply that the partner has a poor identity (e.g., an ongoing behavioral flaw), and being sensitive to the partner's needs for autonomy. This list is clearly not exhaustive, but it illustrates that much more goes into demanding behavior than simply wanting change: A person who demands also must be relatively unfettered by numerous potentially relevant secondary concerns.

A similar analysis can be made for avoiding relational issues. The standard accounts of demand/withdraw suggest that wanting to maintain the status quo leads to withdrawal, but withdrawal is not the only option. One could attempt to maintain existing arrangements by discussing the issue, expressing one's feelings about the topic, or using other cooperative conflict tactics, hoping to resolve the issue without sacrificing whatever arrangements are important to the individual. Moreover, withdrawal is not without risks. Extreme cases of withdrawal, such as leaving a conversation entirely, likely would be viewed as ignoring a relational partner's request for change. To the extent that one wishes to be seen as a reasonable member of a relationship, ignoring one's partner could threaten that person's identity as somebody worthy of attention; indeed, Sillars, Canary, and Tafoya (2004) consider leaving during a discussion a "rejecting act" (p. 421).

Our discussion demonstrates that withdrawing can be a potential threat to relevant identity and relational goals. Based on multiple goals perspectives, these threats have at least two important implications for understanding withdrawal during conflict. First, there are likely occasions when a person would like to avoid explicit discussion of an issue but is constrained from outright withdrawal. Second, even if the person attempts to avoid the topic, secondary goals would shape the manner in which that avoidance is enacted. An individual might, for instance, attempt to avoid substantive discussion but do so in a way that appears to engage in the discussion (e.g., by shifting the topic in a way that is coherent with the previous one but departs from the undesired issue).

Another assumption of a multiple goals perspective is that interaction goals change over time (e.g., Waldron, 1997; Wilson, 2002). Fincham and Beach (1999) described how goals can change over the course of a conflict. They noted, for example, that even if a married couple begins a discussion in a constructive manner, the partners sometimes become concerned about who has the more valid perspective, which can introduce identity concerns into discussions about seemingly innocuous topics. Threats to spouses' identity can lead to increased affective intensity (e.g., anger). Consequently, spouses who begin a discussion with no intention of nagging or leaving may eventually be willing to engage in such behaviors in order to address other concerns (e.g., proving who is right). The hurt feelings associated with some conflicts might lead spouses to be less concerned about goals that involve protecting the other's identity or feelings (Caughlin, Scott, & Miller, in press). Thus, changes in goals may lead to demand/withdraw.

Although this discussion is somewhat speculative, it is congruent with some existing findings in related areas. Research on repeated persuasion attempts, for instance, has shown that people typically become less polite and more assertive after being rebuffed (Hample & Dallinger, 1998). This is consistent with the notion that a person wanting change may try nagging if he or she becomes frustrated by initial (less negative) attempts to influence the partner.

The dynamic nature of goals also may be useful for theorizing about how demand/withdraw emerges over time in relationships. Whereas our discussion to this point has focused on particular encounters, the conversational topics relevant to the demand/withdraw pattern are usually not confined to particular episodes (Christensen & Heavey, 1993; Malis & Roloff, 2006). People often discuss the same issues in many episodes, sometimes over the course of years. Given that goals can change even within a particular encounter, they certainly can change over longer periods as well. For example, the evidence that dissatisfaction with a relationship sometimes leads to increased demand/withdraw in subsequent years (Noller, Feeney, Bonnell, & Callan, 1994) suggests that people who are unhappy may become frustrated with trying to engage in conflicts cooperatively.

In sum, the various features of a multiple goals perspective appear to have the potential to address some of the limitations of previous models. One can examine differences in goals across dyads (e.g., comparing husbands to husbands) as well as within dyads (e.g., comparing husbands to wives), which could be used to explain both variations in demand/withdraw across dyads and variations in roles within dyads. Furthermore, a multiple goals perspective does not contradict previous findings. Prior findings about gender differences and other individual differences can easily be conceptualized as influencing conversational goals, which in turn have a more direct influence on individuals' actions during discussions of conflict issues. Moreover, a multiple goals perspective is congruent with the likelihood that there are multiple ways in which demand/withdraw gets enacted; for instance, as outlined above, a multiple goals viewpoint suggests that people probably withdraw in varying ways. At a theoretical level then, a multiple goals perspective is consistent with what is already known about demand/withdraw and offers explanations for aspects of the pattern that are currently not well understood. A logical next step is to see whether a multiple goals perspective can be usefully applied to conversations that exhibit demand/withdraw.

Application

To explore the potential utility of a multiple goals framework for understanding demand/withdraw, we analyzed existing recordings of conflict discussions by married couples (Caughlin & Vangelisti, 1999) and parent-adolescent dyads (Caughlin & Malis, 2004b). In previous research on these data, audiotapes of the conversations were rated for the extent to which they demonstrated demand/withdraw (see original articles for details). The raters received brief training but relied heavily on their cultural understanding of what constitutes demanding and withdrawing behaviors.

For the current chapter, we analyzed conversations that were rated particularly high on at least one form of demand/withdraw. The ratings referred to the entire conversations, which included discussions of multiple topics. In the married dyads, high demand/withdraw was defined as at least one standard deviation above average on HDWW or WDHW (or both). This definition resulted in eight couples who were high in at least one form of demand/withdraw. Through a similar process, we identified seven parent-adolescent dyads that were high in at least one form of demand/withdraw.

Our analysis of the transcripts involved a finer level of assessment than the previous global ratings. As a preliminary step, we inspected the selected transcripts for passages that may have been considered high in demand/withdraw by the raters. Obviously, no conversation was composed entirely of demand/withdraw sequences, so it was necessary to identify excerpts that could explain the high ratings on demand/withdraw. The examples discussed below represent passages that we agreed were likely to have led to the high demand/withdraw ratings.

The initial goal of our analysis was to assess whether the transcripts suggested that a multiple goals perspective was useful for understanding why demand/withdraw occurs. This involved making inferences about the likely purposes or goals of certain utterances. Although such inferences should be made with caution (Dillard, 1997), this procedure was appropriate to our current purposes because our objective was to determine whether a multiple goals framework provides a promising lens for understanding demand/withdraw (rather than to offer definitive claims about specific individuals' goals).

We first examined the transcripts independently. After meeting, we agreed that there were numerous examples of demanding or withdrawing behavior that seemed aimed at attending to multiple goals. This is not to suggest that the individuals were cognizant of these purposes; in fact, like Kellermann (1992), we assume that people often are unaware of their goal-directed behavior in conversation. Regardless of their awareness, much of what participants said was manifestly purposeful and nonrandom. Below, we provide some illustrations of excerpts that evinced multiple goals. Then we discuss two other pertinent features of the data: the evidence that changes in goals may be important to explaining demand/withdraw and the evidence that there are multiple distinct ways of enacting demand/withdraw.

Illustrations of Multiple Goals

There were numerous examples of people appearing to attend to multiple goals. The following excerpt is one that was rated high in HDWW. In it, a married couple discuss affection in their relationship, an issue about which the husband desires some change from his wife (his rating was 4 out of 7 on a desire-for-change measure):

1. *H:* It's just nice to have a little conversation about issues like—

2. *W:* Yeah, but you get so wrapped up and take it all so personally.

3. *H:* Where are you going?

4. *W:* I'm shutting this window.

5. [Pause]

6. *W:* I understand what you are saying, but I really don't see how that has anything to do with this question.

7. *H:* I do, 'cause it's kind of like talking is a way of showing affection and a lot of times we just don't just sit down and talk about stuff that much.

This example includes two actions from the wife that could be conventionally understood as avoidant. First, she appears to physically distance herself from her husband (see Turns 3 and 4). Her shift in attention to the physical environment rather than the conversation would commonly be coded as withdrawal (Sillars et al., 2004). When her husband asks why she is getting up, her account focuses on the window rather than the apparent withdrawal (Turn 4). One interpretation of this is that the wife is attempting to not discuss the issue in a way that would not be viewed as on-record avoidance. This interpretation is consistent with her second avoidant action: commenting on whether the discussion fits with the topic they were asked to discuss for the experiment (Turn 6). Again, this sort of behavior is often coded as withdrawal (Sillars et al., 2004), but it is not explicit withdrawal. Assuming that the wife's actions were aimed at not discussing the issue further, it is useful to consider other ways she could have accomplished this and how that might have changed the meaning. If she had simply said, "I don't want to talk about this," she could have achieved the goal of preventing further discussion, but it would have had very different identity implications than the actions she actually took. Simply refusing to discuss the topic could present an undesirable identity (e.g., as somebody uncooperative or unconcerned about her partner). Instead, comments suggesting that she intends to make sure they are following the directions seem geared toward casting her as a responsible research participant (and not somebody who is being uncooperative). That is, the particular avoidant behaviors the wife uses appear influenced by identity goals.

There are other similar examples. In one dyad that was rated high in ADPW, the adolescent girl indicated that issues surrounding dating were very salient in her relationship with her father. The following excerpt is from their discussion of dating:

1. *A:* So you would let me go on a date by myself?

2. *P:* It's group—

3. *A:* You know I've gone on dates by myself before.

4. *P:* It's group, group therapy.

5. *A:* Group therapy? What are you talking about? [*Laughs*]

6. *P:* [*Laughs*] Okay. What's the next one? So what else? Is there something else there?

7. *A:* On the sheet?

8. *P:* Let me see that sheet.

By making a joke (Turns 2 and 4) and then asking to see the instructions for the research project (Turn 6), the father manages to avoid discussing the issue in a substantive way while not overtly denying the daughter's request or explicitly refusing to discuss the matter. Again, a plausible explanation of these particular strategies is that the father had relevant identity goals (e.g., not being too authoritarian) and relational goals (e.g., discouraging a heated conflict) that influenced him to enact indirect rather than explicit means of avoidance.

Importance of Changing Goals

Consistent with our contention that the emergence of goals over time may be important, there was evidence that demanding sometimes results from frustration (e.g., from being rebuffed). One wife, for instance, explained that she only tended to "bitch at" her husband after she becomes frustrated. This is consistent with the idea that demanding can result from abandoning certain identity or relational goals after being rebuffed. Also, one husband explicitly argued that what he wanted changed over time. When explaining why he did not want to discuss an issue, he stated, "Well, it's just that I don't want to discuss it now. It doesn't mean I don't want to discuss it over time." It is possible that this is a stalling tactic and the husband never intends to discuss the matter, but this statement suggests that this participant (at least) believes that changes in his desires over time are a viable account. Obviously, the conversations we recorded cannot definitively demonstrate how goals change across conversations (or over the course of a relationship), but there were some indications that it is useful to consider how goals may change over time.

Distinct Types of Demand/Withdraw

Among the conversations rated high in demand/withdraw, we identified four distinct versions of the pattern. This list is not meant to be exhaustive, and it is certainly possible to make even finer distinctions. Our purpose here is not to provide a definitive list of ways of enacting demand/withdraw but, instead, to offer evidence that there are qualitatively different ways of enacting demand/withdraw. The distinctions were partly defined by the apparent attention to goals; for example, as noted above, overt avoidance presents unmitigated risks to certain commonly pursued goals. Thus, demand/withdraw involving one person exiting the conversation (i.e., discuss/exit) would be distinct from the other forms, in which the withdrawal is less direct.

The first demand/withdraw pattern, *discuss/exit,* involves one individual seeking discussion and the other overtly avoiding discussion through physical or communicative exit from the conversation. Even if the person seeking discussion does not explicitly nag, the overt avoidance of the withdrawer casts the relational partner in the role of the demander. Discuss/exit is illustrated in this married couple's discussion about handling disagreements:

1. W: There's been situations in the past where we've had arguments and disagreements and I want to talk about things and you don't. And you'll make me wait sometimes a week before you'll talk about it.

2. H: Well, once I've had a chance to think about it and gather, you know, a battle plan.

3. W: A battle plan almost sounds like you have to get—see, the way I would see it, and I know you're not going to like this, but it's more you need to get your story straight. You got to make sure that every little detail is in place so you don't mess up.

4. H: Okay, next question.

In this example, the husband's communicative exit (Turn 4) casts his wife in the nagging role. One can imagine contexts in which the wife's attempts to discuss this issue (Turns 1 and 3) would seem nonhostile and even analytical, but in the context of the husband's exit, the wife's statements appear accusatory and demanding.

Physical exit is demonstrated in the following interaction between a mother and daughter, which was rated high on ADPW. The discussion begins with the adolescent reading a card that listed the last of three topics the dyad was supposed to discuss:

1. A: Alcohol and drug use among teenagers, number three. Um, I don't know. Where is a good place to start on this one? It's kind of touchy. I mean—

2. P: Well, actually, when it comes right down to it, I think that parents . . .

3. A: Parents what? Come back, Mom!

4. P: Let's back that up.

5. A: Back that up? You can't back that up. You left the room. Don't mess with it. Just say you left the room! You big dork! Now you're going to record the—

6. P: I'm looking for the stop . . .

7. A: What are you doing? Just keep on going, Mom!

After the adolescent's directive to "keep on going" (Turn 7), the recorder was turned off, and we assume that the conversation did not continue. This is a clear example of discuss/exit in which the parent appears to have literally exited. In this case, the parent's withdrawal seems to help define the adolescent's utterances as demanding: The daughter's comments in Turn 1 (e.g., "Where is a good place to start?") are not overtly negative or demanding, but the parent responds as if the comments are something to be avoided. Even a seemingly innocuous introduction of the topic is apparently enough for the parent to respond as if the adolescent is demanding. Obviously, we do not know whether the mother actually perceives this as demanding, but it seems likely that the dyad had discussed this topic before and this influenced the mother's response. This interpretation is consistent with other information we have about this dyad. In their questionnaire responses, the mother reported being a regular smoker (about one pack per day), and the daughter reported that she would very much like to change her mother's behavior regarding smoking (i.e., she scored 7 out of 7 on a desire-for-change item).

In the second form of demand/withdraw, *Socratic question/perfunctory response,* the demander asks a series of questions, and the withdrawer offers an expected response. Although Socratic question/perfunctory response appeared in some interactions between married partners, the form was most salient in discussions between parents and their children:

1. *P:* Who's in charge of you going to bed?

2. *A:* Me.

3. *P:* You. Should you have a bedtime?

4. *A:* Yeah.

5. *P:* That's a good idea. Should get at least, at least 9 hours of sleep?

6. *A:* Probably, yeah.

7. *P:* Okay, what are you going to do to make that happen?

8. *A:* Get to bed on time.

9. *P:* How?

10. *A:* [mumbles]

11. *P:* Well, you haven't been doing it so I don't—

12. *A:* By having all of my stuff that needs to be done.

The parent's first five turns are all questions, which are met with minimal perfunctory responses from the adolescent boy. When the son mumbles instead of giving the expected response (Turn 10), the parent's renewal of her demand (Turn 11) is interrupted by the adolescent giving the obligatory response (Turn 12). At first glance, the adolescent's minimal responses appear cooperative, and indeed brief statements of assent (e.g., "Yeah") are commonly considered cooperative (Sillars et al., 2004). However, such statements are also generally viewed as indirect or not fully engaged (Sillars, 1986; Sillars et al., 2004), which explains why raters would count such responses as withdrawal. The perfunctory responses appear overtly cooperative while at the same time remaining disengaged. That is, the perfunctory responses are consistent with a person who has a goal of avoiding but also has a goal of seeming cooperative (e.g., to maintain an identity as a reasonable child). In short, perfunctory responses to Socratic demands seemed well suited to appeasing demands while ending the discussion quickly.

The third form of demand/withdraw, *complain/deny,* occurs when the demander complains about the relational partner's behavior, and the withdrawer challenges the legitimacy of the complaint. Complain/deny is similar to criticize/defend (see below) in that the demander expresses a desire for the partner's behavior to change, but it differs because rather than explicitly defending oneself, the withdrawer implicitly or explicitly challenges the legitimacy of the complaint. That is, the avoidance takes the form of denying that there is an actual conflict issue. In the context of one spouse insisting that there is a problem, such denials generally are considered avoidant actions (Sillars, 1986). In this example of complain/deny, the husband complains about how his wife plans joint activities (Turns 1 and 3), but the wife implicitly denies that there is a meaningful problem by first suggesting that her husband liked the activity in question (Turn 2) and then claiming that it was an anomalous event (Turn 4).

1. *H:* You brought that up and the idea—and spending the weekend at a bed and breakfast, I wasn't really hot on the idea.

2. *W:* But it turned out to be fun.

3. *H:* Yeah see, you look at the results, but when we plan things, I don't necessarily like planning the things that you like planning. You like planning these cutesy quaint things, like at the bed and breakfast.

4. *W:* You know, the one cutesy thing in how many years that I've known you.

In the fourth form of demand/withdraw, *criticize/defend,* the demander levels a criticism and the withdrawer responds by justifying the criticized behavior. The withdrawer in criticize/defend implicitly recognizes the legitimacy of the criticism, but counters with a defense that is meant to nullify the criticism. This form is illustrated in the excerpt below, in which the husband criticizes his wife's use of pain medicine (Turn 1) and the wife defends her behavior by attributing her use of pain medicine to physicians' instructions for treating her mental illness (Turns 2 and 4).

1. *H:* That's exactly what I used to tell people about drinking whiskey, Julie. "This is for my nerves, this is for my pain."

[Three conversational turns later]

2. *W:* Yeah, but you know what? You're not a manic depressive ADHD kid who had trouble all their life connecting anywhere. I was out of sync with the whole world.

3. *H:* I'm not sure that you had that much of a problem, Julie, really true. I see you differently than you describe yourself.

4. *W:* But I've been sent to doctors all my life and given pills.

The criticize/defend form also is demonstrated in this parent's criticism of her daughter's school performance:

1. *P:* I remember it being a real issue. You had been sick a lot and every teacher I talked to said you were not turning things in.

2. *A:* I was turning things in, I just had seven classes. I did, I had seven classes. How was I going to do it all at once? I couldn't just wake up and be like, "I'm Superwoman," not sleep for 3 days, and do all my homework.

The adolescent defends herself against her mother's criticism by arguing that the situation constrains her ability to change the criticized behavior.

Because defending is not a classic withdrawal behavior, the reader might wonder why criticize/defend counts as demand/withdraw. Indeed, classifications of conflict behaviors typically consider excuses and defenses to be negative forms of engagement, not withdrawal (e.g., Sillars et al., 2004). Yet these conversations were rated high in demand/withdraw, and our reading of the transcripts suggests why. Often, the criticisms were repeated multiple times and appear to involve issues that had been discussed previously. Given the repeated criticisms, the defensive statements seem to convey a plea to be left alone (while simultaneously serving an identity goal by parrying a criticism). Our interpretation is consistent with previous conceptualizations of the demand/withdraw construct, which implicitly subsumes the criticize/defend form. For instance, Christensen's popular measure of demand/withdraw explicitly asks about one partner criticizing, while the other defends (Christensen & Heavey, 1993).

Conclusion

A multiple goals explanation of demand/withdraw provides a more nuanced and complete account of demand/withdraw than previous models. Although future research is needed to confirm some of our ideas, a multiple goals perspective has the potential to explain issues that other perspectives do not address. For example, any model that implies a simple one-to-one connection between a goal (e.g., desiring change, wanting to maintain the status quo) and a communication behavior (e.g., demanding, withdrawing) cannot explain why a person with that goal would not always engage in that behavior. A multiple goals perspective can explain such scenarios; for instance, a person desiring change may forego demanding if he or she is worried that demanding may threaten identity or relational goals.

Moreover, a multiple goals perspective can provide insights into why people may enact demanding and withdrawing in particular ways. Several of the examples discussed above, for instance, involve indirect strategies of avoidance (e.g., talking about the experiment instructions rather than the conflict topic). Clearly, a more direct strategy for avoidance would be to just refuse to discuss the matter. There was also evidence of indirect demanding, as in the example where the adolescent wondered aloud where to start talking about smoking, and the mother appeared to interpret that as nagging. Indirect utterances, of course, are often aimed at pursuing one goal while trying to mitigate the possibility that other objectives will be undermined (Brown & Levinson, 1987). Such examples suggest that individuals' particular constellation of goals in a particular situation do not only predict *whether* they engage in demanding and withdrawing but also *how* they demand or withdraw.

The transcripts also suggested that the broad construct of demand/withdraw encompasses at least four distinguishable types of the pattern. Granted, the data presented here were not sufficient to conclusively prove that these four types of demand/withdraw can be reliably identified as separate patterns. Nevertheless, the distinctions we noted in demand/withdraw were congruent with ones that have previously been made with individual conflict behaviors; for instance, defending and denying are recognizable as distinct behaviors (Sillars et al., 2004). Such consistencies with previous categorization schemes lend credibility to the distinctions made here.

It is also important that the different forms of demand/withdraw appear to function in different ways and that these differences imply different goal configurations. We would expect, for example, that a person willing to engage in the overt avoidance that is part of discuss/exit must be less concerned about appearing cooperative than somebody who makes an apparently cooperative response as part of Socratic questioning/perfunctory response. A more systematic investigation of the goals associated with the different forms of demand/withdraw would be a useful step for future studies.

Presuming that it is possible to create empirical assessments of distinct forms of demand/withdraw, this could provide another avenue for future studies. In previous work (Caughlin, 2002), we argued that some apparently contradictory findings in the demand/withdraw literature may be explained if there is a variety of more specific demand/withdraw patterns, which may be associated with different outcomes. It is plausible that certain forms of demand/withdraw are more harmful to long-term relational well-being than are others.

Finally, we should note that while our analysis of the transcripts was fine-grained relative to previous research on demand/withdraw, it is by no means a microscopic examination of the conversations. Our assessment gave us confidence that there are at least four general ways in which demand/withdraw can be enacted, but clearly much more happened in the conversations than we could analyze in the current chapter. This suggests to us that demand/withdraw researchers may benefit from future collaborations with scholars who are interested in even more microscopic perspectives of interaction.

References

Afifi, T. D., & Schrodt, P. (2003). "Feeling caught" as a mediator of adolescents' and young adults' avoidance and satisfaction with their parents in divorced and non-divorced households. *Communication Monographs, 70,* 142–173.

Berger, C. R. (2005). Interpersonal communication: Theoretical perspectives, future prospects. *Journal of Communication, 55,* 415–447.

Brown, P., & Levinson, S. (1987). *Politeness: Some universals in language usage.* Cambridge, UK: Cambridge University Press.

Byrne, M., Carr, A., & Clark, M. (2004). Power in relationships of women with depression. *Journal of Family Therapy, 26,* 407–429.

Caughlin, J. P. (2002). The demand/withdraw pattern of communication as a predictor of marital satisfaction over time: Unresolved issues and future directions. *Human Communication Research, 28,* 49–85.

Caughlin, J. P., & Huston, T. L. (2002). A contextual analysis of the association between demand/withdraw and marital satisfaction. *Personal Relationships, 9,* 95–119.

Caughlin, J. P., & Huston, T. L. (2006). The affective structure of marriage. In A. L. Vangelisti & D. Perlman (Eds.), *The Cambridge handbook of personal relationships* (pp. 131–155). New York: Cambridge University Press.

Caughlin, J. P., & Malis, R. S. (2004a). Demand/withdraw between parents and adolescents as a correlate of relational satisfaction. *Communication Reports, 17,* 59–71.

Caughlin, J. P., & Malis, R. S. (2004b). Demand/withdraw communication between parents and adolescents: Connections with self-esteem and substance use. *Journal of Social and Personal Relationships, 21,* 125–148.

Caughlin, J. P., & Ramey, M. E. (2005). The demand/withdraw pattern of communication in parent-adolescent dyads. *Personal Relationships, 12,* 337–356.

Caughlin, J. P., Scott, A. M., & Miller, L. E. (in press). Conflict and hurt in close relationships. In A. L. Vangelisti (Ed.), *Feeling hurt in close relationships.* New York: Cambridge University Press.

Caughlin, J. P., & Vangelisti, A. L. (1999). Desire for change in one's partner as a predictor of the demand/withdraw pattern of marital communication. *Communication Monographs, 66,* 66–89.

Caughlin, J. P., & Vangelisti, A. L. (2000). An individual difference explanation of why married couples engage in the demand/withdraw pattern of conflict. *Journal of Social and Personal Relationships, 17,* 523–551.

Caughlin, J. P., & Vangelisti, A. L. (2006). Conflict in dating and marital relationships. In J. G. Oetzel & S. Ting-Toomey (Eds.), *Sage handbook of conflict communication: Integrating theory, research, and practice* (pp. 129–157). Thousand Oaks, CA: Sage.

Christensen, A. (1988). Dysfunctional interaction patterns in couples. In P. Noller & M. A. Fitzpatrick (Eds.), *Perspectives on marital interaction* (pp. 31–52). Philadelphia: Multilingual Matters.

Christensen, A., & Heavey, C. L. (1993). Gender differences in marital conflict: The demand/withdraw interaction pattern. In S. Oskamp & M. Costanzo (Eds.), *Gender issues in contemporary society* (pp. 113–141). Newbury Park, CA: Sage.

Christensen, A., & Shenk, J. L. (1991). Communication, conflict, and psychological distance in nondistressed, clinic, and divorcing couples. *Journal of Consulting and Clinical Psychology, 59,* 458–463.

Clark, R. A., & Delia, J. G. (1979). *Topoi* and rhetorical competence. *Quarterly Journal of Speech, 65,* 187–206.

Dillard, J. P. (1990). A goal-driven model of interpersonal influence. In J. P. Dillard (Ed.), *Seeking compliance: The production of interpersonal influence messages* (pp. 41–56). Scottsdale, AZ: Gorsuch Scarisbrick.

Dillard, J. P. (1997). Explicating the goal construct: Tools for theorists. In J. O. Greene (Ed.), *Message production: Advances in communication theory* (pp. 47–69). Mahwah, NJ: Erlbaum.

Dillard, J. P., Segrin, C., & Harden, J. M. (1989). Primary and secondary goals in the production of interpersonal influence messages. *Communication Monographs, 56,* 19–38.

Eldridge, K. A., & Christensen, A. (2002). Demand-withdraw communication during couple conflict: A review and analysis. In P. Noller & J. A. Feeney (Eds.), *Understanding marriage: Developments in the study of couple interaction* (pp. 289–322). New York: Cambridge University Press.

Feldman, C. M., & Ridley, C. A. (2000). The role of conflict-based communication responses and outcomes in male domestic violence toward female partners. *Journal of Social and Personal Relationships, 17,* 552–573.

Fincham, F. D., & Beach, S. R. H. (1999). Conflict in marriage: Implications for working with couples. *Annual Review of Psychology, 50,* 47–77.

Fogarty, T. F. (1976). Marital crisis. In P. J. Guerin (Ed.), *Family therapy: Theory and practice* (pp. 325–334). New York: Gardner Press.

Gottman, J. M., & Levenson, R. W. (2000). The timing of divorce: Predicting when a couple will divorce over a 14-year period. *Journal of Marriage and the Family, 62,* 737–745.

Hample, D., & Dallinger, J. M. (1998). On the etiology of the rebuff phenomenon: Why are persuasive messages less polite after rebuffs? *Communication Studies, 49,* 305–321.

Heavey, C. L., Christensen, A., & Malamuth, N. M. (1995). The longitudinal impact of demand and withdrawal during marital conflict. *Journal of Consulting and Clinical Psychology, 63,* 797–801.

Heavey, C. L., Layne, C., & Christensen, A. (1993). Gender and conflict structure in marital interaction: A replication and extension. *Journal of Consulting and Clinical Psychology, 61,* 16–27.

Heffner, K. L., Loving, T. J., Kiecolt-Glaser, J. K., Himawan, L. K., Glaser, R., & Malarkey, W. B. (2006). Older spouses' cortisol responses to marital conflict: Associations with demand/withdraw communication patterns. *Journal of Behavioral Medicine, 29,* 317–325.

Kellermann, K. (1992). Communication: Inherently strategic and primarily automatic. *Communication Monographs, 59,* 288–300.

Klein, R. C. A., & Johnson, M. P. (1997). Strategies of couple conflict. In S. Duck (Ed.), *Handbook of personal relationships* (2nd ed., pp. 469–486). New York: Wiley.

Malis, R. S., & Roloff, M. E. (2006). Demand/withdraw patterns in serial arguments: Implications for well-being. *Human Communication Research, 32,* 198–216.

Napier, A. Y. (1978). The rejection-intrusion pattern: A central family dynamic. *Journal of Marriage and Family Counseling, 4,* 5–12.

Noller, P., Feeney, J. A., Bonnell, D., & Callan, V. J. (1994). A longitudinal study of conflict in marriage. *Journal of Social and Personal Relationships, 11,* 233–252.

Noller, P., Feeney, J. A., Sheehan, G., & Peterson, C. (2000). Marital conflict patterns: Links with family conflict and family members' perceptions of one another. *Personal Relationships, 7,* 79–94.

Sillars, A. L. (1986). *Procedures for coding interpersonal conflict* (Revised manual). Missoula: University of Montana, Department of Interpersonal Communication.

Sillars, A., Canary, D. J., & Tafoya, M. (2004). Communication, conflict, and the quality of family relationships. In A. L. Vangelisti (Ed.), *Handbook of family communication* (pp. 413–446). Mahwah, NJ: Erlbaum.

Terman, L. M., Buttenwieser, P., Ferguson, L. W., Johnson, W. B., & Wilson, D. P. (1938). *Psychological factors in marital happiness.* New York: McGraw-Hill.

Vogel, D. L., & Karney, B. R. (2002). Demands and withdrawal in newlyweds: Elaborating on the social structural hypothesis. *Journal of Social and Personal Relationships, 19,* 685–701.

Waldron, V. (1997). Toward a theory of interactive conversational planning. In J. O. Greene (Ed.), *Message production: Advances in communication theory* (pp. 195–220). Mahwah, NJ: Erlbaum.

Wilson, S. R. (2002). *Seeking and resisting compliance: Why people say what they do when trying to influence others.* Thousand Oaks, CA: Sage.

Wilson, S. R., & Feng, H. (2007). Interaction goals and message production: Conceptual and methodological developments. In D. R. Roskos-Ewoldsen & J. L. Monahan (Eds.), *Communication and social cognition: Theories and methods* (pp. 71–95). Mahwah, NJ: Erlbaum.

10

Advances in Deception Detection

Judee K. Burgoon

Timothy R. Levine

Humans expect their interpersonal interactions to be devoid of deception. In fact, our very ability to communicate in some ways depends on a presumption that what others say to us is truthful (Gilbert, 1991; Grice, 1989). Otherwise, we would be faced with a thousand decisions daily about whether to tag each incoming piece of information as truthful or not. Yet deception pervades every corner of our lives, from dealings with the local electronics salesperson, to communications among work team members, to politicians' claims on the news, to the excuses and fibs of family and friends. It occurs not just in face-to-face encounters but also in telephone conversations, voice mails, e-mails, chats, and other forms of mediated communication. Empirical research indicates that as much as one quarter to one third of all conversations entail some form of deception. People completing diary studies report lying as often as once or twice a day, and students report deception in as many as 77% of their interactions with strangers (DePaulo & Kashy, 1998; George & Robb, 2006; Hancock, Thom-Santelli, & Ritchie, 2004; Marett & George, 2004; Turner, Edgley, & Olmstead, 1975). The pervasiveness of deception in our interpersonal interactions thus warrants closer examination of how it can be detected and countered. This chapter is devoted to two streams of research the authors have conducted on how and why deception can (and cannot) be detected.

Deception Detection 101

Deception is typically defined as messages knowingly and intentionally transmitted to mislead another person (Burgoon & Buller, 2008). The inclusion of criteria of awareness and intentionality rules out self-delusion, accidental transmission of faulty information, or faulty conclusions by receivers that are of their own doing. Detection *accuracy* usually encompasses not only detection of deceit but also detection of truth. People are considered accurate to the extent that they judge truthful messages as honest (or more honest) and deceptive messages as dishonest (or more deceptive, less honest).

From a communication perspective, it is useful to distinguish outright lies from other types of deceptive communication. When people think of deception, they most often think of a blatant lie, which involves intentionally saying something that is known to be false. But deception comes in a variety of guises, from flat-out lies, elaborate fabrications, misdirection and exaggerations, to evasions, equivocations, concealments, omissions, strategic ambiguity and deflections, spoofing and phishing, to more subtle misdirection and camouflage. Of course, people can and do also mix truthful information in with false information when deceiving. But probably the most common types of deception are mere omission, or the strategic withholding of information, and equivocation (Bavelas, Chovil Black, & Mullett, 1990; Burgoon, Buller, Guerrero, Afifi, & Feldman, 1996; Levine et al., 2002). Nevertheless, the vast majority of deception detection research is more accurately labeled truth-lie detection research.

Three consistent findings are evident in the literature on detection accuracy, and most deception researchers agree on these. First, people are significantly, but only slightly, above 50% in accuracy (Bond & DePaulo, 2006). The latest and best meta-analysis finds that people are, on average, 54% accurate in deception detection experiments (Bond & DePaulo, 2006). These values are significantly greater than the 50% base rate and are very stable, with few studies reporting values below 45% or above 65%. However, the 54% average includes both truth detection and deception detection. When separate figures are calculated, deception detection rates are more dismal, averaging 47%, or below chance, whereas truth detection is higher.

Second, people overestimate their ability to detect other's lies, yet confidence is unrelated to accuracy (DePaulo, Charlton, Cooper, Lindsay, & Muhlenbruck, 1997; Jensen, 2007). That is to say, people who are supremely confident in their detection abilities are no more accurate than those who harbor serious doubts about their abilities. Study after study has found a near-zero correlation between detection accuracy and confidence. Nevertheless, people (incorrectly) think that they can detect others' lies.

Third, people have a strong proclivity to judge a message truthful rather than deceptive, independent of actual message veracity (Levine, Kim, Park, & Hughes, 2006; Levine, Park, & McCornack, 1999). This tendency, called the *truth bias,* is one of the most well-documented findings in the communication and psychology literature. Truth bias likely stems from how people mentally represent true and false information (Gilbert, 1991) and from tacit assumptions that guide communication (McCornack, 1992). Truth bias is more pronounced in face-to-face interaction (Buller, Strzyzewski, & Hunsaker, 1991; Burgoon, Buller, & Floyd, 2001; Dunbar, Ramirez, & Burgoon, 2003), when communicating with relationally close others (McCornack & Parks, 1986), and when people are not primed to be suspicious (McCornack & Levine, 1990).

There are several reasons why people tend to be inaccurate lie catchers. First, there do not appear to be any strong, cross-situation behavioral cues that would make high accuracy possible. Although statistically reliable cues to deception are observed across studies (DePaulo et al., 2003), many individual cues are inconsistent from one situation to the next, which reduces their utility in detecting specific instances of deception (Levine, Feeley, McCornack, Harms, & Hughes, 2005; Qin, 2007).

Second, people pay attention to cues that lack diagnostic utility. For example, there is a widely held, cross-cultural belief that liars look away (Bond & The Global Deception Research Team, 2006), yet truth tellers and liars do not differ in eye behavior, and amount of eye gaze has no diagnostic utility (DePaulo et al., 2003). Reliance on stereotypical rather than actual signs of deception leads many a detector astray (Miller & Stiff, 1993; Vrij, 2000; Zuckerman & Driver, 1985).

Third, receivers, being "cognitive misers," often turn to mental shortcuts called heuristics that save them mental effort but also can lead them to wrong judgments. The aforementioned truth bias is one such heuristic. If people assume others are truthful, they may not even entertain the possibility that deception is taking place. Other heuristics that have been examined include a tendency to pay more attention to visual than auditory or verbal cues, a tendency to be satisfied with the mere fact of asking probing questions and not the actual answers that are provided, and a tendency to "bite" on whatever is fishy looking, conspicuous, or unusual (e.g., Bond et al., 1992; Buller, Strzyzewski, & Comstock, 1991; Burgoon, Blair, & Strom, in press; Levine & McCornack, 2001; Rosenthal, Hall, DiMatteo, Rogers, & Archer, 1979).

Fourth, even when people are familiarized with some of the most reliable indicators through training, the resultant improvement has been slight. On average, Frank and Feeley (2003) found that training leads only to a 4% improvement in raw accuracy. However, researchers continue to seek ways to make training more effective. Recent research has shown that more extended training periods than those used in most laboratory experiments and use of computer-assisted training tools that supply feedback, intermittent testing, and extra examples yield good results with motivated current and future practitioners (e.g., George, Biros, Adkins, Burgoon, & Nunamaker, 2004; Mann, Vrij, & Bull, 2004).

Fifth, research designs require judgments made without benefit of contextual information. People often detect lies well after the fact, drawing on inconsistencies with prior knowledge, information from third parties, and physical evidence rather than at-the-time verbal and nonverbal behavior (Park, Levine, McCornack, Morrison, & Ferrara, 2002). Most deception detection experiments do not equip subjects with this kind of background information or familiarize them with the subject's normal communication style. Judgments made in such a contextual vacuum are likely to be error prone.

We consider some additional factors that may influence accuracy as we discuss our own independent and intersecting research streams.

Our Deception Research Stories

Burgoon's Interpersonal Deception Research

In the Beginning

Judee's foray into deception research began when she was invited to serve on a panel critiquing current trends in deception research. Feeling it would be rather presumptuous to be a critic without having ever conducted deception research, she decided to team up with former student David Buller, who, under the tutelage of G. R. Miller, was already full sway into conducting deception research. Out of this collaboration emerged *interpersonal deception theory* (Buller & Burgoon, 1996; Burgoon & Buller, 1996, 2008), which has attracted continuous funding from government agencies to develop and test the theory.

Interpersonal Deception Theory (IDT)

The theory endeavors to offer a communication account of deception, as contrasted with the then-prevailing psychological and physiological accounts.

Among the major tenets of the theory are that deception is a goal-directed, intentional, and strategic activity; that deceivers, in concocting their deceits, are cognizant of receiver reactions; and that deceivers attempt to adapt to whatever feedback and suspicions they perceive receivers are communicating so as to appear credible and evade detection. Receivers in turn are not passive recipients of senders' messages. They have their antennae up (albeit often subconsciously) and may engage in active or indirect strategies to ferret out the true state of affairs. Thus, deceptive episodes are not static. Just as with any other form of interpersonal communication, sender and receiver are interdependent. One person's actions influence the other and vice versa. IDT lays out the various assumptions it makes about interpersonal communication generally and deception in interpersonal encounters specifically. It then advances 18 propositions—empirically testable statements—that posit what factors influence how deception is enacted and how it is detected. From these general propositions, specific hypotheses can be derived.

IDT is equally divided between addressing the message production (sender) and message reception (receiver) sides of deceptive interactions. It also considers the emotions and behaviors as well as the cognitions that are involved. Here we present just a snapshot of the portion that addresses receiver detection of deception and present two experiments as illustration of our approach to examining deception detection. Along the way, we identify where our thinking agrees or diverges.

Influences on Receiver Judgments

Unquestionably, there are widely ranging factors that will affect how, and how well, receivers detect deception. IDT highlights just a handful as particularly important in interpersonal communication contexts. They include (a) the *communication skills of receiver and sender* (is the receiver skilled in deciphering social and emotional verbal and nonverbal cues, is the sender skillful in encoding verbal and nonverbal communication), (b) *receiver suspicions* (do receivers enter the interaction with a truth bias or some degree of suspicion, does the interaction itself provoke suspicion), (c) the *relationship between sender and receiver* (how familiar are they with one another and how positively or negatively is the relationship evaluated), (d) the *nature of the medium* through which communication takes place (is it an interactive medium, does it give receivers access to nonverbal cues and other social information), (e) *the sender's performance* (does the sender deviate from normal communication patterns, does the sender say or do certain things that provoke suspicion), (f) the *conversational demands* receivers must meet (are their mental resources overly taxed by fulfilling their responsibilities to maintain the conversation and complete any task at hand or can they devote full cognitive effort to detecting deception), and (g) *time* (how long the interaction is and where in the process the judgment is being made). In other words, there are actor, relationship, and interaction factors at work.

Specifically, IDT predicts the following (Burgoon, Guerrero, & Floyd, in press):

- *Detection accuracy is related to context interactivity, receiver truth biases, receiver familiarity, receiver decoding skills, sender encoding skills, and sender deviations from expected patterns.* Receivers will be less accurate if (a) the context is interactive, (b) they hold strong truth biases, (c) they are well acquainted with the sender, (d) they lack familiarity with the sender's background, with the sender's typical communication, and with diagnostic deception cues, (e) the sender has excellent encoding skills, and (f) the sender adheres to expected communication patterns.

- *Judgments of sender credibility and detection accuracy at the end of an interaction are a function of final receiver cognitions and sender performance.* What matters is not what receivers thought or how senders acted at the outset but where the thoughts and behavior processes end up. That is, there is a recency effect.

For example, a person with only modest sensitivity to nonverbal cues who is in a close, trusting relationship and is carrying on a very intimate face-to-face conversation may fail to pick up on the partner's subtle dissembling and misrepresentations. In signal detection terms, the accuracy in detecting deception will be poor due to too many false negatives (misses).

Illustration: The Deceptive Interviews Experiment

One of the first IDT experiments to examine several of these factors is reported in Burgoon, Buller, Ebesu, and Rockwell (1994). Two different samples participated. The community sample consisted of people who had been called for jury duty or were nontraditional (older) students from a community college. The military sample included civilian and military personnel at a nearby base. Half the participants were assigned the role of interviewer (ER) and half, the role of interviewee (EE). ERs were either induced to be suspicious—by being told that people often are less than completely truthful during such interviews and their task would be to uncover deception—or were in the control condition that lacked this induction. The military interviewers were experts in interviewing and interrogation whereas the community ERs were not.

EEs were told to be truthful on the first few questions and then to depart from "the truth, the whole truth, and nothing but the truth" on their remaining answers.

Results showed, as expected, that people were far more "accurate" judging truth than deception but only because they had such strong truth biases. They were far less accurate in detecting deception. Surprisingly, the novices had higher truth and deception detection accuracy scores than did the experts. The results are shown in Table 10.1.

These results provided support for several of the predictions of IDT, including that receivers' cognitive biases, whether based on predispositions or triggered experimentally, impair judgment. Other experiments that were part of this program of research also confirmed that deceivers altered their behavior over time and that final judgments were highly correlated with degree of suspicion at the end of the interaction (Burgoon, Buller, White, Afifi, & Buslig, 1999; White & Burgoon, 2001).

Table 10.1   Means for Interviewer Honesty Judgments, Accuracy Discrepancies, and Bias on Truthful and Deceptive Questions

Dependent Measure	Suspicion	No Suspicion	Experts	Novices
Honesty judgment				
Truthful responses	7.88	8.39		
Deceptive responses	3.32	3.55		
Accuracy				
Truthful responses	2.08	1.80	2.95	0.80
Deceptive responses	3.93	4.18	4.33	3.99
Bias				
Truthful responses	1.83	1.08		
Deceptive responses	−2.35	−2.51		

Note: On honesty judgments, which represent the mean ER estimates on the truthfulness scale, scores could range from 0 (completely untruthful) to 10 (completely truthful). Accuracy scores represent the absolute discrepancy between EE reports and ER estimates. Higher scores reflect greater discrepancies, that is, less accuracy. Total accuracy combines the truthful and deceptive questions. Bias scores represent the signed difference between EE reports and ER estimates. Positive scores can be interpreted as a truth bias, negative scores, as a lie bias.

Judgments Over Time

One of the points of contention between Burgoon-Buller and Levine has been the extent to which deceivers adapt their behavior and receivers modify their judgments over the course of an interaction. The notion of deception as a dynamic, adaptive enterprise is at the heart of IDT; so it becomes important to demonstrate that senders and receivers are indeed changeable across the course of an interaction. The next experiment was intended to do just that.

The same basic interview paradigm was used, but in this case EEs alternated answering truthfully and deceptively in blocks of three questions at a time. Half followed a truth-deception-truth-deception sequence and the other half, a deception-truth-deception-truth sequence. Of interest here is that we asked ERs to record their judgments of sender truthfulness after each question so we could have a running assessment of their thought processes. One possibility was that they would simply seize on their first judgment and stick with it. Another, proposed in IDT, is that their judgments would vary in concert with changing sender behavior, reflecting receivers' awareness of sender behavioral changes, but that they would still suffer truth biases that would tilt all their judgments toward the truthful end of the scale.

Figure 10.1 shows the results for receiver judgments in the truth-first order.

Note that when EEs are truthful, ER judgments on the 0 (not at all truthful) to 10 (completely truthful) scale are also high, and obviously pretty accurate. When EEs shift to deception during the next three questions, ER ratings decline, which indicates awareness that the answers are not as truthful. Yet results would be scored as inaccurate because they are still truth biased, that is, above the midpoint of the scale. Then, when EEs are truthful again, ERs also rate EEs as more truthful. Finally, when EEs become deceptive again on the last three questions, ER judgments also shift to less perceived honesty. If ERs are given binary scores of accurate or inaccurate, based on whether they perceived truth (scores above the midpoint of the scale) or deception (scores below the midpoint), their accuracy scores would be high on truth judgments but poor on deception judgments. Yet the figure reveals that on average, ERs were aware of changes in sender behavior and adjusted their judgments accordingly.

The implications are fourfold. First, truth biases are quite pronounced. On average, receivers give senders the benefit of the doubt. Second, to obtain a good measure of detection accuracy, continuous as well as dichotomous measures are needed to tap into the subtleties of judgments. Burgoon believes that when receivers are asked to judge sincerity or believability rather than truthfulness (what some would regard as indirect measures), judgments are more accurate. Third, receivers do not lock into their first

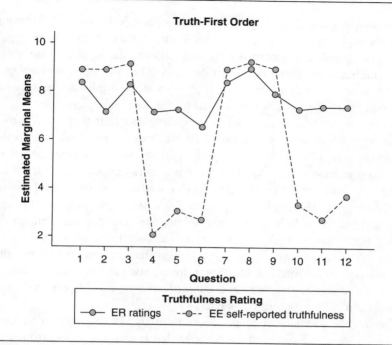

Figure 10.1   Sender Self-Reported Truthfulness (dotted line) and Receiver
Estimate of Sender Truth (solid line) Across 12 Interview
Questions, Truth-First Order

(Results in the deception-first order show similar variability.)

judgments. They are continually updating their judgments in response to
changes in sender behavior. This offers some encouragement for the prospect
of improving detection accuracy if receivers are indeed tuning in to some
cues that are valid indicators. Finally, Burgoon finds these data as strong
support for the interdependent nature of interpersonal deception. This, in
turn, has important ramifications for technologies and techniques for detecting
deception, a topic we take up momentarily.

Levine's Deception Research and the Power of Truth Bias

Levine's research on deception detection began with the questions of how
relational closeness and suspicion influence deception detection accuracy in
interpersonal relationships. At the time, Levine was a graduate student at
Michigan State University working on Steve McCornack's research team.

Steve and Tim's first experiment (McCornack & Levine, 1990) brought dating couples into the lab, videotaped one of them lying and telling the truth on a series of videotaped questions, showed the segments to the partners, and had them make veracity judgments. The judging partner either did not know it was a deception detection study (low suspicion), was casually told that all answers might not be truthful (moderate suspicion), or was told that the partner was definitely lying on some and that they needed to tell which was which (high suspicion). Much to our surprise, even in the high suspicion condition, judges were still truth biased, believing almost two thirds of the messages. So while suspicion did systemically lower truth bias, it did not eliminate it. To this day, Levine has never observed a lie bias in any of his data. The truth-bias rates in Table 10.2 reflect the percentage of messages judged as honest in Levine's detection accuracy experiments. The strong truth bias and poor lie detection accuracy rates are consistent with Burgoon's findings as well, although Judee offers the caveat that the situation is likely to be different with practitioners such as polygraph examiners, customs and border screeners, and military interrogators for whom the usual expectation is that the subject is lying.

During the debriefings of participants in the 1990 experiment, Levine took great care to explain to the subjects that it was just an experiment and the partner had lied only because instructed to do so. However, virtually no one was upset. Many judges simply refused to believe that it was a deception experiment and insisted that their partner did not lie to them. This reaction was observed with surprising frequency. Levine was amazed. What Levine took from this was, "Oh my, this truth bias thing is really powerful."

Table 10.2   Truth Bias and the Veracity Effect in Levine's Detection Studies

Study		Truth Bias	Truth Accuracy	Lie Accuracy
McCornack and Levine (1990)		72%	81.8%	31.3%
Levine et al. (1999)	Study 4	68%	68.5%	37.5%
Levine and McCornack (2001)	Study 1	72%	75.0%	31.0%
	Study 2	69%	76.7%	39.2%
	Study 3	56%	56.8%	44.1%
Park et al. (2002)		66%	67.0%	37.0%
Levine et al. (2005)	Study 1	63%	65.3%	38.6%
	Study 2	62%	66.4%	43.0%
	Study 4	62%	66.4%	43.2%
Levine et al. (2006)		66%	67.1%	34.3%

An important implication of this reliable truth-bias finding for detection accuracy was suggested by Hee Sun Park. Hee Sun's idea was a simple one. We later called the resulting findings the "veracity effect" (Levine et al., 1999).

The idea behind the veracity effect is that a very different understanding of the literature is obtained when truth accuracy and lie accuracy are scored and reported separately. Recall that meta-analysis suggests that (a) people are significantly, but only slightly, better than chance and (b) people tend to be truth biased. If both are true, since people in deception experiments usually judge half-truths and half-lies, then people must be getting the truths right more frequently than the lies and truth accuracy must be greater than lie accuracy. The veracity effect follows from this, and refers to the finding that the a priori veracity of the message judged predicts subsequent detection accuracy. Levine et al. (1999) found that the veracity accounted for between 30% and 60% of the variance in detection accuracy in several previous studies. The veracity effect can be seen in each of the studies listed in Table 10.1 as the difference between truth and lie accuracy.

The findings consistent with the veracity effect naturally led to the issues of truth-lie base rates and the Park-Levine probability model (Levine et al., 1999, 2006; Park & Levine, 2001). The idea is that if a priori message veracity predicts subsequent accuracy as suggested by the veracity effect findings, then the ratio of truths to lies matters a whole lot. So one implication of the veracity effect is that the percentage of accuracy averaged across truths and lies at one base rate does not generalize to other base rates. The studies comprising the detection meta-analyses involve 50–50 base rates. If the veracity effect is true, then the 54% accuracy findings from the meta-analysis reviewed at the beginning of the chapter are strictly limited to averaged rates under conditions of exactly a $p = .50$ probability of deception. Of course, outside the lab the probability of deception is seldom precisely 50–50. Therefore, a common design feature of 40 years of deception detection experiments has led to meta-analysis results with very narrow generality.

The Park-Levine (2001) model was designed to model average detection accuracy rates at different truth-lie base rates. That is, it seeks to answer the question, what if the base rate is something other than exactly 50–50? The model predicts that observed total accuracy will be the product of truth accuracy times the proportion of messages that are true plus the product of lie accuracy times the proportion of messages that are lies. This formula predicts linear effects and, so long as people are truth biased, a positive slope. The more truth biased people are, the steeper the slope. If judges were lie biased, the slope would be negative. The y-intercept is a direct positive function of truth-lie transparency.

An initial test of the model yielded promising results. Levine et al. (2006) had one set of subjects in a control group view a series of truths and lies with a 50–50 truth-lie base rate. Then another set of subjects participated in an experiment in which the base rate was experimentally manipulated. Detection accuracy in eight base-rate conditions was predicted based on the formula, which condition participants were in, and the estimates obtained from the control group data. The base-rate induction substantially affected accuracy, explaining 24% of the total variance in accuracy (it explained 21% of the variance in the earlier Levine et al., 1999, Study 4). The effects were linear, with the linear contrast accounting for 95% of the base-rate effect (98% in Levine et al., 1999). The correlation between predicted values and those obtained was $r = .97$. The model predicted the slope and the intercept of the line best fitting the data to within two decimal places. Raw accuracy was predicted to within a couple of percentage points. The results are portrayed in Figure 10.2. An interesting next step will be to see if the model generalizes to interactive deception experiments.

Another set of important findings are reported in the "How People Really Detect Lies" study (Park et al., 2002). All the judges in most detection

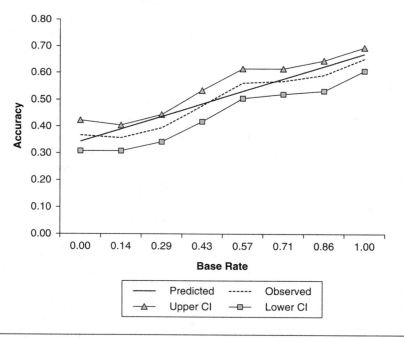

Figure 10.2   Detection Accuracy as a Function of Truth-Lie Base Rate in Levine et al. (2006)

experiments have to go on is the at-the-time verbal and nonverbal behavior of the message sources. Outside the lab, however, people can fact check, talk to others, and so on. Consequently, we expected that most lies outside the deception lab probably get detected well after the fact and by discovery methods other than at-the-time-of-deception verbal and nonverbal source behaviors. Park et al. (2002) simply asked participants to recall a lie that they had detected, to describe what happened, how they found out that the person was lying, and how much time had elapsed between the telling of the lie and its detection. Only 2% of the recalled lies were caught at the time of the telling based on source verbal and nonverbal behaviors. Most were detected after the fact, often much later, and discovery methods often included information from others, physical evidence, and later confessions.

Thus, Levine et al.'s research into deception detection accuracy, as it has progressed, has come to suggest a different picture than portrayed in meta-analyses or the standard review book or chapter. Truth bias is robust and its pervasiveness means that people are actually well below 50% at detecting lies per se. Furthermore, people are probably more truth biased outside the deception lab. After all, there is nothing like knowing you are in a deception detection experiment to pique suspicion. In Levine et al. (2000), participants were not informed that the research involved credibility assessment, and they were extremely truth biased even when exposed to bizarre behavior from a confederate. Thus, outside the lab, people are oblivious to the possibility of deception most of the time and probably correct most of the time as a consequence (because Levine believes that deception occurs at low base rates). When they are suspicious, it is because they project a motive for deception (Levine & Kim, 2007). When lies are detected, most often they are detected well after the fact based on information other than at-the-time source verbal and nonverbal behaviors.

The Future of Deception Research

Below, we have partially sketched some of the issues that beg for further investigation. Here are a handful of some of the larger controversies and directions on the detection side of the interpersonal deception picture that we agree merit attention.

1. *What variables are valid moderators of detection ability?* Among the variables that have attracted substantial attention are receiver expertise, receiver familiarity with sender communication, sender-receiver relationship, extent of interaction, interviewer communication and questioning style, and

motivation. The expertise factor actually is a bundle of variables such as the person's occupation, age, training, and detection experience. Although the most recent Bond and DePaulo (2006) study reports no differences in detection accuracy between novices and experts, Judee's position is that many of the components work in opposite directions (e.g., training improving detection somewhat but longevity in an investigative career fostering excessive skepticism that impairs accuracy) and until these are all "unpacked," it is premature to draw conclusions about expertise. Tim concurs.

The same problem applies to sender-receiver relationship. Tim's view is that the data are solid in showing little effect for relationship because the relationship is mediated by confidence and truth bias (McCornack & Parks, 1986). Judee's view is that the relationship variable is composed of components such as informational familiarity (how much the parties know about each other), behavioral familiarity (how much exposure they have each had to one another's communication patterns under truth and deception), and relational familiarity (how "close" the relationship is), each of which can affect detection accuracy in different, and sometimes opposite, ways.

How the interviewer interacts with the sender is a centerpiece of IDT. Judee's view as expressed in IDT is that participants are worse at detecting deception than nonparticipants. The Bond and DePaulo (2006) meta-analysis bears this out when comparing interacting receivers with third-party observers of interactive deception. However, there is far more to the issue of interactivity that requires investigation. For example, sender interactivity, as tested in Burgoon, Buller, and Floyd (2001), can make a difference. If senders are engaged in monologic communication with their receivers, they are more detectable behaviorally than if they can engage the receiver in a back and forth dialogue. This effect needs to be replicated. The *when* of judgment also matters. Hamel, Burgoon, Humpherys, and Moffitt (2007) found that judgments made near the beginning of interaction (but not its outset) were more accurate than those made later in the course of an interaction. The timing of assessment deserves further exploration.

Tim's view is that interviewer behavior and the extent of interaction generally have small effects on accuracy, at least in everyday deception, and that those effects tend to relate more to truth bias. Both Judee and Tim, however, agree that the kinds of questions asked might have the potential for substantial improvement in accuracy (see Blair & Horvath, 2007). The complex interplay between senders' behaviors, receivers' judgments, and their subsequent behavioral changes is only in the fledgling stages of investigation and merits additional research.

As regards motivation, there is a growing recognition that the distinction between everyday lies (see DePaulo, Kashy, Kirkendol, & Epstein, 1996) and high-stakes lies is a meaningful one. Whereas DePaulo has advanced the claim that motivated deception will make deception more detectable when people have access to nonverbal cues but less so when receivers have access only to verbal ones, Burgoon has argued that motivation can impair or facilitate both verbal and nonverbal communication (see Burgoon, 2005, for the extensive issues and literature involved in this controversy). Uncontroversial is that motivation is a critical moderator with which to contend and one that may necessitate new methods to gauge motivation and its effects.

In general, Judee tends to view many factors as affecting deception detection accuracy and believes that social science research will ultimately provide a basis for reasonably accurate deception detection based on multimodal analyses of behavior. Tim is more skeptical. He believes that few factors have much impact on accuracy, that people do not have the ability to detect lies, and there is not much variance in receiver ability to explain. He sees truth bias as the important dependent variable, and differences in truth bias merely trade off one type of error for another without much impact on overall accuracy.

2. *What is the influence of culture on deception detection?* This moderator deserves special mention because more than any other variable, it is raised by scholars and practitioners as a major fly in the ointment. Virtually all deception research has been limited to the United States and Western Europe, which may place severe limitations on the generalizability of current knowledge. Although there have been surveys on cultural variability regarding the morality and acceptability of deception and surveys on stereotypes regarding what cues are reliable in each culture, virtually no studies have tested whether people are better at detecting deception from those of similar than disparate cultural backgrounds (a typical exception is Al-Simadi, 2000, in which a native culture is compared with one other).

3. *What cognitive and affective mechanisms affect deception displays and their detectability?* If lies are to be detected in near real time, and without extensive background knowledge, whether based on observable behavioral displays or physiological measures, such mechanisms need to be isolated. It is not at all clear, in Tim's opinion, that they reliably exist. For example, Tim questions if lies are necessarily more arousing, emotion producing, or cognitively effortful than truths (see McCornack, 1997). If these are not universals, than perhaps these mechanisms are reliable consequences of deception under some conditions. Judee's view, based on the many interaction experiments she and colleagues have conducted, is that there are reliable indicators, but they appear to be very context-, culture-, and time-dependent and they form very complex conglomerations of substitutable cues, which makes it a folly to rely on any single cue as dependable and valid across situations,

time, and people. Discovery of universals seems unlikely; the quest for them will require a deeper understanding of the cognitive, affective, and communication factors that give rise to them and how those same factors influence receivers' detection abilities.

4. *What are the implications of base rates?* In many real-world applications, the probability of deception occurring is highly variable. Extreme base rates present extreme challenges. For police detectives interviewing suspects, the probability of deception may be high, but for airport screeners, it may be quite low. How to contend with extremes in base rates, and what implicit schemas people hold for deception base rates within a given environment, warrants concerted exploration.

5. *Can deception detection be automated?* One solution to human fallibility in detecting deception is to automate some of the detection tasks. Research we have been conducting on computer vision, automated linguistic analysis, and other techniques for detecting deception (e.g., Burgoon & Qin, 2006; Meservy et al., 2005) are among the many studies that are being explored in vigorous government and industry efforts to find better and more portable lie detectors.

6. *What is the role of ground truth in validating research results?* Perhaps the greatest research challenge facing detection research is enhancing ecological validity while maintaining ground truth. Ground truth means that the actual truthful or deceptive nature of the message must be known so that accuracy can be determined. The need for ground truth leads most researchers to laboratory experiments. This makes studying realistic, higher stakes, unsanctioned lies particularly challenging.

Conclusion

The deception detection literature is intriguing. In one sense, it may be one of the most consistent literatures in all social science. People are truth biased. People are better than chance at deception detection, but much closer to chance levels than perfect accuracy. On these major findings, all pretty much agree. This is fortunate because there exists a solid empirical foundation for future research to build on.

However, there are also several theoretical divides, and no shortage of groups of scholars who disagree about what the findings mean and how to explain them. Just as one example, Judee sees the answers in dynamic interaction over time, whereas Tim sees truth bias as a powerful blinding force.

Judee and Tim do not even agree on disagreeing. Judee thinks that we disagree less; Tim sees the disagreements as more substantial.

But disagreements provide problems to solve. One thing on which Judee and Tim agree is on the appeal to data. Our points of disagreement are empirical questions. Good research is needed to sort them out. Maybe one of our views will prevail. More likely, the truth may lie somewhere in between. But one thing is certain—there is no shortage of important questions to answer.

References

Al-Simadi, F. A. (2000). Detection of deception behavior: A cross-cultural test. *Social Behavior and Personality 28*, 455–462.

Bavelas, J. B., Black, A., Chovil, N., & Mullett, J. (1990). *Equivocal communication.* Newbury Park, CA: Sage.

Blair, J. P., & Horvath, F. (2007). *Detection of deception accuracy using the verbal component of the behavioral analysis interview model.* Manuscript submitted for publication.

Bond, C. F., Jr., & DePaulo, B. M. (2006). Accuracy of deception judgments. *Review of Personality and Social Psychology, 10*, 214–234.

Bond, C. F., Jr., & The Global Deception Research Team. (2006). A world of lies. *Journal of Cross-Cultural Psychology, 37*, 60–74.

Bond, C. F., Jr., Omar, A., Pitre, U., Lashley, B. R., Skagg, L. M., & Kirk, C. T. (1992). Fishy-looking liars: Deception judgment from expectancy violation. *Journal of Personality and Social Psychology, 63*, 969–977.

Buller, D. B., & Burgoon, J. K. (1996). Interpersonal deception theory. *Communication Theory, 6*, 203–242.

Buller, D. B., Strzyzewski, K. D., & Comstock, J. (1991). Interpersonal deception: I. Deceivers' reactions to receivers' suspicions and probing. *Communication Monographs, 58*, 1–24.

Buller, D. B., Strzyzewski, K. D., & Hunsaker, F. G. (1991). Interpersonal deception II: The inferiority of conversational participants as deception detectors. *Communication Monographs, 58*, 25–40.

Burgoon, J. K. (2005). The future of motivated deception detection. In P. Kalbfleisch (Ed.), *Communication yearbook 29* (pp. 49–95). Mahwah, NJ: Erlbaum.

Burgoon, J. K., Blair, J. P., & Strom, R. (in press). Cognitive biases, modalities and deception detection. *Human Communication Research.*

Burgoon, J. K., & Buller, D. B. (1996). Reflections on the nature of theory building and the theoretical status of interpersonal deception theory. *Communication Theory, 6*, 311–328.

Burgoon, J. K., & Buller, D. B. (2008). Interpersonal deception theory. In L. A. Baxter & D. O. Braithwaite (Eds.), *Engaging theories in interpersonal communication: Multiple perspectives* (pp. 227–239). Los Angeles: Sage.

Burgoon, J. K., Buller, D. B., Ebesu, A., & Rockwell, P. (1994). Interpersonal deception: V. Accuracy in deception detection. *Communication Monographs, 61,* 303–325.

Burgoon, J. K., Buller, D. B., & Floyd, K. (2001). Does participation affect deception success? A test of the interactivity principle. *Human Communication Research, 27,* 503–534.

Burgoon, J. K., Buller, D. B., Guerrero, L. K., Afifi, W., & Feldman, C. (1996). Interpersonal deception: XII. Information management dimensions underlying deceptive and truthful messages. *Communication Monographs, 63,* 50–69.

Burgoon, J. K., Buller, D. B., White, C. H., Afifi, W. A., & Buslig, A. L. S. (1999). The role of conversational involvement in deceptive interpersonal communication. *Personality and Social Psychology Bulletin, 25,* 669–685.

Burgoon, J. K., Guerrero, L., & Floyd, K. (in press). *Nonverbal communication.* Boston: Allyn & Bacon.

Burgoon, J. K., & Qin, T. (2006). The dynamic nature of deceptive verbal communication. *Journal of Language and Social Psychology, 26,* 76–96.

DePaulo, B. M., & Kashy, D. A. (1998). Everyday lies in close and casual relationships. *Journal of Personality and Social Psychology, 74,* 63–79.

DePaulo, B. M., Charlton, K., Cooper, H., Lindsay, J. J., & Muhlenbruck, L. (1997). The accuracy-confidence correlation in the detection of deception. *Personality and Social Psychology Review, 1,* 346–357.

DePaulo, B. M., Kashy, D. A., Kirkendol, M. M., & Epstein, J. A. (1996). Lying in everyday life. *Journal of Personality and Social Psychology, 70,* 979–995.

DePaulo, B. M., Lindsay, J. J., Malone, B. E., Muhlenbrick, L., Charlton, K., & Cooper, H. (2003). Cues to deception. *Psychological Bulletin, 129,* 74–118.

Dunbar, N. E., Ramirez, A., Jr., & Burgoon, J. K. (2003). Interactive deception: Effects of participation on participant-receiver and observer judgments. *Communication Reports, 16,* 23–33.

Frank, M. G., & Feeley, T. H. (2003). To catch a liar: Challenges for research in lie detection training. *Journal of Applied Communication Research, 31,* 58–75.

Gilbert, D. T. (1991). How mental systems believe. *American Psychologist, 46,* 107–119.

George, J. F., Biros, D. P., Adkins, M., Burgoon, J. K., & Nunamaker, J. F., Jr. (2004). Testing various modes of computer-based training for deception detection. In H. Chen, R. Moore, D. Zeng, & J. Leavitt (Eds.), *Intelligence and security informatics: Proceedings of the second symposium on intelligence and security informatics ISI 2004, Tucson, AZ, USA* (pp. 411–417). Berlin: Springer-Verlag.

George, J. F., & Robb, A. (2006). *Deception and communication technology: A diaries study replication.* Paper presented to the 39th annual meeting of the Hawaii International Conference on Systems Sciences, Kauai, HI.

Grice, P. (1989). *Studies in the way of words.* Cambridge, MA: Harvard University Press.

Hamel, L., Burgoon, J. K., Humpherys, S. L., & Moffitt, K. (2007, November). *The "when" of detecting deception.* Paper presented at the annual meeting of the National Communication Association, Boston.

Hancock, J. T., Thom-Santelli, J., & Ritchie, T. (2004). Deception and design: The impact of communication technologies on lying behavior. *Proceedings, Conference on Computer Human Interaction, 6,* 130–136.

Jensen, M. L. (2007). *The effects of an expert system on novice and professional decision making with application in deception detection.* Unpublished dissertation, University of Arizona.

Levine, T. R., Anders, L. N., Banas, J., Baum, K. L., Endo, K., Hu, A. D. S., & Wong, N. C. H. (2000). Norms, expectations, and deception: A norm violation model of veracity judgments. *Communication Monographs, 67,* 123–137.

Levine, T. R., Feeley, T., McCornack, S. A., Harms, C., & Hughes, M. (2005). Testing the effects of nonverbal training on deception detection accuracy with the inclusion of a bogus training control group. *Western Journal of Communication, 69,* 203–218.

Levine, T. R., & Kim, R. K. (2007, May). *(In)accuracy at detecting true and false confessions and denials.* Presented at the annual meeting of the International Communication Association, San Francisco.

Levine, T. R., Kim, R. K., Park, H. S., & Hughes, M. (2006). Deception detection accuracy is a predictable linear function of message veracity base-rate: A formal test of Park and Levine's probability model. *Communication Monographs, 73,* 243–260.

Levine, T. R., Lapinski, M. K., Banas, J., Wong, N., Hu, A. D. S., Endo, K., Baum, K. L., & Anders, L. N. (2002). Self-construal and self-other benefit as determinants of deceptive message generation. *Journal of Intercultural Communication Research, 31,* 29–48.

Levine, T. R., & McCornack, S. A. (2001). Behavioral adaption, confidence, and heuristic-based explanations of the probing effect. *Human Communication Research, 27,* 471–502.

Levine, T. R., Park, H. S., & McCornack, S. A. (1999). Accuracy in detecting truths and lies: Documenting the "veracity effect." *Communication Monographs, 66,* 125–144.

Mann, S., Vrij, A., & Bull, R. (2004). Detecting true lies: Police officers' ability to detect suspects' lies. *Journal of Applied Psychology, 89,* 137–149.

Marrett, K., & George, J. F. (2004). Deception in the case of one sender and multiple receivers. *Group Decision & Negotiation, 13*(1), 29–44.

McCornack, S. A. (1992). Information manipulation theory. *Communication Monographs, 59,* 1–16.

McCornack, S. A. (1997). The generation of deceptive messages: Laying the groundwork for a viable theory of interpersonal deception. In J. O. Greene (Ed.), *Messages Production* (pp. 91–126). Mahwah, NJ: LEA.

McCornack, S. A., & Levine, T. R. (1990). When lovers become leery: The relationship between suspicion and accuracy in detecting deception. *Communication Monographs, 57,* 219–230.

McCornack, S. A., & Parks, M. R. (1986). Deception detection and relationship development: The other side of trust. In M. L. McLaughlin (Ed.), *Communication yearbook 9* (pp. 377–389). Beverly Hills, CA: Sage.

Meservy, T. O., Jensen, M. L., Kruse, J., Twitchell, D. P., Tsechpenakis, G., Burgoon, J. K., et al. (2005). Deception detection through automatic, unobtrusive analysis of nonverbal behavior. *IEEE Intelligent Systems, 20*(5), 36–43.

Miller, G. R., & Stiff, J. B. (1993). *Deceptive communication.* Newbury Park, CA: Sage.

Park, H. S., & Levine, T. R. (2001). A probability model of accuracy in deception detection experiments. *Communication Monographs, 68,* 201–210.

Park, H. S., Levine, T. R., McCornack, S. A., Morrison, K., & Ferrara, M. (2002). How people really detect lies. *Communication Monographs, 69,* 144–157.

Qin, T. (2007). *Identification of reliable cues for an automatic deception detection system.* Unpublished dissertation, University of Arizona.

Rosenthal, R., Hall, J. A., DiMatteo, M. R., Roger, P. L., & Archer, D. (1979). *Sensitivity to nonverbal communication: The PONS test.* Baltimore: Johns Hopkins University Press.

Turner, R. E., Edgley, C., & Olmstead, G. (1975). Information control in conversations: Honesty is not always the best policy. *Kansas Journal of Sociology, 11,* 69–89.

Vrij, A. (2000). *Detecting lies and deceit.* New York: Wiley.

White, C. H., & Burgoon, J. K. (2001). Adaptation and communicative design: Patterns of interaction in truthful and deceptive conversations. *Human Communication Research, 27,* 9–37.

Zuckerman, M., & Driver, R. E. (1985). Telling lies: Verbal and nonverbal correlates of deception. In A. W. Siegman & S. Feldstein (Eds.), *Multichannel integrations of nonverbal behavior* (pp. 129–148). Hillsdale, NJ: Erlbaum.

11

Hurtful Communication

Current Research and Future Directions

Anita L. Vangelisti

Alexa D. Hampel

Hurt feelings may be elicited inadvertently or on purpose. They may be experienced as mild or intense and may be concealed or flaunted. Being hurt may be viewed as trivial or important. Although hurt feelings are elicited, enacted, and interpreted in different ways, we believe they can have profound influences both on individuals and on their relationships.

Our purpose in writing this chapter is to advance the study of hurt feelings by providing an account of existing theory and research on hurt and outlining an agenda for future work. We begin our narrative by discussing the various ways that hurt has been conceptualized. Next, we review the empirical literature on hurt feelings. Finally, we describe methodological and theoretical challenges of conducting research on hurtful communication and propose directions for future study.

What Are Hurt Feelings?

Hurt is conceived by most researchers and clinicians as a feeling that occurs in response to an emotional injury (Folkes, 1982; L'Abate, 1977). People feel hurt when they believe that another individual, or group of individuals, communicated or behaved in a way that caused them emotional pain. Supporting this conceptualization, a prototype analysis of emotion concepts conducted by Shaver, Schwartz, Kirson, and O'Connor (1987) revealed that hurt clusters with emotion terms such as *anguish* and *agony* and that people associate hurt with sadness. The suffering that Shaver et al. suggest is common to the emotion concepts that cluster with hurt underlines the centrality of emotional injury to hurt feelings.

Although researchers and theorists generally see emotional injury as core to the experience of hurt, the relationship between hurt and other emotions and the features that distinguish the elicitation of hurt from the elicitation of other emotions are still being debated. One reason that resolving these issues has been challenging is that hurt is difficult to isolate and control—hurt feelings usually are accompanied by other emotions (Feeney, 2005; Leary, Springer, Negel, Ansell, & Evans, 1998). In fact, clinicians have long suggested that hurt is at the root of a number of other emotions—that, for example, when people say that they feel anger or jealousy toward a relational partner, they actually are feeling hurt. The frequent coupling of hurt with other emotions is part of what initially led us to suggest that hurt is an emotion "blend" (Vangelisti & Young, 2000). We noted, more specifically, that hurt is a combination of sadness at having been emotionally injured and fear of being vulnerable to harm. Our argument was that the blending of sadness and fear creates a separate emotion (hurt) that often is defensively masked by emotions marked by less vulnerability (e.g., anger).

Rather than conceptualize hurt as a blend, other researchers have argued that it is a unique emotion in and of itself. For instance, Leary and Springer (2001) examined a number of negative emotions and found that those emotions did not account for all the variance in hurt. Based on these findings, they suggested that although hurt often is accompanied by other negative emotions, it is unique. Feeney (2005) similarly argued that hurt is a distinct emotion, but took the argument one step further. She suggested that the negative emotions that accompany hurt depend on the type of experience that initially evoked individuals' hurt feelings.

The literature clearly suggests, then, that when people are asked to recall hurtful experiences, they describe emotional pain. The pain they describe often is accompanied by other negative feelings but, as noted by Shaver, Mikuliner, Lavy, and Cassidy (in press), "other negative emotions do not share this particular painful quality." Given that people experience hurt as unique, we see it as less useful for researchers and theorists to argue about the hypothetical structure of hurt (e.g., whether it is a blend or whether it is a "basic" emotion) and more useful to further specify the factors that distinguish hurt from other emotions. In fact, this is what a number of researchers have done: They have begun to identify what makes the elicitation of hurt different from the elicitation of other emotions. For instance, Leary et al. (1998) argued that the distinguishing feature of hurt is relational devaluation or "the perception that another individual does not regard his or her relationship with the person to be as important, close, or valuable as the person desires" (p. 1225). In contrast, we suggested that hurt feelings are a consequence of relational transgressions and that the transgressions that elicit hurt feelings, in particular, create a sense of vulnerability (Vangelisti, 2001; Vangelisti & Young, 2000). Seeing merit both in Leary et al.'s perspective and our view, Feeney (2005) argued that hurt feelings are evoked by relational transgressions that imply low relational evaluations. She also noted that when people are hurt, their beliefs about self and others—and thus their attachments to others—are threatened. Shaver and his colleagues (in press) agreed with Feeney's arguments, but suggested that individuals' sense of safety and security may be even more closely linked to hurt feelings than their mental models of self and other.

Although the distinguishing characteristics of hurt that have been noted in the literature reflect a diversity of theoretical and disciplinary approaches, they also share a number of features in common. First, they underline the idea that, as previously noted, emotional injury is core to the experience of hurt. When people feel hurt, they perceive that they have been emotionally wounded by something that someone else said or did. Second, the various causes put forth by researchers all suggest that hurt involves loss. This loss may be reflected by the lack of value a partner places on a relationship, by the unwillingness of a partner to adhere to relational norms, by a partner's tendency to violate others' positive views of themselves, or by the failure of a partner to engage in behaviors that create a safe, secure relational environment. Third, and finally, the different causes discussed by researchers all involve vulnerability to future pain. Once people have been hurt by a relational partner, they know that there is a chance that they may be hurt again. Whether individuals' hurtful experience centers on relational devaluation or a threat to their safety, the possibility looms that they may have a similar experience in the future.

The agreement among researchers concerning many of the essential characteristics of hurt has provided a common focal point for investigation. At the same time, the different theoretical and disciplinary approaches that scholars have brought to the study of hurt have produced a diverse, somewhat fragmented literature. Our effort in the following section is to catalogue existing scholarship on hurtful interaction and highlight new developments in the research. Specifically, we discuss the literature in terms of four categories of variables that are associated with hurtful interactions: (a) characteristics of hurtful behavior, (b) cognitive processes, (c) individual differences, and (d) relationship characteristics.

Review of Literature

Characteristics of Hurtful Behavior

Hurtful behavior that occurs in the context of interpersonal relationships can be characterized by a number of factors that contribute to the experience of hurt feelings. Previous research reveals that people perceive certain types of behavior to be especially hurtful and that the intensity and frequency of hurtful behavior have important implications for hurt feelings.

Types

The messages and events that produce hurt feelings have been categorized by researchers in several ways to reflect both verbal and nonverbal acts involved in the elicitation of hurt. Our initial research on hurtful communication emphasized the messages people perceive to be hurtful (Vangelisti, 1994). Namely, we identified speech acts that evoke hurt feelings during social interaction and proposed that the form, content, and relative intensity of hurtful messages contribute to the ways that people evaluate and interpret hurtful events. Our data yielded nine categories of hurtful messages and indicated that the messages varied with regard to the degree of hurt they evoked (e.g., informative statements often were rated as highly hurtful, whereas accusations usually were perceived as less hurtful).

Although our research elucidated the statements and questions that people perceive to be hurtful, Leary et al. (1998) noted that our data did not account for nonverbal behavior or the absence of behavior(s)—both of which may be quite hurtful. To address this limitation, Leary and his colleagues developed a typology of the instances in which someone "said or did something" to hurt their respondents' feelings (p. 1226). Feeney (2004) then extended Leary et al.'s typology by applying it to situations in which people's hurt feelings were evoked by a dating partner or spouse.

The differences among the aforementioned typologies are interesting, but their similarities may be even more informative. For instance, all three studies suggest that hurtful behavior may be particularly painful when it revolves around feelings or events that the person who is hurt cannot control or change. The studies also provide evidence that the way in which people interpret hurtful behavior may be specific to the type of relationship in which it occurs.

Intensity

Because hurt is an emotion that occurs between people, the way that hurt feelings are elicited is a driving factor in the course and outcome of hurtful episodes. In particular, the intensity with which another's hurtful comment is delivered affects the way that recipients of the message make sense of the situation. Message intensity refers to "the strength or degree of emphasis with which a source states his [sic] attitudinal position toward a topic" (McEwen & Greenberg, 1970, p. 340). Negative nonverbal cues (e.g., yelling) and extreme language (e.g., swearing) are characteristics of intense hurtful communication.

One of our colleagues (Young, 2004) articulated the role of message intensity in hurtful interactions by exploring factors that influence recipients' appraisals of hurtful comments. The results of her study indicated that statements characterized by harsh or abrasive language were evaluated more negatively than those spoken with a neutral or less offensive tone. We similarly found that people sometimes explain their hurt feelings in terms of the way that a hurtful comment was communicated (Vangelisti, Young, Carpenter-Theune, & Alexander, 2005). It is important to note that while the extant literature defines what constitutes the intensity of hurtful communication, researchers have yet to operationalize the intensity of other forms of hurtful behavior.

Frequency

Although the intensity of something someone said or did to hurt another's feelings affects the way that people make sense of the behavior, the effect of intensity can vary across relationships. If the behavior is an isolated occurrence, it is likely to be evaluated differently than if it is perceived as part of a larger ongoing pattern in the relationship. In other words, the frequency with which hurtful behavior occurs in a given relationship influences the experience of hurt feelings. Relatively little is known about ongoing patterns of hurtful behavior, yet existing research provides some evidence about their potential consequences. For instance, we explored hurtful behavior that participants perceived to be part of an ongoing pattern (Vangelisti & Young, 2000). To do this, we measured two different variables. First, we assessed the frequency with which individuals perceived a person to have hurt them (e.g., "It is typical of him or her to hurt my feelings"); second, we measured individuals' perceptions of the general tendency of that person to hurt others (e.g., "He or she often says or does things that hurt people"). Our results indicated that individuals' perceptions of both the frequency with which a partner hurt them and the other person's general tendency to hurt others were positively associated with participants' tendency to distance themselves from their relationship with the partner.

The findings of our research point to another factor that may contribute to the individual and relational effects of hurtful behavior: the expectation of hurt feelings in a given relationship. The degree to which people expect to be hurt by a relational partner may influence the amount of vulnerability that they feel going into an interaction with that person. If hurt is expected, or anticipated, individuals may feel prepared for, and thus less vulnerable to, any emotional pain they may experience.

Cognitive Processes

In addition to various characteristics of hurtful behavior, researchers have studied the way that individuals think about and interpret their hurt feelings. Parkinson (1997) argues that individuals' appraisals of an emotional experience are evidenced in the way that they think and talk about that experience. Likewise, we assume that appraisals of another person's behavior are fundamental to the elicitation of hurt feelings (Vangelisti, 2001). Following this reasoning, scholars have explored the cognitive processes that influence the course and outcome of hurt feelings in relationships. In particular, the ways that individuals make sense of another person's hurtful behavior and the ways that they explain their own feelings have been examined.

Perceived Intent

Discerning whether another's behavior is enacted intentionally or unintentionally can affect the dynamics of a hurtful interaction as well as the influence of hurtful behavior on relationships. Several different factors are considered when people evaluate the intent of another's behavior (see, e.g., Malle & Knobe, 1997). When hurtful behavior is judged as intentional, people are likely to perceive that the individual who enacted the behavior chose to hurt them, wanted to hurt them, had the skill to do so, and planned the behavior. Research suggests that comments or behaviors that are perceived as intentionally hurtful are considered to be more intense and to cause more damage to relationships than are those seen as unintentionally hurtful. For example, we found that people who believed that a relational partner said something to intentionally hurt their feelings reported that the interaction created more distance in their relationship than did those who perceived a partner to have accidentally hurt them (Vangelisti & Young, 2000). Our findings further suggested that individuals who saw their partner's behavior as intentionally hurtful were less satisfied with their relationship and less close to their partner than were those who believed that the partner hurt their feelings unintentionally.

The relative impact of intentional and unintentional hurtful behavior, however, is complicated by the frequency with which people perceive that others hurt them. When we examined the degree of hurt people felt in response to a partner's behavior, we found a significant interaction between perceived intent and perceived frequency (Vangelisti & Young, 2000). To clarify, participants in our study who noted that a relational partner did *not* hurt them frequently reported that the hurtful behavior was much more painful when it was deemed intentional and much less painful when it was perceived to be unintentional. Interestingly, however, those who reported that a partner who hurt them tended to hurt them frequently did not exhibit the same pattern. Rather, these individuals reported experiencing little or no hurt when they perceived that the other hurt them intentionally and moderate levels of emotional pain when they believed that their hurt feelings were unintentionally elicited. In short, people who believed that they were frequently hurt by a relational partner tended to become inured to their partner's intentionally hurtful behavior.

Perceived Causes

Of course, individuals' perceptions of intent are not the only factor influencing the outcomes associated with hurtful events. We suggested that the impact of hurtful interactions on individuals and relationships depends on the way that people explain the causes of their hurt feelings (Vangelisti et al., 2005). In brief, we argued that individuals' appraisals (Lazarus, 1991), or explanations, for *why* their feelings were hurt affect the way that hurtful interactions unfold. The results of our studies indicated that people's explanations for their hurt feelings were linked to their emotional and behavioral responses to another's hurtful behavior. For instance, individuals' tendency to explain their hurt by saying that the other person's behavior denigrated their relationship (i.e., made them feel the relationship was not important) was positively associated with the degree of hurt that they felt. Similarly, there was a direct association between people's tendency to report that their hurt was caused by humiliation (i.e., the other person made them feel ashamed, inferior, or vulnerable) and the intensity of their hurt feelings. Individuals who explained that they felt hurt either because an event denigrated their relationship or because a personal flaw was emphasized by the other were relatively likely to distance themselves relationally from the person who hurt them. Conversely, those who said that their hurt feelings were due to mistaken intent (i.e., they were misunderstood or questioned) were relatively unlikely to engage in relational distancing. In short, the ways that people explain their own hurt feelings are important for their understanding of others' hurtful behavior. Making sense of hurtful interactions by appraising the various causes of hurt feelings may shape the cognitive processes that are activated when hurtful behavior is enacted in relationships.

Habituation and Sensitization

Although hurt feelings are predominantly experienced as aversive, emotional responses to another's hurtful behavior are not necessarily consistent over time. The cognitive processes that occur when people make sense of hurtful interactions may differ as a result of repeated exposure to hurtful behavior. One process by which individuals may react to hurtful behavior involves an increased sensitivity to emotional pain. Zahn-Waxler and Kochanska (1990) argue that repeated exposure to certain stimuli may result in exaggerated emotional responses over time. This sort of sensitization has been investigated by Cunningham and his colleagues (see, e.g., Cunningham, Shamblen, Barbee, & Ault, 2005) in their work on social allergies. These researchers argue that emotion-arousing behaviors (social allergens) may produce hypersensitive responses (social allergies) if such behaviors are encountered frequently or with prolonged exposure. If hurtful interactions can be described using a sensitization model, people who are frequently exposed to hurtful behavior may be especially likely to perceive hurtful cues during interaction, or may need little reason to feel hurt by others.

In contrast, research on social exclusion suggests that the way that individuals respond to hurtful interactions may be better described by a habituation model than by a sensitization model (see, e.g., DeWall, Baumeister, & Masicampo, in press). In other words, when people are repeatedly exposed to hurtful stimuli, they may become emotionally numb to feeling hurt. MacDonald and Leary (2005) presented compelling evidence supporting an overlap between social and physical pain in response to perceived threats to social inclusion. In line with the case put forth by MacDonald and Leary, DeWall et al. (in press) argue that the deficits they found in physical sensitivity following social exclusion "should be accompanied by reduced emotional sensitivity." Indeed, our own research has yielded some support for this perspective. In one study, we found that when people perceive that they are frequently and intentionally hurt by relational partners, they appear to develop "emotional calluses" such that their partner's hurtful behavior elicits less intense feelings of hurt than it would otherwise (Vangelisti & Young, 2000). In another investigation, our findings suggested that repeated, ongoing exposure to certain hurtful behaviors may encourage individuals to become accustomed to emotional pain and, as a consequence, less sensitive to their hurt feelings (Vangelisti, Maguire, Alexander, & Clark, 2007).

Individual Differences

People bring individual qualities to their relationships that shape the way that interactions with their partner unfold. There is theoretical and, in some cases, empirical evidence that at least three individual differences contribute to the experience of hurt feelings in relationships: attachment orientation, self-esteem, and rejection sensitivity.

Attachment Orientation

One of the individual differences that influences the way in which people evaluate and interpret another's hurtful behavior is attachment orientation. Attachment orientation appears to predispose individuals to make sense of hurtful behavior in particular ways. Feeney (2005) investigated the role of attachment when people felt hurt in the context of couple relationships. She argued that because personal injury is central to hurt feelings, and because a sense of vulnerability accompanies most hurtful episodes, people who are hurt experience their feelings in ways that reflect their attachment orientation. To explain further, she noted that as a result of prior attachment-related experiences, individuals develop working models of the self and of others that influence their behavior in relationships, particularly during times of stress or threat. Accordingly, she predicted that attachment dimensions would be associated with participants' reports of their emotional reactions when a romantic partner hurt their feelings. The results of Feeney's study indicated that, indeed, those who were highly avoidant reported relatively low levels of hurt and distress. Conversely, highly anxious individuals reported experiencing relatively high levels of hurt and distress.

Feeney's (2005) findings suggest that individuals' attachment orientation influences the way that they experience hurt in the context of their romantic relationships. Given that hurt feelings are shaped, at least in part, by the type of relationship in which they are elicited, it is possible that attachment orientation affects hurtful interactions in different ways in other relational domains. For instance, hurtful behavior enacted by a family member (e.g., a former primary caregiver) may be more distressing to those who are highly anxious than similar behavior enacted by a romantic partner. Conversely, highly anxious individuals might be more susceptible to distress in romantic relationships than in family relationships because of the voluntary nature of romantic relationships.

Self-Esteem

Another individual difference that may affect the course of hurtful episodes is self-esteem. Leary and colleagues suggested that people have a tendency to appraise their feelings in ways that are consistent with their self-esteem (Leary, Tambor, Terdal, & Downs, 1995). Evidence supporting this argument has surfaced in our research on hurt. We found that self-esteem was inversely related to the degree to which participants felt hurt by another's behavior (Vangelisti et al., 2005). Furthermore, the causes that our participants assigned to their hurt feelings differed based on their self-esteem. Individuals with relatively high self-esteem were likely to say that another's behavior was hurtful because it was a shock or it was unexpected. Those with relatively low self-esteem tended to describe the cause of their hurt feelings in terms of relational devaluation, a personal flaw, or humiliation.

The link between self-esteem and hurt implies that individuals enter social situations with preexisting biases about others' behavior based on the way that they feel about themselves. Although the link between self-esteem and hurt has not been evaluated longitudinally, it is theoretically possible that these biases serve to perpetuate self-esteem over time. People with relatively low self-esteem may perceive their hurt feelings to be caused by reasons such as relational devaluation or personal flaws, which, in turn, may confirm their negative self-perceptions or lead to further decrements in perceived self-worth.

Rejection Sensitivity

A number of researchers have noted that hurt typically is associated with feelings of rejection (e.g., Feeney, 2004; Fitness, 2001; Leary et al., 1998). Although people have a general proclivity to avoid social exclusion (Baumeister & Leary, 1995), individuals differ in their tendency to feel rejected in their relationships. The variation across individuals may be, in part, linked to dispositional traits that guide their interpretation of others' behavior. In particular, researchers have suggested that some individuals have a heightened sensitivity to rejection in their relationships. Downey and colleagues refer to rejection sensitivity as a tendency for some people to "anxiously expect, readily perceive, and intensely react to rejection" (Downey, Mougios, Ayduk, London, & Shoda, 2004, p. 668). While the concept of rejection sensitivity has not been examined directly in relation to hurt, it resonates with findings indicating that perceived rejection is positively associated with the degree of hurt felt in a given situation (Leary et al., 1998). Downey and colleagues argue that people's sensitivity to rejection is developed based on previous exposure to rejection and that it serves to defend against the potential emotional pain linked to rejection situations. They also note that this defense system can be dysfunctional if it is triggered automatically without sufficient rejection cues. When this occurs, the behavior of others may reinforce individuals' expectations concerning rejection, regardless of whether these others intended to reject them (Downey, Freitas, Michaelis, & Khouri, 1998). Individuals' expectations concerning the likelihood that they will experience hurt may result in the premature termination of their relationships or a perceived inability to avoid hurtful partners. Furthermore, exaggerated perceptions of others' hurtful behavior may put additional strain on subsequent interactions. Inasmuch as this is the case, individuals who have been hurt in past relationships may inadvertently become more susceptible to hurt feelings in the future.

Relationship Characteristics

People's perceptions of hurtful behavior and the impact of hurtful behavior on social interaction are influenced by interpersonal relationships. For instance, the literature suggests that the type of relationship in which people are involved informs their perceptions of hurtful behavior and, thus, influences the way that they react to hurtful episodes. Similarly, global relationship qualities offer important insights into the various precursors and outcomes of hurtful interactions.

Relationship Type

Certain types of relationships are characterized by features that are likely to influence the way that relational partners interpret and respond to hurtful behavior. For instance, we have speculated that, because of the extensive knowledge that they often have about each other, family members may be particularly skilled at hurting each other. Indeed, our studies have indicated that hurtful behavior enacted by family members tends to elicit more emotional pain than does hurtful behavior enacted by others in general (Vangelisti & Crumley, 1998). The same research revealed that people who reported their feelings were hurt by a family member perceived that the behavior had less of a distancing effect on their relationship than did those who reported they were hurt by other relational partners. There are at least two reasons why family members may be less likely than others to engage in relational distancing. First, the involuntary, relatively permanent nature of the family bond can influence the experience of hurt in ways that are unlike the influences that occur in other relationships. Second, the lengthy shared history of many family members may be more important for relational outcomes than the relatively small portion of time it takes to enact a hurtful episode.

In contrast to family relationships, romantic relationships are voluntary in nature. Feeney (in press) notes this distinction as a primary reason why hurt feelings are especially relevant in the context of romantic relationships. She also argues that the bonds between committed partners usually are communal, such that partners believe that they "should strive to meet each other's needs and protect each other's welfare." If one partner's behavior is seen as a violation of the communal norm, the other might be particularly likely to engage in relational distancing because partners can leave the relationship if the hurt is too intense (Vangelisti & Crumley, 1998). Additionally, Feeney emphasizes the prevalence of hurt in couple relationships as a reason for studying hurt feelings as a distinct phenomenon in this context. In particular, she notes that romantic relationships and close friendships are the most frequently recalled relational context for retrospective accounts of hurtful events (Leary et al., 1998). Events in which a romantic partner is involved have also been found to receive the highest ratings for the degree of hurt and for perceived rejection. Furthermore, our own research indicates that romantic relationships are the most commonly reported topic of hurtful messages (Vangelisti, 1994).

Although hurt feelings are especially prevalent in close, intimate relationships such as those between romantic partners, family members, and friends, intimacy is not a mandatory precursor for hurt feelings to be elicited. Research suggests that hurt feelings are also likely to occur between acquaintances or even strangers, and that it is not necessarily interpersonal closeness that influences the degree of hurt experienced. Snapp and Leary (2001) argue that although the majority of the literature suggests that people's feelings are hurt more frequently by someone close to them than by those whom they do not know well, this finding may be a result of the retrospective accounts on which it is based. In a laboratory setting, Snapp and Leary explored the moderating effects of interpersonal familiarity on hurt feelings among newly acquainted people. Interestingly, the results of their study indicated that participants were much more hurt when they were ignored by a confederate who barely knew them than when a confederate who was more familiar with them seemed disinterested in what they had to say.

Satisfaction

The qualities of interpersonal associations affect individuals' perceptions of and responses to social interaction. In lieu of this, the way people evaluate another's hurtful behavior is likely shaped by their feelings about that relationship. Research has shown that relationship satisfaction tends to color individuals' attributions concerning their partner's behavior (see, e.g., Murray & Holmes, 1997). For instance, people who are highly satisfied with their romantic relationship tend to evaluate their partner's negative behavior in less negative ways than do those who are dissatisfied with their relationship (e.g., Fincham, 1985).

Evaluations influenced by relationship satisfaction can buffer the negative effects of hurtful behavior. Those highly satisfied with their relationship may have a positive interpretation of an interaction that others (those dissatisfied with their relationship) might see as hurtful. As such, people in more satisfied relationships are likely to experience less hurt than those who are dissatisfied. In support of this notion, we found that people who indicated that they were relatively satisfied with their relationship reported experiencing lower levels of emotional pain as a result of a hurtful interaction. Individuals higher in satisfaction also were less likely to distance themselves from the relationship with the person who hurt their feelings than were dissatisfied partners (Vangelisti & Crumley, 1998).

Of course, the ways that satisfied partners evaluate hurtful interactions are not the only reason that hurt seems to have less of an impact on their relationships. People in satisfying relationships probably hurt each other less frequently than do those in dissatisfying relationships. It also is likely that when those who are satisfied are asked to recall a hurtful behavior enacted by their partner, they remember fewer episodes or report situations in which less intense hurt feelings were elicited, as compared with those in relatively dissatisfied relationships. Furthermore, the extent to which individuals are satisfied with their relationship with the person who hurt them can influence the specific appraisals they make about another person's hurtful behavior. Consistent with this thinking, (Young, 2004) found that factors such as relationship satisfaction shape individuals' appraisals of another's hurtful behavior and may mitigate the aversive interpretations of the behavior.

Structural Commitment

Existing literature highlights the possible implications of structural commitment for the course and outcome of hurtful interactions. When individuals are structurally committed to a relationship, they feel that they must remain with their partner, regardless of their preference for maintaining the relationship (Johnson, 1999). This sort of commitment is particularly evident in family relationships. Indeed, it may be one of the reasons why individuals tend not to distance themselves from family members who hurt them—even though the emotional pain they feel at the hands of family members can be more intense than the pain they feel when others hurt them (Vangelisti & Crumley, 1998).

Although family relationships may be one of the most obvious contexts to study the effects of structural commitment on hurtful interactions, other relationships should be examined as well. For instance, research suggests that women sometimes stay with an abusive partner because of the social and financial resources that their partner controls (Johnson, 2006). The inability of these women to distance themselves from a relational partner who hurts them may both reflect and create an expectation for hurtful behavior. It also is possible that some women who are hurt feel that they must pay the price of being hurt for the resources that they receive in their relationship. Perpetrators may feel that their hurtful behavior is appropriate given what they offer their abused partner. This ongoing pattern likely then shapes the emotional context that serves as a backdrop for subsequent hurtful interactions to be evaluated and interpreted. Breaking this complicated cognitive-behavioral cycle and preventing it from occurring in the future (e.g., after abused partners extricate themselves from abusive relationships) are of paramount importance for future research on hurt.

Emotional Context

The emotional contexts that are created in relationships contribute to the ways that individuals interpret and evaluate others' hurtful behavior. Although research has yet to identify the means by which different emotional contexts affect hurt feelings in relationships, we have begun to explore the nature of hurtful family environments and assess whether individuals' perceptions of their family environment are linked to their perceptions of hurtful family interactions (Vangelisti et al., 2007). The results of our studies indicated that hurtful family environments tend to be characterized by aggression (e.g., general negativity, fighting, yelling), a lack of affection (e.g., not saying "I love you," no hugs, not feeling loved), neglect (e.g., loneliness, disregard, needs unmet), and violence (e.g., physical or sexual abuse). We found that those who perceived that their family environments were characterized by a lack of affection tended to be more verbally hostile and have lower self-esteem. In contrast, individuals who typified their family environments as aggressive tended to have relatively low verbal hostility and low self-esteem. Those who saw their family context as aggressive also tended to perceive a family member's hurtful behavior as intentional. Our findings further suggest that the emotional context that characterizes family environments is linked to the experience of hurtful behavior in important ways. More specifically, those who perceived that their family environment was lacking in affection reported hurtful episodes to be less emotionally painful than did others, suggesting that people tend to habituate to such situations and become relatively numb to their hurt feelings. To this point, the extant work on hurt has neglected the context-specific features that are associated with the elicitation and experience of hurt feelings. Our findings concerning hurtful family environments underline the need to consider others—outside of the dyad under question—who might influence hurtful interactions.

Directions for Future Research

Although the literature shows that scholars from several disciplines, including our own research team, have made substantial progress in studying hurt, it also reveals that our understanding of hurt feelings and hurtful interactions is quite limited. Some limitations stem from conceptual and methodological challenges inherent to investigating hurt; others involve simple, but important, gaps in the literature that we have yet to address.

Conceptual and Methodological Challenges

One criticism of research on hurt feelings is that much of it relies on retrospective data. Participants frequently are asked to recall and describe an incident that hurt their feelings and to respond to any number of questions concerning that event. Undoubtedly, one of the reasons that researchers have relied on these sorts of data is the ease with which they are collected. But another reason that is much more difficult to deal with involves ethical issues. Researchers certainly can elicit hurt in a laboratory setting, but the ways in which they can do so and intensity of the emotion that they can evoke are constrained by important ethical considerations. Some researchers have dealt with these constraints by setting up situations in the laboratory that elicit relatively mild forms of hurt or rejection. For instance, Eisenberger, Lieberman, and Williams (2003) asked participants to engage in a virtual ball-tossing task from which they had been excluded. DeWall and Baumeister (2006) asked participants to complete a personality test and then told some of them that they had a personality type that might result in their ending up alone later in life. While both of these manipulations are creative, they are not likely to evoke hurt feelings that are comparable in intensity to those that are elicited when people are rejected by a relational partner (e.g., with words such as "I don't love you anymore") or reviled by a parent (e.g., with statements such as "I never thought I'd have a daughter as stupid as you are").

Another limitation of research on hurt feelings is that many studies have analyzed relatively salient hurtful episodes. When participants are asked to recall and describe an event that hurt their feelings, the likelihood is that they will recall an incident that is particularly salient to them—one that stands out in their mind because it was extremely hurtful and memorable. As a consequence of focusing attention on hurtful events that are salient, we know very little about those that are more mundane or routine. Importantly, hurtful events may be perceived as mundane for a number of reasons. One is that they may not be very hurtful. When the intensity of hurt feelings is low, individuals are relatively unlikely to focus on and remember the event that elicited those feelings. Another reason is that the events may involve people or circumstances that are viewed as unimportant. In these situations, individuals may feel a fair amount of hurt, but may disregard their feelings after a short period of time because the people involved or the situation itself is not relevant to their goals or their current course of action. Yet another reason that hurtful episodes may be viewed as mundane is that they were quickly resolved. In these cases, the initial pain experienced may have been intense, but that pain may have been quelled by an immediate, very sincere apology. Understanding these and other sorts of mundane, routine hurtful interactions would provide insights into how hurt feelings operate.

The tendency to focus on single hurtful events and on retrospective reports also has limited what researchers know about patterns of hurtful behavior. There are some data on the perceived frequency of hurtful interactions and on the likelihood that a relational partner will repeatedly engage in hurtful behavior (see, e.g., Vangelisti & Young, 2000). There also are data on the perceived influence of hurtful interactions on people's relationships over time (see, e.g., Leary et al., 1998) and on sequences of behavior that may be viewed as hurtful (see, e.g., Caughlin, 2002). But there are almost no data on patterns of hurtful behavior. As a consequence, we know little about how hurtful communication unfolds within a given interaction or how it operates over time within a given relationship. What is it that makes an utterance extremely painful in one interaction but not very painful in another? What makes people in some relationships become more sensitive to their partner's hurtful behavior over time while others become less sensitive to similar behavior? Why does hurtful behavior have a profound influence on the quality of some relationships and relatively little influence on others? The extant literature offers a solid rationale for positing questions such as these, but researchers need to begin to use methods that allow them to examine sequences of behavior in hurtful interactions and to study the influence of hurtful interactions over the course of relationships so as to respond to these questions.

Topics for Study

While some gaps in the literature on hurt feelings are due to conceptual and methodological challenges faced by researchers, others involve important topics that researchers, including our own team, simply have yet to investigate. We see several important but yet-to-be-addressed questions that extend from the intraindividual level to family/peer-network and cultural levels. For example, scholars have yet to systematically consider the role of physiology in hurtful interactions. The degree to which people are physiologically aroused before, during, and after they experience a hurtful event is likely to influence not only the way they feel about the event but also the way they respond to it. We have argued that individuals' ability to respond to hurt in constructive ways might be influenced by the intensity of their hurt feelings (Vangelisti, 1994). It is possible that the link between people's responses to hurt and the intensity of their feelings is mediated by the physiological reactions that they have to being hurt. Those who become highly aroused when they are hurt may have much more difficulty responding to their feelings in constructive ways than those who are not highly aroused—regardless of how intense their initial feelings were. Alternatively, people who are physiologically aroused by hurt may develop coping mechanisms to deal with their arousal. DeWall and Baumeister (2006) argued that individuals who are hurt by being socially excluded experience temporary emotional numbness. It may be that people who are highly aroused when they are hurt become emotionally numb in an effort to regulate their arousal. If this is the case, physiological arousal may moderate the link between hurt and emotional numbness.

Another topic that researchers have yet to study involves the way that people are socialized about hurt feelings. What are the means by which children learn to hurt others and respond to their own emotional pain? Perhaps the most obvious way is through their own direct experience. The literature on bullying in childhood suggests that there is an association between bullying and victimization (Rigby, 2002)—that by being treated badly at home or school, children learn the roles of both bully and victim. Children's direct experiences with hurt likely operate in a similar way. When they are repeatedly hurt at home by parents or at school by peers, children are likely to learn strategies for hurting others and for responding to hurt. But direct experience is not the only way to learn about emotional pain. Children also can learn about hurt indirectly by watching members of their family or peer group hurt each other. Research indicates that interparental conflict and the quality of parents' communication affect the way that children function in their relationships with others (e.g., Howes & Markman, 1989; Lindahl, Clements, & Markman, 1997). Given this, children who frequently overhear their parents saying hurtful things to each other during conflict may develop a different orientation toward emotional pain than those who do not. On the one hand, they may emulate their parents and adopt similarly aggressive, hurtful strategies when they engage in conflict. On the other, they may make a conscious decision to avoid repeating their parents' behavior and, as a result, become extremely passive.

If, indeed, children learn about hurt feelings from their family members and their peers, part of what they learn probably involves cultural values about hurt. As noted by MacDonald and Leary (2005), a wide range of cultures appear to have a term or phrase to describe "hurt feelings," and that term or phase often is associated with social exclusion. However, the cross-cultural linguistic connection between hurt and social exclusion does not preclude the possibility that there are theoretically important differences in how people interpret hurtful behavior and express hurt feelings. The cultural milieu in which children are immersed likely teaches them which behaviors are hurtful, whether and when it is appropriate to hurt others, and how they should express their hurt feelings. For example, because of the premium that people in collectivist cultures place on group membership, they may be more susceptible to experiencing intense hurt when they are socially rejected than may those in individualistic cultures. Similarly, those in collectivist cultures may be less likely than those in individualistic cultures to express their hurt feelings if the expression creates questions about their loyalty to the group and more likely to do so if the expression highlights their loyalty. In other words, the tendency of people in collectivist cultures to express their hurt may be moderated by the degree to which such expression raises questions about their dedication to the group or its values. Examining cultural differences in the way people interpret hurt, engage in hurtful behavior, and express hurt feelings would provide researchers (including our own team) and theorists with important information about the influence of hurt feelings on interpersonal relationships within and across cultural boundaries.

References

Baumeister, R. F., & Leary, M. R. (1995). The need to belong: Desire for interpersonal attachments as a fundamental human motivation. *Psychological Bulletin, 117*, 497–529.

Caughlin, J. P. (2002). The demand/withdraw pattern of communication as a predictor of marital satisfaction over time: Unresolved issues and future directions. *Human Communication Research, 28,* 49–86.

Cunningham, M. R., Shamblen, S. R., Barbee, A. P., & Ault, L. K. (2005). Social allergies in romantic relationships: Behavioral repetition, emotional sensitization, and dissatisfaction in dating couples. *Personal Relationships, 12,* 273–295.

DeWall, C. N., & Baumeister, R. F. (2006). Alone but feeling no pain: Effects of social exclusion on physical pain tolerance and pain threshold, affective forecasting, and interpersonal empathy. *Journal of Personality and Social Psychology, 91,* 1–15.

DeWall, C. N., Baumeister, R. F., & Masicampo, E. J. (in press). Feeling rejected but not much else: Resolving the paradox of emotional numbness following social exclusion. In A. L. Vangelisti (Ed.), *Hurt feelings in close relationships.* New York: Cambridge University Press.

Downey, G., Freitas, A., Michaelis, B., & Khouri, H. (1998). The self-fulfilling prophecy in close relationships: Rejection sensitivity and rejection by romantic partners. *Journal of Personality and Social Psychology, 75,* 545–560.

Downey, G., Mougios, V., Ayduk, O., London, B. E., & Shoda, Y. (2004). Rejection sensitivity and the defensive motivational system: Insights from the startle response to rejection cues. *Psychological Science, 15,* 668–673.

Eisenberger, N. I., Lieberman, M. D., & Williams, K. D. (2003). Does rejection hurt? An fMRI study of social exclusion. *Science, 302,* 290–292.

Feeney, J. A. (2004). Hurt feelings in couple relationships: Towards integrative models of the negative effects of hurtful events. *Journal of Social and Personal Relationships, 21,* 487–508.

Feeney, J. A. (2005). Hurt feelings in couple relationships: Exploring the role of attachment and perceptions of personal injury. *Personal Relationships, 12,* 253–271.

Feeney, J. A. (in press). When love hurts: Understanding hurtful events in couple relationships. In A. L. Vangelisti (Ed.), *Hurt feelings in close relationships.* New York: Cambridge University Press.

Fincham, F. D. (1985). Attributions in close relationships. In J. Harvey & G. Weary (Eds.), *Attribution: Basic issues and applications* (pp. 203–234). New York: Academic Press.

Fitness, J. (2001). Betrayal, rejection, revenge, and forgiveness: An interpersonal script analysis. In M. R. Leary (Ed.), *Interpersonal rejection* (pp. 73–103). New York: Oxford University Press.

Folkes, V. S. (1982). Communicating the causes of social rejection. *Journal of Experimental Social Psychology, 18,* 235–252.

Howes, P., & Markman, H. J. (1989). Marital quality and child functioning: A longitudinal investigation. *Child Development, 60,* 1044–1051.

Johnson, M. P. (1999). Personal, moral, and structural commitment to relationships: Experiences of choice and constraint. In J. M. Adams & W. H. Jones (Eds.), *Handbook of interpersonal commitment and relationships stability* (pp. 73–87). New York: Kluwer Academic/Plenum.

Johnson, M. P. (2006). Violence and abuse in personal relationships: Conflict, terror, and resistance in intimate partnerships. In A. L. Vangelisti & D. Perlman (Eds.), *Cambridge handbook of personal relationships* (pp. 557–576). New York: Cambridge University Press.

L'Abate, L. (1977). Intimacy is sharing hurt feelings: A reply to David Mace. *Journal of Marriage and Family Counseling, 3,* 13–16.

Lazarus, R. S. (1991). *Emotion and adaptation.* New York: Oxford University Press.

Leary, M. R., & Springer, C. A. (2001). Hurt feelings: The neglected emotion. In R. M. Kowalski (Ed.), *Behaving badly: Aversive behaviors in interpersonal relationships* (pp. 151–175). Washington, DC: American Psychological Association.

Leary, M. R., Springer, C., Negel, L., Ansell, E., & Evans, K. (1998). The causes, phenomenology, and consequences of hurt feelings. *Journal of Personality and Social Psychology, 74,* 1225–1237.

Leary, M. R., Tambor, E. S., Terdal, S. K., & Downs, D. L. (1995). Self-esteem as an interpersonal monitor: The sociometer hypothesis. *Journal of Personality and Social Psychology, 68,* 518–530.

Lindahl, K. M., Clements, M., & Markman, H. (1997). Predicting marital and parent functioning in dyads and triads: A longitudinal investigation of marital processes. *Journal of Family Psychology, 11,* 139–151.

MacDonald, G., & Leary, M. R. (2005). Why does social exclusion hurt? The relationship between social and physical pain. *Psychological Bulletin, 131,* 202–223.

Malle, B. F., & Knobe, J. (1997). The folk concept of intentionality. *Journal of Experimental Social Psychology, 33,* 101–121.

McEwen, W. J., & Greenberg, B. S. (1970). The effects of message intensity on receiver evaluations of source, message, and topic. *Journal of Communication, 20,* 340–350.

Murray, S. L., & Holmes, J. G. (1997). A leap of faith? Positive illusions in romantic relationships. *Personality and Social Psychology Bulletin, 23,* 586–604.

Parkinson, B. (1997). Untangling the appraisal-emotion connection. *Personality and Social Psychology Review, 1,* 62–79.

Rigby, K. (2002). Bullying in childhood. In P. K. Smith & C. H. Hart (Eds.), *Blackwell handbook of social development* (pp. 549–568). Oxford, UK: Blackwell.

Shaver, P. R., Mikuliner, M., Lavy, S., & Cassidy, J. (in press). Understanding and altering hurt feelings: An attachment-theoretical perspective on the generation and regulation of emotions. In A. L. Vangelisti (Ed.), *Hurt feelings in close relationships.* New York: Cambridge University Press.

Shaver, P. R., Schwartz, J., Kirson, D., & O'Connor, C. (1987). Emotion knowledge: Further exploration of a prototype approach. *Journal of Personality and Social Psychology, 52,* 1061–1086.

Snapp, C. M., & Leary, M. R. (2001). Hurt feelings among new acquaintances: Moderating effects of interpersonal familiarity. *Journal of Social and Personal Relationships, 18,* 315–326.

Vangelisti, A. L. (1994). Messages that hurt. In W. R. Cupach & B. H. Spitzberg (Eds.), *The dark side of interpersonal communication* (pp. 53–82). Hillsdale, NJ: Erlbaum.

Vangelisti, A. L. (2001). Making sense of hurtful interactions in close relationships. In V. Manusov & J. H. Harvey (Eds.), *Attribution, communication behavior, and close relationships* (pp. 38–58). New York: Cambridge University Press.

Vangelisti, A. L., & Crumley, L. P. (1998). Reactions to messages that hurt: The influence of relational contexts. *Communication Monographs, 65,* 173–196.

Vangelisti, A. L., Maguire, K. C., Alexander, A. L., & Clark, G. (2007). Hurtful family environments: Links with individual, relationship, and perceptual variables. *Communication Monographs, 74,* 375–385.

Vangelisti, A. L., & Young, S. L. (2000). When words hurt: The effects of perceived intentionality on interpersonal relationships. *Journal of Social and Personal Relationships, 17,* 393–424.

Vangelisti, A. L., Young, S. L., Carpenter-Theune, K. E., & Alexander, A. L. (2005). Why does it hurt? The perceived causes of hurt feelings. *Communication Research, 32,* 443–477.

Young, S. L. (2004). Factors that influence recipients' appraisals of hurtful communication. *Journal of Social and Personal Relationships, 21,* 291–303.

Zahn-Waxler, C., & Kochanska, G. (1990). The origins of guilt. In R. A. Thompson (Ed.), *Nebraska symposium on motivation* (pp. 183–258). Lincoln: University of Nebraska Press.

PART IV

Relationships, Media, and Culture

12

Culture and Personal Relationships

Kristine L. Fitch

My first exposures to interpersonal communication research and theory happened between the two seminal volumes (Miller, 1976; Roloff & Miller, 1987) noted as predecessors to this one. There was no specific mention of culture as a factor in interpersonal relationships in those volumes (I have refreshed my memory on this point), because the processes and concepts we studied—self-disclosure, stages of relational development, nonverbal immediacy, communication apprehension—were implicitly assumed to be universal aspects of human communication. When culture was mentioned, it was considered relevant only in contexts of difference: People in different cultures might do interpersonal communication differently, in which case predictions might need tweaking, but theoretical substance would remain the same. In the social science approach to communication scholarship, culture was generally synonymous with nation-state, and was largely the domain of intercultural communication. That approach separated interpersonal communication processes from culture, and examined contact between distinct cultural systems of values and attitudes, and differences in communication behavior rooted in those systems. Some research in this vein also focused on cultural differences among racial groups within the United States, often in an effort to describe and explain miscommunication.

This pattern was broken, for me, in a graduate seminar taught by Robert Hopper in which we read "Speaking Like a Man in Teamsterville" (Philipsen, 1975) and "Places for Speaking in Teamsterville" (Philipsen, 1976). Those two articles, sometimes described as among the most influential of their time, offered a view of interpersonal communication as inseparable from culture, as situated on every level and in every nuance within systems of meaning specific to groups of people. In this chapter, I will describe the contribution of the ethnography of speaking to research and theory in interpersonal communication, in particular its approach to communication as always and everywhere situated within particular cultural contexts. I begin with a brief sketch of the historical context of this theoretical program, then trace three stages of my own work in the area, and conclude with a discussion of some current challenges and possible future directions.

Personal Relationships as Situated Within Cultural Codes

The idea that all communication practices are situated within cultural codes of meaning is based on the work of Dell Hymes (1962, 1972), who described the unit of analysis for studying codes such as *speech communities*. This term emphasized that boundaries of cultural groups consisted of patterns of communication that were intelligible and symbolically significant for members of the group (rather than, e.g., geography or ethnicity). Membership in a speech community was later framed by Philipsen (1992) as a verb: *Membering* is the action of participating as a member of a speech community by using, or showing understanding of others' uses of, valued ways of speaking. "Speaking," in the Hymesian approach to culture, includes all forms and modes of communication. The Teamsterville studies we read in Hopper's seminar expanded the concept of culture beyond nation-state and race, given that the people he observed and interviewed were all U.S. Americans and most were white, working-class males.

An illustration of how this approach to interpersonal communication diverged from the received view of the time may be instructive. In a widely cited state-of-the-art essay, Miller (1978) proposed a developmental definition of interpersonal communication. He claimed that all initial communication is impersonal, and that communicators encountering one another for the first time could only relate to one another on the basis of social roles, rather than personal characteristics. From this view, interpersonal communication is the result of moving beyond broad "cultural and sociological, rather than psychological information" (p. 167)—such as age, race, and sex—to communication based on knowledge of the other as a unique, specific individual. In truly interpersonal communication, participants can move beyond the social norms and constraints imposed on them to more "mutually negotiated, idiosyncratic rules" for their communication and their personal relationship (p. 169).

In contrast, Katriel and Philipsen (1981), building on Philipsen's Teamsterville studies, argued that this view of interpersonal communication was in fact a culture-specific one, rather than a universal characteristic of human communication. This insight was available to the two authors because in Tamar Katriel's native language of Hebrew, there was no word for *communication* in its culturally symbolic sense, for example, "What we need is communication." In her home country of Israel, there was no parallel to the idea that *relationships* were something formed by *real communication,* or that both relationships and selves could be *worked on* through *communication.* All these were, however, taken-for-granted assumptions among middle-class white Americans. Katriel and Philipsen focused on uses of the term *real communication* (and its contrast term *mere talk*) in everyday talk and in certain media texts. The cultural code they described as revolving around these key terms matched quite precisely the interpersonal end of the developmental continuum proposed by Miller: Close relationships were those in which the participants came to know one another as unique individuals, and based on that knowledge they developed unique systems of expectations and interpretations for their actions. Katriel and Philipsen described a "communication ritual" as the cultural practice through which such closeness was understood to develop; they further argued that this ritual was specific to a particular (though loosely defined) cultural group. The theoretical program of some ethnographies of speaking since then has been to show that other, also supposedly universal aspects of interpersonal communication are in fact culturally situated ideas. That has been a particular emphasis of the work that I do.

Urban Colombians: A Basis for Theoretical Development Through Contrast

I studied the communication practices of urban Colombians not because I thought that the field of communication would find them intrinsically worth knowing, but because of the illumination a contrasting case study could make of the culturally situated nature of all communication practices. The conceptual emphasis in my work has thus been on communication *practices* rather than on *processes.* I focus on historically transmitted, symbolically meaningful ways of communicating specific to loosely defined groups of people, not on the properties and characteristics of human communication in its most generalizable form. This emphasis assumes that the ways people use language and other modes of communication in their encodings of intentions and their interpretive, often evaluative decodings are grounded in templates of expectations (norms) and taken-for-granted, unspoken assumptions about meanings of choices made between alternative possibilities for action (premises). Beyond the seminal work of Hymes and Philipsen, the theoretical underpinnings for the work I do include ordinary language philosophy (Austin, 1962; Grice, 1975; Searle, 1969, 1975, and others), pragmatics (Brown & Levinson, 1987; Buttny, 1993, and others), and discursive psychology (Antaki, 1994; Edwards, 1995; Potter & Wetherell, 1987, and others).

Within those theoretical and conceptual parameters, I argued first in a general way that construction of meaning occurred through pragmatic structures such as personal address, and was realized through culture-specific resources for communication. The data for that study were 10 Colombian address terms related to the central term *mother,* the range of meanings for those terms hearable in everyday interaction, and the categories of interpersonal action they accomplished (Fitch, 1991). I suggested that understanding metaphorical uses of address terms, and knowing how to distinguish multiple meanings of language use more generally, required detailed examination of naturally occurring interaction within and about personal relationships. I proposed that any study of interpersonal relationships needed to be situated within—or at least take seriously into account—communal systems of resources, linguistic and otherwise, for understanding and negotiating relationships.

I then pursued the more specific point that what was widely studied in interpersonal communication as compliance gaining could be more fully understood from a cultural perspective of what resources existed for attempts to influence peoples' behavior (Fitch, 1994). Following an initial study that set a particular agenda of research questions and methods (Miller, Roloff, Seibold, & Boster, 1977), compliance-gaining research focused primarily on matching strategy types or techniques (Dillard, 1988) with either situational or personality variables (Seibold, Cantrill, & Meyers, 1984). Although critiques of that approach appeared as I pursued the cultural aspects of social influence (e.g., Kellermann & Cole, 1994), discursive enactment of compliance-gaining attempts was not a specific focus of attention. Contextual variation was limited to situational differences, rather than looking for systems of meaning that defined situations as meaningfully similar or different. Personal qualities and situational differences were examined as central to compliance-gaining attempts, and the likelihood of their success or failure, independent of both the speech community in which they were situated and the particular formulation and sequential placement through which they were enacted.

In contrast, I argued that the primary resource for compliance seeking was the speech act defined by Searle (1975) as directives, a category of action that included hints, requests, advice, commands, threats, and so forth. Directives had long been established through anthropological linguistic case studies as indices of cultural norms and premises related to power, personhood, and coordination of meaning and action (Blum-Kulka, House, & Kasper, 1989; Ervin-Tripp, 1976; Goodwin, 1990; Rosaldo, 1980, 1982; Rushforth, 1981; Weigel & Weigel, 1985). A communication perspective needed to broaden the Searlian concept of directives as a type of utterance to include metaphorical as well as literal meaning, a shift that involved looking at directives as a kind of sequence. Only by examining the response to an utterance, I proposed, could the hearer's interpretation of it as a directive be determined. I presented a comparison of directive sequences and natives' reflections on them in Boulder, Colorado, and Bogotá, Colombia, less to establish the unremarkable fact that preferences for particular directive types differed across them than to show that those preferences were grounded in communal systems of norms and premises. To the extent that U.S. American compliance-gaining research focused entirely on techniques and strategies as evaluated and used by U.S. American research subjects, the logic behind preferred and dispreferred choices would never be discovered. As long as variation in strategy selection was linked to personality, situational context, and relational type, the existence of a particular interpersonal ideology (Fitch, 1998) that enabled, constrained, and generally set evaluative parameters around individual choices would remain unheard and invisible.

The final argument I put forth in this vein related to cultural norms and premises, and relationships formulated within particular systems of meaning, as integral to persuasion (Fitch, 2003a). I compared three ethnographic case studies, none focused specifically on persuasive attempts, to show that culture is the basis, not only for *how* persuasion happens—the typical focus of cross-cultural studies of both interpersonal persuasion (Cai & Wilson, 2000; Kim, Shin, & Cai, 1998; Neuliep & Hazleton, 1985) and rhetoric (e.g., Garrett, 1999; Ma, 1999)—but for *what* people regard as contingent and thus open to persuasive attempts. I explored with particular emphasis the available resources—*with what*—people may be persuaded in a particular speech community. Based on the comparison across ethnographic case studies, I proposed that cultural influence on persuasion be conceptualized as a range of contingency. Within each culture is an array of action and thought that is sufficiently contingent—possible but not certain—about which its members may be persuaded. Outside that array are, first, matters that are not subject to persuasion because they are taken for granted, which members of a group learn through socialization. Few U.S. American white middle-class children need to be persuaded to leave home at age 18, for example, because there is a cultural imperative that all must do so. In contrast, Colombian children are expected to live at home until they marry; to persuade them to do otherwise, in the absence of some extraordinary circumstance, would be close to impossible.

Matters of this kind, ones so contrary to the norms and premises of the group that members could not ordinarily be persuaded of them, lie outside the range of persuasion in a quite different way. This class of nonpersuadables I termed *coercibles,* with the assumption that people may be, and observably are, brainwashed or forced into doing many things that they ordinarily would not do. Few wealthy Americans could be persuaded to rob a bank, but heiress Patricia Hearst claimed that she was both brainwashed by the group that kidnapped her and forced at gunpoint to do so. I also discussed relational codes—systems of meaning developed within particular relationships, described by some as relational cultures (Baxter, 1987; Wood, 1982)—as able to exert particular persuasive force on the people involved in the relationship, in close parallel (although sometimes in an opposing direction) to the persuasive force of culture. As with the studies of personal address as an index of identity and relationships and of directive sequences as an index of communal understandings of power and human nature, I hoped that this essay would expand theories of interpersonal persuasion by showing that cultural influence extended beyond surface variation of persuasive strategies. I meant the sum of these three studies to be an amplification of interpersonal theory and research into considering the cultural frameworks of norms, premises, and symbolic terms characteristic of all human communication activity.

The work I have described so far was oriented toward the face-to-face instantiations of culture. Given my focus on interpersonal communication and personal relationships, this might seem to be common sense. A profound challenge to that understanding of culture—one I had never noticed—came when I moved to the University of Iowa in 1995. I had studied or taught in three quite different departments of communication—two were named, significantly, departments of *speech communication*—with no exposure to media studies of any kind. At Iowa, I heard people use the word *culture,* the concept I felt most sure I understood, in ways that were mysterious to me: "We all know, of course, that culture is something people are *paid to produce.*"

Another: "I approach intercultural communication in the usual way—as a site of oppression and resistance" (*the usual way?*).

The shift was more than a matter of what my colleagues examined as data, partly because they never referred to collection or analysis of data. It was a passage from social science, a world in which I thought that, given my interpretive approach, I was as marginal as a person could be, into critical cultural studies. The pass I got was a transit visa rather than a green card: I can move freely, but only for short periods of time and in a limited area. In the critical cultural studies world, I am always and forever destined to be a social scientist. Thankfully, that makes questions of data and methods—ones I understood to be at the heart of the work I do—still relevant.

Methods

The methods involved in ethnographic research used to be, from a social science perspective, a straightforward issue. We observe people, usually doing the most ordinary activities of their lives, sometimes participating to some degree in what they are doing. We ask questions about what they do and how they do it and what other ways they might be doing it, sometimes in sit-down sessions with lists of questions and a tape recorder and at other times in spare moments during the activities themselves. I also ask people to turn on audio recorders when they are likely to be talking, again in very ordinary, everyday ways, either when I am present or when I am not. I have learned to ask relational partners to interview themselves, rather than asking the questions myself. Increasingly, I have watched television and films, collected parts of newspapers and magazines that had something to do with personal relationships, and sometimes followed people into their instant messenger screens or their e-mail chains.

The guiding principle behind data collection, for me and to some degree for most ethnographers, has been to immerse myself as fully as possible within the way of life of a group of people. Research questions are narrow enough to focus on some subset of the total stream of experience: How do urban Colombians use formal and informal second-person pronouns? What native terms for persons and talk do English people from the East Midlands use to refer to personal relationships, and what evaluative load do these terms carry? At the same time, research questions in ethnographic work are fluid and expected to change, depending on what emerges as meaningful and important in the group or setting under study. My original question about formal versus informal second-person pronouns in Colombia, for example, spread into five categories of address terms: Three, not two, second-person pronouns are used in Colombian Spanish (*vos* is closer to the informal than the formal, but not quite *tú*, and is regionally distinctive). These three pronouns index the rest of the personal address system that includes proper names, kinship terms, nicknames, and titles.

Data collection thus begins from midrange and flexible research questions and spreads across as many forms of, and settings for, interaction as are theoretically relevant to the phenomenon under study (described as theoretical sampling by Honigmann, 1970) with the expectation that analysis of data will begin during, not after, data collection. Analysis of ethnographic data is an inductive, iterative process of tentatively grouping particular instances of the phenomenon into categories of similarity and difference. What counts as an instance of the phenomenon may change during the course of the study due to the understanding that language use is meaningful only in context (another way of saying that all communication is culturally situated). When I started to study directives, for example, I followed Searle (1969, 1975) and assumed that they were a type of utterance. Confronted with exchanges such as this one, I had to rethink that assumption:

Fragment I. Boulder, Colorado.

Preschool teacher: Matthew (child looks up), I see someone throwing dirt.

Child: Oooookay (sighs, puts down handful of dirt). (Fitch, 1994, p. 199)

Grammatically, it is difficult to hear the declarative sentence "I see someone throwing dirt" as a command. Interactionally, a 4-year-old child clearly understood it as such. The only empirical way to count an utterance as a directive turned out to be a consideration of sequence: Any grammatical construction could count as a directive, or as something else, depending on what came before and/or after it. That was as true in Bogotá as in Boulder; therefore, the boundaries of an instance of the phenomenon of *directives* were a conversational sequence, rather than an utterance. The fluidity of this aspect of data collection, in the sense that it actually emerged during early stages of data analysis, makes *instances* a more interpretive variety of the social science standard *unit of analysis.*

Another distinction between ethnographic data analysis and much qualitative social science is the activity described in qualitative work as "coding." To the extent that coding is understood to be a process oriented toward objective, reliable, and replicable sorting of instances into mutually exclusive categories, ethnographic analysis is, again, a more fluid version of that activity. Although instances are compared with one another, and although at a basic level the comparison is one of similarities and differences, the range of possible relationships between instances is extensive. Such possibilities are described by Spradley (1979, 1980) as semantic relationships. He notes that although there are some universal semantic relationships (following Casagrande & Hale, 1967), others will be specific to the group being studied. The sorting and comparison activities of ethnographers are thus better understood as interpreting, rather than coding, data. Data interpretation involves noticing the complexity of social life and the resulting need to describe nuances of difference within categories of apparent similarity. Although not all ethnographic analysis is grounded theory—a fashionable and therefore much-misused term (Suddaby, 2006)—the first goal of an ethnographic case study is sometimes described as building a theory internal to the case. In other words, the patterns and meanings of language use observed (or by other means discerned) within the speech community are described in systematic ways that constitute an explanation of some aspect of the symbolic life of that group of people.

In much of my work with Colombians, for example, the central symbolic element I focused on was the notion that a person is first and foremost a set of connections to other people. The connections are to individuals, of course, but more important, they are connections to groups: families, neighborhoods, schools, professions, and natives of each geographical region. That central conceptualization of the person emerged through personal address, through directives, through narratives told about reaching goals through *palanca*—literally, a lever; symbolically, a personal connection (Fitch, 1998). My analysis of ethnographic data focused on distinguishing patterns of those language features—address terms, speech acts, and a narrative genre—and their meanings as reflected in natives' terms for talk (Carbaugh, 1989).

The interpretation that led to the central claim of connectedness as more salient than, for example, the autonomy of unique individuals, was one I discussed at length with Colombian participants, particularly in the later stages of analysis. They offered contradictory instances and observations, describing individuals who lived their lives exactly as they pleased, with no apparent regard for the expectations of those they were presumably connected to. They noted people who rose from humble origins to achieve great success in politics or the arts, despite the lack of personal connections generally assumed to be indispensable to such success. They pointed out couples and families who were joined in particularly tight relationships, yet at odds with the ways of life typical of their region or class. It would be an oversimplification to say that many such "exceptions" to the patterns I claimed actually highlighted the meaningfulness and evaluative weight of those patterns. Nonetheless, the talk that constructed those contradictions and corrections to patterns did itself orient—in a useful variety of ways—to the cultural code I hoped to discern. Certainly individuals, couples, and families had room to go against (and to improvise within) cultural norms. The talk that described those people as aberrations, whether with admiration or disapproval, was both offered to me as a researcher and hearable in more everyday, naturally occurring interaction. Gossip, advice, moral tales told of those who behaved inappropriately, and accounts offered to explain and justify actions sanctionable as inappropriate are some of the forms of talk through which Daena Goldsmith and I, among others, have sought to show the discursive force (Philipsen, 1992) of cultural norms for behavior (Fitch, 2003a, 2003b; Goldsmith & Baxter, 1996; Goldsmith & Fitch, 1997).

Focusing on native terms for talk as an analytic approach highlights another distinctive characteristic of ethnographic methods described by Geertz (1976) as an emphasis on experience-near, as opposed to experience-distant, analytic concepts. Connections between people are referred to as *vínculos* in Colombian Spanish, and there were native terms for categories of actions—speech events with names—that created, reinforced, made deeper, or threatened those connections. *Coger confianza* (to create or "catch" trust, i.e., to establish a connection to another person characterized by some degree of trust and affection), for example, is a speech event accomplishable through personal address, by directives, and by other linguistic and nonlinguistic means. *Echar cepillo* (literally, to run a brush; figuratively, to curry favor) is an evaluative term for the same linguistic and nonlinguistic actions when put to more instrumental uses. The *vínculo* created or deepened when someone curries favor is evaluated as insincere and thus problematic, though all too common, within the Colombian interpersonal ideology of connectedness. Creating and maintaining relationships with an appropriate level of *confianza,* on the other hand, was the activity on which personal happiness as well as success in life depended.

In contrast to these experience-near concepts, the social world of urban Colombians I observed might be described and explained by any number of experience-distant analytic terms, that is, ones the natives themselves would not use in everyday talk, nor in research interviews, with regard to their lives. Social class stratification is a ubiquitous feature of Colombian life, visible in personal appearance, clothing, and where, what, and how one eats. It is also hearable on all levels of verbal communication, from accent to pronoun use to directive forms to narratives. Social class is also a term and a concept familiar to most educated Colombians. It is not, however, an explanation or description used in everyday talk in the way that *coger confianza* and *echar cepillo* are. Social class is thus an experience-distant concept for Colombians and a significantly larger interpretive leap from the data. Experience-distant analytic categories are crucial to ethnographic work as links to research and theory beyond the case study. The theory of the case, then—the systematic description and explanation of the ways of speaking within the group and their symbolic importance—connects to theories external to the case by way of such analytic categories.

A final methodological point worth noting has to do with writing itself as a research method, rather than a neutral medium for conveying results of research. Writing is posited as the method most definitive of, and thus crucial to, ethnography. Postmodernist challenges to traditional ethnography began with epistemological questions about the position and perspective of a researcher who claimed the authority to describe the way of life of a group of people, despite, in most cases, being an outsider to the group. Beyond the ethical questions raised by doing so, traditional ethnography's implicitly objectivist stance was contradicted by the mandate of immersion, to the extent possible, within the group (for cogent expressions of this and other critiques of traditional ethnography, see Conquergood, 1991; Stewart, 1997). Both the attempt at objectivity and the representation of another's way of life, rather than one's own, are, however, mandates of social science writing. One response to postmodernist criticism was to turn the focus of ethnography away from lives of others to one's own lived experience. Third-person objectivity gave way to the presumed honesty of self-reflexivity and first-person ownership of perceptions and biases that were inseparable from experience, including research. Beyond the people who do it, autoethnography is regarded by some—though certainly not all—communication scholars as offering valuable contributions to research and theory without being considered social science.

There is no denying the impact that autoethnography has had on ethnographic research, even among those whose work does not go in that direction. Autoethnography is a siren song, particularly for some beginning scholars to whom social science writing seems too stiff and foreign, an inauthentic language they fear to master as much as they desire to. I have written personal narratives about aspects of culture and language about which it would have been difficult to do traditional ethnographic inquiry, some of them more empirical (Fitch, 2003b), some of them closer to autoethnography's open subjectivity (Fitch, 2005). Teaching writing as an ethnographic method remains a challenge because of the Janus face of ontology and epistemology unveiled by postmodernism: Writing social science means striving for some degree of objectivity, from the first framing of research questions through the final draft of the article.[1] Objectivity rests on distance between subjects and researchers that makes close attention to writing uncomfortable, very much like attention to what the cook was thinking and feeling while cooking rather than to the taste of the soufflé. Autoethnography, in contrast, embraces writing as definitive of the process as well as the product. I talk to graduate seminars about adapting messages to particular audiences and listen to them condemn as old fashioned those who dismiss autoethnography as journalism or creative nonfiction. In a methods class, writing matters as deeply these days as gaining access to the field site and formulating rich interview questions have done in the past.

My Current Work:
Relational Codes in Four Cultures

I studied urban Colombians for 15 years in an attempt to expand the scope of interpersonal communication research and theory to explicit consideration of culture. From there, I moved to a more explicitly cross-cultural study of personal relationships. Intrigued by dialectal differences between peninsular Spanish and Colombian Spanish, and the parallel comparisons of British and American English, I wondered what I could find out about personal relationships by comparing them across those four reference points. The four countries, as nation-states, were joined clearly by language and history, and separated just as clearly by dialect and, more hazily, by culture. Strongly influenced by the critical cultural studies work of my Iowa colleagues, I knew any comparative study I did would have to include a focus on media, integrated in some way with face-to-face interaction. I had also read enough conversation analytic work (and other forms of discourse analysis) to know that collection and transcription of audiotaped interaction would be more central to the effort than would field notes and interviews, as my earlier work had been.

I spent 8 months in the East Midlands of England in 1999, 6 months in Madrid in 2000, and made brief trips to Colombia in 1998 and 2003. The data I collected in those three places and in Iowa consisted of case studies, in which relational partners first audiotaped 1 to 3 hours of their naturally occurring conversation and then conducted a self-interview, that is, the relational partners talked through a list of questions and tape-recorded that interaction. The interview questions included the story of their relationship, the barriers to staying together, memorable moments they had shared, and media consumption. I also collected a wide range of media texts: videotaped television shows, newspaper and magazine articles, audiotaped radio call-in programs, and so forth. Living, or having lived, in all four places made for opportunities to observe interaction going on around me, and occasionally I took fieldnotes. That was ethically problematic with friends and family, although those were both the people I had most complete access to and the ones most aware of the details of my research. My fieldnotes for this study are thus the kinds of public behavior people ordinarily do not expect privacy for: groups around a lunch table or work task, fellow passengers on public transportation, parents and children in parks and supermarkets. Although that description can only sound random, some wonderful instances of natives using means of communication in ways I had heard about through the media or the self-interviews have come along in such moments.

As is typical for ethnographic work, the focus of the study—relational codes—emerged along the way. I started with broad questions, hoping to find culturally situated, specific answers to all of them: Why do some personal relationships flourish, making the people involved in them happier, healthier, and even longer lived than they might otherwise be? Why do other personal relationships seem to have largely negative effects, not only on the people who construct and live in them but on their social and family networks? How do communities facilitate or even coerce some personal relationships into being, and how—and why—do they constrain or prohibit other relationships? This study approaches relational codes as the specific systems of meaning worked out by relational partners within a particular interpersonal ideology, understood as evaluative premises that both constrain and enable such negotiations between partners. It proposes to show that personal relationships and culture are inseparable systems of norms, premises, and symbols. The consequences of this position are to consider that what happens within a relationship may be at least as dependent on the social and cultural context in which it unfolds as on any individual trait, intention, or practice of the partners in the relationship. Traits, intentions, attachment styles, and the relational histories of particular partners are the focus of a great deal of research and theory in personal relationships. In contrast, my goal is to show the extent and magnitude of cultural influence on personal relationships.

The breadth of this endeavor can sound ludicrous. I hope to show it as reasonable through an example of data and the kind of claims I make on the basis of such data. The fragment below comes from an interview with a middle-class Colombian woman in her 50s, asked to tell the story of her relationship with her husband of 33 years. Before this point, she has described meeting him on a bus when she was 17, her reluctant agreement to his romantic overtures, and the outrage of the nuns at her high school when she did not hide the fact of having a boyfriend (translation mine):

Maritza: I astutely quit school before the final exams to keep from giving them the pleasure of failing me . . . I went home to where I was born, and I missed him a lot . . . I came back in January and he said OK, we're getting married

now or never, and he talked to my mom and one very special day he invited us
[out to dinner] and asked for my hand . . . and she said yes so we got married.
He won my mother's affection, she always saw him as the ideal man for me,
so the three of us went to Venezuela to get married . . . I was a minor, so of
course she had to be there . . . What's more, we got married *por lo civil* when
that was a scandal—we had to go across the border to Venezuela because [civil
marriage] didn't exist in Colombia [in 1970].

The power of cultural norms to define and constrain the relationships of
individuals resonates throughout the story: In 1970, a 17-year-old female
openly involved in a romantic relationship was scandalous enough that
Catholic nuns in an all-girls' school could plausibly be suspected of failing a
student to remove her from the school,[2] in order to protect its reputation.
Although the teller's feelings for her future husband are relevant to the
progress of the relationship—she "missed him a lot" when she went home—
her mother's opinion is described as at least as important as her own. Her
mother is, in fact, described as a participant in their marriage: She "always
saw him as the ideal man" for her, and "one very special day he invited us
[out to dinner] and asked for my hand . . . and she said yes so we got married." Maritza's narration of the marriage proposal, one of life's most sto-
ryable events in North American culture (see Chang & Fitch, 2002), suggests
that the mother was the one who was asked and made the decision. More
strikingly, she says that "the three of us went to Venezuela to get married."
Even if the mother's role is exaggerated for comic effect, that phrase is one
that is difficult to imagine hearing from a U.S. American, given the ideological framing of marriage as a matter of love between two people.

The fact of getting married before a judge rather than in a church is noted as
even further outside the cultural norms for marriage of the time, although the
limits of the norm are also hearable in the story: Civil marriage did not exist in
Colombia at that time, necessitating a trip across the border to Venezuela. To
say "it didn't exist in Colombia then" invokes an institutional constraint and a
reasonably easy solution: Go across the border to Venezuela. To note that it
was a scandal to have a civil ceremony rather than a Catholic one suggests that
Maritza knew that there would be gossip about these events. Such gossip would
then serve, at that time, as a warning to other young women about how people
would talk about *them* if they did the same. Her knowing that she would be
gossiped about is an example of what Philipsen (1992) describes as discursive
force: The strength of the norm is shown in the certainty of predictions about
the talk that will occur when the norm is violated. I contend that although the
norms of Colombian culture in the 1970s did not prevent Maritza from engaging in behavior she knew would be negatively evaluated—openly having a
boyfriend and then marrying in a civil ceremony—their relevance and weight

had to be quite significant to be part of the story 30 years later. Similarly, to describe her mother's role in her marriage as that of an active participant verbalizes a distinctively Colombian understanding of family. In the course of this study of personal relationships across four cultures, I hope to map in rich detail the interplay of cultural norms and premises with specific, individual relational systems of meaning.

Challenges and Future Directions in Cross-Cultural Ethnographic Research

Among the conceptual and analytic challenges I consistently face in this work, there is space to discuss only two. First, to describe any phenomenon as culturally situated raises the question of sorting out the cultural from the individual and the merely demographic. Without representative samples that would allow for ruling out such explanations, arguments must be based on talk itself: which actions are accounted for, gossiped about, explicitly challenged or praised, or narrated for particular listeners on particular occasions. Those are matters rarely dissolvable into race, age, *or* gender; the nature of cultural codes is to cut across those kinds of groupings through symbolically meaningful ways of speaking.

A second challenge is to understand the ontological nature of media texts and processes with regard to personal relationships. My first stab at that challenge (Fitch, 2002) got as far as showing that unscripted (so-called reality) television is, at least in its less heavily edited versions, useful to the relationships researcher as data. The communicative resources drawn on by participants in such shows—the native terms, the sequential organization of talk, the vocabularies of motives (Burke, 1950) available to them for interpersonal purposes—are exactly those available to relational partners in life off the screen. There is much more to be discovered about how people draw on media products and processes to construct their personal relationships. Given the increasingly media-saturated lives led by people in all four cultures I study, the importance of understanding the blurred line between mediated life and the rest of it—assuming there is a "rest of it"—seems obvious.

The conceptual objective of ethnographies of speaking is to show what is truly universal about interpersonal communication by showing what is specific to particular groups of people. A more traditional social science approach to these questions informs Kim's (2002) extensive review of interpersonal communication theories' bias toward individualism, self-interest, and competitiveness. Kim offers findings from a wide range of empirical research to suggest that East Asian models of interdependence show marked cultural differences in communication preferences, evaluations, and behavior. Beyond demonstrating these measurable differences, Kim's work proposes to expand interpersonal communication theories by consideration of East Asian philosophical traditions and their links to cultural norms and premises. That approach to theory building is exactly the agenda pursued in the ethnographic work described in this chapter, with obvious epistemological and methodological differences.

I began by noting that earlier versions of this volume did not consider culture as an influence on personal relationships, in contrast to this one that includes a chapter devoted to that idea. Ethnography's hope is to enrich social science approaches to interpersonal communication and personal relationships research methodologically through a more broadly interpretive stance that centers on language use captured in something close to its natural state. I look forward to seeing the state of cultural approaches to interpersonal communication research and theory the next time this kind of volume is taken up.

Notes

1. Writing books, I found, allows you to have some cake and eat it too—see the epilogue of Fitch (1998).
2. My Colombian niece who graduated from such a high school in 2006 tells me that little has changed since then: If students have boyfriends, they carefully conceal that fact from the school staff.

References

Antaki, C. (1994). *Explaining and arguing: The social organization of accounts.* London: Sage.

Austin, J. L. (1962). *How to do things with words.* Cambridge, MA: Harvard University Press.

Baxter, L. A. (1987). Symbols of relationship identity in relationship cultures. *Journal of Social and Personal Relationships, 4,* 261–280.

Blum-Kulka, S., House, J., & Kasper, G. (1989). *Cross-cultural pragmatics: Requests and apologies.* Norwood, NJ: Ablex.

Brown, P., & Levinson, S. (1987). *Politeness: Some universals in language usage.* New York: Cambridge University Press.

Burke, K. (1950). *A rhetoric of motives.* Berkeley: University of California Press.

Buttny, R. (1993). *Social accountability in communication.* London: Sage.

Cai, D. A., & Wilson, S. R. (2000). Identity implications of influence goals: A cross-cultural comparison of interaction goals and facework. *Communication Studies, 51*(4), 307.

Carbaugh, D. (1989). Fifty terms for talk: A cross-cultural study. In S. Ting-Toomey & F. Korzenny (Eds.), *Language, culture and communication: Current directions* (pp. 93–120). Newbury Park, CA: Sage.

Casagrande, J. B., & Hale, K. L. (1967). Semantic relationships in Papago folk-definitions. In D. Hymes & W. E. Bittle (Eds.), *Studies in southwestern ethnolinguistics* (pp. 165–196). The Hague, the Netherlands: Mouton.

Chang, Y., & Fitch, K. (2002, July). *"Will you marry me?" An ethnographic study of communicative practices leading to marriage.* Paper presented at the International Communication Association, Seoul, South Korea.

Conquergood, D. (1991). Rethinking ethnography: Towards a critical cultural politics. *Communication Monographs, 58,* 179–194.

Dillard, J. P. (1988). Compliance-gaining message selection: What is our dependent variable? *Communication Monographs, 55,* 162–183.

Edwards, D. (1995). Two to tango: Script formulations, dispositions, and rhetorical symmetry in relationship troubles talk. *Research on Language and Social Interaction, 28*(4), 319–350.

Ervin-Tripp. (1976). Is Sybil there? The structure of some American English directives. *Language in Society, 5,* 25–66.

Fitch, K. (1991). The interplay of linguistic universals and cultural knowledge in personal address: Colombian madre terms. *Communication Monographs, 58,* 254–272.

Fitch, K. (1994). A cross-cultural study of directive sequences and some implications for compliance-gaining research. *Communication Monographs, 61,* 185–209.

Fitch, K. (1998). *Speaking relationally: Culture, communication, and interpersonal connection.* New York: Guilford Press.

Fitch, K. (2002). Unscripted television and social interaction: An exploration of possibilities for data in "Big Brother." In J. Gabalda, C. Gregori, & R. Rosello (Eds.), *La cultura mediática* (pp. 73–88). Valencia: Universitá de Valencia.

Fitch, K. (2003a). Cultural persuadables. *Communication Theory, 13,* 100–123.

Fitch, K. (2003b). Taken-for-granteds in (an) intercultural communication context. In P. Glenn, J. Mandelbaum, & C. LeBaron (Eds.), *Studies in language and social interaction* (pp. 91–102). Mahwah, NJ: Erlbaum.

Fitch, K. (2005). Both sides now: Raising Colombian-Americans. In W. Leeds-Hurwitz (Ed.), *From generation to generation: Raising bicultural children* (pp. 297–318). New York: Hampton Press.

Garrett, M. M. (1999). Some elementary methodological reflections on the study of the Chinese rhetorical tradition. *International and Intercultural Communication Annual, 22,* 53–65.

Geertz, C. (1976). "From the native's point of view": On the nature of anthropological understanding. In K. H. Basso & H. Selby (Eds.), *Meaning in anthropology* (pp. 221–239). Albuquerque: University of New Mexico Press.

Goldsmith, D., & Baxter, L. (1996). Constituting relationships in talk: A taxonomy of speech events in social and personal relationships. *Human Communication Research, 23,* 87–114.

Goldsmith, D., & Fitch, K. (1997). The normative context of advice as social support. *Human Communication Research, 23,* 454–476.

Goodwin, M. H. (1990). *He-said-she-said: Talk as social organization among black children.* Bloomington: Indiana University Press.

Grice, H. P. (1975). Logic in conversation. In P. Cole & J. L. Morgan (Eds.), *Syntax and semantics: Vol. 3. Speech acts* (pp. 41–58). New York: Academic Press.

Honigmann, J. J. (1970). Sampling in ethnographic fieldwork. In R. Naroll & R. Cohen (Eds.), *A handbook of method in cultural anthropology* (pp. 45–70). Garden City, NY: Natural History Press.

Hymes, D. (1962). The ethnography of speaking. In T. Gladwin & W. C. Sturtevant (Eds.), *Anthropology and human behavior.* Washington, DC: Anthropological Society of Washington.

Hymes, D. (1972). Models of the interaction of language and social life. In J. Gumperz & D. Hymes (Eds.), *Directions in sociolinguistics: The ethnography of communication* (pp. 35–71). New York: Holt, Rinehart, & Winston.

Katriel, T., & Philipsen, G. (1981). "What we need is communication:" "Communication" as a cultural term in some American speech. *Communication Monographs, 48,* 301–317.

Kellermann, K., & Cole, T. (1994). Classifying compliance gaining messages: Taxonomic disorder and strategic confusion. *Communication Theory, 4,* 3–60.

Kim, M.-S. (2002). *Non-Western perspectives on human communication: Implications for theory and practice.* Thousand Oaks, CA: Sage.

Kim, M.-S., Shin, H. C., & Cai, D. (1998). Cultural influences on the preferred forms of requesting and re-requesting. *Communication Monographs, 65,* 47–66.

Ma, R. (1999). Water-related figurative language in the rhetoric of Mencius. *International and Intercultural Communication Annual, 22,* 119–130.

Miller, G. (Ed.). (1976). *Explorations in interpersonal communication.* Beverly Hills, CA: Sage.

Miller, G. R. (1978). The current status of theory and research in interpersonal communication. *Human Communication Research, 4,* 164–178.

Miller, G. R., Roloff, M. E., Seibold, D., & Boster, F. (1977). Compliance-gaining message strategies: A typology and some findings concerning effects of situational differences. *Communication Monographs, 44,* 27–51.

Neuliep, J., & Hazleton, V. (1985). A cross-cultural comparison of Japanese and American persuasive strategy selection. *International Journal of Intercultural Relations, 9,* 389–404.

Philipsen, G. (1975). Speaking "like a man" in Teamsterville: Culture patterns of role enactment in an urban neighborhood. *Quarterly Journal of Speech, 61,* 13–22.

Philipsen, G. (1976). Places for speaking in Teamsterville. *Quarterly Journal of Speech, 62,* 15–25.

Philipsen, G. (1992). *Speaking culturally.* Albany: State University of New York Press.

Potter, J., & Wetherell, M. (1987). Discourse and social psychology: Beyond attitudes and behaviour. London: Sage.

Roloff, M., & Miller, G. (Eds.). (1987). *Interpersonal processes: New directions in communication research.* Newbury Park, CA: Sage.

Rosaldo, M. (1980). *Knowledge and passion: Ilongot notions of self and social life.* New York: Cambridge University Press.

Rosaldo, M. (1982). The things we do with words: Ilongot speech acts and speech act theory in philosophy. *Language in Society, 11,* 203–237.

Rushforth, S. (1981). Speaking to "relatives-through-marriage": Aspects of communication among Bear Lake Athapaskan. *Journal of Anthropological Research, 37,* 28–45.

Searle, J. (1969). *Speech acts.* New York: Cambridge University Press.

Searle, J. (1975). A taxonomy of speech acts. *Language in Society, 4,* 1–23.

Seibold, D., Cantrill, J., & Meyers, R. (1984). Communication and interpersonal influence. In M. Knapp & G. Miller (Eds.), *Handbook of interpersonal communication* (1st ed., pp. 551–611). Beverly Hills, CA: Sage.

Spradley, J. P. (1979). *The ethnographic interview.* New York: Holt, Rinehart, & Winston.

Spradley, J. P. (1980). *Participant observation.* New York: Holt, Rinehart, & Winston.

Stewart, J. (1997). Developing communication theories. In G. Philipsen & T. Albrecht (Eds.), *Developing communication theories* (pp. 157–192). Albany: State University of New York Press.

Suddaby, R. (2006). From the editors: What grounded theory is not. *Academy of Management Journal, 49,* 633–642.

Weigel, M., & Weigel, R. (1985). Directive use in a migrant agricultural community: A test of Ervin-Tripp's hypotheses. *Language in Society, 14,* 63–79.

Wood, J. T. (1982). Communication and relational culture: Bases for the study of human relationships. *Communication Quarterly, 30,* 75–83.

13

New Technologies and New Directions in Online Relating

Joseph B. Walther

Artemio Ramirez, Jr.

New directions in research on the interpersonal dimensions of computer-mediated communication (CMC) are often driven as much by the evolution of the Internet's sociotechnological systems and the uses to which these systems are put, as much as they are by advances in formal research. Although the study of CMC is a relative infant among communication research foci, its rapid evolution has seen several theoretical approaches come and some of them go. New technological formats are stretching the applicability of even the most contemporary theories of CMC; which ones will break and which ones will accommodate new phenomena is not certain. In some cases, new technological developments are showing that some theories may be quite robust, albeit within more clearly defined boundaries. New theories are emerging, as well, the utility of which seem especially apt and potentially agenda setting as technology advances catch up to illuminate them.

This chapter focuses on a few of the current and most stimulating developments in the area of communication technology and interpersonal relations. It reviews the emergence of some specific aspects of communication technologies that affect interpersonal interaction, relationship processes that have newly come to prosper online, and predictions for emerging research that may conceptualize and explore the simultaneous presentation of mass and interpersonal messages via CMC. The Internet's greater capacity to transmit multiply cued forms of information, such as photos, avatars, virtual reality, and other online self-representations causes popular theories to be reevaluated and reparameterized. The retention of "plain text" CMC, in light of these alternatives, has been met with detailed and revealing research about the potency of language and adaptive media uses in the management of impressions and relationships in personal and professional settings. The diffusion of the Internet as a commonplace venue to pursue relationship initiation and maintenance impels new research on information management and mode sequences in relationship development, including mixed-mode relationships and their trajectories. We will also suggest how systems collectively referred to as Web 2.0 are beginning to be approached and beg for more research from the perspectives of identification and relational impacts on noninterpersonal sources.

Naturally, any such review, assessment, or projection reflects the authors' perspectives and biases. In this case, our (Walthers and Ramirez) similar academic training and views reinforce a certain approach to what constitutes important developments and how they fit with the past. These experiences and perspectives have influenced our own work, as well. Thus, in the interest of accounting for what was considered in this review, and in sharing perspectives on technology and communication generally, the chapter begins with some background that might help contextualize not only the present matter but research on communication technology writ large.

A Functional Perspective on CMC

Some common fundamental assumptions about communication and how to approach its analysis have shaped our perspectives, conceptual thinking, and empirical research on CMC. We both took doctoral study in Communication at the University of Arizona and both studied nonverbal and relational communication with Dr. Judee K. Burgoon, theory and research methods with Dr. Michael Burgoon, and related foci with Dr. David Buller and others. Arizona's doctoral program at that particular time fostered a relatively coherent focus on theory-driven empirical research (see Burgoon, 1989) and a strong dedication to a "functional" approach to communication analysis. We tried to focus our research not on specific channels such as mass media versus interpersonal settings, or to define domains based strictly on contexts such as political communication or organizational communication. Rather, we focused on social influence, impression formation and management, information processing, and relational dynamics, in a variety of settings. In nonverbal communication, we did not study what certain cues meant per se. The functional approach to nonverbal communication is articulated quite explicitly in the influential text published at that time, *Nonverbal Communication: The Unspoken Dialogue,* by J. K. Burgoon, Buller, and Woodall (1989), which dictates as follows:

- A single nonverbal cue may serve multiple functions.

- A single function may be accomplished through multiple nonverbal cues.

- A single function typically requires the coordination of verbal and nonverbal behaviors. (p. 26)

Although both Walther and Ramirez committed to midterm memory the seven basic sets of nonverbal cue systems, their subtaxonomies, coding systems, and various kines and morphs, they learned these approaches in subservience of a larger principle: that no single nonverbal behavior, or specific set of behaviors, had a monopoly on the conveyance of social meanings. To study communication was to study the fluid encoding and decoding of complex interactions of appearance, proximity, touch, and other cues, while communicating verbally, and as relational contexts varied.

During this same time, research began to appear in a new field of study, a domain of communication without nonverbal cues: CMC. Most of the early studies of online groups focused on the lack of nonverbal cues as the primary explanatory difference between CMC and offline behavior. Moreover, the lack of nonverbal cues was often alleged to deplete, occlude, or prevent CMC users from being able to relate in socially and interpersonally normal ways. Early CMC research indicted nonverbal cues, wholesale; it sometimes provided a list of them with no particular differentiation with regard to cause.

This approach was an intellectual problem for Walther and Ramirez, as well as others who had similar training in the area of personal relationships (e.g., Parks & Floyd, 1996). From a functional perspective, it was difficult to accept that nonverbal cues alone (much less, no specification of which among them) could bear the entire communicative responsibility for interpersonal affect, online or elsewhere. As if individuals who could not see or hear could have no relationships; as if writing, from poetry to pornography, could not arouse.

We developed alternative positions that reflected a functional orientation. Our work explicitly assumes that communicators use whatever cues they have at their disposal when they wish to communicate sociably, and that the study of CMC is best premised on the interactions of time, cues, and interpersonal motivations on the relational functions which it may reflect. The original theories and empirical studies that the authors have developed since then have attempted to stay attuned to this premise, assuming that through that lens researchers can focus on technology effects in theoretically describable processes, rather than focus on more descriptive research about each new Internet application. Because some of the technologies have become mainstream staples of relationships, this lens has had a good deal of utility. As technologies change and their applications morph, the applicability of this and other lenses warrants appraisal.

Image-Based CMC

Challenges for Contemporary CMC Theories

The rapid diffusion of communication technologies that involve photographs of users provides a shake-up to contemporary CMC theories. Boundaries for theories of CMC that were previously quite broad in scope are no longer as applicable to the expansive realm of CMC, and if more online interactions include visual imagery, some theories will wither while others will stretch insofar as their application is concerned. At the same time, some theoretical approaches will be more robust even if their boundaries shrink. Research in the near future should have much to say on these issues.

The potential to imbue electronic communication with images has dramatically changed in recent times, due to changes in cost and access of technologies that enable it. Bandwidth is greater: Cable systems and wireless connectivity have brought high-speed Internet into homes and coffee shops for relatively little more expense than maintaining extra telephone lines for much inferior dial-up access. Digital cameras have replaced the need to scan photographs, as have cameras in cellular phones.

The dominant theories related to interpersonal relations presently are premised on the absence of visual and other nonverbal cues (for review, see Walther, 2006).

The social information processing theory of CMC (Walther, 1992), as suggested above, was the first to apply a functional perspective to the absence of nonverbal cues, including physical appearance cues, from CMC. This theory argues that the social functions for which communicators rely on nonverbal cues offline are translated into verbal content, linguistic, stylistic, and chronemic cues in text-based CMC. The model also holds that when interpersonal functions, in addition to instrumental functions, must be conveyed through the single conduit of text, it takes more messages, over a longer time, to encode and decode sufficient information with which to develop and modify impressions and relationships. This position, too, has placed a premium on what happens when communicators cannot see one another. In this case, however, researchers have already placed photos into the theoretical calculus, along with offline biographical material, as extrainteractional "head starts" to impression formation (Tanis, 2003). That is, visual information affects impressions just as communication behavior might, but it conveys more information more quickly relative to slower and leaner text-based signals. Future research on parallel or sequential transmission of both forms may be needed for the theory's growth.

The hyperpersonal model of CMC has also been premised on a lack of visual information about CMC partners. The hyperpersonal model of CMC was developed by Walther (1996) in an attempt to explain how people create intimate and sociable relational communication online that exceeds parallel offline relations. The model includes explanations of how users (a) idealize unseen online partners; (b) send voluntaristic and controllable cues about themselves via language, and exclude uncontrollable cues such as physical appearance; (c) exploit the channel's editing and composing capabilities as well as the channel's conduciveness to sequester oneself when using it; and (d) intensify these elements through mutually reinforcing prophecy effects. Some research has suggested that these effects may take place between face-to-face meetings, but the premise of the absence of visual cues in this model, as in the social identification/deindividuation model, seems intractable. The future of such models depends on the continued use of sightless CMC.

It was formerly projected that an imageless, text-based Internet would equalize the conversational playing field; that discussions sans physical cues to race, gender, age, and other features would democratize the electronic public sphere (Landow, 1992). It has become clear that for some purposes people quite adamantly want to learn about others' demographic classifications and individual appearances, using photographs and descriptions. The impulse to learn who others are, and to present oneself for others' reciprocal identification, was quite doable using text, by means of overt disclosure and subtle linguistic behavior (for review, see Walther, Loh, & Granka, 2005). Now the simplicity of uploading photos of oneself, friends, or places has fed into an apparently innate desire to see and be seen—in some contexts, but not as much in others. Research has yet to determine which contexts or communication functions seem to draw out the impulse to see and be seen. Indeed, as we will discuss further, the selection and display of photos, some of which may provide contradictory information about individuals, remain to be studied.

Avatars, Icons, and Virtual Representations

Another form of visual self-representation online does not depend on photos. There is a resurgence of activity using avatar-based chat systems, in which users represent themselves in virtual interaction spaces by the use of some graphic character. These characters typically range from abstract and cartoonish to somewhat anthropomorphic. Such has been the case for some time on graphical chat systems such as Habitat in the 1980s and The Palace or The Sims in the 1990s, which has been the focus of several monographs related to the psychodynamic and/or psychoanalytic potential to go into a communication space, invent a character, and occupy and animate the character as a projection of some entity other than one's more-or-less true self (Turkle, 1995). Recently, a newer avatar-based chat system, Second Life, has gained popularity. Although Second Life operates similarly to The Palace, there are some significant differences. Second Life includes more advanced graphics in backgrounds and character definition, commensurate with advances in computer science, online gaming systems, and the greater diffusion of high-speed Internet connections that allow more fluid movement in terms of frequently changing graphics data. It also includes the "user-extensible" ability to program new virtual objects with interactive capabilities that avatars can deploy, and then buy and sell these objects privately and profitably among users to enhance the experience of online interaction. For example, one can enhance the visual appearance (i.e., virtual physical appearance) of one's avatar, options of which range from adornments and clothing, to virtual body parts that can facilitate graphical aspects of online sexual activity between avatars. These developments enhance communication encounters among users in advanced ways. Nevertheless, the issues, attractions, and social gratifications of Second Life seem very similar to the graphical spaces of the past despite advancements in technology, and it is worthwhile reexamining speculations offered by creators of the Habitat graphical chat space several decades ago. As Morningstar and Farmer (1991) observed,

> Cyberspace is defined more by the interactions among the actors within it than by the technology with which it is implemented. While we find much of the work presently being done on elaborate interface technologies—DataGloves, head-mounted displays, special-purpose rendering engines, and so on—both exciting and promising, the almost mystical euphoria that currently seems to surround all this hardware is, in our opinion, both excessive and somewhat misplaced. We can't help having a nagging sense that it's all a bit of a distraction from the really pressing issues. At the core of our vision is the idea that cyberspace is necessarily a multiple-participant environment. It seems to us that the things that are important to the inhabitants of such an environment are the capabilities available to them, the characteristics of the other people

they encounter there, and the ways these various participants can affect one another. (p. 274)

These comments reflect that, throughout the short history of the Internet, developers have come to realize that the interpersonal issues sustained by the technology, rather than technological advances themselves, are what command enduring attention albeit through new technological lenses.

In addition to avatars, a related direction has to do with how individuals respond to virtual representations of themselves and of others when they are depicted by static graphics in chat rooms. Several studies have examined how the nature of relatively inanimate icons (a face or cartoon character representing a chat user) or avatars anchor and bias information processing and influence in online spaces. Lee's (2004, 2005) robust experiments have shown that the stereotypical gender appearance of an icon can have a profound effect on users, even when they should rationally discount the icon as representing other users. Lee (2004) led research participants to expect that they were randomly assigned a male- or female-appearing icon to represent them in dyadic chat sessions—the subjects could see the icon they were assigned—and that an icon was also being randomly assigned to their partner. In actual experimental tests, the icon's gender was not randomly assigned. Rather, it was the opposite gender of the subject. This mismatch should have reinforced to the subjects that the icon's gender had no necessary relationship to themselves, and presumably the same should be true for their partners. Participants were presented topics to discuss with their partners, which the researchers had selected for their stereotypical association as women's topics or men's topics. In online conversations, participants were relatively less attentive to and influenced by their partner when their partner's icon reflected the gender opposite to that which was stereotypically associated with the topic, and this was the case whether the actual "real-life" partner was male or female. The sex-related appearance of the icon anchored participants' perceptions of the sex of the partner and biased their information processing, despite the case that they should have known better.

These findings raise profound questions about the perception of others in chat spaces based on superficial stereotypical characteristics that may or may not pertain to the chat user. Gender and racial characteristics, among other stereotypes, were once thought of or hoped for as a relic of traditional, pre-Internet communication that the text-based universe of online communication would render moot. CMC was once hoped or hyped to be the environment that would "democratize" communication and make participants' ideas more salient than their hereditary-based appearances. Although many online chat spaces continue to allow users to converse appearance-free, it cannot be ignored that in many cases users do wish to signal who they think they are (or wish to be seen as being), and that perceivers quite strongly anchor on visual representations of online conversants almost against their better judgment.

Future research on bias and prejudice online, their manifestations and consequences online, and whether they are gaining or receding in potency relative to other social venues is certainly worth pursuing as the Internet continues to diffuse. A recent study by Gong (2007) offers a disconcerting yet potent step in this direction. Gong explored what preferences a sample of Caucasian Midwestern American students expressed in choosing among an array of onscreen icons they might use to represent themselves online. Gong had hypothesized that an ingroup/outgroup preference dynamic should appear: Individuals would prefer to be represented by a cartoon with human appearance, including a variety of icons with phenotypic variations suggesting racial differences, compared with cartoon characters resembling the outgroup, robots. Gong's predictions were not supported. Subjects most strongly preferred Caucasian-looking cartoon characters, followed by aliens, followed by African American–looking characters. Research on the potential effects of cross-race representations in virtual chats, and their effects on self, interactions, and others, are currently beginning. Further research on the extent to which Internet users employ available visual cues to ghettoize their online social networks is also worthy of study.

The Continued Importance of Plain Text

It is clear that in a variety of arenas, visual representations online may have profound effects on CMC users. Whether nonvisual CMC can affect diversity is not a new topic, but one receiving renewed attention. Speculation has arisen about the Internet's propensity to help users diversify their online social networks (e.g., Dimmick, Ramirez, Lin, & Wang, 2007). Some have envisioned language translation systems so that people from different nations, who speak different languages, could talk to one another in their own languages, transparently, and in doing so achieve interpersonal understandings (Ishii, Kobayashi, & Grundin, 1993). We have speculated that research/practitioners might learn to use text-based online interaction to hold at bay visually cued intergroup perceptions sufficiently long for interethnic collaborators to become friendly colleagues (Walther, 1997, 2004; see also Amichai-Hamburger & McKenna, 2006). In an attempt to use CMC to enhance interethnic understanding, Mollov (2006) employed CMC to conduct dialogues among Jewish Israeli and Palestinian students. Rather than masking differences, discussions focused specifically on Jewish and Islamic religious practices. Factual learning about the groups' holidays increased for both groups, and postdiscussion attitudes about the exchanges were very positive. The absence of obvious differences and the development of common ground are good beginnings. Such efforts may be enhanced by the application of interaction rules that enhance relationships among strangers. Our research has tested a set of collaboration rules that, when virtual groups are required to use them, demonstrably promote trust and liking (Walther & Bunz, 2005).

It would be easy to assume that visual information might be desired in any context, and where it is not used, some barrier occludes it. Such is the position taken by Cummings, Lee, and Kraut (2006), who explored how college students stay in touch with their friends from high school. Cummings et al. predicted that friendships require rich media—for simplicity, those conveying nonverbal cues—to communicate the emotional nuances that friendships entail. Therefore, face-to-face communication, followed by telephone, was predicted to displace e-mail and instant messaging (IM) as preferred channels. Such was not the case: Results found that IM and e-mail were more frequently used among these individuals. Cummings et al. (2006) attempted to explain these findings by reference to the greater costs involved to make long-distance phone calls, identifying cost as a barrier that defied theoretically based expectations. New applications such as Skype that allow free voice calls over the Internet cast doubt on the confound assertion by Cummings et al. A rival hypothesis is that high school and college students actually *like* plain text. Cummings et al.'s dismissal of CMC as communicationally inferior yet cheaper than voice cannot be reconciled with the continued strong use of text-based CMC in a variety of settings in which users could use multimedia but do not, and prefer the advantage of text—not just asynchronous, but real-time text.

The growing adoption of IM in youth leisure as well as professional contexts (Shiu, 2005) is well established. Young people in particular use IM for social conversations alongside other task-related activities they perform on their computers. Ramirez and Broneck's (in press) research also provides an alternative perspective to that of Cummings and colleagues. The authors examined how college students employ IM across social and personal relationships. They found that (a) females were more likely than males to use IM to maintain their relationships; (b) a higher percentage of interactions via IM were conducted with physically distant, cross-sex partners; (c) lovers and best friends were the most likely IM partners; and (d) IM was used routinely alongside other channels (e.g., e-mail, telephone, face-to-face interaction) to sustain relationships. The use of synchronous, text-based IM technology plays an important role in sustaining ongoing associations, and the growth of text-messaging via mobile phones also suggests that the centrality of text-only communication may not subside anytime soon.

Adults as well as teens use dyadic and group chat systems recreationally, to meet people with similar interests, and sometimes as escapist amusement. For many individuals, it appears, chatting online with potentially interesting people and forming relationships in these spaces provides significant gratifications. In these spaces, the hyperpersonal model of CMC seems particularly dynamic, as users invent personae online that bear varying degrees of resemblance to the "typist." Selective self-presentation, idealization, exploiting the channel's editing and entrainment affordances, and mutual feedback enhancements seem rampant in certain online discussion spaces. Chat rooms and similar group discussion settings continue to attract teens and adults who select pseudonyms by which to discuss common concerns as well as to flirt. The use of CMC to adopt fictitious personae and develop questionable but intense relationships still takes place and still receives flamboyant press (Labi, 2007), despite decades-old warnings and lessons about the similar issues (Van Gelder, 1985). Whitty suggests that using deception to shield one's identity is important for many participants (Whitty, 2002; Whitty & Gavin, 2001). In a survey of chat room participants, women reported concealing their identity for safety reasons, such as avoiding harassment. Men, on the other hand, reported using identity deception to allow themselves, somewhat paradoxically, to be more expressive and reveal secrets about themselves.

Recent research provides greater insight into the mechanisms of selective self-presentation online through textual CMC, whether for the purpose of identity deception, romantic distortion, or simple relational pleasantry. As part of a series of tests of the hyperpersonal model, one of our experiments focused on the microbehavior of CMC to hone and craft relational messages (Walther, 2007): keyboard editing (backspaces, deletions, insertions). Student subjects wrote messages to partners whom they believed to be either a professor (whose description was rather elaborate), a vocational high school student (with an elaborate description), or another college student (with no description provided other than gender). Among the complex interaction effects, a pattern revealed that participants edited more for messages directed to an undescribed college-age partner of the opposite sex. More editing was associated with greater relational affection as well. In a much different study with equally strong implications for the microbehaviors of selective self-presentation, Herring and Martinson (2004) coded language use from an online contest, the "Turing Game," in which individuals communicated textually in efforts to convince judges of a gender. Sometimes participants tried to convince judges that they were female and sometimes male. The performance assignments were randomly assigned to participants. Most participants chose names and selected discussion topics stereotypically associated with men or women; judges discounted names but were influenced by topics. Although judges appeared not to attend to them, Herring and Martinson found that the microlinguistic behaviors of participants—hedges, qualifiers, possibility modals, clausal mitigation, questions, boosters, universal quantifiers, profanity, insults, and message length—were more consistent with players' actual gender than with the gender they tried to perform in cross-gender contests (although real-life males seemed to be able to switch codes somewhat more effectively than real-life females).

The development of multimedia interpersonal and group communication technology shows us much by the contexts in which it is not used as much as from those in which it is used. Text-based online communication remains a mainstay of Internet communication, and it appears as though this is so not only because of the way it reduces opportunity costs but also because of the situational and interpersonal affordances it bestows (see also Ramirez, Dimmick, Feaster, & Lin, 2008).

Mixed-Mode Relationships

Another arena that is receiving research attention is heralded by both new technologies and new relationship processes that involve alternating online/offline sequences, or hybrid systems that meld and extend online and offline relationships. Research has grown concerning what Walther and Parks (2002) call "mixed-mode relationships," that is, relationships that start in one channel and progress into another, such as from online to offline or vice versa. The progression from an online to offline relationship, Walther and Parks argued, raises users' needs to assess the reliability of the information partners have disclosed to one another via text and occasional photos, for the sake of their prospective relationship trajectory if not for their personal safety. The ways in which users approach their own needs and those of their partners has generated interesting new research focusing on technologies designed for starting and maintaining relationships.

Matching and Dating Systems

One platform focused on forming relationships includes online match-finding systems. Match-making or date-finding sites include match.com, eHarmony, JDate, and so on. In such sites individuals are "looking" for others among whom they can initiate a dating relationship. It is normative to post a photo of oneself in these sites, and according to Ellison, Heino, and Gibbs (2006), failure to do so raises suspicion that the individual wishes to hide his or her appearance. It is unclear whether the utility of photographs relates to impressions about the physical attractiveness of the poster, or whether individuals make personality or other kinds of inferences from pictorial information. Ellison et al. (2006) point out that when individuals compose their online profiles for match-seeking sites, many are cognizant of the capacity of a photo to substantiate claims they might make about themselves that would otherwise have questionable veracity. A male claiming that he likes to work out, for instance, may post a muscular-looking photo to corroborate the claim. Claims about enjoying spending time with one's children or traveling to exotic destinations, similarly, can be supported quite efficiently with visual information.

The utility of photos to substantiate otherwise verbal online claims about the self helps illuminate Donath's (1999) concerns that verbal messages online, generally, convey few *assessment* signals rather than *conventional* signals. Drawing on anthropological notions, Donath argues that, when it comes to some traits or characteristics, there are some signals or behaviors associated with those characteristics that are difficult or impossible to convey unless one actually possesses the characteristic. Among animals, for instance, a ram with very large horns signals physical strength; the ability to stand with large horns could not be faked by a weaker animal. Among humans, wealth can be signaled by liberally spending money in a way poor individuals cannot easily do. *Verbally* claiming to be rich offers conventional signals: Verbal symbols do not invoke direct corroboration of the characteristic in the way that assessment signals confer. Creating an impression of actual verbal alacrity or expressiveness should be demonstrable in a verbal medium. For other possessions or abilities, conventional signals vastly outnumber assessment signals in text-based discussions, leading to considerable wariness about whether online discussants can be trusted entirely to be who they say they are. The advent of systems that easily capture and display photographs may be doing much to address these concerns.

Older research on relationship-seeking online suggested more paradoxical conclusions about the importance of photographs in the courtship process. Baker's (1998) research about romantic couples who met online and eventually continued offline inquired about the role that the exchange of photos played in relationship trajectories. Baker's research was initiated before matching sites were well-known, and her findings reflect a different context than those who meet using systems expressly designed for dating. Nevertheless, the couples Baker interviewed all exchanged photos of themselves well into their virtual courtship, but prior to their face-to-face meeting. Each couple said that the photograph did not really have an effect on their impressions or feelings about their partners. Ironically, as superfluous as this information was credited as being, it was exchanged by 100% of the subjects. While photos may provide assessment signals where only conventional signals once prevailed, there is still manipulation with respect to the photographs that individuals exchanged: Men exchanged more outdated and flattering photos to women than women did to men; women sent photos that were less flattering than their actual appearances. No research has explored whether women did this in order to lower expectations in anticipation of providing a positive surprise on initial face-to-face encounters, or whether women wanted the men to appreciate them for characteristics other than their physical appearance. Research on these motives, and how they are manifested on dating and matching systems, deserves renewed attention for the insights on human courtship dynamics it has the potential to reveal.

Several studies have now examined the progression of strictly online friend or romantic relationships, whereas fewer have explored the dynamics of relationships that move from online to offline. In terms of strictly online relationships, the social information processing theory's proposition that relational development accrues more slowly online than offline, in proportion to the information exchanges between users, has been borne out in several studies. Chan and Cheng (2004) documented that levels of friendship development differed between face-to-face and CMC partners at several points along their progression over time, with equivalent levels of development ultimately. At a more microscopic level, Liu, Ginther, and Zelhart (2002) documented correspondence between impression development online due to the frequency and duration of messages between partners. Hian, Chuan, Trevor, and Detenber (2004) found that intimacy increased over 3 days' time among experimental CMC dyads but did not change in face-to-face dyads. Other studies have also demonstrated that online relationships increase in intimacy as a result of the accumulation of messages and/or time using asynchronous CMC (Peter, Valkenburg, & Schouten, 2005) or using synchronous systems (Henderson & Gilding, 2004).

Studies examining impressions and relations in the migration of online to offline encounters reflect mixed reactions by participants. As Ramirez and Zhang (2007; see also Ramirez & Wang, 2008) reviewed, some observers suggest that face-to-face interaction provides more interpersonal information than CMC, and therefore moving from online to offline should enhance interpersonal affect and intimacy (e.g., Whitty & Gavin, 2001). Others, however, have reported that the impressions that online partners form of one another are inaccurate, and that meeting one's virtual partner in the flesh can be disorienting and/or disappointing (e.g., Jacobson, 1999). Ramirez and Wang (2008) argued that a critical factor distinguishing positive changes from negative changes in online/offline transitions may be how long online partners had been involved prior to their face-to-face encounter. Consistent with the hyperpersonal model and social information processing theory, online partners may develop inflated perceptions and expectations of one another over time, whereas short-term couples do not reach a great level of idealization. To test this contention, 86 unacquainted dyads communicated asynchronously with one another for 3 weeks, while another 86 did so for 6 weeks. Crossing the short-term/long-term factor in a 2 × 2 experimental design, half of the dyads in each condition met each other face-to-face at the end of the interaction period, while the other half did not.

Results showed that those who switched from online to offline were surprised by their partners' characteristics, no matter whether the dyad interacted for a longer or shorter period. With respect to judgments of physical attractiveness, there was greater disappointment with one's partners' looks among the longer-term dyads who met than among shorter-term dyads. In fact, there was no difference in attractiveness ratings between short-term dyads that did or did not actually meet their partners offline, in contrast to a significant disparity between the long-term dyads who did or did not meet face-to-face.

These results were consistent with Ramirez and Zhang's (2007) findings on perceptions of relational communication. In that study, participants were assigned to one of six interaction conditions, each beginning with either CMC or face-to-face interaction, to complete three tasks over a 9-week period. Briefly, the three CMC conditions involved a CMC-only condition and two other CMC conditions that shifted to offline interaction after completion of either the first or second task; the accompanying offline conditions mirrored the CMC ones. Findings showed that remaining online exclusively yielded the highest terminal level of intimacy and social attraction ratings, relative to the remaining conditions in which face-to-face interaction occurred. Moreover, among the CMC conditions, remaining online and not shifting to face-to-face interaction produced reports of greater social orientation and more positive relationship forecasts than either of the conditions that did shift. The within-condition findings also suggested that whereas shifting to face-to-face interaction early in the partnership (following the initial task) modestly enhanced relational message perceptions, doing so later (following the second task) significantly depressed relational messages.

The implications of this line of research stand in contrast to studies of online-only relationship development, where more time online facilitates relationship quality. When a relationship moves from online to offline, the hyperpersonal dynamics from lengthier online relationships may backfire upon the first physical encounter. There may be some as yet undiscovered optimal level of virtual relationship development prior to a modality switch, beyond which relationships that develop online inflate expectations too greatly.

Social Networking Systems

Another blended system of relationships appears on social networking sites such as Facebook, MySpace, and similar systems. Social networking sites are typified by three elements, the first of which is profile pages. Users have some design latitude for their profiles on MySpace, but in this and other systems, users populate preestablished information categories with their own responses, which are displayed for others to see online. These categories include a central photograph, and such personal information as hometown, birthday, preferred activities, music, and entertainment, and so on. Second, individuals link to other individuals through requests to have "friend" status, which when granted places a small photo and name of ones' friends on one's own profile page. These photos and names constitute hyperlinks to the friends' profiles, and thus *n* degrees of separation friendship networks are clickable and visible to participants. Third, friend status allows others to leave messages by posting statements to each other's profile "walls." These messages are not only visible to the profile owner, but to anyone else allowed to observe the site (including no less than a profile owner's other "friends," but potentially anyone in the world).

On these sites, individuals manifest exceptionally large social networks. Whereas individuals traditionally maintain close relationships with up to 10 to 20 other people (Parks, 2007), and the total number of relationships people traditionally manage is estimated to be around 150, studies report *average* Facebook friend counts of 246 (Walther, Van Der Heide, Kim, Westerman, & Tong, 2008) and 272 (Vanden Boogart, 2006). "Friending" large numbers of people is one of the main activities of Facebook (Ellison, Steinfield, & Lampe, 2007). Bare acquaintances often establish friend links, and otherwise weak ties—friends of friends—link as well. But there can be too much of a good thing: There is a curvilinear effect on positive impressions when friend counts exceed high levels (Tong, Van Der Heide, Langwell, & Walther, 2008).

Online social networking systems are novel with respect to more established forms of CMC because the information displayed about an individual includes both information provided by the profile creator as well as by others—the creator's friends. Recent research has begun to examine the implication of these multiple sources of information. Walther et al. (2008) experimentally found that statements made by profile owners' friends had significant impacts on observers' ratings of the social attractiveness and credibility of profile owners. Wall postings alluding to sociable behavior by the target increased favorable ratings of targets, whereas postings suggesting excessive drinking and philandering prompted a reversal. Moreover, the physical attractiveness of a profile owner's friends (as seen on the profile's wall) has a positive relationship with observers' ratings of the profile owner's physical attractiveness.

We believe that the greatest utility of social networking systems has yet to be explored. These systems provide a dramatically new way to enact *relational maintenance*. The systems are used to keep track of previously made (offline) acquaintances in many cases. One individual (with 1,402 Facebook friends) reported how the system allows him to

> catch up on my social life without telephone tag, awkward lunches, and five-, 10-, (and) 15-year reunions. We write on each other's Wall, a message board, when we want to say happy birthday . . . When I'm having a hectic week at my internship, I can change my (online status indication) so that people know why I haven't returned their telephone calls. (Soller, 2007, p. 44)

Donath and boyd (2004) speculate that online social networking systems can help individuals maintain a larger number of ties than people can typically maintain without such technology. Along with e-mail, which has become a mainstay for families' relational maintenance (Stafford, 2004), we expect that the role of technologies in the preservation, strengthening, reestablishing, or loosening of established bonds will occupy a growing focus in research on CMC and relationships in the near future, from social networking sites to soldiers' blogs and beyond.

Web 2.0 and Renewed Research Agendas

Finally, as outlined by Carr et al. (2008), we foresee great opportunities for communication researchers to set the agenda for research on the communication technologies referred to as Web 2.0: Web-based technologies that rely on content provided by readers in addition to that which original creators contribute. The common features of these technologies—peer-generated messages—offer communication researchers the opportunity to bring familiar approaches to these new settings. Of particular importance will be how perceptions of similarity, liking, and relationship potential with the contributors of message postings affect the processing of adjacent noninterpersonal messages. How do individuals process news stories on CNN.com as they chat about the content at the same time, in IM? How do messages by peers affect perceptions and interpretations of other contiguous information online? For example, Edwards, Edwards, Qing, and Wahl (2007) experimentally investigated how computer-mediated comments ostensibly left by other students on RateMyProfessors.com affected perceptions of a videotaped lecture shown to subjects. The comments affected students' perceptions of the teacher as well as students' motivation to learn. Elsewhere, presentation of other buyers' feedback about an eBay seller causes significant effects on the bid prices a seller garners (Resnick, Zeckhauser, Swanson, & Lockwood, 2006). David, Cappella, and Fishbein (2006) examined how adolescents' chat room discussions could reverse the intended influence of public service announcements they watched online. Wang, Walther, Pingree, and Hawkins (2008) explored online support groups and health-related Web sites and found that sources' homophily to the readers drove attitude change about a health-related recommendation or coping advice more strongly than source expertise in both online settings.

The implications for the influence of interactive online communication are great. We expect that new communication technologies that present both mass, peer, and interpersonal messages will reinvigorate research on simultaneity, sequencing, and repetition cycles in the exposure to and interpretation of mass and interpersonal messages, as these sources share the screen. The relatively young area of communication and technology has generally drawn on both mass media and interpersonal communication principles, although seldom at the same time. The activities and uses that technology promote demand integration of traditionally distinct processes to recognize and understand what people do and what it means in online communication.

References

Amichai-Hamburger, Y., & McKenna, K. Y. A. (2006). The contact hypothesis reconsidered: Interacting via the Internet [Online]. *Journal of Computer-Mediated Communication, 11*(3), article 7. Retrieved June 1, 2007, from http://jcmc.indiana.edu/v0111/issue3/amichai-hamburger.html

Baker, A. (1998, July). Cyberspace couples finding romance online then meeting for the first time in real life [Online]. *CMC Magazine.* Retrieved December 1, 2000, from www.december.com/cmc/mag/1998/jul/baker.html

Burgoon, J. K., Buller, D. B., & Woodall, W. G. (1989). *Nonverbal communication: The unspoken dialogue.* New York: Harper & Row.

Burgoon, M. (1989). Instruction about communication: On divorcing dame speech. *Communication Education, 38,* 303–308.

Carr, C. T., Choi, S. S. W., DeAndrea, D. C., Kim, J., Tong, S. T., Van Der Heide, B., et al. (2008, May). *Interaction of interpersonal, peer, and media influence sources online: A research agenda for technology convergence.* Paper presented at the annual meeting of the International Communication Association, Montreal, Quebec, Canada.

Chan, D. K.-S., & Cheng, G. H.-L. (2004). A comparison of offline and online friendship qualities at different stages of relationship development. *Journal of Social and Personal Relationships, 21,* 305–320.

Cummings, J. N., Lee, J. B., & Kraut, R. (2006). Communication technology and friendship during the transition from high school to college. In R. E. Kraut, M. Brynin, & S. Kiesler (Eds.), *Computers, phones, and the Internet: Domesticating information technology* (pp. 265–278). New York: Oxford University Press.

David, C., Cappella, J. N., & Fishbein, M. (2006). The social diffusion of influence among adolescents: Group interaction in a chat room environment about antidrug advertisements. *Communication Theory, 16*, 118–140.

Dimmick, J., Ramirez, A., Jr., Lin, S.-F., & Wang, T. (2007). "Extending Society": The role of personal networks and gratification-utilities in the use of interactive communication media. *New Media & Society, 9*, 795–810.

Donath, J. (1999). Identity and deception in the virtual community. In M. A. Smith & P. Kollock (Eds.), *Communities in cyberspace* (pp. 29–59). New York: Routledge.

Donath, J., & boyd, d. (2004, October). Public displays of connection. *BT Technology Journal, 22*(4), 71–82.

Edwards, C., Edwards, A., Qing, Q., & Wahl, S. T. (2007). The influence of computer-mediated word-of-mouth communication on student perceptions of instructors and attitudes toward learning course content. *Communication Education, 56*, 255–277.

Ellison, N., Heino, R., & Gibbs, J. (2006). Managing impressions online: Self-presentation processes in the online dating environment [Online]. *Journal of Computer-Mediated Communication, 11*(2). Retrieved March 12, 2007, from http://jcmc.indiana.edu/v0111/issue2/ellison.html

Ellison, N. B., Steinfield, C., & Lampe, C. (2007). The benefits of Facebook "friends": Social capital and college students' use of online social networks sites [Online]. *Journal of Computer-Mediated Communication, 12*(4). Retrieved August 6, 2007, from http://jcmc.indiana.edu/v0112/issue4/ellison.html

Gong, L. (2007, May). *Testing the boundary of racial prejudice with robots.* Paper presented at the annual meeting of the International Communication Association, San Francisco.

Henderson, S., & Gilding, M. (2004). "I've never clicked this much with anyone in my life": Trust and hyperpersonal communication in online friendships. *New Media & Society, 6*, 487–506.

Herring, S. C., & Martinson, A. (2004). Assessing gender authenticity in computer-mediated language use: Evidence from an identity game. *Journal of Language and Social Psychology, 23*, 424–446.

Hian, L. B., Chuan, S. L., Trevor, T. M. K., & Detenber, B. H. (2004). Getting to know you: Exploring the development of relational intimacy in computer-mediated communication [Online]. *Journal of Computer-Mediated Communication, 9*(3). Retrieved January 3, 2007, from http://jcmc.indiana.edu/v019/issue3/detenber.html

Ishii, H., Kobayashi, M., & Grundin, J. (1993). Integration of interpersonal space and shared workspace: ClearBoard design and experiments. *ACM Transactions on Information Systems, 11*(4), 349–375.

Jacobson, D. (1999). Impression formation in cyberspace: Online expectations and offline experiences in text-based virtual communities [Online]. *Journal of*

Computer-Mediated Communication, 5(1). Retrieved May 18, 2000, from www.ascusc.org/jcmc/vol5/issue1/jacobson.html

Labi, N. (2007, September). An IM infatuation turned to romance. Then the truth came out. *WIRED, 15*(9), 149–153.

Landow, G. P. (1992). *Hypertext: The convergence of contemporary critical theory and technology.* Baltimore: Johns Hopkins University Press.

Lee, E.-J. (2004). Effects of gendered character representation on person perception and informational social influence in computer-mediated communication. *Computers in Human Behavior, 20,* 779–799.

Lee, E.-J. (2005). Effects of the influence agent's sex and self-confidence on informational influence in computer-mediated communication: Quantitative vs. verbal presentation. *Communication Research, 32,* 29–58.

Liu, Y. L., Ginther, D., & Zelhart, P. (2002). An exploratory study of the effects of frequency and duration of messaging on impression development in computer-mediated communication. *Social Science Computer Review, 20,* 73–80.

Mollov, B. (2006, June). *Results of Israeli and Palestinian student interactions in CMC: An analysis of attitude changes toward conflicting parties.* Paper presented at the annual meeting of the International Communication Association, Dresden, Germany.

Morningstar, C., & Farmer, F. R. (1991). The lessons of Lucasfilm's Habitat. In M. Benedikt (Ed.), *Cyberspace: First steps* (pp. 273–301). Cambridge, MA: MIT Press.

Parks, M. R. (2007). *Personal relationships and personal networks.* Mahwah, NJ: Lawrence Erlbaum.

Parks, M. R., & Floyd, K. (1996). Making friends in cyberspace. *Journal of Communication, 46,* 80–97.

Peter, J., Valkenburg, P. M., & Schouten, A. P. (2005). Developing a model of adolescent friendship formation on the Internet. *Cyberpsychology and Behavior, 8,* 423–430.

Ramirez, A., Jr., & Broneck, K. (in press). "IM Me": Instant messaging as relational maintenance and everyday communication. *Journal of Social and Personal Relationships.*

Ramirez, A., Jr., Dimmick, J., Feaster, J., & Lin, S.-F. (2008). Revisiting media competition: The gratification niches of instant messaging, e-mail, and the telephone. *Communication Research, 35,* 529–547.

Ramirez, A., Jr., & Wang, Z. (2008). When on-line meets off-line: An expectancy violation theory perspective on modality switching. *Journal of Communication, 58,* 20–39.

Ramirez, A., Jr., & Zhang, S. (2007). When online meets offline: The effect of modality switching on relational communication. *Communication Monographs, 74,* 287–310.

Resnick, P., Zeckhauser, R., Swanson, J., & Lockwood, K. (2006). The value of reputation on eBay: A controlled experiment. *Experimental Economics, 9,* 79–101.

Shiu, E. (2005). *How Americans use Instant Messaging.* [Online] Pew Internet and American Life Project. Retrieved January 7, 2007, from www.pewinternet.org/pdfs/PIP_Instantmessage_Report.pdf

Soller, K. (2007, August 20). Why I love it. . . . *Newsweek,* p. 44.

Stafford, L. (2004). *Maintaining long-distance and cross-residential relationships.* Mahwah, NJ: Lawrence Erlbaum.

Tanis, M. (2003). *Cues to identity in CMC: The impact on person perception and subsequent interaction outcomes.* Unpublished doctoral dissertation, University of Amsterdam, the Netherlands.

Tong, S. T., Van Der Heide, B., Langwell, L., & Walther, J. B. (2008). Too much of a good thing? The relationship between number of friends and interpersonal impressions on Facebook. [Online] *Journal of Computer-Mediated Communication, 13*(3), 531–549.

Turkle, S. (1995). *Life on the screen: Identity in the age of the Internet.* New York: Simon & Schuster.

Van Gelder, L. (1985). The strange case of the electronic lover. *Ms., October, 94,* 99, 101–104, 117, 123–124.

Vanden Boogart, M. R. (2006). *Uncovering the social impact of Facebook on a college campus.* Unpublished master's thesis, Kansas State University, Manhattan, KA.

Walther, J. B. (1992). Interpersonal effects in computer-mediated interaction: A relational perspective. *Communication Research, 19,* 52–90.

Walther, J. B. (1996). Computer-mediated communication: Impersonal, interpersonal, and hyperpersonal interaction. *Communication Research, 23,* 3–43.

Walther, J. B. (1997, June). *Fahrfugnugen auf der Infobahn.* Presentation at the biennial meeting of the Society of Social Psychology in the German Psychological Society, Konstanz, Germany.

Walther, J. B. (2004). Language and communication technology: An introduction to the special issue. *Journal of Language and Social Psychology, 23,* 384–396.

Walther, J. B. (2006). Nonverbal dynamics in computer-mediated communication, or : (and the net : ('s with you, :) and you :) alone. In V. Manusov & M. L. Patterson (Eds.), *Handbook of nonverbal communication* (pp. 461–479). Thousand Oaks, CA: Sage.

Walther, J. B., & Bunz, U. (2005). The rules of virtual groups: Trust, liking, and performance in computer-mediated communication. *Journal of Communication, 55,* 828–846.

Walther, J. B. (2007). Selective self-presentation in computer-mediated communication: Hyperpersonal dimensions of technology, language, and cognition. *Computers in Human Behavior, 23,* 2538–2557.

Walther, J. B., Loh, T., & Granka, L. (2005). Let me count the ways: The interchange of verbal and nonverbal cues in computer-mediated and face-to-face affinity. *Journal of Language and Social Psychology, 24,* 36–65.

Walther, J. B., & Parks, M. R. (2002). Cues filtered out, cues filtered in: Computer-mediated communication and relationships. In M. L. Knapp & J. A. Daly (Eds.),

Handbook of interpersonal communication (3rd ed., pp. 529–563). Thousand Oaks, CA: Sage.

Walther, J. B., Van Der Heide, B., Kim, S., Westerman, D., & Tong, S. T. (2008). The role of friends' behavior on evaluations of individuals' Facebook profiles: Are we known by the company we keep? *Human Communication Research, 34,* 28–49.

Wang, Z., Walther, J. B., Pingree, S., & Hawkins, R. (2008). Health information, credibility, homophily, and influence via the Internet: Web sites versus discussion groups. *Health Communication, 23,* 358–368.

Whitty, M. T. (2002). Liar, Liar! An examination of how open, supportive and honest people are in chat rooms. *Computers in Human Behavior, 18*(4), 343–352.

Whitty, M., & Gavin, J. (2001). Age/Sex/Location: Uncovering the social cues in the development of online relationships. *CyberPsychology & Behavior, 4,* 623–630.

14

Interpersonal Relationships on Television

A Look at Three Key Attributes

Stacy L. Smith

Amy Granados

The purpose of this chapter is to review what we know about interpersonal relationships on television. By perusing the table of contents of any edited interpersonal communication text, you will see that such a task can be daunting to a media effects scholar. Elements of interpersonal relationships can involve communicator attributes such as speech acts, emotional displays, physical appearance, and personality traits. Aspects of communicating relationally also may be defined in terms of culture, assessing similarities and differences in group norms, or exploring issues of passing, stereotyping, and prejudice. Interpersonal relationships also can be defined in terms of the roles of participants, looking at communicative signals and patterns among acquaintances, friends, romantic partners, families, or coworkers. Finally, interpersonal relationships can involve a dark side, which incorporates deception, stalking, physical and verbal aggression, and the misuse of power.

All these topics cannot be covered in one book, let alone a single chapter. As a result, some strategic decisions had to be made about what to include and exclude in this chapter. We have chosen to examine three areas on television germane to interpersonal relationships. These three may not be *the* most important, but we believe that they are central to how relationships are shown on television and the positive and negative effects that viewing such depictions may have on individuals and society. The three elements seem to incorporate many of the aspects of interpersonal interactions discussed in the paragraph above. Also, each area encompasses topics that Stacy has devoted some time and energy researching over the past decade. Thus, the chapter will privilege autobiography over exhaustiveness when it comes to the three areas.

The first area is aggression. The issue of television violence is still a hot topic for many parents in this country, as some have alleged that exposure may be contributing to violent and criminal activity. The second area concerns gender roles. One of the primary ways in which individuals are defined relationally is through their gender, which can exert an influence on appearance cues, psychological traits, relational roles, power, and even occupational options. Given that television plays a part in the socialization of sex roles, we thought that it was important to include it in this chapter. Finally, we wanted to examine sex and romance on television. These attributes are central to the initiation, maintenance, and dissolution of romantic relationships, and often appear on popular shows such as *Desperate Housewives* and *Grey's Anatomy*. Because such depictions may have a particular influence on developing youth and, thus, real-world interpersonal relationships, we included sex and romance in this chapter.

The structure of this chapter is as follows. Within each area, content patterns and their effects are delineated. We spend very little time explicating theory, as many other scholars have devoted considerable attention to discussing explanatory mechanisms (Bryant & Zillmann, 2002). The last section of the chapter addresses limitations of previous work and directions for future research. It is here that we step back, reflect on our own work, and offer some insights based on lessons learned along the way.

Television Violence

Television violence has long been a concern of parents, teachers, and policy-makers. The anxiety over TV violence ebbs and flows in the United States, with trepidation seemingly being triggered when crime statistics rise or a school shooting occurs. The early 1990s was one of those time periods when there was mounting congressional concern over media violence in this country. As a result, the National Cable Television Association awarded a $3.3 million dollar grant in 1994 to a consortium of scholars working under the auspices of the National Television Violence Study. The goal of that study was to examine a variety of aspects related to the amount and context of violence on television. Stacy worked as a research assistant on this project at the University of California, Santa Barbara, site for more than 3 years. That experience concretized her knowledge of content patterns and effects of exposure to violent portrayals, which we will now review.

Content Patterns

How much violence is on American television? This question has been asked by a variety of scholars and research teams across decades. Looking at instances of physical aggression across 23 channels airing programming between 6:00 a.m. and 11:00 p.m., Smith et al. (1998) found that roughly 60% of all shows depict violence. Much of the violence shown on television is sanitized, glamorized, trivialized, and not chastised. Of the 17,638 violent interactions coded, most are committed by men, adults, and Caucasians. Similar trends were observed for the targets of violence, suggesting that women may not be portrayed as the victimized as much as the popular press purports.

Several scholars have examined violence in prime time (Smith, Nathanson, & Wilson, 2002), or evening, shows. Potter et al. (1995) found 471 minor assaults on evening shows, with almost half of all acts directed at someone close to or at least an acquaintance of the perpetrator. Examining 13 different samples of prime-time content, Signorielli (2003) found that 19% of women perpetrated violence in prime time, and 17.4% were victims. Genre also affects the presentation of violence. Children's shows are more likely to feature violence than all other types of programming (Wilson et al., 2002), as indicated by percentage of programs with aggression (69% vs. 57%) or rate per hour (14.1 acts vs. 5.6 acts). Studies have also assessed violence in music videos. Rich, Woods, Goodman, Emans, and DuRant (1998) found that only 14.7% of 518 music videos sampled contained an instance of aggression, which is remarkably similar to the results (15%, $N = 1,962$ music videos) obtained by Smith and Boyson (2002). Rich et al. (1998) found that males were portrayed as 78.1% of the perpetrators and females accounted for 46.3% of the victims.

The most common form of aggression on television occurs verbally, however. Yet very little research has been conducted on the prevalence of verbal aggression or conflict on television. Of the 105 conflicts coded by Brinson

(1992) in prime-time shows, opposite-sex clashes occurred most frequently, followed by male dyad conflict and then female dyad conflict. The research found that conflict was often characterized by the following: aggressive behavior (M = 43%, F = 33%), physical withdrawal (M = 26%, F = 42%), emotional withdrawal (M = 25%, F = 28%), raised voice (M = 30%, F = 38%), use of sarcasm (M = 45%, F = 39%), and use of "I" statements (M = 54%, F = 64%). Such findings suggest that a great deal of conflict on television may include verbal and physical aggression.

Potter et al. (1995) also looked at verbal aggression in evening shows. The researchers coded nearly 4,000 instances of antisocial behavior. Hostile remarks accounted for the largest category, with 27.3% of all acts categorized as "harsh criticism, insults, put downs" (p. 505). Among these caustic remarks, most were directed at a close relation (45.4%) or an acquaintance (24.1%). Almost one fifth of comments were directed at strangers and an even smaller number were self-directed (7.5%). Two hundred and one instances of deceit (e.g., fraud, cheating, lying) were observed in evening shows, most often occurring between those in a close relationship. Roughly half of such deceitful acts took place between acquaintances (22.5%) and strangers (24.5%).

Overall, aggression is a common element in television. Verbal aggression and minor assaults both seem to occur between characters with some relational tie. Gender exerts an influence on how conflict and aggression are shown, with females often the victims of violence in music videos.

Effects of Exposure

The effects of exposure to television violence also has attracted a great deal of empirical attention. Most investigations have focused on the effects of exposure to physical violence rather than verbal aggression or conflict. Research reveals that three negative effects are associated with viewing television violence. First, viewing television violence can effect aggressive tendencies. Experiments show that TV violence can lead to short-term systematic increases in aggressive thoughts and behaviors (see Bushman & Huesmann, 2001), consistent with a priming perspective (Jo & Berkowitz, 1994). Surveys also reveal a correlation between viewing TV violence and aggressive behavior (Dominick & Greenberg, 1972; McIntyre & Teevan, 1972). Longitudinal evidence documents an overtime link (Huesmann, Moise, Podolski, & Eron, 1998), with one study showing that boys' early exposure to TV violence at the age of 8 years was a significant and positive predictor of later aggressive behavior at age 30 (Huesmann, 1986). Huesmann has explained this effect using a social developmental perspective, which indicates that heavy viewing of television violence at a young age can lead to the development and enactment of aggressive scripts for social problem solving long into adulthood. Paik and Comstock's (1994) meta-analysis of 217 studies reveals a medium-sized effect ($r = .31$) between viewing TV violence and antisocial behavior.

Next, research indicates that intervening variables can affect the TV violence/aggression tie. Studies show that the context or way in which violence is shown on television can influence its effect. To illustrate, weapon violence (Berkowitz & LePage, 1967), violence that is rewarded or not punished (Bandura, 1965), justified violence (Meyer, 1972), realistic violence (Atkin, 1983), violence lacking pain cues (Baron, 1971), humorous violence (Berkowitz, 1970), and violence that is extensive (Huesmann et al., 1998) can all *increase* the probability of aggressive responding. Other characteristics such as age (Paik & Comstock, 1994), perceived realism of TV violence (Huesmann et al., 1998), and trait aggressiveness (Bushman, 1995) may also moderate exposure effects.

Another outcome associated with exposure to television violence is fear. There are two types of fear effects. Viewing television violence can trigger fright (Cantor, 2002) in the form of negative affect or behavioral manifestations of upset. Wilson, Hoffner, and Cantor (1987) found that roughly 75% of preschool and elementary school–age children self-report being frightened by something in the media. Cantor (2002, p. 291) has argued that certain types of stimuli elicit fear: (a) dangers/injuries, (b) distortions/deformities, and (c) seeing liked characters in threatening scenarios. She indicates that such effects operate through a process of stimulus generalization, whereby real threats can trigger the same, but weaker response when depicted on television or in film (Cantor, 2002).

Research shows that fear effects are influenced by several variables. Females often report more fear in response to media dangers and threats than do males (Peck, 1999), which may be due to sex-role norms surrounding the discussion and expression of emotions. Age also affects fear responses to television violence. Younger children are more frightened by fantastic portrayals that look scary, whereas older viewers are more frightened by possible or probable threats (Cantor & Sparks, 1984; Sparks, 1986). This trend is presumably due to cognitive differences in the ability to differentiate fantasy versus reality and to be persuaded by perceptual characteristics of stimuli (Melkman, Tversky, & Baratz, 1981; Morison, Kelly, & Gardner, 1978).

Cultivation scholars have also established that viewing television may have a cumulative effect on social reality perceptions (Gerbner, Gross, Morgan, Signorielli, & Shanahan, 2002). Because television is filled with stories involving crime and violence, heavy viewers may be more likely than light viewers to perceive the world as a mean and scary place. Indeed, studies show that repeated exposure is positively associated with (a) interpersonal mistrust, (b) worry about walking alone at night, and (c) estimates of violence (Hawkins & Pingree, 1982).

The third outcome of exposure to TV violence is desensitization. Studies show that viewing TV violence is associated with decreases in physiological arousal to media and real-life aggression (Cline, Croft, & Courrier, 1973). TV violence exposure can "spill over" and affect individuals' tolerance and perceptions of real-world aggression (Molitor & Hirsch, 1994). Drabman and Thomas (1974) found that children viewing an 8-minute violent clip took significantly longer to seek help when exposed to a mediated portrayal of a physical confrontation between two children than did those in the non-viewing control. Even more pronounced desensitization effects have been observed in adults' responses to sexualized violence (Linz, Donnerstein, & Penrod, 1984).

The literature reviewed above reveals that viewing television violence can contribute to aggression, fear, and emotional desensitization, all of which affect personal relationships. The effects are influenced, however, by content features, amount of exposure, and individual differences.

Gender Roles

After conducting content-analytic and effects studies on violence in television, I (Stacy) collaborated (as second author) on an analysis of gender roles in video games with graduate student Edward Downs. It was my first exposure to assessing characters as the unit of analysis (rather than violent interactions or scenes), and I was surprised by the lack of gender parity found in the popular console-based games (e.g., ratio of over 5 males to every 1 female). That study proved timely as it laid the groundwork and began my thinking about gender roles in entertainment. Little did I know that on the heels of that investigation, I would receive a grant with funds raised by Academy Award winner Geena Davis to examine the prevalence of males and females in media aimed at children. My knowledge of media violence informed that work greatly, as we assessed the frequency *and* context of characters in popular films and television. To date, we just finished our fifth investigation assessing gender roles in the media that has involved multiple graduate students (i.e., Elaine Chan, Marc Choueiti, Amy Granados, Katherine Pieper) and more than 150 undergraduates at the Annenberg School for Communication at the University of Southern California. The research on gender roles, including some of our own work, is presented below.

Content Patterns

Most of the gender research examines the distribution of characters' biological sex. Some of that research also assesses indicators such as demography, occupations, and personality traits. Many of the content-analytic studies focus on prime-time programming. Females make up approximately 40% of all speaking characters in this time slot (Signorielli & Bacue, 1999). Some studies evidence a genre effect, in which women appear more frequently in prime-time sitcoms than in other types of programming (Glascock, 2001; Signorielli & Bacue, 1999). Even more variation exists in the distribution of gender roles by character importance. Only 17.7% of the major characters in Elasmar, Hasegawa, and Brain's (1999) study were female. However, other studies (Lauzen & Dozier, 1999, 2004) have observed that women were cast in roughly 40% of all major roles. Given that female comprise roughly half of the population, such empirical trends suggest a lack of gender symmetry in prime-time shows.

Other demographic indicators covary with gender. Females are shown as *younger* than their male counterparts (Davis, 1990; Signorielli & Bacue, 1999). The overemphasis on female youth is not surprising, given Hollywood's fixation with physical appearance and aversion to aging. Several studies also show that *marital status* is more easily identifiable for female characters than for males (Davis, 1990; Glascock, 2001; Lauzen & Dozier, 1999). This tendency may indicate that family life is not prioritized for men or that domesticity cues are overemphasized for women. A similar trend is found when examining characters' *parental status*. Males evidence more ambiguity in parental status than do females. When parental status is ascertainable, women are nearly twice as likely as men to be caregivers (Glascock, 2001). Finally, females are more likely than males to be unemployed or to have an indeterminable *occupational status* (Signorielli & Kahlenberg, 2001). For those who are employed, men are more often shown than women to have occupational power (Lauzen & Dozier, 2004) and higher-paying jobs (Glascock, 2001).

Besides demographics, the way in which gender influences communication patterns has been assessed (Lauzen & Dozier, 1999). Zhao and Gantz (2003) also found that prime-time males interrupt more than do prime-time females. Men are more likely than women to use a disrupting strategy and less likely to use a cooperating one. Lauzen and Dozier (2002) also examined appearance comments. The researchers found that women are almost twice as likely as men to be the targets of appearance-related comments. Of those women who receive appearance-related comments from men, 10% are insults, 68% are compliments, and 22% are neutral.

Outside prime time, scholars have also examined sex roles in children's shows. We (Smith, Granados, Choueiti, & Pieper, 2006) recently examined gender roles across a composite week of 1,034 randomly sampled children's shows airing between 6:00 a.m. and 8:00 p.m. across 12 broadcasting outlets. A total of 15,371 speaking characters were evaluated across the sample, and 63.2% were male and 36.8% were female. This calculates into a ratio of 1.72 males to every 1 female in children's programming. The percentage of males to females varied by shows' style of presentation (i.e., live action vs. animation) and rating (i.e., TVY = all children, TVY7 = 7 and older, and TVG = general audience). Shows presented in live action and rated G almost featured parity (55.3% males, 44.7% females).

Notable differences also emerged in family roles. Females were more likely than males to be shown as a caregiver or partner in a romantic relationship. Other studies have documented gender-related differences in occupations and personality traits. Thompson and Zerbinos (1995) found that males are more likely to have a recognizable occupation than are females across 175 children's cartoons. Such jobs are often shown in a gendered light. Analyzing 15 episodes of *Sesame Street,* Jones, Abelli, and Abelli's (1994) content analysis revealed that males and females are 10 times as likely to be shown in stereotypical occupations than in counterstereotypical ones. Investigating personality characteristics, Barner (1999, p. 559) found that males are more likely to be portrayed as active, aggressive, and dominant, whereas females are more likely to be shown as deferent, dependent, and nurturing.

Depictions of males and females in children's shows and prime-time programming are highly stereotyped. Females are more likely than males to be younger and minor characters, with nurturing and domestic traits. Males, on the other hand, are more likely to be single, use commanding communication, and possess occupational power.

Effects of Exposure

A fair amount of the research in this area has focused on children, given how impressionable they may be to exposure effects. Despite exceptions (e.g., Repetti, 1984), some survey research has indicated that repeated exposure may contribute to sexist beliefs. Heavy viewers are more inclined to endorse sex-typing household chores and personality traits (McGhee & Freuh, 1980; Morgan, 1987; Signiorelli & Lears, 1992). Longitudinal data also suggest that there is a link between exposure to televised content and stereotypical attitudes and beliefs. Research reveals that early heavy viewing among girls is correlated with later sexism (Morgan, 1982). Morgan and Rothschild (1983) observed that this relationship only held for youth without many social affiliations and for those who have access to cable. In a naturalistic design, Kimball (1986, p. 278) found that children's perceptions were more sex-typed 2 years after TV had been introduced. The findings also show that girls were more likely to sex-type peer and authority relations, whereas boys were more likely to sex-type actions and occupations.

There is ample evidence that viewing television contributes to sex-role stereotyping. A meta-analysis of more than 20 studies supports the trends illuminated here. Herrett-Skjellum and Allen (1996) found that heavy viewing was positively correlated with the endorsement of sexual stereotypes across multiple experimental ($r = .21$) and nonexperimental ($r = .10$) studies. Among the nonexperimental research (p. 174), the effect for stereotyping occupations ($r = .22$) was greater than the effect for sex roles ($r = .075$) or sex-typed behavior ($r = .105$).

Two prominent theories have been advanced to explain how television may contribute to or reinforce sex-role stereotyping. Bandura's (1986) social cognitive theory suggests that children learn sex-typed actions by way of reinforcement of their own behaviors or by observing the behaviors of others (i.e., modeling). Information-processing theories, in comparison, focus on schema development and enactment. Gender is one powerful organizing schema (Calvert, 1999), which focuses attention to and encoding of detailed information about the child's own as opposed to the opposite sex. Television presents countless examples of sex-typed behavior to develop and enrich these schemas or teach positive and/or negative response consequences to sex-typed and/or counterstereotypical actions to male and female role models.

A few studies have indicated that parental involvement in children's media selections may counteract the effects of viewing stereotypical content. Experimentally, Nathanson, Wilson, McGee, and Sebastian (2002) found that among younger children (kindergarten to second graders), a counter-stereotypical mediation strategy (i.e., "The show is wrong. Lots of girls like camping") increased youngsters' endorsement of females participating in activities conventionally reserved for males. Although these findings suggest that parental involvement can allay the negative effects of viewing, considerably more research is needed to substantiate this claim.

Sex and Romance

Perhaps one of the hottest topics of media effects research pertains to content patterns and effects of exposure to sexual portrayals. Our own work, unexpectedly, has found its way into this body of research, which we will overview below.

Content Patterns

Using a liberal definition, Kunkel, Eyal, Finnerty, Biely, and Donnerstein's (2005) research has examined the amount of sex (talk or behavior) on television. The researchers' content analyzed the landscape of television programming for sexual behavior across multiple broadcast and cable channels, viewing seasons and day parts (7:00 a.m. to 11:00 p.m., PST). Three major findings are important. The first is that televised sexual content is on the rise. Over half of all shows during the 1997/1998 season featured one or more instances of sex. In the 2004/2005 season, sex appears in 70% of all programs.

The second result is that much sexual activity on TV is taking place increasingly outside the context of an explicit relationship. In 2002, a total of 39% of all scenes with implied or depicted sexual intercourse involved two people who were not in a committed relationship. That figure jumped to 47% in the 2004/2005 viewing season. This trend may communicate to young, naive viewers that sex is a frivolous commodity, readily exchanged between mere acquaintances.

The last major finding is that the risk and responsibilities associated with intimate behavior are rarely portrayed. Fewer than one in five shows with any sexualized content in the 2004/2005 season had a reference to the potential consequences associated with such mature intimate behavior. While this percentage is 9% higher than in 1997/1998, it remains relatively the same as 2001/2002.

Ward (1995) examined sexual talk in prime-time programs popular with children and adolescents during the 1992/1993 viewing season. Out of the 1,145 interactions assessed, 29.4% were about sexuality. Looking at segments of spoken dialogue, almost a third (31.3%) of all sexual messages focused on the male's sex role (p. 604). The most frequently occurring themes were about men perceiving women as sex objects and valuing females for how they look. Also common were statements about the male sex drive and being "always ready and willing for sex, anytime, anywhere" (p. 606). There were substantially fewer messages about the female's sex role (18.9%), with the greatest number of those comments focusing on attributes of a potential partner's attractiveness, wealth, and sweetness. Outside gender, the most frequently discussed theme was sexual competition where "women, and men especially (approximately 74% of the speakers), discussed scoring, cheating on partners, stealing partners, and fighting over dates" (p. 607). Thus, even content popular with children and adolescents is rife with sexualized and objectifying information.

Genres have also been assessed for actions with sexual overtones. Kunkel et al. (2005) found that 85% of soap operas feature some form of sexual dialogue or action. Examining 97 hours of content across 10 daytime soaps,

Heintz-Knowles (1996, p. 3) found 594 sexual behaviors that occurred at a rate of 6.12 acts per hour. The most frequent type of behavior was kissing, accounting for 45% of all sexual behavior. Very little intercourse between characters was shown, with 16 out of 17 of these depictions occurring in the context of a committed relationship. Greenberg, Sherry, Busselle, Hnilo, and Smith (1997) assessed conversational topics across 11 popular daytime talk shows during the summer of 1995. These shows tend to feature topics surrounding sex, with 37% of the programs focusing on discussions about marriage/dating and 36% on sexual activity. Reality series, according to Kunkel et al.'s (2005) research, are the least likely of all genres to feature sexual behavior (28%). Examining dating reality shows in particular, Ferris, Smith, Greenberg, and Smith's (2007) results reveal that typical messages include "women are sex objects," "dating is a game," and "men are sex-driven" (pp. 500–501).

Children's shows are also saturated with a specific type of sexualized content. Drawing from the research with Edward Downs on video games (Downs & Smith, 2005; see also Children Now, 2001), we examined the frequency of hypersexualized males and females in a composite week of ($N = 1,034$) children's television shows. Hypersexuality refers to an overemphasis on a character's thinness, physical beauty, and/or alluring attire. The results were nothing short of provocative, no pun intended. Females were almost four times as likely as males to be shown in scanty or tight attire (20.7% vs. 5.4%), thereby illuminating provocative parts of the body (for definitions, see Downs & Smith, 2005 or Smith et al., 2006). Over a quarter (25.6%) of the females had diminutive waistlines, leaving little room for a womb or any other internal organ. Only 14.4% of males had such a small midsection. Females are more likely to be shown with an exaggerated hourglass figure than are males, who are shown with a hypermuscularized frame. Not surprisingly, animated females are substantially more likely to be hypersexualized than are live-action females.

G-rated films evidenced trends similar to those observed in children's television. Looking at hypersexuality in 100 top-grossing G-rated films theatrically released between 1990 and 2006, we observed that characters in these kid-friendly films are just as sexualized in terms of body shape and dress. To see how a heavy focus on sexualized appearance might relate to the types of journeys taken by female characters, we conducted a qualitative analysis (Granados & Smith, 2007). Examining 13 general audience films with a female protagonist revealed that romance is typically present and often a chief aim of the leading lady. Love at first sight regularly sparks these romantic pursuits, highlighting the preeminence of physical attractiveness. The use of deception to lure a romantic mate is also a common plot device. Looks can also be deceiving, as extreme makeovers frequently transform the heroine

296 Part IV • Relationships, Media, and Culture

from an eyesore to an eyeful. Given the parallel depiction of the female body in children's television and G-rated films, it becomes imperative that scholars examine the nature of stories children are exposed to across media.

Television paints the picture that sex is a recreational pursuit, potentially as harmless and ubiquitous as any other leisure-time activity. Independent of genre or time of day, the conversation about sex seems to be omnipresent on the small screen. A different type of sexual content is shown in children's fare. In this genre, an emphasis is put on hypersexualizing females' figures, thereby potentially increasing the likelihood of viewer or other character gaze and objectification.

Effects of Exposure

What impact does exposure to televised portrayals of sex have on viewers? Greeson and Williams (1986) observed that adolescents exposed to MTV rated premarital sex as more acceptable than did those adolescents not exposed to such content. Kalof (1999) found that participants who viewed a sexualized, performance-based music video segment scored higher on the Adversarial Sexual Beliefs Subscale than did those participants who viewed a concert-based music video segment devoid of sexualized content. Bryant and Rockwell (1994) found that teens massively exposed to scenes of sexual relations between unmarried couples rated subsequent sexual improprieties as significantly *less bad* than did those teens massively exposed to scenarios of marital intimacy or nonsexual relations.

Survey research has also looked at the association between exposure to racy television content and outcomes surrounding sex. Knight's (2001, p. 5) results show that viewing media with sexual overtones is significantly related to perceiving the rewards of sexual behavior despite multiple controls. Among undergraduates, Ward (2002) found that viewing content that often incorporates sexualized scenarios (i.e., music videos, soaps) was a significant and positive predictor of perceiving increased peer sexual experience. Attitudinal findings indicate that females who frequently watch prime-time content are also more likely to support attitudes that emphasize sex as a sport or recreational activity (Ward & Rivadeneyra, 1999, pp. 241, 243).

To ascertain directionality, a series of longitudinal investigations have been undertaken. At least one study has demonstrated no overall relationship between exposure to televised content and sexual activity (Peterson, Moore, & Furstenberg, 1991). As the authors note, these findings may be attributable to the measures used in the study. Other research has documented a correlation between viewing and self-reports of sexual behavior, but the association is influenced by race. Among whites, Brown et al. (2006)

found that adolescents with a heavy sexual media diet (SMD) were more likely than those with a light SMD to have initiated sexual activity 2 years after baseline assessment. Using multivariate analyses with multiple controls, Collins et al. (2004) found that Time 1 viewing of sexualized TV content had a positive association with sexual initiation at Time 2. The same study also found that African Americans heavily exposed to the consequences or safety concerns associated with sexual activity at baseline were less likely to engage in such mature behavior at follow-up a year later. This latter finding is consistent with a social cognitive approach, which reveals that negative reinforcements can teach or inhibit risky behavior.

Previous research in this area has placed a strong emphasis on the sexual beliefs, attitudes, and behaviors of youth. Though important, this focus has largely neglected the role that viewing habits may have on children's body esteem. Given the well-documented hypersexualization of characters in children's film and television content, it becomes important to investigate what young viewers may be learning about what it means to be male and female in terms of physical appearance, particularly in the context of romantic relationships. Girls as young as 5 years have been found to evidence weight concerns and body dissatisfaction (Davison, Markey, & Birch, 2000). Although the relationship to body image issues and media exposure has not been clearly established for young children, Dittmar, Halliwell, and Ive (2006) found that exposure to images of Barbie was related to depressed body satisfaction in girls of ages 5 to 7 years. Currently, we (Smith and Granados) are working on a series of experiments funded by the University of Southern California designed to assess the relationship between exposure to hypersexualized media characters from popular children's content and young girls' body esteem and satisfaction.

A few intervening variables have been identified in the literature. Dissatisfaction with the home environment may make some youth vulnerable viewers to sexual content (Strouse, Buerkel-Rothfuss, & Long, 1995). Among females who are dissatisfied with the family context, Strouse et al. (1995) found that heavy consumers of music videos were 3.7 times more likely than light consumers to be nonvirgins. Further risk may be incurred when youths' viewing habits go unmonitored (Ashby, Arcari, & Edmonson, 2006; Peterson et al., 1991). Turning our attention to body esteem variables, currently very little is known. However, a recent meta-analysis (Groesz, Levine, & Murnen, 2002) reveals that females under the age of 19 years and those with preexisting body disturbance are more likely to be adversely affected by viewing thin ideals. Thus, a child's age, level of development, and family beliefs about diet and thinness are all potential moderators that may ameliorate or exacerbate negative effects.

Future Directions for Research

Stepping back, the literature reveals that we know quite a bit about the types of roles, characters, and actions that are a part of interpersonal relationships on television. After summarizing all this work, it is clear that there are four specific directions for future research that scholars should be mindful of when conducting studies on content patterns of or effects surrounding exposure to TV.

1. Content Studies Need to Incorporate Different Units of Analysis

Most of the content-analytic studies focus on negative behaviors (e.g., violence, sex) and/or the types of characters (e.g., males, females) engaging in such acts. As a result, most investigations simply tally up the number of males engaging in aggression and compare that with the number of females engaging in such acts. In this case, the violent action or the character shown might be the unit of analysis. Such an approach may be fitting for measuring violence or sexual content. But it will simply not do when trying to assess the nature of interpersonal relationships on TV (i.e., friendships, romantic relationships, family dynamics) and how such associations may change over time. By nature, interpersonal relationships involve at least two people. Interlocutors influence the rhythm, direction, and tone of conversation, not to mention nonverbal behavior, the presence of sexual overtones, or verbally aggressive acts. All the meaning that emerges from interaction takes place because of two or more people. Consequently, media scholars should figure out ways to unitize dyads and groups that complement what interpersonal scholars have been doing for years. Then, we can begin to compare and contrast real-world interactions with those that take place in the "reel" world of television and film.

2. Researchers Need to Capture the Full Range of Interpersonal Relationships

We decided to present three areas of research that have received a great deal of empirical attention, presumably due to their potential for increasing the risk of negative effects. Although a lot of other research has taken place in the field outside these areas, many messages germane to interpersonal relationships remain completely underexplored. We still know very little about deception or lying on television and the effects exposure to such messages has on viewers, especially children. Deceptive messages occurring in the context of a developing romantic relationship may be powerful portrayals for social learning. Additionally, we still know very little about family communication (i.e., husband and wife, parent and child, sibling and sibling) and relational interactions between and among different cultures (i.e., race, class, religion). To better understand the role of television in the lives of children, adolescents, and adults, we need to capture the frequency and multidimensional nature of these types of messages on television and their immediate and cumulative effects.

3. Researchers Need to Think About How Individuals Are Watching Television

In light of the changing nature of the entertainment industry, it may be important to assess the impact of *how* individuals watch television content. With DVR technology and entire series now available for purchase on DVD, viewers no longer have to wait a week between episodes to watch their favorite programs. They now have the choice to immerse themselves in an entire season of a series at their own pace. This accessibility may lend itself to extended periods of viewing or exposure to selected episodes repeatedly. These types of viewing patterns may hasten the effect of viewer identification with television characters. Extended viewing may also accelerate cultivation effects, particularly if viewers are consuming negative or skewed content from specific genres. New technologies may also make children's and adolescents' patterns of exposure more difficult for parents to mediate.

4. Researchers Need to Consider How Outcomes Relate to One Another

As noted above, TV violence can contribute to three negative effects: (1) aggressive tendencies, (2) desensitization, and (3) fear. To date, however, we have no idea how these outcomes relate to one another. Is it that heavy viewing cultivates fear; or, does repeated exposure to television violence desensitize the viewer? Can it do both? If it can, what are the mechanisms responsible for these effects? Clearly, these types of questions need to be grappled with by communication scientists in the 21st century so that we have a more complete understanding of the impact of viewing TV content.

Overall, this chapter covered three common aspects of interpersonal relationships on television: (1) gender roles, (2) sex/romance, and (3) conflict/aggression. Though not exhaustive or comprehensive, this chapter serves as a snapshot of what we currently know and do not know about these areas in the media effects arena as it relates to interpersonal relationships.

References

Ashby, S. L., Arcari, C. M., & Edmonson, B. (2006). Television viewing and risk of sexual initiation by young adolescents. *Archives of Pediatric and Adolescent Medicine, 160,* 375–380.

Atkin, C. (1983). Effects of realistic TV violence vs. fictional violence on aggression. *Journalism Quarterly, 60,* 615–621.

Bandura, A. (1965). Influence of models' reinforcement contingencies on the acquisition of imitative responses. *Journal of Personality and Social Psychology, 1,* 589–595.

Bandura, A. (1986). *Social foundations of thought and action: A social cognitive approach.* Englewood Cliffs, NJ: Prentice Hall.

Barner, M. (1999). Sex-role stereotyping in FCC-mandated children's educational television. *Journal of Broadcasting & Electronic Media, 43*(4), 551–564.

Baron, R. A. (1971). Magnitude of victim's pain cues and level of prior anger arousal as determinants of adult aggressive behavior. *Journal of Personality and Social Psychology, 17,* 236–243.

Berkowitz, L. (1970). Aggressive humor as a stimulus to aggressive responses. *Journal of Personality and Social Psychology, 16,* 710–717.

Berkowitz, L., & LePage, A. (1967). Weapons as aggression-eliciting stimuli. *Journal of Personality and Social Psychology, 7,* 202–207.

Brinson, S. L. (1992). TV fights: Women and men in interpersonal arguments on prime time television dramas. *Argumentation & Advocacy, 29,* 89–105.

Brown, J. D., L'Engle, K., Pardun, C. J., Guo, G., Kenneavy, K., & Jackson, C. (2006). Sexy media matter: Exposure to sexual content in music, movies, television, and magazines predicts Black and White adolescents' sexual behavior. *Pediatrics, 117,* 1018–1027.

Bryant, J., & Rockwell, S. C. (1994). Effects of massive exposure to sexually oriented prime-time television programming on adolescents' moral judgment. In D. Zillman, J. Bryant, & A. C. Huston (Eds.), *Media, children, and the family: Social scientific, psychodynamic, and clinical perspectives* (pp. 183–195). Hillsdale, NJ: Lawrence Erlbaum.

Bryant, J., & Zillmann, D. (2002). *Media effects* (2nd ed.). Mahwah, NJ: Lawrence Erlbaum.

Bushman, B. (1995). Moderating role of trait aggressiveness in the effects of violent media on aggression. *Journal of Personality and Social Psychology, 69*(5), 950–960.

Bushman, B., & Huesmann, L. R. (2001). Effects of television violence on aggression. In D. G. Singer & J. L. Singer (Eds.), *Handbook of children and the media* (pp. 223–254). Thousand Oaks, CA: Sage.

Calvert, S. (1999). *Children's journey through the information age.* Boston: McGraw-Hill.

Cantor, J. (2002). Fright reactions to mass media. In J. Bryant & D. Zillmann (Eds.), *Media effects* (pp. 287–306). Hillsdale, NJ: Lawrence Erlbaum.

Cantor, J., & Sparks, G. (1984). Children's fear responses to mass media: Testing some Piagetian predictions. *Journal of Communication, 34*(2), 90–103.

Children Now. (2001). *Fair play: Violence, gender, and race in video games.* Oakland, CA: Author.

Cline, V. B., Croft, R. G., & Courrier, S. (1973). Desensitization of children to television violence. *Journal of Personality and Social Psychology, 27,* 360–365.

Collins, R. L., Elliott, M. N., Berry, S. H., Kanouse, D. E., Kunkel, D., Hunter, S. B., et al. (2004). Watching sex on television predicts adolescent initiation of sexual behavior. *Pediatrics, 114*(3), 280–289.

Davis, M. D. (1990). Portrayals of women in prime-time network television: Some demographic characteristics. *Sex Roles, 23,* 325–332.

Davison, K. K., Markey, C. N., & Birch, L. L. (2000). Etiology of body dissatisfaction and weight concerns among 5-year-old girls. *Appetite, 35,* 143–151.

Dittmar, H., Halliwell, E., & Ive, S. (2006). Does Barbie make girls want to be thin? The effect of experimental exposure to images of dolls on the body image of 5- to 8-year-old girls. *Developmental Psychology, 42,* 283–292.

Dominick, J. R., & Greenberg, B. S. (1972). Attitudes toward violence: The interaction of television exposure, family attitudes, and social class. In G.A. Comstock & E. A. Rubinstein (Eds.), *Television and social behavior: Vol. 3. Television and adolescent aggressiveness* (pp. 314–335). Washington, DC: Government Printing Office.

Downs, E. P., & Smith, S. L. (2005, May). *Keeping abreast of hypersexuality: A video game content analysis.* Paper presented to Mass Communication division for the annual conference of the International Communication Association, New York.

Drabman, R. S., & Thomas, M. H. (1974). Does media violence increase children's toleration of real-life aggression? *Developmental Psychology, 10,* 418–421.

Elasmar, M., Hasegawa, K., & Brain, M. (1999). The portrayal of women in U.S. prime time television. *Journal of Broadcasting & Electronic Media, 44,* 20–34.

Ferris, A. L., Smith, S. W., Greenberg, B. S., & Smith, S. L. (2007). The content of reality dating shows and viewer perceptions of dating [Online]. *Journal of Communication, 57*(3), 490–510.

Gerbner, G., Gross, L. G., Morgan, M., Signorielli, N., & Shanahan, J. (2002). Growing up with television: Cultivation processes. In J. Bryant & D. Zillmann (Eds.), *Media effects* (2nd ed, pp. 43–68). Mahwah, NJ: Lawrence Erlbaum.

Glascock, J. (2001). Gender roles on prime-time network television: Demographics and behaviors. *Journal of Broadcasting & Electronic Media, 45*(4), 656–669.

Granados, A., & Smith, S. L. (2007). *A qualitative analysis of female protagonists in G-rated films.* Research report submitted to the See Jane Program at Dads and Daughters, Duluth, MI.

Greenberg, B. S., Sherry, J. L., Busselle, R. W., Hnilo, L. R., & Smith, S. W. (1997). Daytime television talk shows: Guests, content, and interactions. *Journal of Broadcasting & Electronic Media, 41*(3), 426–441.

Greeson, L. E., & Williams, R. A. (1986). Social implications of music videos for youth: An analysis of the content and effects of MTV. *Youth Society, 18,* 177–189.

Groesz, L. M., Levine, M. P., & Murnen, S. K. (2002). The effect of experimental presentation of thin media images on body satisfaction: A meta-analytic review. *International Journal of Eating Disorders, 17,* 81–89.

Hawkins, R., & Pingree, S. (1982). Television's influence on social reality. In D. Pearl, L. Bouthilet, & J. Lazar (Eds.), *Television and behavior: Ten years of scientific progress and implications for the eighties* (Vol. 2., pp. 224–247). Rockville, MD: U.S. Department of Health and Human Services.

Heintz-Knowles, K. E. (1996). *Sexual activity on daytime soap operas: A content analysis of five weeks of television programming.* Menlo Park, CA: Kaiser Family Foundation.

Herrett-Skjellum, J., & Allen, M. (1996). Television programming and sex-stereotyping: A meta-analysis. *Communication Yearbook, 19,* 157–185.

Huesmann, L. R. (1986). Psychological processes promoting the relation between exposure to media violence and aggressive behavior by the viewer. *Aggressive Behavior, 42,* 125–139.

Huesmann, L. R., Moise, J., Podolski, C. L., & Eron, L. (1998, July). *Longitudinal relations between children's exposure to television violence and their later aggressive and violent behavior in young adulthood: 1977–1992.* Paper presented at the meetings for the International Communication Association, Jerusalem, Israel.

Jo, E., & Berkowitz, L. (1994). A priming effect analysis of media influences: An update. In J. Bryant & D. Zillmann (Eds.), *Media effects* (pp. 43–60). Mahwah, NJ: Lawrence Erlbaum.

Jones, R. W., Abelli, D. M., & Abelli, R. B. (1994, August). *Ratio of female:male characters and stereotyping in educational programming.* Paper presented at the meeting of the American Psychological Association, Los Angeles.

Kalof, L. (1999). The effects of gender and music video imagery on sexual attitudes. *Journal of Social Psychology, 139*(3), 378–385.

Kimball, M. M. (1986). Television and sex-role attitudes. In T. M. Williams (Ed.), *The impact of television: A natural experiment in three communities* (pp. 265–301). Orlando, FL: Academic Press.

Knight, M. G. (2001). *Mass media use and teen sexuality: Findings from the National Longitudinal Study of Adolescent Health.* Paper submitted for review for AEJMC National Convention Washington, DC.

Kunkel, D., Eyal, K., Finnerty, K., Biely, E., & Donnerstein, E. (2005). *Sex on TV IV: A biennial report to the Kaiser Family Foundation.* Menlo Park, CA: Kaiser Family Foundation.

Lauzen, M. M., & Dozier, D. M. (1999). Making a difference in prime time: Women on screen and behind the scenes in the 1995–96 season. *Journal of Broadcasting & Electronic Media, 43*(1), 1–19.

Lauzen, M. M., & Dozier, D. M. (2002). You look mahvelous: An examination of gender and appearance comments in the 1999–2000 prime-time season. *Sex Roles, 46*(11/12), 429–437.

Lauzen, M. M., & Dozier, D. M. (2004). Evening the score in prime time: The relationship between behind the scenes women and on-screen portrayals in the 2002–2003 season. *Journal of Broadcasting & Electronic Media, 48*(3), 484–500.

Linz, D., Donnerstein, E., & Penrod, S. (1984). The effects of multiple exposures to filmed violence against women. *Journal of Communication, 34*(3), 130–147.

McGhee, P. E., & Frueh, T. (1980). Television viewing and the learning of sex-role stereotypes. *Sex Roles, 6*(2), 179–188.

McIntyre, J. M., & Teevan, J. J. (1972). Television violence and deviant behavior. In G. A. Comstock & E. A. Rubinstein (Eds.), *Television and social behavior: Vol. 3. Television and adolescent aggressiveness* (pp. 383–435). Washington, DC: Government Printing Office.

Melkman, R., Tversky, B., & Baratz, D. (1981). Developmental trends in the use of perceptual and conceptual attributes in grouping, clustering, and retrieval. *Journal of Experimental Child Psychology, 31,* 470–486.

Meyer, T. P. (1972). Effects of viewing justified and unjustified real film violence on aggressive behavior. *Journal of Personality and Social Psychology, 23,* 21–29.

Molitor, F., & Hirsch, K. W. (1994). Children's toleration of real-life aggression after exposure to media violence: A replication of the Drabman and Thomas studies. *Child Study Journal, 24*(3), 191–207.

Morgan, M. (1982). Television and adolescents' sex role stereotypes: A longitudinal study. *Journal of Personality and Social Psychology, 43*(5), 947–955.

Morgan, M. (1987). Television, sex-role attitudes, and sex-role behavior. *Journal of Early Adolescence, 7*(3), 269–282.

Morgan, M., & Rothschild, N. (1983). Impact of the new television technology: Cable TV, peers, and sex-role cultivation in the electronic environment. *Youth & Society, 15*(1), 33–50.

Morison, P., Kelly, H., & Gardner, H. (1978). Reasoning about the realities on television: A developmental study. *Journal of Broadcasting, 25,* 229–241.

Nathanson, A., Wilson, B. J., McGee, J., & Sebastian, M. (2002). Counteracting the effects of female stereotypes on television via active mediation. *Journal of Communication, 52*(4), 922–937.

Paik, H., & Comstock, G. (1994). The effects of television violence on antisocial behavior: A meta-analysis. *Communication Research, 21,* 516–546.

Peck, E. Y. (1999). *Gender differences in film-induced fear as a function of type of emotion measure and stimulus content: A meta-analysis and a laboratory study.* Unpublished doctoral dissertation, University of Wisconsin–Madison.

Peterson, J. L., Moore, K. A., & Furstenberg, F. F. (1991). Television viewing and early initiation of sexual intercourse: Is there a link? *Journal of Homosexuality, 21,* 93–118.

Potter, W. J., Vaughan, M. W., Warren, R., Howley, K., Land, A., & Hagemeyer, J. C. (1995). How real is the portrayal of aggression in television entertainment programming? *Journal of Broadcasting and Electronic Media, 39,* 496–516.

Repetti, R. L. (1984). Determinants of children's sex stereotyping: Parental sex-role traits and television viewing. *Personality and Social Psychology Bulletin, 10*(3), 457–468.

Rich, M., Woods, E. R., Goodman, E., Emans, S. J., & DuRant, R. H. (1998). Aggressors or victims: Gender and race in music video violence. *Pediatrics, 101,* 669–674.

Signorielli, N. (2003). Prime time violence 1992–2001: Has the picture really changed? *Journal of Broadcasting & Electronic Media, 47*(1), 36–57.

Signorielli, N., & Bacue, A. (1999). Recognition and respect: A content analysis of prime-time television characters across three decades. *Sex Roles, 40*(7/8), 527–544.

Signorielli, N., & Kahlenberg, S. (2001). Television's world of work in the nineties. *Journal of Broadcasting & Electronic Media, 45*(1), 4–22.

Signorielli, N., & Lears, M. (1992). Children, television, and conceptions about chores: attitudes and behaviors. *Sex Roles, 27*(3/4), 157–170.

Smith, S. L., & Boyson, A. (2002). Violence in music videos: Examining the prevalence and context of physical aggression. *Journal of Communication, 52*, 61–83.

Smith, S. L., Granados, A., Choueiti, M., & Pieper, K. (2006). *Equity or eye candy: Exploring the nature of sex-roles in children's television programming.* A report prepared for the See Jane program at Dads and Daughters, Duluth, MN.

Smith, S. L., Nathanson, A. I., & Wilson, B. J. (2002). Prime-time programming: Assessing violence during the most popular viewing hours. *Journal of Communication, 52*, 84–111.

Smith, S. L., Wilson, B. J., Kunkel, D., Linz, D., Potter, W. J., Colvin, C., et al. (1998). Violence in television programming overall: University of California, Santa Barbara Study. In *National television violence study* (Vol. 3, pp. 5–220). Thousand Oaks, CA: Sage.

Sparks, G. G. (1986). Developmental differences in children's reports of fear induced by the mass media. *Child Study Journal, 16*, 55–66.

Strouse, J. S., Buerkel-Rothfuss, N., & Long, E. C. J. (1995). Gender and family as moderators of the relationship between music video exposure and adolescent sexual permissiveness. *Adolescence, 30*(119), 505–521.

Thompson, T. L., & Zerbinos, E. (1995). Gender roles in animated cartoons: Has the picture changed in 20 years? *Sex Roles, 32*(9/10), 651–673.

Ward, L. M. (1995). Talking about sex: Common themes about sexuality in prime-time television programs children and adolescents view most. *Journal of Youth and Adolescence, 24*(5), 595–615.

Ward, L. M. (2002). Does television exposure affect emerging adults' attitudes and assumptions about sexual relationships? Correlational and experimental confirmation. *Journal of Youth and Adolescence, 31*(1), 1–15.

Ward, L. M., & Rivadeneyra, R. (1999). Contributions of entertainment television to adolescents' sexual attitudes and expectations: The role of viewing amount versus viewer involvement. *Journal of Sex Research, 36*(3), 237–249.

Wilson, B. J., Hoffner, C., & Cantor, J. (1987). Children's perceptions of the effectiveness of techniques to reduce fear from mass media. *Journal of Applied Development Psychology, 8*, 39–52.

Wilson, B. J., Smith, S. L., Potter, W. J., Kunkel, D., Linz, D., Colvin, C., et al. (2002). Violence in children's television programming: Assessing the risks. *Journal of Communication, 52*, 5–35.

Zhao, X., & Gantz, W. (2003). Disruptive and cooperative interruptions in prime-time television fiction: The role of gender, status, and topic. *Journal of Communication, 53*, 347–362.

Author Index

Foregger, S., 14
Forgas, J. P., 107
Forthofer, M. S., 125
Frank, M. G., 204
Freitas, A., 231
Freuh, T., 292
Friedman, A. L., 106
Frinelli, L., 35
Fritz, H. M. H., 135
Fritz, J. M. H., 139
Furstenberg, F. F., 296, 297

Gadjah, M., 149
Gaff, C. L., 104
Gailliard, B., 142
Gangestad, S. W., 37
Gantz, W., 291
Gardner, H., 289
Gardner, R. R., ix, x
Garrett, M. M., 249
Gavin, J., 273, 276
Gay, C. D., 87
Geertz, C., 254
George, J. F., 201, 204
George, L., 117
Gerbner, G., 289
Gibbs, J., 274, 275
Giddens, A., 137
Gilbert, D. T., 100, 201, 203
Gilbert, S. J., ix, x
Gilding, M., 276
Giles, H., 138
Gill, E. A., 100, 171
Gill, J. N., 168
Gillihan, S. J., 165
Giner-Sorolla, R., 101
Ginther, D., 276
Given, B., 121
Given, C. W., 122
Glascock, J., 291
Glaser, R., 181
Goffman, E., 147
Goldsmith, D. J., 75, 86, 95, 161, 163, 254
Golish, T. D., 59
Gong, L., 271
Goodman, E., 287
Goodwin, M. H., 249
Gordon, G. H., 69

Gossett, L., 149
Gottman, J. M., 184
Graen, G., 139
Graham, E. E., 116
Graham, M. L., 79
Granados, A., 292, 295
Granka, L., 268
Graves, A. R., 165
Greenberg, B. S., 13, 225, 288, 295
Greenberg, L. S., 173
Greene, J. O., 166
Greenspan, M., xi
Greeson, L. E., 296
Greil, A. L., 124, 125
Grice, H. P., 248
Grice, P., 201
Groesz, L. M., 297
Gross, L. G., 289
Grove, T. G., 72
Grundin, J., 271
Gudykunst, W. B., 69, 71, 72, 75, 76
Guerrero, L. K., 120, 138, 141, 202, 206
Guo, G., 296

Haas, S. M., 75, 86, 95, 97, 100
Habbema, J. D. F., 37
Hagemeyer, J. C., 287, 288
Hale, J. L., 116, 138
Hale, K. L., 253
Hall, J. A., 203
Hallam, M., 37
Hallett, J. S., 39
Halliwell, E., 297
Hamann, H., 104
Hamel, L., 214
Hamilton, W. D., 33, 34
Hample, D., 188
Hanasono, L., 168, 171, 172
Hancock, G. R., 162
Hancock, J. T., 201
Harden, J. M., 186
Hardie, E. A., 140
Harms, C., 203, 210
Harper, A. M., 59
Harré, R., 141
Harrington, N. G., 11, 12
Harrison, R. P., x, 6, 7
Harrison, T., 7, 95

Subject Index

About the Editors

Sandi W. Smith (PhD, University of Southern California) is Professor in the Department of Communication at Michigan State University, where she teaches courses in persuasion, communication theory, and interpersonal communication, and Director of the Health and Risk Communication Center. Her research interests parallel these course topics, and her research has been funded by foundations and government agencies such as the Kaiser Family Foundation, the Fetzer Institute, the U.S. Department of Education, and the National Cancer Institute. In particular, she has focused her research on the impact of memorable messages received from important others on health behaviors; persuading people to carry signed and witnessed organ donor cards and to engage in family discussion about their decisions related to organ donation; encouraging college students to consume alcohol moderately, if at all; and the portrayal of interpersonal relationships on television. Among her more than 60 publications are articles that appeared in *Communication Monographs, Human Communication Research, Health Communication, Journal of Health Communication, Journal of Communication,* and the *Journal of Applied Communication Research,* among others. She is active in the National Communication Association and the International Communication Association, where she served as Chair of the Interpersonal Communication Division. She has received honors for her teaching and research from student groups, professional associations, and the universities at which she has worked. In 2007, she was honored with the Distinguished Faculty Award at Michigan State University, and in 2008 she received the B. Aubrey Fisher Mentorship Award from the International Communication Association.

Steven R. Wilson (PhD, Purdue University) is Professor in the Department of Communication at Purdue University. He also has been a faculty member at Michigan State, Northern Illinois, and Northwestern Universities. His research and teaching focus on interpersonal communication, social influence, and aggression/conflict. He is the author of *Seeking and*

Resisting Compliance: Why Individuals Say What They Do When Trying to Influence Others (Sage, 2002), for which he received the Gerald R. Miller book award from the National Communication Association's Interpersonal Communication Division in 2005. He also has published more than 50 articles and chapters in communication journals such as *Communication Monographs, Communication Research,* and *Human Communication Research,* interdisciplinary journals such as *Child Abuse & Neglect, Journal of Social and Personal Relationships,* and *Journal of Language and Social Psychology,* and edited volumes such as the *Handbook of Communication and Social Interaction Skills* and the *Handbook of Communication Science* (2nd ed.). His recent research explores patterns of parent-child interaction in families at risk for child maltreatment as well as patterns associated with children's school readiness (funded by the Lilly Endowment). He is active in both the National Communication Association and the International Communication Association, and has served as chair of the Interpersonal Communication Division for both associations. From 2001 to 2003, he served as one of five associate editors of the interdisciplinary journal *Personal Relationships.* In 2008, he was honored with the Bernard Brommel Award for Outstanding Scholarship or Distinguished Service in Family Communication from the National Communication Association.

About the Contributors

Walid A. Afifi (PhD, 1996, University of Arizona) is an Associate Professor in the Department of Communication at the University of California–Santa Barbara. He is an author of more than 50 articles and chapters, has served as Associate Editor for both the *Journal of Social and Personal Relationships* and *Personal Relationships,* and has been active as a member of several editorial boards. His program of research revolves around uncertainty and information-management decisions and has led to the development and refinement of the Theory of Motivated Information Management. His program of life revolves around, and the (usually) calming influence on his personal experiences of uncertainty are, his wife, Tamara, their two young children (Leila and Rania), and two dogs (Mashi and Maddi).

Leslie A. Baxter is F. Wendell Miller Distinguished Professor of Communication Studies at the University of Iowa, where she has taught and conducted her program of research for the past 15 years. She has published 130 books, chapters, and articles on a variety of topics, but her research is centered on understanding the communication contradictions that animate family life. She is honored to be the recipient of several scholarly awards, including the Brommel Award for Family Communication, the Woolbert Research Award, the Knower Best Article Award, and the Miller Book Award, all from the National Communication Association.

Dawn O. Braithwaite (PhD, University of Minnesota) is Willa Cather Professor of Communication Studies at the University of Nebraska–Lincoln. She focuses her scholarship on communication in times of change and challenges in personal and family relationships, via studying relational dialectics, rituals, and social support. She has published 70 articles and chapters, along with four books. Her most recent book is *Engaging Theories in Interpersonal Communication,* with Leslie A. Baxter (2008, Sage). She received the National Communication Association's Brommel Award in family communication and is a past president of the Western States Communication Association. She has served as the director of the National Communication Association's Research Board and will be the association's president in 2010.

Judee K. Burgoon is Professor of Communication, Family Studies and Human Development at the University of Arizona, where she is Site Director for the Center for Identification Technology Research and Director of Research for the Center for the Management of Information in the Eller College of Management. She has authored seven books and monographs and more than 250 articles, chapters, and reviews related to deception, nonverbal and relational communication, computer-mediated communication, research methods, and media use. Her current research, which has been funded by the National Science Foundation, Department of Defense and Department of Homeland Security, is examining ways to automate analysis of nonverbal and verbal communication to detect deception. She is a Fellow of the International Communication Association, which has also honored her with its B. Aubrey Fisher Mentorship and Steven B. Chaffee Career Achievement Awards. She has also been honored by the National Communication Association with its Distinguished Scholar Award, Golden Anniversary Monographs Award, and Charles H. Woolbert Award for Research with Lasting Impact.

Brant R. Burleson (PhD, University of Illinois, Urbana-Champaign, 1982) is Professor of Communication and Affiliate Professor of Psychological Sciences at Purdue University. His research examines supportive forms of communication (such as comforting) and their effects on varied forms of well-being, and focuses on how people both produce and process supportive messages. Other research interests include communication skill acquisition and development, the effects of communication skills on relationship outcomes, and the role of emotion in communication and relationships. He has authored more than 140 articles, chapters, and reviews, and has edited several publications, including *The Handbook of Communication and Social Interaction Skills, Communication of Social Support,* and *Communication Yearbook.* He is a Fellow of the International Communication Association, a Distinguished Scholar of the National Communication Association, and a recipient of the Berscheid-Hatfield Award for Distinguished Midcareer Achievement from the International Association for Relationship Research.

John P. Caughlin (PhD, University of Texas at Austin, 1997) is an associate professor of communication at the University of Illinois at Urbana-Champaign. His research examines communication in families and other close relationships focusing on the causes and consequences of avoiding communication. Recent work has appeared in journals such as *Communication Monographs, Human Communication Research, Journal of Social and Personal Relationships, Communication Research,* and *Personal Relationships.* He is a winner of the Knower Outstanding Article Award from the Interpersonal Division of the National Communication Association, and in 2004 he received the Gerald R. Miller Award for Early Career Achievement from the International Association for Relationship Research. Currently, he is serving as an associate editor of the *Journal of Social and Personal Relationships.*

Kristine L. Fitch (PhD, University of Washington) is Professor of Communication Studies at the University of Iowa. Her research and theory are centered on the ethnography of speaking based on fieldwork in Colombia, England, Spain, Finland, and Texas. Her current work centers on persuasion and personal relationships in cultural context, particularly in moments of poaching and improvisation at the intersections of public (media representations and discourses) and private (everyday conversation between, and relational narratives of, relational partners). She is the author of three books, including *Speaking Relationally: Culture, Communication, and Interpersonal Connection.* Her research has appeared in journals such as *Communication Monographs, Human Communication Research, Communication Theory, Journal of Applied Communication Research,* and *Discourse Studies,* among others.

Kory Floyd (PhD, University of Arizona, 1998) is Professor of Human Communication and Director of the Communication Sciences Laboratory at Arizona State University. His research focuses on the communication of affection in personal relationships and on the interplay between communication, physiology, and health. He has authored or edited seven books and nearly 75 journal articles and book chapters and recently served as editor of the *Journal of Family Communication.* His work has been supported by the National Institutes of Health and has earned several awards, including the Gerald R. Miller Award for Early Career Achievement from the International Association for Relationship Research.

Amy Granados is a doctoral student at the Annenberg School for Communication at the University of Southern California. Her research interests include media and gender. In particular, she is focused on the role of women behind the scenes and their relationship to onscreen portrayals of gender; the impact of exposure to idealized content across the life span; and the experiences of working actors, especially as they relate to sexual harassment.

Alexa D. Hampel (MA, University of Texas at Austin) is a doctoral student in communication studies at the University of Texas at Austin. Her research interests include interpersonal and family communication. Specifically, her research examines communication processes in close relationships, focusing on the causes and consequences of emotional communication for relationship quality and development.

Leanne K. Knobloch (PhD, University of Wisconsin–Madison, 2001) is an associate professor in the Department of Communication at the University of Illinois. Her research focuses on how communication shapes and reflects people's understandings of close relationships, particularly with respect to relationship development, relational uncertainty, and interdependence. Her work has appeared in outlets such as *Communication Monographs, Human Communication Research, Communication Research, Journal of Social and Personal Relationships,* and *Personal Relationships.* In 2008, she received the Gerald R. Miller Award for Early Career Achievement from the International Association for Relationship Research.

Ascan F. Koerner (PhD, University of Wisconsin–Madison, 1998) is an associate professor of Communication Studies and the Donald V. Hawkins Professor for 2008–2009 at the University of Minnesota–Twin Cities. His research focuses mainly on Family Communication Patterns and the cognitive representations of relationships and their influence on interpersonal communication, including message production and message interpretations. His research has appeared in communication journals such as *Communication Monographs, Communication Theory,* and *Human Communication Research,* and interdisciplinary journals such as the *Journal of Marriage and Family* and the *Journal of Social and Personal Relationship,* and a number of edited volumes.

Timothy R. Levine (PhD, Michigan State University) is a professor in the Department of Communication at Michigan State University. Prior to Michigan State University, he held appointments at the University of Hawaii and Indiana University. His research interests include deception, interpersonal communication, personal relationships, persuasion and social influence, intercultural communication, communication traits, and measurement validation. He has published more than 70 journal articles, including approximately 30 articles in *Communication Monographs* and *Human Communication Research.* He is currently working on a new theory of deception to be called truth bias theory. The theory will merge findings on the veracity effect and the probability model with work on deception motives and projective motives.

Karen K. Myers (PhD, Arizona State University) is an assistant professor in the Department of Communication at the University of California, Santa Barbara. Her primary areas of research are organizational socialization and assimilation, vocational socialization, organizational identification, organizational knowledge, emotion management, conflict, and leadership. Much of her research focuses on how group processes influence member integration, group coordination, and the development of relationships. Her work has appeared in *Human Communication Research, Journal of Applied Communication Research, Management Communication Quarterly,* and *Communication Yearbook,* among other publications.

Artemio Ramirez, Jr., PhD, is an assistant professor in the Hugh Downs School of Human Communication at Arizona State University in Tempe. His research focuses on the interpersonal aspects of computer-mediated communication, including relationship development and maintenance, social information seeking, and modality switching. His research has appeared in several major journals of the field of communication, including *Communication Monographs, Communication Research, Human Communication Research, Journal of Communication,* and *New Media & Society.* He also serves on the editorial boards of the *Journal of Applied Communication Research, Journal of Computer-Mediated Communication,* and *Journal of Social and Personal Relationships.*

Michael E. Roloff (PhD, Michigan State University) is Professor of Communication Studies at Northwestern University. He researches in the area of conflict management. He wrote *Interpersonal Communication: The Social Exchange Approach* and coedited *Persuasion: New Directions in Theory and Research* (with Gerald R. Miller), *Interpersonal Processes: New Directions in Communication Research* (with Gerald R. Miller), *Social Cognition and Communication* (with Charles R. Berger), and *Communication and Negotiation* (with Linda Putnam). He has published in journals such as *Communication Monographs, Communication Research, Human Communication Research, International Journal of Conflict Management, Journal of Language and Social Psychology, Journal of Social and Personal Relationships,* and *Personal Relationships.* He is also Senior Associate Editor of the *International Journal of Conflict Management.* He served as editor of *The Communication Yearbook* and is currently coeditor of *Communication Research.*

Allison M. Scott (MA, University of Illinois at Urbana-Champaign, 2006) is a doctoral student in communication at the University of Illinois at Urbana-Champaign. Her research examines health communication within families and close relationships. She has published in *AIDS Patient Care and STDs* and has been a graduate fellow in the Department of Communication.

Stacy L. Smith (PhD, University of California, Santa Barbara, 1999) is Associate Professor of Entertainment at the Annenberg School for Communication at the University of Southern California. Her research assesses content patterns and effects of media (i.e., television, film, video games, point of purchase advertising) violence, gender roles, and hypersexuality. She has published roughly 50 book chapters and journal articles, with some of her research appearing in journals such as *Journal of Communication, Communication Research, Journal of Broadcasting & Electronic Media* and *Media Psychology.*

Denise Haunani Solomon (PhD, Northwestern University) is Professor of Communication Arts and Sciences and Associate Dean for Graduate Studies at the Pennsylvania State University. Her research focuses generally on the causes and consequences of turbulence in romantic associations as well as on how communication participates in those experiences. Her research has examined how relationship qualities, including interpersonal power, relational uncertainty, and interdependence, shape people's perceptions of and communication about relational irritations, problematic events, uncertainty-provoking events, changes in sexual intimacy, jealousy experiences, hurtful messages, and sexually harassing statements. This work has culminated in the relational turbulence model, which is a theory describing how transitions in romantic relationships promote relationship qualities that polarize cognitive, emotional, and communicative reactions to both ordinary and extra-ordinary experiences. She serves on the editorial boards of five journals, and she is currently an associate editor for *Personal Relationships.*

Keli Ryan Steuber (MA, University of Delaware) is a PhD candidate at the Pennsylvania State University. Her research examines how married partners negotiate relational transitions across the life span. She is specifically interested in how transitions influence communication between spouses and how partners share private information with individuals outside their marriage. Her most recent work acknowledges the medical, social, and marital stressors that accompany infertility by considering how social networks can facilitate or complicate a couple's efforts to cope with infertility. She has contributed to projects relating to relational uncertainty and partner interference in transitions, management of secrets within families, and perceptions of marital support.

Anita L. Vangelisti is the Jesse H. Jones Centennial Professor of Communication at the University of Texas at Austin. Her work focuses on the associations between communication and emotion in the context of close, personal relationships. She has published numerous articles and chapters and has edited or authored several books. Vangelisti has served on the editorial boards of more than a dozen scholarly journals. She has received recognition for her research from the National Communication Association, the International Society for the Study of Personal Relationships, and the International Association for Relationship Research.

Joseph B. Walther (PhD, University of Arizona, 1990) is a professor in the Department of Communication and the Department of Telecommunication, Information Studies, and Media at Michigan State University. His research focuses on the interpersonal dynamics of communication via computer networks, in personal relationships, work groups, social support, and educational settings, areas in which he has published original theories and empirically based research articles. He has previously held appointments in Psychology, Information Technology, and Education and Social Policy at universities in the United States and England. He was chair of the Organizational Communication and Information Systems division of the Academy of Management, and the Communication and Technology division of the International Communication Association. His professional honors include the National Communication Association's Woolbert Award for an article that has stood the test of time and influenced thinking in the discipline for more than 10 years.

Kirsten M. Weber (MA, Pennsylvania State University) is a PhD student in the Department of Communication Arts and Sciences at the Pennsylvania State University. Her research interests lie at the intersection of interpersonal and health communication. Specifically, she is interested in understanding how interpersonal relationships both influence and are an influence on illness experiences. Her work has been published in the *Journal of Communication* and *Health Communication*, and she is coauthoring a book chapter on family communication during health transitions. Her professional affiliations include the National Communication Association and the International Communication Association. Additionally, she is a new scholar reviewer for *Personal Relationships* and served as professional development officer for the Department of Communication Arts and Sciences graduate forum at Penn State.